MARKETING
ASIAN PLACES

MARKETING ASIAN PLACES

Attracting Investment, Industry, and Tourism to Cities, States and Nations

PHILIP KOTLER
MICHAEL ALAN HAMLIN
IRVING REIN
DONALD H. HAIDER

John Wiley & Sons (Asia) Pte Ltd

This publication is designed to provide accurate and authoritative information in regard to the subject matter covered. It is sold with the understanding that the publisher is not engaged in rendering professional services. If professional advice or other expert assistance is required, the services of a competent professional person should be sought.

Other Wiley Editorial Offices

John Wiley & Sons, Inc., 605 Third Avenue, New York, NY 10158-0012, USA
John Wiley & Sons Ltd, Baffins Lane, Chichester, West Sussex PO19 1UD, England
John Wiley & Sons (Canada) Ltd, 22 Worcester Road, Rexdale, Ontario M9W 1L1, Canada
John Wiley & Sons Australia Ltd, 33 Park Road (PO Box 1226), Milton, Queensland 4064, Australia
Wiley-VCH, Pappelallee 3, 69469 Weinheim, Germany

Library of Congress Cataloging-in-Publication Data
0-471-47913-6 (cloth)

Typeset in 11/15 points, Times Roman by Linographic Services Pte Ltd
Printed in Singapore by Craft Print International Ltd
10 9 8 7 6 5 4 3 2 1

Contents

To Asian decision-makers in their capacities
as creative place marketers

Acknowledgments

Inspiration for this book stems from many local and regional actors — public and private — throughout Asia. Their struggle to improve place attraction has resulted in a profound knowledge base waiting to be structured and diffused to others.

The cross-Pacific dialogue preceding this book has added a new dimension to what is taking place in Asia. New and exciting comparative aspects emerged as Asian, European and American place marketing was studied in more detail. This book was written during a very exciting period of Asian development. Asian development is remarkable in many ways, and among its most remarkable qualities is the rapid rate of growth. Asia's modern capacity for rapid growth is now threatened by the continuing financial crisis (which began in 1999) and the threat of global recession.

But the challenge of sustaining Asia and its rate of growth under vastly different circumstances has served to bring out the best in Asian place marketers. Extreme duress produced exemplary instances of innovative thinking, value proposition development and competitive marketing. We found insights into these developments from a number of sources. Particularly meaningful, however, were the one-on-one interviews and correspondence with many of the individuals at the helm of shaping the New Asia. The authors are grateful to these experts and leaders who took time from their busy schedules so that we might better understand how and why Asia will continue to be among the best-marketed regions on earth despite, or perhaps because of, its challenges.

We are likewise grateful to senior researcher Jemma Jadwani and her assistant, Rhea Marie Santos, both of TeamAsia. This small team provided instrumental assistance in researching, editing and organizing the manuscript.

We also thank Kevin O'Donnell, who provided valuable assistance in research and editing, Rachel Blank, who skillfully provided editing advice, and Matthew Miller, who carefully edited the proofs. All are from Northwestern University's Department of Communication Studies in Evanston, Illinois.

Finally, we wish to express our appreciation to our publisher, Nick Wallwork of Wiley Asia, and to his patient team of editors and marketers for making this book possible.

Philip Kotler
Irving Rein
Don Haider
Evanston, Illinois

Michael Alan Hamlin
Manila, Philippines

Foreword

On its title alone, *Marketing Asian Places* paints a broad canvas of the region that will prompt debate and discussion. Indeed, within the book there are assertions that some of us in the region may well take issue with. But the underlying theme carries a message that can benefit Asian places by changing their marketing techniques. Places must assign higher importance to strategic planning processes. The book's message is to challenge us all to understand what is required to become more competitive and to build stronger relationships between the public and private sectors.

Asia's problems in recent years may well have persuaded some investors that their money may be better placed somewhere else. *Marketing Asian Places* is a timely reminder of Asia's fundamental strengths and long term potential. The concepts in the book provide some significant guide posts to foreign investors who want to understand more about, and become involved in, Asia and its future. And that future is certainly bright.

Hong Kong could be described as the definitive example of one of the great truisms of our time: the one constant in today's global environment is change. Living in a place of less than 1,100 square kilometres, and with the only natural resource being its fabled deepwater harbour, the people of Hong Kong have had to trade globally to make a living. In doing this, they have developed a perspective of their environment which extends far beyond its physical boundaries. In other words, globalization has had a long currency in Hong Kong. It has been an economic factor of life for generations – well before the term was defined in the latter part of the 20th century.

Hong Kong has not been alone in the Asian region in recognising the importance of globalization to the economy and in raising the standard of living. In most other places, however, it may not have been part of a long-developed economic condition needed for survival. Rather, it was one embraced in more recent times as barriers between countries and economies have tumbled. Or was it hastened by the Asian financial crisis which swept through the region with such force in 1997-98 — a crisis from which most Asian countries are only beginning to recover?

Today, Asia accounts for 60% of the global population and a quarter of the world's exports and global GDP. Just under half of all Asians are below the age of 25; and East Asia alone accounts for 40% of global official foreign exchange reserves. There would be few regions anywhere that provide a gateway to new opportunities in such a young, dynamic and affluent market. The publication of *Marketing Asian Places* at this juncture is particularly timely as it is now a theme central to the agenda of government leaders, politicians and business people from Sydney to Shanghai and from Mumbai to Manila.

The Asian financial crisis no doubt exposed some fundamental weaknesses and frailties in the make-up of the region. While the turmoil caused economic dislocation and human misery, in an historical context it was also a watershed. If the bubble had not burst as it did, the eventual and almost inevitable fallout would have been even more debilitating. Nevertheless, that is cold comfort when decades of exponential growth came to a halt with alarming suddenness, and brought with them some suspect official and corporate governance and more than a touch of hubris.

In many ways, what happened served as a wake up call. It resulted not only in economic restructuring, but some soul searching and character re-building throughout the region. And while we can all be confident about the future, the lessons learned by governments during the crisis must continue to be pursued with vigor, perhaps even more so with the possibility of further economic problems on the horizon.

In the future, more reasoned debate should be held on two other issues that have the potential to bring a further measure of financial maturity and stability to the region and, at the same time, increase the marketability of Asian places. They are the development of an Asian debt market and the much longer-term possibility of the introduction of a single Asian currency.

Both issues have been raised on and off over the past few years, particularly following the financial crisis of 1997-98. With the introduction of the Euro as a circulating currency from January 2002, has the time come for more serious discussion of a single Asian currency? It is certainly not something that will happen overnight, nor in the next few years. But such a currency could have the advantage of reflecting the strong trade links in the region. And it would also have the effect of creating bigger and more liquid markets that are less susceptible to manipulation – a factor which exacerbated the Asian financial crisis.

Because of the many obstacles that need to be overcome, the advent of a single currency would take a very long time. The widely different economic regimes under which the economies of the region operate, and the complex issue of setting up an institution to administer the system with the politics involved are just some of the problems. Remember, it took 50 years for the Euro to become a reality.

As for stable and transparent Asian debt markets, such a proposition could be implemented more quickly. It is one of the ironies of history that our failure to establish a strong and robust Asian bond market was among the reasons for the Asian financial crisis. What needs to be done is a fresh examination of the barriers to the development of Asian bond markets. We must bring together market practitioners, government agencies and international financial institutions to tackle these barriers and clear the path for developing an Asian debt market.

So what does *Marketing Asian Places* bring to this debate? I believe the insights provided by the authors suggest that the time is upon us to make a start on bringing Asian markets together. The book serves as a catalyst for progress for those of us involved in the development of public policy as administrators or legislators, those in the private sector, and the overseers of regulatory and other critical institutions. This will provide an opportunity to manage the changes that will invariably take place in Asia, rather than simply react to them. And we'll be far better off for it.

Donald Tsang
Chief Secretary for Administration of the
Hong Kong Special Administrative Region

The Marketing Challenge in the New Asia

T he competition in Asia has never been more intense, and the stakes for winning have never been greater.

During the five-year span which encompassed the Asian financial crisis, Shanghai transformed its Pudong area from sleepy grassland to an impressive, world-class financial and industrial center. Over a 20-year period, Shenzhen, which shares a border with Hong Kong, saw its population increase from a few hundred thousand to around five million, which helped attract China's highest density of PhDs as well as the highest average income in the country.[1] Two years before the 1997 handover of Hong Kong to the Mainland Government, Fortune magazine forecast the death of Hong Kong. That was not to be. Six years later, financial secretary Antony Leung Kam-Chung noted dryly that the former colony was not yet buried, and was prospering as Asia's leading financial center.[2]

China has consistently defied analysts' frequent and dire predictions of doom. At the onset of the financial crisis, Pudong became one more symbol of Asian excess as the media reported vacancy rates in its gleaming towers and its possession of perhaps the most unsightly television broadcasting tower in the world. As the area prospered and the rates rose, the critics fell silent. Shenzhen absorbed its neighbor's manufacturers, who were fleeing high-cost Hong Kong's exorbitant rents and high pay scales, and became a magnet for ambitious workers throughout China. Meanwhile, Hong Kong's challenge was to remain more than just another Chinese city. One way was to make it the only Chinese city that will have a Walt Disney theme park, including its HK$148 billion in economic benefits and 36,000 jobs. Despite stiff competition from Singapore, Hong Kong also remained the most popular location for regional headquarters of multinational firms.[3]

> *Malaysia fixed its currency at 3.8 ringgit to the dollar as Asia's financial crisis worsened, a move MIT economist Paul Krugman not only applauded, but also took credit for apparently influencing the decision-makers to finalize the controversial move. During the crisis, Malaysia was the only country to introduce capital controls that included penalties for "early" withdrawal of foreign invested funds during the crisis. There was a price to pay. In 2000, Malaysia's stock market losses were equivalent to 44.1% of annual economic output.[4] Worse, foreign reserves were down sharply as portfolio investors stayed away, local exporters circumvented controls to keep proceeds in foreign currencies, and foreign direct investors frowned at the country's high cost of doing business. The peg had backfired when other currencies bowed to market pressure in the region.[5]*

State bailouts of banks and big businesses that were allied to top government officials increased the financial burden on Malaysia, as did widespread political tension in the aftermath of the arrest and conviction of popular former deputy prime minister Anwar Ibrahim. Malaysia managed to postpone the day of reckoning by instituting capital controls. But insulating its inefficient private sector from reform proved to be no guarantee that Malaysia would remain the investment star it had become during Asia's miracle years.

> *It may not be fair, but in many minds Thailand "owned" Asia's financial crisis. After all, it was the baht that was the first domino to fall, pushing along most of the rest of the region into one of the most gruesome financial panics the world had ever seen. With the financial ashes still smoldering in 1998 — and threatening to burst into another fireball — most consultants probably would have advised against running a tourism campaign under the banner "Amazing Thailand." But not Thailand.[6]*

Fortunately for Bhanu Inkawat, the creator of the "quirky" campaign, it "helped Thailand pull in 8.65 million tourists in 1999, some 370,000 more than the target."[7] The Tourism Authority of Thailand was so pleased that it extended the campaign, even advertising on international broadcaster CNN. The campaign increased the number of visitors by

10%, resulting in more than nine million tourists. In fact, the campaign was good enough to be widely emulated and awarded, and not just in Asia. Have you heard the tagline "Amazing Finland?"

Although Taiwan was left largely unscathed by Asia's financial crisis, it had other problems to deal with. The Hsinchu Science-Based Industrial Park illustrates just how difficult dealing with the problems of success can be. The park is a textbook example of how to build and develop an industrial cluster. Covering 580 hectares occupied by 272 tenants, the park, with close ties to two national universities, is situated near 12 research facilities at the Industrial Technology Research Institute. It also provides grants for innovative high-tech research and development projects. The park's "ecosystem" includes shops, sporting facilities, a large apartment complex and efficient transportation links.[8] At the same time, it's also bursting at the seams and suffering regular brownouts.

The creaky infrastructure has gotten so bad that Taiwan semiconductor-maker Macronix International doesn't think it will be able to expand. Intent on taking over government land adjacent to the park, president Miin Wu laments, "Even if [the government] gives you the land they may not allow you to build because they have only so much power and water. We may have to look elsewhere."[9] The park's problems include lack of space for the expansion of existing clients, profit-sapping power shortages and even water shortages. Meanwhile, there are plenty of other places to look in Asia, places that may begin to look increasingly attractive even to existing clients.

Chronically strife-torn Cambodia is trying a different approach from Thailand to lure visitors, and leveraging its ancient culture isn't the principal value proposition, although the magnificent 12th-century Angkor Wat monument plays a part. Instead, officials are counting on Hollywood's filming in Cambodia of Tomb Raider, *starring Angelina Jolie, to boost the country's chronically flagging tourism industry. If the impact of the country on Jolie is any indication, the bet may pay off. When fighting erupted in Phnom Penh, an hour away by plane from Angkor Wat where filming was taking place, she said, "There was a moment of concern. [But] if anything was to happen to me here, it would be worth it."[10]*

Nick Lord, author of the *Lonely Planet Cambodia* guide, thinks the country deserves a break too. "Tourism is going to go crazy," Lord says. "People who see the film are going to look at Cambodia and know it's a real place and will want to come here. They'll say, 'If Hollywood can go, then I can go.'" Not everyone is happy with those prospects. For years, Cambodia has been a profitable source of artifacts for smugglers who took advantage of the chaos associated with decades of war and violent transition to a sort of pseudo-democratic government. Many are more worried about conserving Cambodia's treasures than showing them off. One thing is certain: the desperately poor country needs the money tourists will bring.

WINNING IN ASIA

What places will be successful in 21st-century Asia? Who will be the new Asian winners? The challenges and threats to Asian prosperity have never been greater, as new opportunities arise and new threats mount at an increasingly faster rate. Yet, for the responsive place — community, city or region — new competitive forces such as technology and global competition will invigorate and produce new partnerships and star performers. In this highly competitive environment for attracting investment, industry, residents and visitors, there will be winners and losers. The places that adopt and implement strategic planning will emerge as strong economic contenders.

Places need to understand their role and function in a fast-changing competitive marketplace (see Exhibit 1.1).

Exhibit 1.1: WHAT IS A PLACE?

A place is a nation-state, a geopolitical physical space.
A place is a region or state.
A place is a cultural, historical or ethnic bounded location.
A place is a central city and its surrounding populations.
A place is a market with various definable attributes.
A place is an industry's home base and a clustering of like-industries and their suppliers.
A place is a psychological attribute of relations between people internally and their external views of those outside.

The decade of the 1990s prompted several highly publicized writings on places. Each gave various interpretations to how politics, economics, technology and trade affected places within a rapidly changing world economy. What these authors and their works have in common is the view that the nation-state is in significant decline in the world order. The collapse of the Berlin Wall and resulting end to communism accelerated the triumph of markets and global forces. A technology-driven information revolution hastened the pace of change by decreasing the traditional boundaries of distance and interference by sovereign countries. Where nation-states once set the rules for economic activity and place development, today a newly integrated, yet locally competitive, world order determines the rules. No longer do they control people, economic activity, investments and trade. In the Internet age where capital, technology and ideas flow freely across national borders, places have assumed a new importance.

In *The Competitive Advantage of Nations*,[1] Harvard Business School Professor Michael Porter develops a new classification of stages of economic growth and factors responsible for growth, particularly localized economies. His case studies illustrate how the competitive success of firms depends largely on the economic and cultural environments of the countries in which they are based. Porter provides a great deal of analytical and conceptual insight into the complex mixture of regional synergies between competing firms within an industry, their clustering and unique supplier networks.

The triumph of regionalism over sovereign nation-states is given a further boost by Neil Peirce in *Citistates: How Urban America Can Prosper in a Competitive World*[2] and Japanese-American economist Kenichi Ohmae in *The End of the Nation State*.[3] Peirce's thesis is that, across America and across the globe, "citistates" are emerging as a critical focus of economic activity, of governance and of social organization for the 1990s as well as the century to come. Peirce sees geopolitically constrained cities replaced by highly competitive metropolitan regions linked by strong core communities and strong corporate partners. Ohmae sees region-states as being more important than national boundaries. The primary linkages of region-states tend to be with the global economy and not with their nation-states. Ohmae offers the view that such units will be in the range of five to 25 million people which, not coincidently, approximated the size of Hong Kong and Singapore when Ohmae wrote. He finds this population to be sufficiently small to share certain economic and consumer interests, but large enough to accommodate investment in and development of a human and physical infrastructure.

In *World Class: Thriving Locally in the Global Economy*[4] Rosabeth Moss Kanter, also of the Harvard Business School, finds the nation-state diminishing as globalization increases. She projects that the new competition will be in vying to be world centers of thinking, making and trading. While economics are globalizing, politics in many parts of the world are localizing, Kanter notes.[5] This localization is at the heart of Samuel Huntington's provocative book *The Clash of Civilizations*,[6] in which the Harvard political scientist argues that in the future the great divisions on the globe will be dominated by cultural rather than ideological or economic conflict. Huntington sees conflict and cooperation among groups of nations that constitute different civilizations; Confucian, Japanese, Islamic and Hindu, for example. This conception has vast implications for future Asian development.

Each of these authors defines places differently and renders his or her own independent weighting to global forces and local impacts. With the exception of Huntington, each provides various prescriptions for public and private leaders, and each sees numerous challenges that all places face to compete successfully in the new world order. There are two important issues for places to consider: their new role in the changing competitive market-place, and the effect to which changing conditions and forces will influence decision-making.

Sources:

1 Michael E. Porter, *The Competitive Advantage of Nations*, The Free Press, New York, 1990.
2 Neil Pierce, *Citistates: How Urban America Can Prosper in a Competitive World*, Seven Locks Press, Washington D.C., 1993.
3 Kenichi Ohmae, *The End of the Nation State*, The Free Press, New York, 1995.
4 Rosabeth Moss Kanter, *World Class: Thriving Locally in the Global Economy*, Simon and Schuster, New York, 1995.
5 *Ibid*, p. 24.
6 Samuel P. Huntington, *The Clash of Civilizations and the Remaking of World Order*, Simon and Schuster, New York, 1998.

Nowhere in the world are the stakes for rejuvenation more acute. As the new century began, Asia emerged from an intensely debilitating two-year financial and structural crisis to find itself in dramatically changed circumstances. Regionally, China had become a formidable competitor for foreign investment and tourism. Internationally, Central and South America and Eastern Asia had become attractive destinations for all kinds of investment. With increased pressure to recruit higher value-added investment of all kinds, much of Asia was no longer a cost-effective base for labor-intensive, low-cost manufacturing. Yet, poor educational infrastructure made it difficult for Asia to produce the number and quality of people required by value-creating enterprises, despite the region's huge population.

This book argues that in this changing and challenging environment, places need to adopt a strategic marketing plan to take advantage of the advances Asian places have already achieved. Strategic market planning is not a singular attempt to solve a crisis or a financial shortfall, but involves an ongoing process that is flexible and broad-based to enable a place to face and adapt to the ever-changing world marketplace. A place dedicated to a comprehensive marketing plan will have developed a template that is flexible and avoids hasty and ill-conceived quick fixes.

There are six main issues that will shape the success of Asian places' marketing efforts. The first is the necessity of place excellence in the New Asia. Asia has some of the strongest branded places in the world that excel in investment, resident and visitor attractions. Whether it is the tourism magnetism of Hong Kong, Singapore or Thailand, the automotive strength of South Korea, or the financial prowess of Tokyo, these places have enormous brand equity. Asia has a unique history and culture in comparison to other continents. Furthermore, Asia's vast resources include not only ancient castles and other architectural masterpieces, but also skilled workforces, important clusters of industries, and a rich diversity of people and languages.

There are hundreds — perhaps thousands — of places in Asia that enjoy superiority in some area of place marketing. The challenge in the 21st century is to create a structure big enough to support the many market leaders while concurrently encouraging new players to build their own reputations for excellence as preferred places to invest, reside or visit. Recent trends toward monetary regionalism, the easing of travel regulations, and regional Internet strategy mean that, for the first time, all Asian places, large and small, may finally share an emerging common identity other than one tied to geography.

A second issue is that places are increasingly responsible for their own marketing. Local places will be empowered to find strategies that stand out in a marketplace crammed with competitors. This challenge is the natural outcome of an Asia that is highly competitive and locally based. Winning strategies will include comprehensive self-auditing, sourcing outside financing to meet goals, building meaningful buyer-seller relationships, managing and marketing infrastructure, and skillfully promoting products. Such marketing efforts may appear overwhelming to small or historically under-marketed places. However, success stories abound all over Asia as strong leadership and systematic marketing applications overcome size and location problems.

The third issue is the integration of information technology — "infostructure" — into the marketing plan. The pace of technology is so rapid that it enables even the smallest town access to new markets. Many places will face the dilemma of deciding when to buy into technologies and at what cost. While infrastructure, capital and skilled workforces are essential to entrepreneurial ventures, technology enhances the opportunities. For example, location is no longer a primary consideration for some industries and services. Technology now enables places around the world to compete on a level playing field for a large number of jobs that were previously confined to major markets.

The fourth issue concerns the importance of managing the communication process. The marketing of places involves image-making, promotion, and information distribution. Technology has facilitated the use of the Internet, fax, and desktop publishing, but all these breakthroughs demand the management of communication skills and strategies. Many places will be developing image campaigns, writing proposals and communicating across a wide variety of media. All these responsibilities demand an understanding of how communication strategy is integral to the overall marketing plan.

The fifth issue relates to the conflicting trend towards localism and regionalism in Asia (known as *divergence*), on the one hand, and, on the other, the trend toward harmonizing rules and standards in Asia and the world (known as *convergence*). Asia is decentralizing from an economy of nations and cities into regions of manufacturing and service. At the same time, East Asia recently begun to generate a degree of collective enthusiasm for a common market. If fully developed, this convergence initiative will immediately present the fastest-growing aggregation of exporting states in the world. Paradoxically, this huge market will create an endless number of opportunities for individual places. Indeed, as the Commission of the European Communities acknowledged with respect to the European Union, "Cohesion and diversity are not conflicting objectives, but can be mutually reinforcing."[11]

The sixth issue reflects the increasing shortage of trained workers and the need for places to retain, recruit, and excel in the management of their talent pool. The aging world population in North America, Europe and parts of Asia has created the "brain-drain" phenomenon. It is routine in some places for skilled workers to be extensively trained and then quickly move to more lucrative sites. Britain, for example, is suffering from a depletion of its information technology talent to the Eastern European countries, which offer more money and promising business opportunities. The race for highly skilled talent demands new initiatives, focused targeting of the potential labor pool, and cooperation of governmental agencies, educational institutions and labor associations.

All of these issues are now set in a competitive context that can only be characterized as intense. There are many more places that are willing and capable of developing marketplace investment strategies. The influence of multinational companies and the emergence of the worldwide market impel every community to assess its identity. The global economy, with its unrelenting movement toward interconnected goods and services, creates a greater urgency for excellence and a higher standard of performance in all places. Rosabeth Moss Kanter implores places to upgrade their education and training systems, their export efforts and their entire place marketing operations to meet the global challenge.[12] The higher standards require that communities recognize their strengths and weaknesses and systematically upgrade their services and products.

A BOTTOM-UP APPROACH TO THE ASIAN GROWTH CHALLENGE

For purposes of developing an Asian concept of the marketing of places for investment-, resident- and visitor-attraction, our focus follows a "bottom-up" process of how places, communities and regions manage to compete in the global economy. We have researched how many individual places in the New Asia are managing to improve their competitiveness and secure economic growth. While Asia, as a whole, faces formidable growth, development and economic transition problems, there are Asian "hot spots" which can teach other places how to achieve positive growth. Such lessons are vital for creating jobs and opportunity.

The high achievers are models to emulate given that much of Asia remains characterized by poverty (47.5% of the population in Bangladesh, for instance, lives in poverty), particularly in rural communities. Unemployment (at around 5% in the first six months of 2000) is at historic highs in Japan, the world's second-largest economy, and reaches double digits in many of Asia's emerging economies. Yet, many of their capitals do not know how to take the necessary steps to understand the importance of unlocking Asia's potential for long-term economic growth.

The Asian Development Bank (ADB) reported in early 2000 that 1999 had "brought a shift from crisis toward recovery: Estimates indicate that all the crisis countries except Indonesia saw substantial gross domestic product (GDP) growth, ranging from 3.2% in the Philippines to around 10.7% in South Korea."[13] (See Table 1.1 for GDP of selected Asian economies). At the same time, the report cautioned that the "recovery, while impressive, masks substantial problems, particularly in the corporate and financial sectors. Distress in the financial sector and restructuring costs have proved to be far larger than anticipated." The Bank and other analysts highlighted a need for stronger economic infrastructure and entrepreneurial practices if Asia was to avoid another crisis. Concerns included:

- Enormous non-performing loans (NPLs). It was believed that 60–85% of loans in Indonesia, and 50–70% in Thailand, were non-performing, compared to 20–30% in South Korea.
- An ailing corporate sector, as indicated by the high incidence of NPLs.
- A lack of acceleration in restructuring. Although the crisis countries had begun to restructure, they needed to pick up the pace.

Table 1.1: Growth rate of GDP in selected Asian economies

Economy	Growth rate of GDP (% per year)					
	1996	1997	1998	1999	2000	2001
Newly industrialized economies						
Hong Kong, China	4.5	5.0	−5.1	2.9	10.5	4.0
Korea, Rep of	6.8	5.0	−6.7	10.7	8.8	3.9
Singapore	7.5	8.0	1.5	5.4	9.9	5.0
Taipei, China	6.1	6.7	4.6	5.7	6.0	5.1
People's Republic of China	9.6	8.8	7.8	7.1	8.0	7.3
Southeast Asia						
Indonesia	7.8	4.7	−13.2	0.2	4.8	4.2
Malaysia	10.0	7.5	−7.5	5.4	8.5	4.9
Philippines	5.8	5.2	−0.5	3.2	3.9	3.1
Thailand	5.9	−1.8	−10.4	4.1	4.2	3.5

Source: *Asian Development Outlook 2000*, Manila, 2001, p. 208.

The magnitude of financial and corporate restructuring required to restore Asia's economies to long-term health will depend on increased levels of foreign investment and revenues from product and service exports. Increased earnings from international sources such as tourists and international residents will also be important to improve corporate and financial buoyancy. Revenue generation is an Asia-wide problem and is not confined to the crisis economies or intra-Asian groups such as the Association of Southeast Asian Nations (ASEAN) and the Asia-Pacific Economic Cooperation forum (APEC). With greater than 10 times the number of consumers in Europe and tens of millions of small- and medium-sized enterprises, cities from Tokyo to Bombay and Beijing to Canberra are affected. The questions are: How should Asia-Pacific economies improve their investment climate? Which new methods should be used to create new jobs? As questions of this type become central to strategic planning, there is an increased interest in and openness towards new solutions, often worked out on a local or regional level.

Asia also continues to wrestle with the evolution of its political culture. Its governments bore the blame for the financial crisis. Japan, South Korea, Indonesia and Thailand all saw governments thrown out of office, sometimes violently, as outraged voters called for accountability. Even when governments were retained, significant political upheaval took place. In Hong Kong, Beijing-appointed chief executive Tung Chee-hwa was held responsible for the perceived failure of the government to counter the crisis with strategies to shift the economy's reliance on speculative investment to value-generating enterprise. Malaysia's Prime Minister Mahathir Mohamad fired his deputy, Anwar Ibrahim, for what were, in the Prime Minister's view, a number of political transgressions. These included aggressive reforms and restructuring that impacted negatively on the Prime Minister's political supporters. Mahathir eventually fired his deputy on the basis of what appeared to be crudely invented — and controversial — sexual misconduct charges.[14] Anwar's unsettling removal led to large public demonstrations in the streets of Kuala Lumpur for the first time in decades. Subsequent elections in 2000 saw the ruling coalition lose support among its traditional Malay constituency.

Even when conditions improved dramatically, the trauma and insecurity constituents had suffered — layoffs and firings from once-secure lifetime jobs and the loss of life savings tied up in the region's once high-flying stock markets — kept the pressure on new governments in Thailand, South Korea and Indonesia to perform. (See composite stock price indices in Figure 1.1).

Figure 1.1: Composite stock price indices, crisis countries,
April 1997–December 1999 (1997 Q2 = 100)

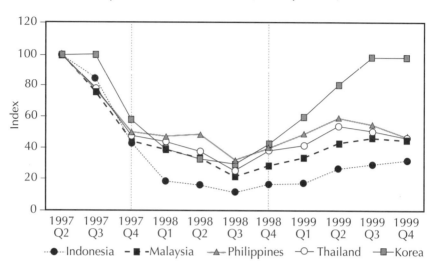

Source: *Asian Development Outlook 2000*, Manila, 2000, p. 24.

The Asian insecurity, the puzzled spectators and the problems of managing change are obvious on a macro level. On the other hand, there is another structure on the micro level that suggests how to manage change. There are thousands of positive growth communities and dynamic local clusters that are unevenly spread all over the Asian continent. For example, although unemployment remains a serious problem in much of Asia, there is already a shortage of Internet and technology workers. The demand in Asia for these skilled workers far exceeds the supply. Developed economies, particularly the United States, are recruiting many of Asia's best and brightest. It is estimated that Asia will be short of 600,000 knowledge workers by 2004.

Still, high-achieving areas are creating technology and other value-added jobs that stimulate already attractive clusters of businesses. Many winning places are the generators of these new businesses. However, many overly ambitious areas have poorly conceived government intervention that tends to foster cluster development, particularly in technology sectors. The clusters are unlikely to succeed. On the other hand, high-achieving places in Asia can provide positive examples of how to maintain effective place-marketing strategies for other communities, cities and regions.

Many hot spots are also confronted with the problem of attracting employable people. This raises a long-term challenge: Over the next 20 years Asia runs the risk of a massive decrease in the labor force. The ADB has warned that although "Asia's population is young, it is aging rapidly. As fertility rates continue to fall and life expectancy continues to rise, a demographic structure with relatively few young people and a large elderly population will emerge. In China, Hong Kong, Singapore, Sri Lanka, and Taiwan's capital Taipei, those aged 60 or more will make up more than 20% of the population by 2050. In these economies, there will be five old people for every two people of working age."[15] Already, 60% of East Asia's population is aged 60 or older, and "continuing population shifts in Northeast Asia, Malaysia, Singapore, and Thailand will be a drag on growth over the next 25 years," according to Harvard University economists Jeffrey G. Williamson and David E. Bloom.[16] As Asia's aging population shifts more and more into retirement, many Asian places will find themselves in a situation where a lack of employable people, rather than unemployment, is the foremost obstacle.

The skilled-worker drought is magnified by two factors: Asia's neglect of educational infrastructure during its miracle years, and the aggressive recruitment of promising young knowledge workers by multinational technology companies. Strategic investment-, resident- and visitor-attraction planning can be an effective solution in this challenging situation. Singapore, Malaysia and Taiwan have adopted resident-attraction programs that are, in many respects, as important as their investment-attraction programs. However, international competition for scarce knowledge workers means these economies must continue to develop innovative marketing strategies.

There are other problems that affect growth. Economic analyses on macro levels, such as nations and mega-regions, tend to overlook the complex realities underlying the development of local strategies for growth. The broad sweep prevents us from discovering how to create a growth dynamic and make it flourish. In traditional post-war thinking up until the Asian financial crisis, many regarded Asia as a high-growth "miracle," which started in Japan, moved rapidly south and west towards South Korea, and encompassed Hong Kong and Taiwan. The end probably began where the miracle started, with the onset of Japan's decade-long recession in the early 90s, but it is more frequently associated with Thailand's sensational surrender to currency speculators in July 1997.

Today, Asia is rarely referred to as a miracle; nevertheless, its rapid emergence from crushing poverty and rampant political instability was no mirage either. Despite its problems, Southeast Asia emerged rapidly from the worst financial crisis since the Great Depression. Japan remains the second most powerful manufacturing nation in the world, and much

Table 1.2: Incidence of poverty measured by surveys, selected Asian developing economies, selected years (%)

Sub-region and country	Survey year	Head-count index (nat'l poverty line)	Survey year	Head-count index (nat'l poverty line)	Survey year	Head-count index ($1-a-day)
Newly industrialized economies						
Korea, Rep of	1970	23	1984	5	1998	>1
Southeast Asia						
Indonesia	1976	40	1996	11	1996	8
Malaysia	1970	49	1992	16	1995	4
Philippines	1971	52	1997	38	1994	27
Thailand	1975	32	1992	13	1992	>2
Vietnam	1993	58	1998	37		
South Asia						
Bangladesh	1973	73	1996	36		
India	1972	52	1994	35	1994	47
Nepal	1979	61	1996	42	1995	50
Pakistan	1975	43	1992	28	1991	12
Sri Lanka	1983	22	1997	21	1994	4

Some years in the earliest survey may refer to the midpoint of the period covered. Data for $1-a-day poverty are estimates based on the most recent surveys.

Source: Asian Development Outlook 2000, Manila, 2000, p. 181.

of South Asia is showing encouraging signs that it intends to follow the example of North and Southeast Asian economies in enhancing quality of life. The emphasis is upon reducing poverty, which is already almost non-existent in Hong Kong, South Korea, Singapore and Taiwan. (Table 1.2 surveys poverty levels of developing economies.) Although obstacles to financial reform and corporate restructuring remain, the outlook is positive. Asia is making consistent progress towards addressing the basic principles of sustainable growth.

The drive to transform Asia into a marketing leader has encouraged the creation of advanced products and services. Already, many Asian governments have identified technology and the Internet as growth sectors. They have invested substantial funds in the development of research parks, and projects that are intended to stimulate technology clusters. Whether direct government intervention can create technology clusters remains to be seen, but it is clear that new economic sectors are forcing dramatic changes in the way Asians live and how enterprises do business.

However, these sectors — as they do elsewhere in the world — overshadow other value-added sectors such as medicine, fashion, publishing, graphic arts and entertainment. As the cluster-growth map of Asia (see Figure 1.2) shows, Asia owes its future prosperity to more than technology and the Internet. Indeed, there are many dynamic and some unexpected clusters of excellence spread throughout Asia. The growth map indicates that successful measures have been taken within a specific

Figure 1.2: Selected Asian clusters

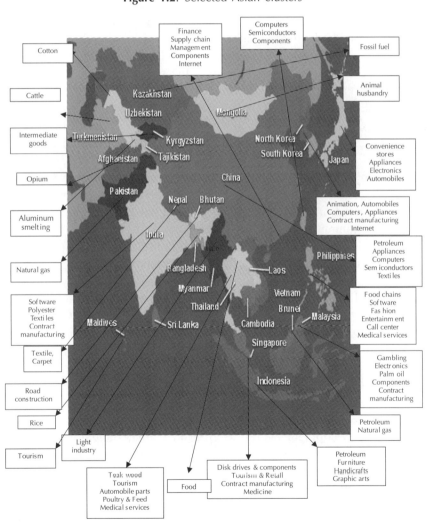

Asian city, community or region. In one way or another — by design or not — these places have developed strategies to increase their attractiveness to investors, industries, residents and visitors.

In this book, we examine and describe strategies that Asian communities have implemented to achieve a stronger position as markets and destinations for investment, residents and visitors. Many Asian places with weak identities can reverse their decline and experience a rebirth and revitalization through the process of strategic market planning.

STRATEGIC MARKET PLANNING OUTSIDE ASIA

Many places outside of Asia have achieved significant identity and growth by applying the principles of strategic market planning. In Europe, Paris works hard at sustaining its image as a world fashion and cultural center. Frankfurt is emerging as Europe's financial capital. Cambridge capitalizes on its university location to develop a reputation as an important center for biotechnology research.

Some European countries have specialized in attracting service-related firms. Ireland has marketed itself, for example, as a source of knowledge workers and has encouraged foreign investment. Many firms from traditional and non-traditional sectors are together making Ireland an international-customer-relationship call center. Others have established back-office administration functions. Major international companies such as Intel, Dell Computer, Microsoft, and Digital Equipment are among many now committed to this European economic tiger.

U.S. cities such as St. Paul, Indianapolis and Baltimore are prospering after a period of stagnation. North Carolina, which 40 years ago was the second-poorest state in the U.S., now provides an exceptionally attractive business climate. Many Asian regional and business managers are visiting North Carolina and its successful cities of Durham, Chapel Hill and Raleigh to experience first-hand their strategic marketing. Neighboring South Carolina managed an even more dramatic turnaround by creating a world-class training program for workers and attracting major companies such as BMW.

An example of the radical shifts in the fortunes of places is shown by the decision of IBM to choose four unlikely cities to constitute its "round-the-clock development cycle:" Beijing in China, Bangalore in India, Minsk in Belarus and Riga in Latvia. Twenty years ago, the list would probably have included London, Brussels or New York. In a rapidly changing worldwide market, there is broader opportunity for places to develop a niche and reposition their mix of workers and businesses.

WHAT IS ASIA?

The Asian area of the world we discuss in this book covers an immense tract: from China and Mongolia to the north; Japan and the islands of the Pacific Ocean and New Guinea to the east; Australia to the south; and Pakistan and Kazakhstan to the west. These areas span six international time zones. Moreover, the world's most populous nations are in Asia. China, India and Indonesia alone account for about 2.5 billion people. Indonesia is the largest Muslim nation on earth, and 16 of the world's largest cities are in Asia. (Table 1.3 compares Asia's population figures.)

Table 1.3: The countries of Asia

Economy	Population (million)	Economy	Population (million except *)
Newly industrialized		Tonga	108,207*
economies		Tuvalu	10,444*
Hong Kong, China	7	Vanuatu	185,204*
Korea, Rep. of	46	**People's Republic of China**	
Singapore	3	**and Mongolia**	
Taiwan	22	China, People's Rep of	1.227
Southeast Asia		Mongolia	3
Cambodia	11	**Central Asian republics**	
Indonesia	200	Kazakhstan	16
Lao People's Democratic Rep.	5	Kyrgyz Republic	5
Malaysia	21	Tajikistan	6
Myanmar	47	Uzbekistan	24
Philippines	73	**South Asia**	
Thailand	61	Bangladesh	124
Vietnam	77	Bhutan	2
Pacific DMCs		India	961
Cook Islands	19,989*	Maldives	290,211*
Fiji Island	802,611*	Nepal	23
Kiribati		Pakistan	137
Marshall Islands	63,031*	Sri Lanka	18
Micronesia, Federated		**Northeast Asia**	
States of	129,658*	Japan	126
Nauru	10,501*	**Australasia**	
Papua New Guinea	5	Australia	19
Samoa	62,093*	New Zealand	4
Solomon Islands	441,039*		
Total all countries			3,275
* Actual population shown for very small states.			

Source: World Development Report: Knowledge for Development (1998/1999), pp. 190–91.

Asia's vast geographical area — a total of 44,936,000 sq km — encompasses a market estimated in 2000 to be more than 3.6 billion inhabitants living in 40 countries, or about 60% of the world's population. Here, about 400 million consumers have disposable incomes equal to those of the world's developed economies.[17] Although Asia covers only one-third of the total global area, it contains 60% of the world's population. Altogether, it easily comprises the biggest market in the world. However, Asia only accounts for approximately 30% of the gross world product, compared to around 55% for North America and Europe combined.[18]

At the local level, there are large numbers of organizational groups working to improve the reputations and identities of their economies. Japan, Asia's newly industrialized economies and Southeast Asia have 449 metropolitan centers, over 1,200 regions and more than 600,000 communities. In most Asian countries, the first level of public organization is at the neighborhood level. Each community has its own image, problems and positioning possibilities.

Above the local level, Asia's regions are best characterized by their incredible ethnic and cultural diversity. This diversity is apparent between indigenous Chinese territories, special administrative regions and republics, such as Singapore, Taiwan and Hong Kong, as well as between the regions of China, where dialect, cuisine and physical appearance differ dramatically. Those contrasts are even greater between the northern and southern regions of Asia, and are equaled only by the contrasts between eastern and western regions.

The economic potential of this vast market has drawn many investors. From 1993 to 1998 investors poured US$432 billion into Asia, not including Japan. Portfolio investments were almost five times greater before Asia's financial crisis, but quickly evaporated in 1997. Some of that investment, however, began to return in 1999. The Asian market has, contrary to conventional wisdom, failed to attract as much American investment as Europe (see Figure 1.3). While the U.S. and Japan have for decades dueled for the status of largest source of FDI (Foreign Direct Investment), that competition has distorted the overall Asian picture.

When it comes to FDI-flows to emerging economies, Asia continues to be the principal destination for investment (see Figure 1.4). About half of that investment is intra-Asian (ex-Japan), and Japan and the United States are the principal investors. Competition for FDI from Latin America presents a significant competitive threat to Asia, highlighting the dangers of complacency.

The reasons for lower U.S. investment in Asia than in Europe vary, but the most obvious factor is that the potential of the Asian market is

Figure 1.3: American dollar investment (U.S. cumulative direct investment)

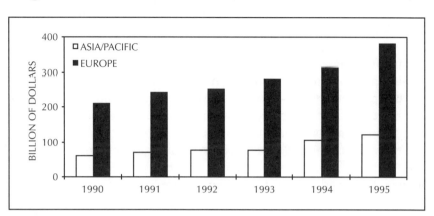

Source: "Old World, New Investment." Data from U.S. Commerce Department, published in *Business Week*, October 7, 1996, p. 16.

Figure 1.4: FDI-flows in emerging economies

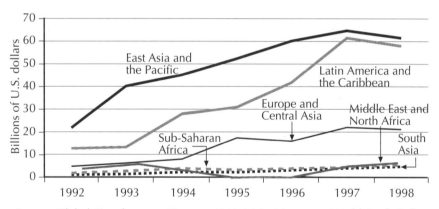

Source: Global Development Finance 1999 Main Messages, World Bank Debtor Reporting System, (http://www.worldbank.org/prospects/gdf99/slides/sld012.htm, viewed on September 18, 2000).

strategic. Investors in Asia, especially in China, are positioning themselves for the future, while investors in developed Europe, where consumers enjoy higher purchasing power, seek to realize returns much more quickly. An apparent lack of intra-Asian competitive zeal seems to be another factor. Asian underachievement is profiled in The World

Competitiveness Scoreboard compiled annually by the International Institute for Management Development (see Table 1.4). The scoreboard represents a benchmark by which Asian countries can measure themselves. Europe clearly dominates the list, and Asian economies account for only about 26% of the 47 countries ranked.

Singapore's number-two ranking demonstrates that an Asian economy can compete at a world-class level. While its small population offers advantages for moving forward, Singapore has transformed itself from a poor to a rich nation in less than 50 years.

Striving for world-class competitiveness is an important issue for Asia. Although most Asian economies are not overly reliant on the U.S. or other developed markets for the lion's share of their trade, the value of exports to the United States, as a percentage of GDP (Gross Domestic Product), is alarmingly high (see Figure 1.5). When economic

Table 1.4: The World Competitiveness Scoreboard

Rank	Country	Score	Rank	Country	Score
1	USA	100.00	26	Japan	57.52
2	Singapore	87.66	27	Hungary	55.64
3	Finland	83.38	28	Korea	51.08
4	Luxembourg	82.81	29	Malaysia	50.03
5	Netherlands	81.46	30	Greece	49.96
6	Hong Kong	79.55	31	Brazil	49.66
7	Ireland	79.20	32	Italy	49.58
8	Sweden	77.86	33	China	49.53
9	Canada	76.94	34	Portugal	48.36
10	Switzerland	76.81	35	Czech Rep.	46.68
11	Australia	75.87	36	Mexico	43.67
12	Germany	74.04	37	Slovak Rep.	43.59
13	Iceland	73.75	38	Thailand	42.67
14	Austria	72.54	39	Slovenia	42.48
15	Denmark	71.79	40	Philippines	40.60
16	Israel	67.92	41	India	40.41
17	Belgium	66.03	42	South Africa	38.61
18	Taiwan	64.84	43	Argentina	37.51
19	U.K.	64.78	44	Turkey	35.44
20	Norway	63.10	45	Russia	34.57
21	New Zealand	61.73	46	Colombia	32.84
22	Estonia	60.20	47	Poland	32.01
23	Spain	60.14	48	Venezuela	30.66
24	Chile	59.84	49	Indonesia	28.26
25	France	59.56			

Source: IMD http://www.imd.ch/wcy/ranking/index.cfm, viewed on May 22, 2001.

Figure 1.5: Asia is vulnerable to a U.S. downturn

DESTINATION U.S.				
Exports from Southeast Asia			Impact of a sharp downturn in U.S.	
	To the U.S. as percentage of total	Value of exports as percentage of GDP	Predicted percentage-point declines in national GDP in 2001	
Philippines	29.8%	51.3%	Philippines	2.1
Thailand	21.6	57.2	Thailand	1.0
Singapore	19.0	97.5	Singapore	2.2
Indonesia	13.0	35.0	Indonesia	0.3
Malaysia	21.9	124.1*	Malaysia	2.8

* Includes value-added transshipments through Malaysia
Source: ING Barings

Source: Robert Frank, "Suddenly, Southeast Asia's Recovery Looks Dubious: Weakness in U.S. Could Hit Exports," *The Wall Street Journal*, June 13, 2000, p. A19.

slowdowns in U.S. and European markets occur, Asian economies have limited alternatives for generating revenue and jobs.

THE ASIAN MARKETING CHALLENGE

Asian cities, communities and regions are trying to develop their own strategies for the future. Millions of local and regional decision-makers are involved. The common denominator today is the struggle for more jobs and investment. Intense competition between markets is evident in investment-attraction battles fought between Thailand and the Philippines for automobile manufacturing capacity, and between Hong Kong and Singapore for financial-center and technology-hub supremacy.

Many cities, communities and regions that have succeeded in attracting substantial investment have spurred others to identify and pursue opportunities. In Asia, public interest in a story seems to be even greater if a region has managed to outbid another. When General Motors decided in 1996 to build a US$650 million plant in Thailand rather than the Philippines it created media headlines in both countries. The Philippines rebounded somewhat in 1998 when Ford announced a US$150-million investment. Ford's move into the Philippines, like the earlier GM move into Thailand, elicited considerable media attention and renewed speculation on future competition among Asian nations.[19]

Despite many high-profile triumphs, the future of outside investment remains uncertain:

- Asia's share in world FDI doubled from 9% to 18% in the last decade, but its share of FDI to developing countries has remained stable at 55%.[20]
- FDI into South Asia grew by a multiple of 15 in the last decade, largely due to the opening of India and interest in China. India's FDI was around US$2.7 billion in the late 1990s, but was dwarfed by China's US$41 billion received from 1995 to 1998.[21]
- The main source of FDI has been the region itself, as both newly industrializing and emerging economies sought to shift manufacturing capacity to low-wage economies.[22] Now, markets are more exposed to foreign competition following liberalization, and the historical low-labor-cost advantages are dissipating. This puts pressure on Asian economies to focus on increasing value-added products and services with, in many cases, inadequate educational infrastructure.
- A large number of major investments are regularly announced in the Asian business press, but they are almost exclusively intra-Asian, as in the case of Pacific Century Cyberworks' takeover of Cable & Wireless Hong Kong Telecom, which dwarfs other recent merger and acquisition activity in Asia.

There is hope for the future as Asia begins to restructure:

- Many Asian places are moving towards liberalization and their markets are now significantly more open for attracting new companies and investors. Former monopolies are disappearing, most notably in telecommunications, energy, and transportation, leaving room for new initiatives and enterprises. A restructuring boom and consolidation is apparent in a broad spectrum of strategic sectors, including banking and financial services, manufacturing, telecommunications and construction throughout Asia. While this process has not been smooth, mostly as a result of local opposition by owners and employees, pressure to rationalize unproductive sectors has been constant because of globalization, liberalization and technology. That's unlikely to change.
- Privatization is opening up opportunities for new investors.
- Asia's economies are aggressively competing in New Economy sectors such as information technology, the Internet and communication businesses.

Strategic market planning is a systematic process that meets these competitive challenges.

CONCLUSION

The challenges to excel in both the Asian and global marketplace have never been greater. At the very least, success requires more dynamic and aggressive investment-attraction activity and commitment to longer-term strategic planning. Although Asia has not been without strategic planning, much of this has been characterized by heavy public subsidies, limited public-private partnerships, public officials without commercial experience, and a lack of innovative endeavor. With the impact of globalization on how business is done and an accelerating pace of change worldwide, past practices are often no longer workable. The emerging global economy demands new thinking to harness future opportunities. Inevitably, local decision-makers face two fundamental questions: How can we move up the scoreboard of competitiveness to excel in attracting investment, residents and visitors for economic advancement? Where can we find successful lessons to guide our own planning?

The next chapter identifies many of the problems Asian places face in global competition and outlines some of the solutions for overcoming such problems.

1 Jim Rohwer, "China on the Move," *Fortune*, May 14, 2001, p. 74
2 May Sin-Mi Hong, "HK not dead but thriving as finance hub: Antony Leung," *South China Morning Post*, May 11, 2001, Internet edition.
3 "The RHQ question: How are multinational companies organizing themselves in the Asia Pacific, and why do they choose to site their regional headquarters the way they do?," *Business Asia*, December 11, 2000, pp. 1–4.
4 "What shoots up must fall down," *Asiaweek*, May 11, 2001, pp. 80–81.
5 Michael Shari, "Mahathir's About-Face: A drop in foreign reserves leads to friendlier policies," *BusinessWeek*, May 28, 2001, p. 59.
6 Julian Gearing, "That Thai Touch: It's the award-winning, sales-boosting formula of Bangkok's admakers," *Asiaweek*, February 9, 2001, p. 42.
7 *Ibid.*
8 "What Asia's science and technology parks have to offer," *Asia-Inc.*, April 2001, p. 44.
9 Bruce Einhorn, "The Big Squeeze: Tight space and poor infrastructure threaten Taiwan's Silicon Valley," *BusinessWeek*, March 12, 2001, p. 18.
10 Alexandra A. Seno, "Lights, Camera, Tourists!," *Asiaweek*, March 2, 2001, p. 38.
11 "First Report on Economic and Social Cohesion," Commission of the Asian Communities, Brussels/Luxembourg, 1996, p. 15.
12 Rosabeth Moss Kanter, *World Class: Thriving Locally in the Global Economy* (New York: Simon & Schuster, 1995).
13 *Asian Development Outlook 2000*, Asian Development Bank, Manila, 2000, p. 24.
14 John Funston, "Malaysia's Tenth Elections: Status Quo, Reformasi or Islamization?", *Contemporary Southeast Asia* (Dow Jones Interactive, April 2000).

15 *Asian Development Outlook 2000*, Asian Development Bank, Manila, 2000, p. 201.
16 Pierre G. Goad, "Fundamental Factors: Study Cites Demographics for Asia's Rapid Growth", *Asian Wall Street Journal*, July 27, 1998, p. 1.
17 Jim Rohwer, *Asia Rising* (Singapore: Butterworth-Heinemann Asia, 1995), p. 32.
18 *Ibid.*
19 http://media.ford.com/article_display.cfm?article_id=2399, viewed on June 14, 2001.
20 "Five-fold Rise in FDI Flow to Asia-Pacific Region," *Business Standard*, February 19, 2000, p. 8.
21 *Ibid.*
22 "ADB: Foreign Direct Investment Spurs Asia's Development," M2 Presswire, April 21, 1999.

CHAPTER 2

Asian Places
in Trouble

POSITIONING PLACES FOR INVESTMENT: PROBLEMS
AND OPPORTUNITIES

S uccessful brand positioning for investment attraction is dependent
on the ability of a place to adapt to the demands of a constantly
changing global marketplace. Since places are competing for a
narrowing pool of investment dollars, adaptation must be both rapid and
effective. Those places that don't adapt, or don't adapt rapidly enough,
see their reputations decline as desirable destinations for investment,
tourists and new residents. At the extreme are places experiencing severe
economic difficulties as a result of economic crises and political and
social restructuring. These places lack even the internal resources to
launch a recovery. Some small towns and cities have lost major
industries or business — often at the hands of new technologies and
changing market circumstances. The repercussions are high
unemployment, bankrupt businesses, abandoned property and
burgeoning slums. People and businesses migrate, leaving a weak tax
base from which the community struggles to fund schools and other
public services.

The migration of rural residents to urban areas with inadequate
support infrastructure and few job opportunities creates other problems.
For instance, depressed areas become vulnerable to crime and drugs,

accelerating their decline. Jakarta, Manila, Bangkok and many other major metropolitan centers in Asia struggle to contain violence and drug addiction among poor communities. It can take decades to reverse the negative images of socioeconomic decline once entrenched and reinforced by regional and international media.

Nonetheless, some acutely depressed places still show some potential for revival. While Jakarta, Bangkok, Manila and other metropolitan centers may have severe problems, many of them also possess historical, cultural, underdeveloped commercial and, sometimes, even political assets that could support a turnaround if the right leadership and vision should emerge.

Other places historically exhibit boom-and-bust characteristics. Their mix of industries and growth-hungry companies is generally highly sensitive to business cycle movements. Hong Kong is one place that has dealt successfully with the threat of boom-bust cycles by turning from labor-intensive production to services such as banking and finance, property development, telecommunications and supply chain management. Hong Kong's shift to services also helped it to emerge as the region's principal gateway to China.

Hong Kong has weathered further economic and political change, following its return to China and the impact of the Asian financial crisis of 1997 and 1998, which brought on five consecutive quarters of decline. The administration of Tung Chee-hwa and many private-sector supporters focused subsequent reforms on reducing a perceived over-reliance on the more speculative service industries such as investment banking and real estate. As a result, the government has taken initiatives to support the development of high value-added industries, particularly in the high-technology sector.

Hong Kong's high-technology initiatives include a Science Park — 22 hectares are being developed at a cost of US$640 million[1] in the first of three phases[2], and a HK$15.8 billion (US$2 billion) Cyberport.[3] The Cyberport and Silicon Harbor are being developed in partnership with the private sector, while the Science Park has as its chairman a private-sector representative, Victor Lo, chairman and chief executive of Gold Peak Industries. Despite criticism that the projects favor business leaders supportive of Tung and his administration, the projects have moved forward.

The government has also liberalized key sectors of the Hong Kong economy, including banking and telecommunications, in order to stimulate competition and to reduce operating costs for business. The Asian Development Bank (ADB) observed that "Liberalizing the international calls market in January 1999 and implementing mobile phone number portability in March 1999 saw an increase suppliers and fierce competition for market share throu cheaper services."[4] Banking reform has likewise been rigoi Kong standards. Reforms have allowed foreign banks to ha᷈ local branches and deregulated the rules governing intei... .... reduce dependence on the local equity market and banking sector for long-term funding, the Hong Kong Monetary Authority "moved aggressively to build capital development," including the introduction of mortgage-backed securities.

The challenges continue. First, educational infrastructure does not produce the quantity or quality of knowledge workers Hong Kong needs to become a technology hub. Shanghai and other emerging Mainland enterprise centers are competing aggressively for many of the service industries that have underpinned Hong Kong's economy. To complicate matters further, the center of political power has shifted to Beijing, Hong Kong residents and investors as increasing anxiety among challenges to social and political freedoms become more frequent. Their unease was heightened in January 2001 when popular chief secretary Anson Chan retired following reports of strained relations with the chief executive and Beijing leaders.

Nevertheless, there is evidence that Hong Kong and many other places in Asia are orchestrating healthy transformations. They have devised place-marketing plans to create new conditions that improve their attractiveness. Manila is gradually transforming itself from an economic backwater into a high-technology human resource center, following in the footsteps of similar success in Bangalore in India. Singapore is attempting to position itself as Asia's financial services center by emulating Hong Kong and deregulating its banking and communication sectors. Other examples of transformations in Asia are Boat Quay in Singapore and Penang in Malaysia (see Exhibits 2.1 and 2.2).

Exhibit 2.1: SINGAPORE DISCOVERS URBAN RENEWAL

Singapore is more widely known for its squeaky-clean image than for urban renewal. However, like any growing metropolitan center, the city-state has had to deal with urban decline in areas affected by economic change. Singapore's Boat and Clarke Quays are characterized by crowded "shophouses" — old townhouse-like structures that combine business and residential premises. As the center of commerce shifted away from these traditional enterprise centers and customers dwindled, the shophouses fell into decline. Singapore decided to restore the areas and, in so doing, enhanced the city-state's image as an interesting place to shop and be entertained.

As Singapore continued to transform itself over time from an economy dominated by small business and trading to an international center for computer and IT products and financial services, the traditional business centers moved to high-rise office buildings, new industrial zones and business parks. As tourism grew, many merchants moved to boutique spaces in shopping malls and department stores along Singapore's fabled Orchard Road.

There were skeptics to the plan of converting older neighborhoods. "How commercially viable is it in the long term to convert old shophouses or landmarks into retail and food and beverage outlets?"[1] asked journalist Jaime Ee in 1999. Already, a number of derelict shophouses had been successfully converted into trendy art-deco offices and restaurants, with somewhat mixed results. Boat Quay and Clarke Quay, separated by the once-polluted Singapore River, demonstrate why the idea worked in some places and not in others.

Boat Quay experienced the greater success. This bustling development was an overnight hit, commanding the highest rentals of the rebuilt projects[2] (although average rental rates remain substantially below those in the Central Business District), which it adjoins. Boat Quay is the short riverside street that, on most evenings, is crowded with executives and tourists alike. The area appealed to a new generation of young Singaporean and expatriate executives — which helps to explain why the street's trendy bars and restaurants are so popular. Just across the river, Clarke Quay hasn't been as successful in attracting patronage, despite the fact that it offers more entertainment, many restaurants and a large new hotel. The difference is simply one of location. It is easy to get to Boat Quay from Singapore's main business district while Clarke Quay is less accessible.

Clarke Quay's developers — DBS Land — realized that there was little hope of competing for Boat Quay's nightlife-seeking crowds of executives and tourists initially. So, instead, it turned Clarke Quay into a family entertainment center, focusing on the weekend leisure-seeker. This strategy increased Clarke Quay's rental occupancy to about 95% by 1999.[3] The developer is now seeking to attract more evening trade with improved land and water transportation, including an underground tunnel to Boat Quay. Both Quays have been transformed into business, dining and entertainment centers, creating value where there was formerly very little.

The lessons of Boat Quay and Clarke Quay are instructive for urban planners and marketers:

- World trends show new-generation consumers value more authentic and culturally interesting entertainment locations. Therefore, places that have old, unrestored neighborhoods have the opportunity to add value to the prosperity of local communities by investing in relevant urban renewal. Consider, for example, the restoration and now-favorable image of New York City's formerly run-down Lower East Side, with its successful mix of apartments and small-scale retail stores.

- Transforming older areas often creates cooperation between public and private sectors that generates flow-on benefits to public services and infrastructure. For example, the Quay restorations in Singapore included a river cleanup that improved the environment, and new water taxis were added to the public transport infrastructure.

Sources:

1 Jaime Ee, "Conservation for Consumers," *Business Times*, 1999, Dow Jones Interactive.
2 *Ibid.*
3 *Ibid.*

Exhibit 2.2: PENANG LEVERAGES CRISIS

"Penang is booming, and it has got the Asian Crisis to thank for the good times,"[1] the *Far Eastern Economic Review* reported in a story about Malaysia's Silicon Island in the summer of 2000. This article appeared at the same time Malaysia's finance minister was warning that lower Foreign Direct Investment (FDI) flows could hinder the nation's capacity to sustain a recovery. Both FDI and portfolio investors were wary of political unrest and worried about the government's reluctance to address financial reform and corporate restructuring. Nevertheless, the government of Penang and its technology-oriented economy was able to retain the confidence of its long-time trading partners.

Penang undertook important initiatives and the results were impressive. The most important initiative was to leverage the depreciation of the ringgit (unlike the national government), which plummeted as a result of the crisis. The depreciated currency significantly lowered costs in U.S.-dollar terms. This provided a good reason for companies to stay. Lower production costs also enabled investors to upgrade facilities, some of which now exceed those in the United States. For example, Intel's Penang facility is so advanced that problems that can't be solved in the United States are often sent there.

The Penang government also deserves credit for staying in contact with investors and providing innovative programs to help them remain competitive. For example, to ensure international supply standards from Penang's small- and medium-size enterprises (SMEs) to local multinational operating facilities, the government launched a Skills Development Center to "nurture Malaysian companies into world-class suppliers."[2] The program provides training in critical skills and matches up MNCs (multi-national companies) with local suppliers. Three progressive levels of competency-training assist in providing a steady supply of skilled knowledge workers.

The retention rate was outstanding. In the summer of 2000, Penang boasted 148 foreign companies, including technology leaders Motorola, Dell and Robert Bosch, which do business with 1,200 SMEs. Foreign investment in 1999 rose by 80%, to US$1.25 billion (most of it from existing companies) and the electronics industry was forecast to grow by 10.5% a year.[3] It did better in 1998. That year, US$2.1 billion of reinvestment flowed into Penang.[4] All of this was accomplished in an environment where some companies were seriously considering China and other locations as better alternatives for low-cost production prior to the Asian financial crisis.

Penang's future, of course, is far from assured. Like many other Asian technology hubs, problems remain. The availability of skilled people remains a serious issue, and FDI growth is still hampered by the lack of a strategic human resource pool. While current investors are prospering, new industrial investment is not growing. Nevertheless, Penang and its SME sector have solved difficulties before, and it is probably safe to assume that more proactive, clear thinking — and continued good luck — will provide a solution to the human resource problems, too. Indeed, Penang is working with local universities to build up a local skills base in such value-added fields as photonics to push investment up the food chain by luring investors fleeing Taiwan's crowded technology parks.[5]

───

Sources:

1 Simon Elegant, "All Wired Up: State-of-the-art Technology, Skilled Workers and a Savvy Government Keep Penang Humming," *Far Eastern Economic Review*, July 6, 2000, p. 72.
2 Marina Emmanuel, "Penang the Silicon Island," *The New Straits Times*, June 6, 2000, Dow Jones Interactive.
3 *Ibid.*
4 Lorien Holland with Simon Burns, "Penang Sees the Light: The country's 'silicon isle' is diversifying from chipmaking into the promising and potentially lucrative field of optonics," *Far Eastern Economic Review*, April 12, 2001, p. 48.
5 *Ibid.*

Many places in Asia may eventually be successful in transforming their economies, as illustrated by Manila, Hong Kong, Shanghai and Taiwan. The stakes are high. Places compete for billions of dollars in investment, job creation, and a move to value-added manufacturing and services. Failure to successfully manage economic transition successfully in the face of global change can have such an impact on socioeconomic stability that it is capable of threatening the very fabric of Asia's political systems.

Finally, some places have earned their place among the "favored few." Despite the impact of the Asian financial crisis, they continue to enjoy strong investment positioning, and to draw business people, new residents and tourists. Penang is one such place. Taiwan and Singapore also remain strong, but former tiger South Korea suffered hugely through Asia's financial crisis. To illustrate the changing fortunes of Asia's economies, investment banker Marc Faber asked investors to:

> ...visualize themselves (sic) as a powerful person wishing to invest in Asia in the year 1800. Your most logical choices would have been Calcutta, which was the administrative center of the British Empire, or Batavia, the capital of the Dutch East Indies. Today Calcutta has lost its luster; and Batavia, now called Jakarta, is one of the region's poorer performers.
>
> Imagine if you were making the same decision a century or so later, say in 1920. The most important city in Asia was Shanghai, a lively, bustling place known as "the Paris of the East". Other places which looked set to boom were Canton (now Guangzhou), Macau, Saigon (Ho Chi Minh City), Rangoon, and Manila — none of which thrived.
>
> At that time, both Singapore and Hong Kong were already relatively important trading centers and bases for British garrisons. But they had no industries of their own, so they didn't seem to be worthwhile conduits for investment. Seoul and Taipei? You probably wouldn't even have heard of them. If you had, you wouldn't have paid them much notice, as both were controlled by Japan. Even after the Second World War, there were few signs that the fastest growing economies in the world would be Japan, Hong Kong, Singapore, South Korea, and Taiwan.[5]

And how would a "powerful person" view today's investment hot spots in Asia? Guangzhou and the Pearl River Delta are enjoying dramatic growth primarily because of Hong Kong-led investment in manufacturing capacity. The lower cost of living and real estate threaten Hong Kong's still sky-high real-estate market. Shanghai shrugged off the debilitating effects of hurried, speculative growth that has made it vulnerable to Asia's financial crisis and contributed to a slowdown in FDI-flows to emerge as a real contender with Hong Kong and Singapore for regional headquarters of multinational firms. Meanwhile, most Asian places are still struggling to find their place in the sun. History tells us that while Singapore, Taipei and Hong Kong may be Asia's new favored few, these places must be diligent in preserving their positioning.

WHY DO PLACES LAND IN TROUBLE?

The Asian continent, with its many competing communities, regions and nations, continues to experience economic turbulence in the aftermath of the Asian financial crisis. This turbulence is often attributed to a slowing of economic reform and private-sector restructuring following most of Asia's return to growth in 1999. Other experts believe it is the result of the dot-com and technology sector downturn in the United States. The sector's revaluation came just as dot-com businesses were emerging in Asia, which dampened investor enthusiasm for non-traditional enterprise. Another view is that efforts by the U.S. Federal Reserve to slow down the U.S. economy have held back the pace of recovery in Asia. Regardless of the influence of any particular factor on investment-attraction competition at any one time, all places are subject to both internal and external forces. Competition is affected by internal growth and decline cycles and also by external impacts.

Internal Forces

Many places experience a period of growth followed by a period of decline, which is commonly seen in Asia and can be repeated many times. The growth period inevitably ends because growth lays the seeds of its own destruction. The processes underlying growth-and-decline dynamics can occur independently of the business cycle. However, these processes may be accelerated by sudden changes in the economic climate.

Figure 2.1 illustrates a well-documented city-growth dynamic and how the process of decline can follow. Imagine a city that is initially attractive. It might be blessed with expanding industries, an exceptional climate or natural beauty, and a remarkable historical heritage. Assuming that job opportunities are strong and the quality of life is appealing, this city inevitably attracts new residents, visitors, businesses and investment. However, the inward migration of people and resources raises housing and real-estate prices and puts pressure on the existing resources for infrastructure and social services. This process can be observed in many European and Asian cities, such as Paris, London, Tokyo, Seoul and Taipei. A city will typically raise taxes on residents and businesses to pay for additional services, such as transportation, communication, energy and social assistance. Some residents and businesses react by moving out of the city to reduce their costs which, in turn, reduces the tax base. Ironically, the attractions of a place can unleash forces that ultimately hurt its desirability, as Hong Kong and Tokyo have found to their dismay.

As a place begins to lose its attractiveness, forces can be released that further undermine the situation (see Figure 2.2). For example, a major

Figure 2.1: Growth dynamics

company or organization in a community might falter or depart. Jobs decline and real-estate prices fall. Soon the infrastructure deteriorates. These developments accelerate the outward migration of residents and businesses. Banks tighten credit and bankruptcies rise. Unemployment leads to more crime and drugs, and social problems increase, further tarnishing the image of the place. The community raises taxes to maintain or improve the infrastructure and meet social needs, but the higher taxes only accelerate the outward migration of resources.

Unfortunately, there are numerous examples of decline in Asia. Consider the shattering of Indonesia's economy and the splintering of its political cohesion. Up until the onset of Asia's financial crisis, Indonesia was often cited by institutions such as the World Bank and the International Monetary Fund as an excellent example of a large nation working effectively to alleviate poverty. From 1994 to 1996, per capita GDP growth was between 5.8 and 6.5%[6], a remarkable accomplishment for an emerging economy of 200 million people. The government of discredited former president Suharto successfully reduced the country's traditional reliance on agriculture and petroleum exports. In 1970, agriculture accounted for 35% of GDP, but only 17.4% in 1999. In contrast, industry and services accounted for over 82% of GDP that year.[7]

Figure 2.2: Dynamics of decline

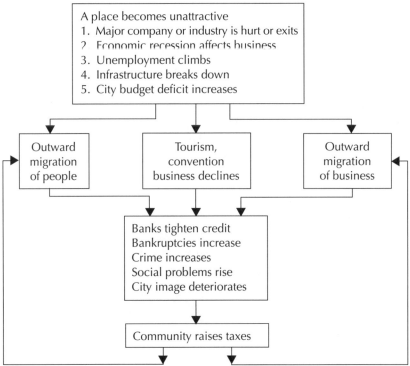

Overall, the incidence of poverty decreased from around 18% to just over 10% in 1997, compared to approximately 37% in the Philippines.[8]

However, the foundation for these gains proved to be extremely fragile when the crisis hit. Although the crisis was a region-wide phenomenon that "officially" began in Thailand, the structural weaknesses that made places vulnerable were internal. They comprised weak government institutions, mismanaged banks, private-sector inefficiencies and low productivity.

For example, uncompetitive firms controlled by the former president and his family dominated the Indonesian economy. As inadequately capitalized and incompetently run banks propped up these firms and their frequently speculative investments, the economy and the currency quickly crumbled. The government was unable to sustain subsidies on rice and other staples, such as cooking oil, and the Indonesian people took to the streets to hold their government accountable. The ensuing riots also targeted other areas of the community thought to have profited at the expense of the Indonesian people, such as the commercially successful indigenous Chinese. The economy soon contracted, by more than 13% in 1998.[9]

Indonesia's problems are far from over. Composed of 300 ethnic groups and 365 languages and dialects, Indonesia, according to Michael Backman, author of *Asian Eclipse* and an authority on corporate Asia, is "an amalgam of nations. Such amalgams were a creation of the 20th century and have largely died with it."[10] There are very real reasons to believe that Indonesia in its present form will not survive far into this century, as those who opposed independence in East Timor violently demonstrated. Until the country — or the states it evolves into — becomes more stable, repositioning itself for sustainable growth will be largely impossible.

External Forces

Places are also vulnerable to external factors over which they can exert little, or no, control. Three major forces upsetting the economic equilibrium of communities are:

- rapid technological change
- global competition
- political power shifts.

Rapid Technological Change

After the Second World War, Asia was principally a low-cost manufacturing center. It needed to create jobs — any jobs — to feed its billions, and the developed economies began shifting low value-added jobs offshore to achieve or maintain cost advantages. Then, as many of Asia's emerging economies rapidly transformed themselves into more prosperous nations, their cost advantages (such as taxes, wages, living expenses) eroded. Many Asian and multinational enterprises had to decide between increasing efficiencies and productivity or moving to lower-cost sites such as Vietnam, Cambodia or Laos. Many manufacturers found it more profitable to move.

This was particularly true for Hong Kong manufacturers, who moved their production to the mainland, principally Guangdong just across the border. Those same Hong Kong companies, however, are once again finding the need for new competitive strategies as China's policies evolve and costs rise. This time, the choice is not so simple. There are fewer places to move to, and the transfer of manufacturing is vulnerable to fast-changing global economic conditions. It is harder to compete on price, and businesses are under pressure to adopt universal standards and operational efficiencies because of the effects of liberalization and globalization. All of these factors point to a strong need in Asia for higher value-added jobs if its economies are to achieve growth.

The question of how to exploit developments in information technology and e-commerce is high on the region's agenda. As we've already seen, places and communities throughout the region are trying to identify their positions in what might be called the New Asian Economy. Many places are eagerly looking for a unique role in the new information society. Places anywhere in the world can now be competitive if they encourage and accommodate the arsenal of information technology available to the globetrotting workforce. Hong Kong, Singapore and Malaysia have chosen to compete by developing world-class information infrastructure and, belatedly, upgrading educational infrastructure. A national task force on information technology and software development in India's Ministry of Information Technology has been established to "boost India's information technology industry."[11] To stem shortages of IT specialists, India is seeking ways to keep its IT professionals at home. However, "stifling government regulation and creaky infrastructure make running a business in India frustrating,"[12] which hinders progress.

In Malaysia, about 250 companies have set up operations in the country's Multimedia Super Corridor (MSC). In some other parts of Asia, development takes place without the benefit of dedicated infrastructure. Like India's Bangalore, Manila and Cebu in the Philippines have become centers for software programming on the strength of their relatively plentiful intellectual resources. In fact, the shortage of IT workers in the U.S. could potentially create more than half a million jobs in Asia every year, about the same number of IT professionals at work throughout the region in 2000. The challenge for Asia is to be able to educate these workers.

Thousands of Asian-based projects and programs have been launched to stimulate the application of new technologies. Top-level seminars, with themes such as "Ready, set, exploit the Internet," promote new possibilities in Asia. Throughout Asia, there are projects proposed and implemented for distance learning, call centers, business processing administration, wireless Internet-application development, and e-commerce proposals including business-to-business, business-to-consumer and business-to-government. In Hong Kong, the Chief Executive's Commission on Innovation and Technology reported that "Hong Kong has the capability to become an innovation and technology center, [but] must leverage on its areas of strength and develop its own niches."[13]

An ever-increasing number of local decision-makers are participating in IT strategy meetings. The questions are action-oriented: "How shall we act in order to join the club of peak performers?" "What is our unique IT image going to be?" Places now realize that targeting, image-making, and performance need to be executed swiftly and decisively.

Asia's economies are feeling the full impact of the revolution in technology and communication. The old notion that only the bigger cities such as Tokyo or Hong Kong can be leaders in finance or information services is no longer valid. These services could just as well be provided from Bangalore, Noida or Sydney — and are. The internationally renowned cities may eventually find themselves facing serious competition from smaller places. For example, "Silicon Alley" — an IT corridor connecting the former U.S. Subic and Clark military bases in the Philippines — is attracting the attention of multinational technology and Internet firms such as AOL, Cisco and Oracle. With the help of the Ministry of International Trade and Development, Japan's Kyushu region is setting up science centers to support IT investment and local start-ups. Asia's emerging economies are full of surprises as communities and sectors seeking to build a strategy for growth exploit the new technologies.

Global Competition

Cities and regions in Asia are not only competing with each other, but are also facing competition from other global locations. South American economies are serious contenders for FDI that was once almost exclusively destined for Asia. Eastern Europe is becoming a fierce competitor. In the Middle East, the Jebel Ali Free Zone Authority in Dubai, building on the momentum of the 1,600 international companies that established themselves in the area, promotes "Freedom to do business" (see Figure 2.3). This business base offers a tax-free market, a stable economy, world-class facilities and a huge potential market. The sphere of competition for investment has spread right around the world, and Asia's communities find themselves competing with places as far away as Dublin and Buenos Aires.

According to an OECD (Organization for Economic Cooperation and Development) study, globalization leads to greater specialization of regions and places. The OECD data demonstrate that incoming foreign investment reinforces patterns of regional specialization in 60–70% of the cases studied.[14] This implies that regions geared toward a particular industry have a higher chance of attracting specialized investment. Thus, an important task for regional policy-makers is to clarify which industries they should support in accordance with their relative strengths and weaknesses.

Figure 2.3: Plan for growth

Source: Jebel Ali Free Zone.

For the first time, some of the smallest Asian cities and regions are competing in a global marketplace. After the Second World War, Asia focused on urban and business reconstruction. It protected strategic sectors and domestic industries alike through import substitution policies, including high tariffs on imported products. At the time, a global strategy was not as high on the agenda as local and national issues.

In the late 1970s, much of Southeast Asia realized that to grow rapidly it was necessary to open up to foreign investors, but liberalization of local markets was slow. With the advent of the European Union (EU) and the North American Free Trade Association in the 1990s, pressure on Asia to trade more openly, particularly with the U.S., became more intense, and the Asean Free Trade agreement resulted. The Asian crisis, however, proved to be the most important catalyst for structural reform, in large part because troubled Asian economies had to agree to open up to receive International Monetary Fund (IMF) relief. Since then, liberalization and globalization trends throughout the world have increased pressure on Asian economies and enterprises to become more competitive and global. Places needed to show reliable and cost-effective labor supply, attractive housing and educational developments, as well as friendly and stable governments to maximize funding.

Political Power Shifts

Extensive debates about the appropriate role of government intervention in troubled places or industries have been on the rise at all levels of the public sector — across communities, cities, nations and regions — due to technological advances and global competition. The Asian unemployment and underemployment situation is a factor that has raised public interest in government intervention — but questions remain as to how to carry it out.

The governments of Japan, Hong Kong, Singapore and Malaysia have been particularly interventionist in making progress toward the New Asian Economy. They have allocated billions in funds and venture capital to nurture domestic IT clusters, and they have all tried to make large multinational corporations such as Intel and Microsoft part of the plan. However, each place faces serious shortages of IT workers, engineers and technicians.

More to the point, there is no evidence that direct state intervention results in cluster development of any kind. There is, however, a strong argument to be made for indirectly intervening to develop support services, or the basic building blocks of cluster development. Such intervention would probably include the development of strong educational institutions. It would also include tax breaks for investment in a variety of infrastructure, as well as entrepreneurial enterprise and other efforts to attract the intellectual resources required for value-added cluster development.

On a national level there are many sophisticated intervention programs to encourage new behaviors, both regionally and locally. Singapore's senior minister Lee Kuan Yew set in motion a complete reorientation towards a less regulated and more market-oriented economy, as shown in his deregulation of the banking and telecommunications sectors. Despite his reputation as an autocrat, Lee encouraged young Singaporeans to think and act more creatively, and promoted less emphasis on rote learning in educational institutions.

On a local and regional level, where problems and opportunities are found in concrete form, the political landscape can quickly change. Old personalities can disappear and new ones can emerge. A review of the Asian experience indicates that the most important factor for change is the capacity for new leadership to see the necessities and opportunities latent in the global market and to press for a local alignment with these opportunities.

Asia lives in a political climate where increased decentralization is encouraging local and regional bodies to make decisions. In Indonesia's case, there's little alternative for the significantly weakened central government. But in cases like the Philippines and Thailand, the momentum for moving decision-making down to local levels is significant, and that momentum will increase as capacity-building programs that target local government institutions begin to take effect.

Increasingly, strong leadership is recognized as the crucial factor in revival. In July 2000, the Ramon Magsaysay Awards — a regional Nobel-type awards program administered in Manila — acknowledged the efforts of former mayor Jesse M. Robredo to transform the once-languishing Naga City into a thriving enterprise center. His administration has also been praised by the United Nations for excellence in improving housing. *Asiaweek* recognized Naga as one of the most improved in its 1999 survey of Asia's best cities.[15]

WHAT ARE PLACES DOING TO SOLVE THEIR PROBLEMS?

Troubled places exhibit a variety of responses when confronting their problems. The first and least desirable response is to do little, in the hope that problems will diminish of their own accord. Some places even consider their individual situations to be their "divine destiny.". A common pattern is to scramble for more economic resources from the central government or multilateral lending institutions. Indonesia has received massive funding for a number of projects — including highways, ports and energy generation plants — that may appear promising but lack connectivity and long-term benefits. Political instability and separatist movements in East Timor, Aceh, and other parts of the country indicate a deep sense among rebel leaders of long-term neglect by the central government. Their cry is: "We want our fair share of the pie!" In the end, these places become recognized for crisis and unemployment.

By contrast, the second response consists of an ever-increasing number of places conserving their financial resources while planning aggressive growth programs to attract industry, investment and visitors. These programs include grant offerings and other financial incentives to lure investors. For example, Malaysia, Thailand and the Philippines have competed fiercely to lure FDI with investment incentive packages. India, with a consumer base of 320 million and increasingly liberal investment policies, is struggling to emerge as one of the region's top FDI destinations, but receives much smaller infusions than Malaysia and Thailand, which have a fraction of the population.

Today, many Asian nations and communities offer competing incentive packages of little distinction or variance. Many represent promotion programs rather than systematic marketing programs. Marketing would call for more comprehensive problem-diagnosis and planning, of which promotion is only a small part.[16]

A third response focuses on developing sophisticated informal measures to dissuade businesses from relocating. When an enterprise signals discontent to local, regional or national decision-makers, intensive discussions often follow in an attempt to find an agreeable solution. However, at this point it is often too late; the hurdles are too great.

Discontent with a place of business is a particularly important issue for Asian economies as the pace of globalization accelerates. As a result of high tariff barriers, many multinational and Asian firms found it necessary to maintain manufacturing operations in multiple Asian economies. However, they are now finding that lower tariffs make manufacturing from one location more economical, due to greater economies of scale. Notable examples are consumer products companies such as Johnson & Johnson, Nestlé, and Procter and Gamble, which have centralized much of their manufacturing capacity in Asia. Previously, they mirrored production capacity in multiple locations to avoid import tariffs. Textile firms that were previously located across the region to capitalize on distributed import quotas are also finding they are able to consolidate their operations. This is a trend that will continue to affect the movement of labor across the region.

A fourth response is to compete by investing in expensive new infrastructure or attractions such as a new cultural center (the Hong Kong International Convention Center, for example), a conference center (such as Suntec City in Singapore) or a Disneyland (as in Tokyo and Hong Kong). This approach is generally characterized by ad hoc actions that seek a single solution for multi-faceted problems. In some cases, ad hoc investments have generated more costs than revenue. The Philippine Centennial National Exposition in Clark Field, for example, cost the government more than P9 billion (US$178.5 million) when built.[17] It was originally intended to promote development and economic activity in the area but was a drain on national coffers during the brief period it operated. Poor conceptualization, allegations of corruption and a change in political administration combined to create a white elephant instead of a white knight. New international airports in Brunei and Kuala Lumpur are other examples of loss-leading infrastructure development. Indeed, there is a risk in Asia today that grandiose projects and infrastructure — such as Malaysia's Cyberjaya and the Petronas Twin Towers — are increasingly seen as the panacea to a place's many problems.

A fifth response is to undertake strategic market-oriented planning. For example, a top-level commission is appointed with mixed representation from the public and private sectors. Together the members examine a place's current and potential strengths, weaknesses, threats and opportunities. They work toward establishing a long-term vision (five to 20 years) of what the community could achieve. Strategic market-oriented planning is not only viable for the larger and more resourceful places. Small and even very troubled communities need to take that path as well.

HOW CAN PLACES IMPROVE THEIR EFFORTS TO SOLVE THEIR PROBLEMS?

A central proposition in this book is that Asian communities and regions are under heavy pressure of competition in both the world market and within Asia. Places compete for investors, experts and tourists in a climate that could best be described as a place war. Asia's competition has intensified as Latin America and Eastern Europe move into the place-market arena as viable alternatives for investment.

In fast-changing and demanding Asian and global economic conditions, each place faces a challenge to deliver something superior or unique for the marketplace. A place's ability to secure a unique position and positive image in the huge Asian market is a crucial part of strategic place marketing. Each place must formulate a combination of offerings and benefits that can meet the expectations of a broad number of investors, new businesses and visitors.

Place marketing, at its core, embraces four activities:

- Developing a strong and attractive positioning and image for the community
- Setting attractive incentives for current and potential buyers and users of goods and services
- Delivering a place's products and services in an efficient, accessible way
- Promoting a place's attractiveness and benefits in such a way as to ensure that potential users are fully aware of the advantages.

Too often, communities fall into the trap of concentrating on only one or two of these marketing tasks — often concentrating on the promotional functions. They may spend money on expensive advertisements or poorly orchestrated slogans without first carrying out requisite diagnostics and planning.

A fairly common Asian model is to organize a planning group made up of local and/or regional officials from the public sector. Sometimes an external consultant is contracted to provide a broader outsider's perspective. However, to be successful, the planners should involve representatives from the local business community from the beginning of the process, as in the case of Hong Kong's Chief Executive's Commission on Innovation and Technology. Sound planning includes commercial knowledge at the outset because collaboration between the public and private sectors has proven to be a prerequisite for achieving success.

When comparing Asian and American models, it is apparent that local business people in Asia are generally less involved in the regional planning process, and this is especially so outside Hong Kong and Singapore. In the U.S., a mix of public and private representatives has existed for decades. There are many examples of this, including the Economic Development Partnership of Alabama, Arkansas Electric Cooperative Corporation and New York's Empire State Business Alliance. This interactive model includes business partners such as local banks, real-estate companies, the local electricity company, telecommunications providers, water suppliers, and so on. It is inevitable that these types of alliances will continue to emerge with more force in Asia. The formation of the e-Asian Task Force and the private-sector meetings that parallel meetings of the Asia Pacific Economic Cooperation (APEC) forum suggest that this is already happening.

The planning group's charter is threefold. It must:

- Define and diagnose the community's condition. The major strengths and weaknesses of the community should be identified, along with major opportunities and threats (see SWOT analysis on page 163).
- Develop a vision of long-term solutions based on a realistic assessment of the community's problems. This vision must be founded on a combination of factors that are unique and commercially viable, upon which a value-added process can be implemented.
- Design a long-term plan of action that involves several intermediate stages of investment and transformation. Developing value-added processes takes time. A 10–15 year period is realistic for most successful cases.

The strategic marketing of a place involves a number of elements, as shown in Figure 2.4.

Figure 2.4: Levels of place marketing

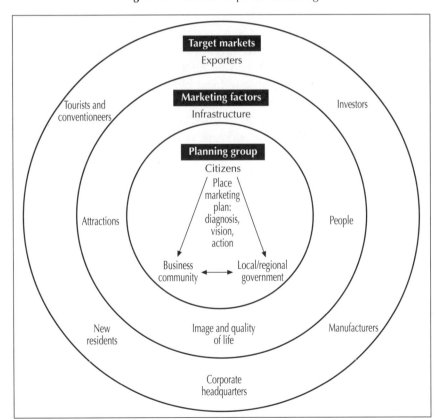

The creation of value-added processes to sustain investment in a community involves four major marketing steps: First, the process must ensure that basic services are provided and infrastructure is maintained to the satisfaction of citizens, businesses and visitors. Second, a place may need new attractions to sustain current business and public support and to bring in new investment, businesses or people. Third, a place needs to communicate its features and benefits through a vigorous image and communication program. Fourth, a place must generate support from its citizens, leaders and established institutions to make it open to, and enthusiastic about, attracting new companies, investments and visitors to the community.

These marketing requisites influence a place's success in attracting and satisfying its potential target markets:

- Producers of goods and services
- Corporate headquarters and regional offices
- Outside investment and export markets
- Tourism and hospitality
- New residents.

In the final analysis, the fortunes of a place depend on the collaboration of the public and private sectors. Asian places must learn to encourage better teamwork among local public units and business firms as well as voluntary and civic associations. Unlike purely business or commercial product marketing, the marketing of a place requires the active support of public and private agencies, interest groups and citizens. Successful Asian places will be those that are most skillful at promoting collaboration among the many stakeholders.

A place's potential depends less on location, climate and natural resources than it does on its human will, skill, energy, values and organization. For example, the fulfillment of potential, whether it is in Beijing in the north or Jakarta in the south, depends increasingly on a place's ability to carry out the following tasks:

- Interpreting what is happening in the broad environment
- Understanding the needs, wants and behavioral choices of specific internal and external constituencies
- Identifying specific strengths and weaknesses
- Building a realistic, commercially viable vision of what can be achieved
- Creating a plan of action to complement the vision
- Strengthening internal consensus and effective organization for operational activities
- Evaluating progress using the action plan.

CONCLUSION

The competition for investment attraction between places in Asia has never been more intense. The market in Asia includes more than 600,000 communities that, in many cases, are in head-to-head competition over tourist and business attraction. To complicate matters, Asia is shrinking as communication technology has an impact on the business community and global competition grows. The rapidly changing world market means that Asian communities must deliver products that will appeal to carefully targeted audiences. The winners will be those that develop a strong and attractive package of benefits. In the next chapter we examine strategies that are designed to reach targeted markets.

---

1 http://www.feer.com/9908_12/p26hongkong.html, viewed on October 9, 2000.
2 "Hong Kong Science Park Launches with University Alliances," Provisional Hong Kong Science Park Company (news release) November 23, 1999, p. 1.
3 http://www.info.gov.hk/itbb/english/cyberport/index_n.htm, viewed on September 25, 2000.
4 *Asian Development Outlook 2000*, Asian Development Bank, Manila, 2000, p. 45.
5 Nury Vittachi, *Doctor Doom: Riding the Millennial Storm*, (Singapore: John Wiley & Sons (Asia) Pte Ltd, 1998), p. 47.
6 *Asian Development Outlook 2000*, p. 243.
7 *Ibid.*, p. 255.
8 *Ibid.*, p. 183.
9 *Ibid.*, p. 90.
10 Michael Backman, "So, Farewell Then, Indonesia", *Asia-Inc.*, August 2000, p. 10.
11 http://www.mit.gov.in/atrnt.htm, viewed on October 9, 2000.
12 Manjeet Kripalani, "Techies Wanted," *Business Week*, October 16, 2000, p. 22.
13 *Chief Executive's Commission on Innovation and Technology: Second and Final Report*, Hong Kong, June 1999, p. iii.
14 "Globalisation and Local & Regional Competitiveness", OECD, Paris, July 29, 1992, p. 40.
15 Raissa Espinosa-Robles, "Pride Restored", *Asiaweek*, August 4, 2000, p. 47.
16 Philip Parrish, "Money Bag Moves", *Corporate Location*, January/February 1997, pp. 12–13.
17 http://www.pcij.org.ph/stories/1999/expo.html, viewed on May 17, 2001.

3

How Places Market Themselves

I f we follow today's global press, there is a clear observation to be made: places are increasingly competing with one another to attract investment, businesses and visitors. Between 5% and 10% of today's advertising space in newspapers and magazines is devoted to marketing places, regions and nations. In addition, special surveys describing regions and places in detail are published regularly.

The marketing of places has become a leading economic activity. Consider a few examples:

■ By the mid 1980s, Malaysia had changed from a sleepy, agriculture-based economy, chiefly reliant on palm-oil exports, into a global production center for appliances and electronic components. Its excellent infrastructure, relatively affordable workforce and receptive government made it a superb destination for high-quality, low-cost manufacturing. However, as Malaysia's economy expanded, upward pressure on wages and other operating costs weakened its attractiveness as a cost-competitive, contract-manufacturing base. In their public remarks, Malaysia's leaders acknowledged the need to develop more value-added production. At the same time, the impact of information technology on the U.S. economy had made it clear that a country's ability to embrace technology would become a prerequisite for sustained economic growth. To stimulate a transition to a high-value-added economy, Malaysia embarked on the development of a

49

massive technology park, the Multimedia Super Corridor (MSC), in the mid-1990s. The MSC spans 60 kilometers, from central Kuala Lumpur to the new international airport. It encompasses 700 square kilometers, provides office space, residential accommodation and educational facilities along with leading-edge IT infrastructure. Over 250 companies, including many global IT leaders such as Microsoft and Sun Microsystems, have established operations in the park.

■ The Philippines' Board of Investment (BOI) claims that, compared to its neighbors, the country offers distinct advantages for investors. First, it says, the Philippines has capitalized on the region-wide shortage of knowledge workers by marketing itself as a source of intellectual capital. The Information Technology and E-commerce Council — an IT policy advisory body composed of private- and public-sector representatives and chaired by the Philippines' president — says the Philippines' tertiary education institutions graduate 350,000 knowledge workers a year.[1] Regular surveys by the Economist Intelligence Unit rate the country as number one or two for the quality of skilled labor in Southeast Asia. Factors taken into consideration include English-language proficiency and training efficiencies. Cultural affinity is also an issue. E-marketplace software developer Enterworks set up its Asian hub in Manila because the Philippines is a "former U.S. colony whose people speak English with an American accent and share many things culturally with the world's biggest economy."[2] Second, the BOI points to the Philippines' progressive record in the areas of democratic rights and liberalization as an added investment attraction. Regulatory reform has also stimulated key sectors of the economy, such as telecommunications, shipping, banking, energy and insurance. Third, the Philippines provides a superior quality of life, according to recent surveys of expatriates and foreign residents. (See Table 3.1).

Table 3.1: Expatriate ratings of quality of life

Country	2000 Rating	1999 Rating
The Philippines	3.27	3.46
Singapore	3.28	3.50
Japan	3.84	4.24
Hong Kong	4.10	4.63
Taiwan	4.49	4.84
Thailand	4.90	4.70
Malaysia	5.00	4.08

Rating scale: 0 = best, 10 = worst

Source: Political and Economic Risk Consultancy (PERC), April 2000.

The Philippines has become an increasingly popular site for companies that need workers with good technical and English-speaking skills. "The Philippines has the best market in Asia for brains,"[3] says enterprise systems consultant Darcy Lalonde of DFI Consulting, a firm headquartered in Kuala Lumpur. America Online has created 800 new jobs by transferring its support services from the United Kingdom, Australia and Hong Kong to the Philippines. TrendMicro, PeopleSoft, Bechtel, Amkor, Intel, iCom, Caltex and Sun Life are among other international companies that have set up customer call, administration and development centers in the country. Japanese engineering firm JGC Philippines has transferred its engineering procurement and construction services operations to the Philippines. Large domestic firms such as Philippine Long Distance Telephone, Ayala Corporation and the Lopez Group have established call centers to service firms based outside the Philippines that wish to outsource their call-center services.

■ Business enterprises can play an important role in place marketing. A good example is Singapore Airlines, which has added considerable value to the island nation's aggressive marketing and promotion of Singapore as a welcoming and modern destination offering world-class efficiencies. Multinational corporations such as Intel also promote places by communicating their commitment to a country, region or community (see Figure 3.1).

The desire and push for economic development by places, communities, regions and nations are not new and, for many, has been a priority for centuries. A good example is the Han Dynasty, which ruled China from 206 BC to 220 AD. In many ways it rightly considered itself the center of the world, or the Middle Kingdom. It was during the Han Dynasty that the Silk Route became a regularly traveled link to the Roman Empire, made secure by the largest standing army on earth — the Han's. The Han Dynasty established a tributary system, where neighboring states were allowed to trade independently and maintain autonomy in return for symbolic acknowledgment of Han rule. In so doing, the Han Dynasty and its vassal states practiced a form of marketing, evident in their coordination and cooperation. Of course, it is a significant leap forward from those cooperative actions to the implementation of systematic marketing strategies for attracting investment, residents and tourists.

Only in the past decade have a few Asian places shifted from a narrow view of economic development to a broad set of strategies to attract new business, retain existing business, develop overseas networks, build tourism and attract outside investors. A growing number of places

Figure 3.1: Intel's Commitment to China

Intel demonstrates its commitment to China with the launch of Intel Teach to the Future program supported by the Ministry of Education. Pictured (from left) are: Zhang Minsheng, deputy director of the Shanghai Education Commission; Jim Jarrett, vice president of Intel Corporation and president of Intel China; Wang Zhan, vice minister, Ministry of Education; and Ni Yichen, president Beijing Institute of Education. The program is expected to train 500,000 teachers worldwide.

Source: *http://www.intel.com/pressroom/archive/BACKGRND/AW050598.HTM,* viewed on September 22, 2000.

are attempting to transform their ad hoc economic campaigns into sophisticated marketing strategies designed to build competitive advantages. They want to create a strong identity, target specific buyers and position the community's resources to respond to specialized buyer needs and desires.

Organizing a program to develop and market a place requires a thorough grasp of target markets. In this chapter, we address three questions:

- What are the main target markets of those marketing the attractions of a place?
- How do marketers go about marketing their community, economy, country or region?
- Who are the major place marketers?

WHAT ARE THE MAIN TARGETS OF PLACE MARKETERS?

Places are interested in a particular kind of growth that can contribute to sustained employment and add value to the tax base. It is useful to distinguish between three specific categories of people and businesses that might be drawn to a place:

- People and businesses worth attracting.
- People and businesses that are acceptable but do not need to be specifically targeted.
- People and businesses to avoid or discourage.

Too often, places fail to define whom they want to attract or to distinguish between the three categories. Some places, however, do define their targets (see Exhibit 3.1).

Exhibit 3.1: A NEW DIMENSION TO HONG KONG

"Hong Kong is already a business and shopping destination," says MJT Rowse, the former tourism commissioner who negotiated the sometimes-controversial joint government venture with U.S. entertainment company Walt Disney. "Disneyland in Hong Kong adds a new dimension. It makes us a family destination as well. We become an alternative for families planning their vacations, and we're not that now."

Rowse believes the added dimension is important for two reasons. First, the obvious: Hong Kong expects to benefit from increased revenue flows associated with family spending into the Special Administrative Region (SAR). Many shoppers who jet into the former colony have had one thing on their mind: clothes. However, Hong Kong is rapidly losing its cost advantage, as regional economies liberalize and reduce their own tariffs on garment imports. While Hong Kong is likely to retain its cosmopolitan appeal among well-heeled visitors for whom shopping in the former British colony is a status-affirming pastime, there is now little incentive to go bargain hunting. As a result, fewer shoppers arrive, although the number of visitors to Hong Kong increased in 1999 as Asia recovered from its financial crisis.

The high costs associated with maintaining expatriate executives in Hong Kong has likewise diluted the number of foreigners with high levels of disposable income. As a result, more jobs are being created for local residents, but the disposable income available for consumption remains constrained. For Rowse, Hong Kong clearly needed new attractions to recover lost revenues, which remained depressed despite a post-crisis upturn in visitor arrivals.

His solution was to turn Hong Kong into a family playground, and his decision was influenced by Tokyo Disneyland's status as the most profitable Disney theme park in the world. He considers Asia a stable market for entertainment, given that Asian parents are notorious for spending money on their children, even when they are otherwise conserving funds in difficult economic times. When the Hong Kong Disney Park opens in 2005, Rowse expects at least 30% of visitors to come from around the region. As the market in China develops and consumers become more affluent, he expects mainland visitors to account for 50% of the park's market.

Source: Interview with MJT Rowse, conducted on September 16, 2000.

Other places build — or try to — on existing strengths to attract new markets. Consider Phuket, in Thailand, that thrives on tourist expenditures. Possessing some of the world's most beautiful beaches, Phuket attracts visitors from around the world who want to escape the pressures of modern life. They do not represent a singular market, but a complex one that consists of many different nationalities, ages and income groups. They are young travelers, backpackers, single Japanese women, large tourist groups, family vacationers and honeymooning couples. Among them is a steady stream of foreign software programmers looking for quality downtime. Government planners believed that enticing them to stay could jumpstart a second local industry: software and e-commerce. Indeed, "'For many software programmers it is the relaxed and creative atmosphere that attracts them to Phuket,' says Will Hebler, managing director of Cyber Village, a project-development operation that bills itself as 'online and on the beach.'"[4] This link between the original target group — vacationing tourists — and more business-like target groups — such as information technology workers — is a prime target for exploitation. It is so important, in fact, that Phuket has plans to transform itself into a digital paradise. Unfortunately, the transition from plan to reality hasn't gone smoothly. This isn't because the plan is infirm; rather, the problem lies in its implementation. Bureaucracy and poor infrastructure are to blame.

Singapore has achieved a global reputation as a center for value-added manufacturing, transportation and business — especially technology. Singapore exploits its high-tech image through aggressive marketing to the international IT industry. It is liberalizing its telecommunications and Internet service sectors with a goal of enhancing services and lowering costs. It has installed fiber-optic cable throughout the island, making bandwidth a non-issue for dot-com start-ups and established firms alike. In 1999, Singapore began to liberalize its banking sector in a bid to leverage its success in other sectors to become a center for Asian finance. Unlike Hong Kong, Singapore has opened its doors to international educational institutions in a bid to increase the quality and quantity of education available, not just to Singaporeans but to bright people outside Singapore. In an economy where competitive advantage is increasingly tied to intellectual resources, Singapore hopes to attract the best and brightest from around the region, and to keep them after graduation.

Now let's examine in detail the four broad target markets of place marketers as outlined in Table 3.2.

Table 3.2: The four main target markets

---

1. **Visitors**
   - Business visitors (attending a business meeting or convention, viewing a production site, or coming to buy or sell something)
   - Non-business visitors (tourists and travelers)

2. **Residents and employees**
   - Professionals (scientists, physicians, etc.)
   - Skilled employees
   - Telecommunications workers
   - Wealthy individuals
   - Investors
   - Entrepreneurs
   - Unskilled workers
   - Senior citizens and pensioners

3. **Business and industry**
   - Heavy industry
   - "Clean" industry assembly, high technology, service companies, etc.
   - Entrepreneurs

4. **Export markets**
   - Other localities within regional markets
   - International markets

Visitors

The visitor market has expanded globally and throughout Asia during the past few decades. It is estimated that intra-Asian tourism will continue to grow, and that the depreciated currencies of the region will stimulate travel from Europe and the United States. The trend toward greater transparency of airfares and hotel rates as a result of liberalization and the advent of the Internet will continue to force prices down.

The term "travel and tourism" is used by the World Travel and Tourism Council (WTTC) to cover both business and leisure markets — domestic and international. This economic sector is already responsible, directly and indirectly, for more than 10% of global GDP and investment, and Asia accounts for 10% of global travel and tourism GDP and a total of 96.9 million travel- and tourism-related jobs.[5] A closer look at Asia shows that 60.2 million of these jobs are in Northeast Asia. "By 2011, this should grow to 71,447,100 jobs, or 8% of total employment, or one in every 12.5 jobs."[6] In Southeast Asia, employment opportunities in this sector already account for 8% of new jobs. "By 2011, this should grow to 25,444,000 jobs, 8.6% of total employment, or one in every 11.6 jobs."[7]

Furthermore, in specific Asian nations, regions and places, the travel-and-tourism sector contributes disproportionately high revenues compared to other sectors. In 1997, five countries and Hong Kong accounted substantially for tourist visits to Asia: Singapore had the highest with US$3.4 billion; followed by Thailand with US$483 million; Japan took third place with US$309 million; fourth was Indonesia with US$228 million; and the fifth place went to Taiwan, with US$207 million.[8]

These national figures overshadow the smaller "hot spots," which depend almost entirely on their performance in the visitor market. The local economies of places such as Bali (Indonesia), Phuket (Thailand), Langkawi (Malaysia) and Boracay (the Philippines), among many others, are based almost entirely on revenue generated from visitors. These places are in a permanent struggle to improve their travel and tourism revenue. Their strategic objective must be to protect, maintain and improve their position.

The visitor market consists of two broad groups; business and non-business visitors. For place marketers, it is important to prepare to meet these two distinct markets. Business visitors congregate in a place to attend a business meeting or convention, to check out a site, or to buy or sell something. Non-business visitors include tourists who want to see the place, and travelers who are visiting family and friends. Within these two groups there are a number of important sub-groups that need to be targeted.

Unfortunately, there is often a failure to prioritize targets. Typically, tourist brochures are sent everywhere, to anyone, and one publicity campaign follows another. Instead of employing a professionally developed marketing strategy, place marketers frequently invest increasing amounts of resources in new tourist brochures or place advertisements without careful consideration of market needs and differences.

The concept of "destination development" calls for a place to develop a systematic and long-term marketing strategy directed towards nurturing and developing the natural and potential attributes of an area or region. A central priority in developing such a strategy is to identify the specific target group to which the area should direct its resources.

A destination must continuously create new value. This requires a value-added process that develops new benefits to appeal to specific target groups. The smaller the destination, the more important it is to offer something of unique and group-specific value. A quick trip around Asia via the Internet already reveals some progress toward specific target group definitions. Some examples of specific target groups are presented in Table 3.3.

Table 3.3: Specific target groups and matching sites and attractions.

Target group	Sites and attractions
Ocean-fishing enthusiasts	Charters are available in Malaysia, Indonesia, the Philippines and Thailand
IT workers and executives	Singapore, Hong Kong and Bangalore have become major IT and telecommunications conference centers
Connoisseurs of fine food	National and regional specialties are available throughout the region, and in great variety
Fashion designers, buyers and related groups	Fashion shows are held in Manila and Hong Kong
Café lovers and tourists	Manila has a traditional café culture
Golf enthusiasts	Malaysia, Indonesia, the Philippines and Thailand all offer high-class facilities
Physicians	Singapore, Thailand and Manila
Train-travel enthusiasts	Eastern & Oriental Express
Children	Disneyland in Hong Kong and Japan; the Singapore zoo
History-seekers	Taj Mahal, Great Wall of China, Hiroshima Peace Memorial and temples, shrines and palaces in many locations throughout Asia

The list in Table 3.3 is just a sample and a visitor's interests will vary enormously depending on available time and money. In spite of the fact that Asia has over 600,000 communities, there is always the possibility of identifying a unique combination for each community. Target groups can range from the smallest niche market hobbyists (for example, visitors interested in the Japanese or Chinese tea ceremonies) to mass-market interest groups (such as golfers).

Singapore and Hong Kong have both been successful in targeting and attracting a significant portion of Asia's conference and exhibition business. Both destinations boast expansive, modern facilities. The Singapore International Convention and Exhibition Center (SICEC) and the Hong Kong Convention and Exhibition Center (HKCEC) are Asia's top conference destinations (see Figure 3.2). From January to June 2000, 530 meetings took place at the SICEC, involving 1.8 million visitors. Meetings included a World Summit on Small Business; SEMICON 2000, a semiconductor exhibition; and a number of IT and medical events. Some 44 IT events were staged in 2000, including Comdex Asia, and 12 medical and health events. Both centers actively promote themselves to the region and the world (see Figure 3.3).

Competition for visitors in Southeast Asia is intense, and characterized by sleek campaigns intended to communicate the unique qualities of each country or community. The "Amazing Thailand" campaign launched in 1997, for example, is especially notable because of its effectiveness during a severe economic downturn, and the tourism sector's impact on the national economy as a result. At the height of the Asian financial crisis, Thailand received 7.7 million visitors, compared to 2.1 million for the Philippines, which has failed to promote its tourism industry as effectively as its neighbors or otherwise promote the sector's development. As we saw in Chapter 1, Thailand's campaign was so successful it was extended — twice — and continued to produce "amazing" results.

Malaysia's almost hyperactive "Truly Asia" campaign produced 4.4 million visitors in its first four months (see Figure 3.4). Other examples of initiatives and entities that promote Asia and Asian tourism are: Asia Tourism Ltd (tour organizer in Central Asia), Eastern and Oriental Express Trains and Cruises (journey through the heart of Asia), Asiana and Air Asia (airlines), and magazines *AsiaMoney* (Asian banking and finance) and *Asiaweek* (reporting on Asian places, economies and politics). There are also Asian Credit Consultant and Business Services and Asian Demographics Ltd (business centers); Asia Market Intelligence and Asia Art Culture (about the arts in Asia); CNN-Asia TV's daily broadcast, *What's on in Asia* (a pan-Asian events service), *Biz*

Figure 3.2: Lobbies of the Hong Kong (top) and Singapore conference and exhibition centers

Source: Singapore International Convention and Exhibition Centre, Hong Kong Convention and Exhibition Centre.

Figure 3.3: HKCEC advertisement

Source: Conferences Exhibitions Incentives Asia Pacific (cei), November/December 2000, p. 9.

Asia, Asia Tonight, Q&A Asia and *Inside Asia*, which also aired on CNN. Also, CNBC Asia has its own schedule of programs about Asia. Places are quick to capitalize on any potential for marketing their attractions to a global audience.

These examples show how the natural amenities of a place are used as marketing attributes by both the community itself and by commercial enterprises. This strategy has everything to do with the search for an identity. A community or region must create and send "identity signals" that companies in the travel-and-tourism industry can recognize, understand and communicate to others.

Residents and Employees

A second target market is residents and employees. As prosperity increased in Asia's "dragon" economies in the 1980s, a number of these countries employed a strategy to attract low-skilled labor from poorer countries in the region. Singapore, Hong Kong and Taiwan actively recruited workers from the Philippines, Indonesia, Sri Lanka and Thailand. Now, priorities have changed. During Asia's heady miracle years, educational infrastructure was largely neglected, despite the common perception that education is highly valued in Asia. There is now a shortage of knowledge workers and marketing strategies are emphasizing the need to attract professionals and skilled labor. The search for civil engineers, researchers, multilingual people, inventors, wealthy and healthy seniors, and stable tax-paying residents is an important trend.

This strategy takes many forms, as illustrated by Singapore's effort to attract bright, young people looking for a top-grade education. The Singapore government provides scholarships covering up to 80% of tuition to qualified students with no strings attached, other than the hope that the student will grow attached to Singapore and decide to stay after graduation. The government is so serious that in certain circumstances a full scholarship and living expenses are provided.[9] "Unless we succeed in this game," says George Yeo, Singapore's minister of trade and industry, "we will lose in every other game. Talent attraction is the foundation of everything we do."[10]

In other instances, Asian countries are working to win back citizens who are studying or working overseas. China, in particular, has aggressively recruited graduating students in both technology- and business-related fields to return home to help build a new economy. About one-quarter of an estimated 200,000 (some estimates place the number of overseas students at more than 300,000, with about one-third having returned by 2000[11]) students who have studied abroad since 1978 have returned, but mostly to small private companies or multinationals. While China's lumbering state-owned corporations are desperate for Western graduates, their old-time bureaucratic cultures are a significant

Figure 3.4: Malaysia's Truly Asia advertisement

Source: *Time*, February 5, 2001, p. 11.

disincentive. At many state companies, "when you go into a meeting, nobody sits down until the chief sits down," says Celia Pan, executive producer at Haowan Information Technologies. "They're not as open [as private firms] to new ideas."[12]

Although China's regular cultural and political upheavals discouraged many Chinese from returning home, in recent years that trend has been reversing (see Figure 3.5). "In 1998, the last year for which figures are available, 7,379 students came back — up from 1,593 in 1990."[13] These results reflect the priority China places on getting students back. In 1991, it set up a China Returned Students Services Center, and government officials travel to U.S. cities "to explain how they would help graduates find work."[14] Cities, science parks and investment zones alike compete vigorously for returnees, offering streamlined bureaucracy, funding and tax incentives for start-ups.

Perks are not the only reason people return. For many, life in the West just isn't exciting enough. "In the States I feel nothing's going to change much," says Zhu Xiaobing, a U.S.-trained certified public accountant on her fourth day back in China and her third day as finance manager at KPMG's Shanghai office. "Here is really a challenge for me. I came back to work in China because it's more exciting."[15]

The example of Chinese graduates returning home makes it clear that marketers must determine the views of their target group. Lipstick and make-up manufacturer Revlon advertised their product as a way of life: "You don't sell lipstick — you sell hope." You have to sell the right concept. China is not just selling itself to overseas citizens with the promise of unlimited financial rewards — it's selling a chance to make a profound difference.

China is not alone. Most of Asia's economies are racing to get a head start in the high-technology fields by seducing bright young people to state-owned incubators. Target groups are also offered venture-capital funding and special incentives to establish businesses at home. Even in highly regulated Singapore, where zoning laws are strictly enforced, the new incentives are significant breakthroughs. The bottom line for winning back overseas-based citizens, however, can be complex. Stephen Lin, Ernest Chen and Albert Chu — all Hong Kong-born business people who met at a U.S. high school — started Seamatch Technology in their home territory. "They cite the Asian recovery, Hong Kong's entrepreneurial spirit, and the proximity of the biggest potential market in the world, as the main reasons for choosing Hong Kong as the base for their web-based community for small office/home office (Soho) businesses."[16]

Figure 3.5: Asian Boomerangs

Source: *Asian Business*, July 2000.

An American guide to the selling points of small towns sums up the main message by asking **"Are you fed up with big-city living? Would you like to start a new life in a place with clean air, safe streets, good schools and friendly neighbors? If so, here are one hundred all-American** small towns where you can find your dream!"[17] This type of place-message is spreading across Europe and all over Asia. Sometimes, as in the case of China, the accessibility of a nice home has been a major selling point in marketing campaigns. The selling of lifestyle dreams will increase as Internet usage increases and reaches more Asian homes. Businesses, families and local decision-makers in Asian cities such as Hong Kong, Manila and Singapore are considering what *teleworking* can mean from a lifestyle point of view, and a new target market is being created: teleworkers.

To attract families, place marketers should be aware of several sub-groups:

- Families without children.
- Families with small children.
- Families with pre-teenage and teenage children.
- Families with children who have moved out of the house ("empty-nesters").

Each target group has specific characteristics and needs. For example, some communities build and emphasize fine schools. Education quality appeals to families with young children and teenagers but is less appealing to empty-nesters.

If a community wants to attract specific professional groups, it can offer and promote the benefits of residing in a particular country or place. As we've seen with Singapore's efforts to attract bright students to its universities, the recruitment theme can appear in many different levels and from many different perspectives. The *Xiamen Investguide* Web site (see Figure 3.6), for example, seeks to attract foreign professionals by easing immigration procedures and selling a high quality of life: "Xiamen, a garden by the sea, has always been one of the world's most popular cruise ship ports of call because of her scenic attractions and natural beauty. Surrounded by sea dotted with an assortment of islets, visitors to Xiamen see scenic spots at every turn."[18]

Even within larger cities, different districts have their own residential marketing strategies. For example, even separate districts in Singapore compete with one another for new residents. David Ng, executive director of Chesterton International, says of the Clarke Quay developments, for example, "I think we can draw a comparison of the area with Orchard Road because they are both shopping and entertainment belts,"[19] suggesting that the two areas must seek to competitively differentiate themselves. Clarke Quay might choose to market itself on the basis of its informal, relaxed atmosphere, compared to the bustling, touristy conditions along Orchard Road. Such targeted

Figure 3.6: Xiamen Investguide promotes its attractions to expatriates

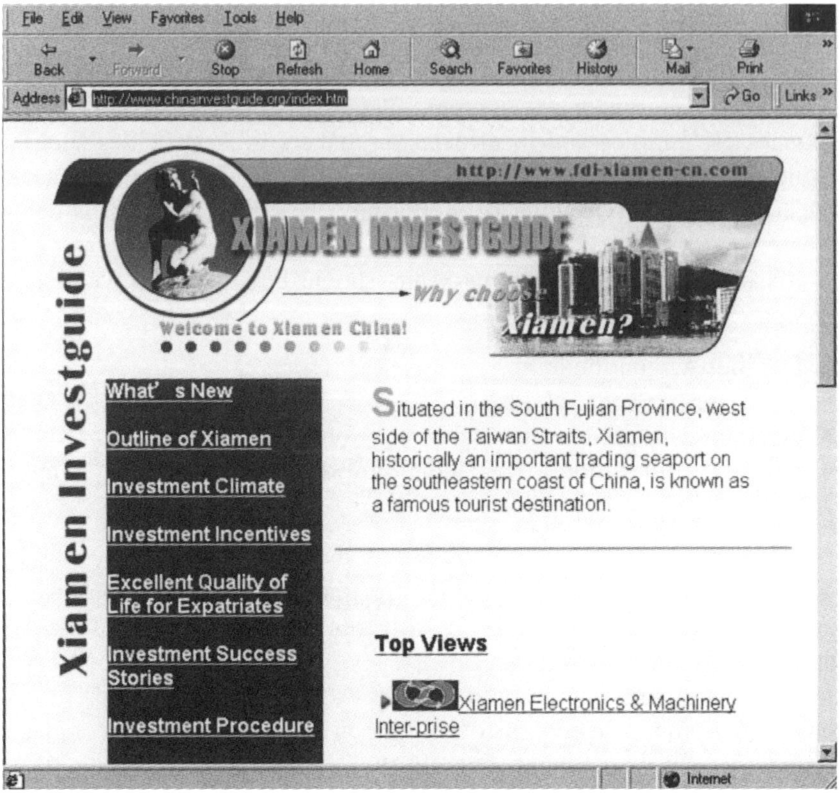

Source: *http://www.chinainvestguide.org/index.htm,* viewed on September 14, 2000.

messages can be communicated via traditional print media, trade publications and even international exhibitions. But this is only the beginning of selective differentiation. Each Singapore district can communicate its own appealing characteristics directly to the global market via the Internet marketplace.

Business and Industry

A desire to attract business, industry and economic investment constitutes a third target market category. This category has the longest tradition and is also the hottest market today, which is understandable given the extent to which the Asian financial crisis eroded the job market. With unemployment in traditional sectors within Asia reaching record levels, it is not surprising that attracting business and industry has become a priority.

As a result, this target market has begun to place growing demands on Asian place marketers. Businesses are becoming increasingly professional in searching for and selecting the right place. Not surprisingly, an increasing number of consulting companies offer their services to companies seeking to invest. In some cases, banks and real-estate brokers offer services to investors. Expatriate communities, such as foreign chambers of commerce, also organize specialized location-advisory services. Services include location-strategy development, labor market evaluations, operating cost and conditions comparisons, business tax comparisons, real-estate searches, incentives evaluation, negotiation, and even relocation-project management. Evidence of this quickly rising volume of knowledge is the increasing number of Asian place-ranking lists that have appeared in recent years. Regions and nations are ranked in all the possible — and improbable — dimensions one can imagine (see Chapter 4).

Several tools are used by places to meet the needs of businesses seeking to invest. Investment seminars are arranged in almost every country. One country or region after another is producing road shows in high-priority target markets. Almost all Asian countries and territories today have established inward investment agencies offering free services. One of the forerunners of these was the Hong Kong Trade Development Council. More recently, Hong Kong has established InvestHK, to augment the Council's work. Other national organizations include Thailand's Board of Investment, the Sri Lanka Board of Investment and the Malaysian Industrial Development Authority.

In addition to the many national initiatives, there are numerous local investment agencies. These are rich both in variety and in their differing economic and personnel resources. Examples include:

Regional Investment Agencies:

- Department of Commerce and Trade, Western Australia
- Western Visayas Regional Tourism Congress
- ASEAN Focus Group
- E-Asean Task Force
- West Bengal Industrial Development Corporation.

Local Investment Agencies:

- Cebu Investment Promotions Center, the Philippines
- Hyogo Investment and Support Center in Kobe, Japan
- Perak Darul Ridzuan Development Corridor in Malaysia.

It is important for place marketers to understand how businesses make investment and location decisions. As a rule, businesses rate places as potential sites after considering various factors that define the overall local business climate of a given place. We call these indicators "attraction factors," and they can be divided into "hard" and "soft" categories (see Table 3.4). The hard factors are those that can be measured in more-or-less objective terms. Soft factors are not so easily measured and represent the more subjective characteristics of a place.

Place marketers can use these factors as guides for improving their attractiveness to a target market. Not all factors can be easily maximized, making it critical to develop the right combination. (Exhibit 3.2 describes the efforts of Sydney to position itself as an important Asian destination for tourism and foreign direct investment in conjunction with the 2000 Summer Olympics).

Table 3.4: Hard and soft attraction factors

Hard factors
- Economic stability
- Productivity
- Costs
- Property concept
- Local support services and networks
- Communication infrastructure
- Strategic location
- Incentive schemes and programs

Soft factors
- Niche development
- Quality of life
- Professional and workforce competencies
- Culture
- Personal relationships
- Management style
- Flexibility and dynamism
- Professionalism in contact with the market
- Entrepreneurship

Exhibit 3.2: SYDNEY OLYMPICS AS A MARKETING TOOL

Sydney, with its laid-back lifestyle and beautiful setting, has been traditionally viewed as a tourist destination rather than a place to do business or enjoy high culture. Today, that image is rapidly becoming outmoded. Government and the private sector are working together to position the city as "Australia's first international city" as well as "the Wall Street of East Asia."[1]

That is an ambitious task for a city in a country that finds itself in the uncomfortable position of not easily fitting in, either geographically or culturally. Australia is physically distant from its European colonial heritage, and despite high immigration from Asia it still seems culturally distant from the region it badly wants to call home — mostly for economic reasons.

Sydney wants to change all that by marketing its positive qualities and establishing a clear, international identity. First among those qualities is its highly talented pool of human resources. The country's excellent educational system has produced skilled professionals and workers well suited to most fields of work. Second, its infrastructure is comparable to the best in the world. Also, Australia was not much affected by the Asian financial crisis and offers "stable financial waters in a region known for its volatility."[2] These factors make Sydney attractive to investors wary of Asia's volatility. Australian authorities believe that Sydney stands a chance of competing with other regional financial hubs, such as Hong Kong and Singapore, despite its distance from other Asian cities and its high corporate and personal tax rates.

Sydney offers an excellent quality of life for business people, including a wide choice of recreational activities and beautiful surroundings. "Giving executives time to take in the view — and enjoy the outdoors — may yet turn out to be one of Sydney's biggest business advantages."[3] Sydney's place marketers view the attractive elements as a draw for new business. It is not unusual for a visiting business executive to find an excuse to develop a long-term business relationship.

That's why the 2000 Summer Olympics presented an excellent opportunity for Sydney to market itself. The event not only represented the chance to overcome stereotypes but also to showcase its talented and skilled workforce and other strengths. The event is said to have brought in a total of 110,000 international visitors who spent about $500 million; it also attracted a television audience of almost three billion. Australia's tourism chief John Morse says the games "presented a new image of Australia, focusing on culture, food and wine, and lifestyle, that reached countries — including France and Italy — where Down Under traditionally has been off the map."[4] What did it take to market Sydney to the world? Australia invested A$1.8 billion (US$952 million) in construction for the Olympics with the "aim to get beyond the images of bounding kangaroos or shrimps on the barbie, and to show the world something uniquely Australian."[5]

The Olympic Games were a smash hit. Many experts proclaimed the Sydney version the best ever, and the city and Australia have elevated international perception to new levels of appreciation. It was anticipated that, as a direct result of the Olympics, the number of international visitors to New South Wales in 2001 would increase by more than 200,000, the vast majority of whom would visit Sydney.[6] The real test will be whether Australia's new image will sustain higher levels of visitors, and whether that will prove to be a reasonable tradeoff for the US$26 million the Olympic site cost taxpayers to operate the year after the successful games.

Sources:

1   Leora Moldofsky, "Cash Point," *Time*, August 7, 2000, pp. 46–47.
2   *Ibid.*
3   *Ibid.*
4   Andrew Browne, "Tourism Takes Gold in Sydney: Post-games Glow Forecast to Draw an Extra 1.6-million Visitors Over the Next Decade," *The Globe and Mail*, October 18, 2000, p. T3.
5   Cathleen McGuigan, "Reinventing Sydney," *Newsweek*, June 12, 2000, pp. 10–13.
6   Tourism NSW Web site, www.tourism.nsw.gov.au/corporate/downloads/01FactNSW. pdf, viewed on August 18, 2001.

A place can maintain and strengthen its economic base in four ways. Firstly, it must retain its current businesses or at least the desirable ones. This is all the more important in a world with increasingly "rootless" enterprises on the Asian market. Every day we can see how businesses leave or threaten to leave one place for another. Cross-border migration is increasing. For Johnson & Johnson, it was profitable to centralize its manufacturing in Malaysia. Globalization and agreements within the APEC forum to reduce tariffs for intra-Asian trade made centralization of

Asian productive capacity logical for both efficiency and productivity. Although other Asian countries, such as the Philippines, were dismayed to see manufacturing capacity and jobs move to a neighboring competitor and tried hard to convince Johnson & Johnson to stay, the company was unmoved.

To retain its businesses, a place must establish a regular dialogue with its businesses. Local decision-makers must understand how they measure up against other places. For the first time, representatives in the public sector need an understanding of the world. Perhaps more importantly, they must acknowledge that their places face increasing competition for a limited pool of available investment.

Secondly, a place must devise plans and services to help existing businesses expand. When these businesses sell more products and services to more distant markets, they produce more income and jobs for the local economy. To a large extent, a city can identify hard and soft factors that it can influence, and on that basis it can begin to develop unique offers. This is the core of the value-added process. The following three examples illustrate what can be achieved.

In Kyoto, Japan, there are a number of competing pottery manufacturers. Some, such as Kaolin and Imari, have well-recognized global brand names. To further strengthen their prominence, a new slogan was created — "the center of enameled pottery."[20] The pottery manufacturers communicated this message to Japanese and international enthusiasts in a bid to increase the number of visitors to their "factories." Today, over two million tourists and shoppers visit "the center of enameled pottery" each year. It is an example of successful place marketing that has given local pottery manufacturers an advantage in an internationally competitive sector. By promoting an attractive destination and not just a visit to a factory, marketers and businesses have together created a brand or trademark with which to compete.

Ho Chi Minh City (formerly Saigon) is an attractive destination for tourists and travelers and for the business sector. The city's rich historical past and multicultural influences are very much evident in its museums, the Chinese district and Dong Khoi Street — formerly Rue Catinat during the French era and Freedom Street during the American war. The street is the location for many of the city's most popular restaurants, clubs and shopping malls.

The city remains Vietnam's commercial headquarters as well as its major port, which is fueled by a booming industrial sector. The city owes its relative prosperity to its strategic location and its status as the departure point for destinations such as the Mekong Delta, the Cu Chi tunnels and Phan Thiet Beach.[21] Because of Vietnam's long, revolutionary past, the city has been the focus of several films, as well as the famous Broadway production *Miss Saigon*. It is also known as "the most stubbornly romantic city on Earth."[22] This rich assortment of assets adds to the country's marketing portfolio.

Hong Kong has become known as the "Hollywood of the Far East."[23] In the Special Administrative Zone, international blockbusters are often no competition for local films, especially now that the industry is maturing. Hong Kong-produced films are box-office hits, not only locally but all over Asia and in the United States. Action star Jackie Chan and acclaimed director John Woo, natives of Hong Kong, are big names internationally. In Japan and the United States, *The Replacement Killers* and *Rush Hour* were big hits. Hong Kong is also the home of renowned stars such as Michelle Yeoh (originally from Malaysia), Chow Yun Fat and the late Bruce Lee. As a result, the city is drawing more international attention. Famous directors and actors want to work in Asian films for the same reasons multinational corporations want to exploit Asian markets.

Thirdly, a place must make it easier for entrepreneurs to start new businesses. Programs to stimulate SMEs — small- and medium-size enterprises — are numerous. During the 1990s many nations, regions and communities in Asia visited U.S. cities to get practical guidance on how to improve the business climate for entrepreneurs. The need to create value-added jobs in Asia stimulated Asian planners to travel to the United States and Europe to observe entrepreneurial support programs.

As a result, there are growing numbers of places in Asia introducing aggressive entrepreneurial support programs. These programs include developing local SME agencies to train and advise entrepreneurs; encouraging local banks to get involved in helping start-up businesses; providing loans; bringing together venture capitalists and entrepreneurs; promoting research parks; helping to secure government contracts; and providing various incentives to starts-ups. Taiwan is one of the best Asian examples of combined efforts to improve the local climate for entrepreneurs (see Exhibit 3.3).

Exhibit 3.3: TAIWAN: AN ENTREPRENEURIAL UMBRELLA

Taiwan is one of Asia's most successful Dragon economies and the 14th-largest trading entity in the world. The tiny island nation's GDP per capita is US$12,850, making it third in Asia after Singapore and Hong Kong. Even during the Asian financial crisis, the economy continued to grow, with GDP expanding 6.7% in 1997 and 4.6% in 1998. What accounts for this tiny country's dramatic success and rapid development?

Some observers suggest the key to Taiwan's success lies in its government's policies on liberalization and international cooperation. To others, it's the entrepreneurial culture that explains how, in just three decades, the country has evolved from a mere exporter of labor-intensive products to a producer of highly capital- and technology-intensive products.

Taiwan is the third-largest producer of information products in the world. In many respects its value-added products differ greatly from those of other East Asian countries and are, increasingly, on par with those of developed economies. Companies like Acer Computer — a former OEM manufacturer, founded in a garage with US$5,000, that now manufactures its own branded products — and Taiwan Semiconductor Manufacturing Company (TSMC) compete in the global market with the international heavyweights — IBM, Compaq, HP, Dell, Texas Instruments, Toshiba and Hitachi.

There are at least five factors that help account for Taiwan's success in fostering commerce and entrepreneurship:

1. The country's 75 universities and centers of technology educate more than 8,000 engineers annually. "There are 43 research scientists and engineers for every 10,000 people in Taiwan, compared with 33 in South Korea, and 28 in Singapore. These institutes spawned specialized technical knowledge, making indigenous technology available to priority sectors early in the country's march toward industrialization. And government allowed researchers to focus on specific industries, rather than individual companies as in South Korea, which substantially multiplied their work."[1]

2. Taiwan has focused on high-growth sectors: computers, telecommunications and semiconductors. As a result, Taiwan is home to Asia's only global computer brand and the world's most profitable semiconductor and wafer manufacturer.

3. There are few real restrictions on business people traveling to China, other than through direct links. This has facilitated new business ventures by local business people anxious to capitalize on mainland opportunities.
4. There are virtually no restrictions on foreign investment in the country, which represents a dependable source of investment.
5. There is a close government–private sector partnership that works diligently at communicating the quality of products produced in the country.

These five factors combine to create a value-added process in Taiwan. What is the next step? "Asians usually rely on real-estate appreciation and tangible goods for wealth, but I'm trying to change that model,"[2] says Acer founder Stan Shih about the urgency with which he was compelled to push his company into value-added software development — and up the value-added food chain — instead of investing profits in speculative real estate, as many successful Asian companies had in the period leading up to the crisis. Although that initiative didn't produce the results Shih hoped for — a new, high value-added source of profitability related to the company's principal source of revenues — the entrepreneur's concern with creating greater value was, and remains, legitimate. In fact, Shih's not alone. TSMC and United Microelectronics have bet their own futures on their capacity to develop new 300mm silicon wafers on the basis of their own research and development.

These companies are able to do this because of the five factors that helped make Taiwan what it is today. And it's reassuring that they will likely continue to work in its favor as it faces new, empowered competitors (many of then right next door across the Taiwan Strait), and looks to a future in which competition for investment and opportunity has never been greater.

—————

Sources:

1 *http://www.gio.gov.tw/taiwan-website/fignertip/g-index5-1.htm*, viewed on September 18, 2000.
2 Louis Kraar, "Taiwan Does It Right," *Fortune*, August 17, 1998, pp. 39, 42.

http://www.taipei.org/press/gio04301.htm, viewed on September 14, 2000; Michael Alan Hamlin, *The New Asian Corporation: Managing for the Future in Post-Crisis Asia*, San Francisco, Jossey-Bass, 2000, p. 230; *Asian Development Outlook 2000*, Asian Development Bank, Manila, 2000, pp. 242 and 243.

Fourthly, a place must try to attract strategically relevant development projects. Such projects often create valuable side contacts with commercial consequences. Singapore provides a good example of how an aggressive marketing strategy can attract both investors and interesting projects. As an indication of its ambition to draw special projects to the nation, the Singapore Economic Development Board was created by the government to formulate and implement economic and industrial development strategies for the country.

Most Asian nations and regions have launched place-marketing programs to attract investment, industry, residents and tourists. Some rely on government employees distributing brochures, while others have developed more sophisticated programs that incorporate all four strategies outlined earlier. To slide into a market strategy in a *laissez-faire* manner will bring success only as an exception. A growing place is most likely to produce first-rate results with a clearly defined, comprehensive strategy. Generally, it is a clear that a comprehensive strategy creates fertile results.

Export Markets

The fourth target market is export expansion — the ability of a city or region to produce more goods and services that other places, people and businesses want to buy. Consider the small city of Rangsit in Thailand, whose economy revolves around computer components and electronics exports to Asia, North America and Europe. Similar stories are found in China, Indonesia, Malaysia, the Philippines and Indochina. Products range from garments to value-added, high-technology components. "Export competitiveness is especially important as a potential tool to reduce poverty in developing countries, as it can lead to higher economic growth and can increase the likelihood of lower prices and better products for consumers," says J. Shivakumar, the World Bank's country director in Thailand.[24]

Shivakumar believes that efforts to stall market liberalization in the aftermath of Asia's financial crisis form a black cloud over Asia's continued prosperity. "Worldwide experience has shown that inward-looking strategies eventually fail, for such policies almost always result in low-quality, high-cost products, greater poverty, disadvantaged consumers, and all with only a well-connected and privileged minority benefiting."[25]

The Hong Kong based Esquel Group is an example of a company that has expanded export markets throughout Asia by producing world-class quality export garments. The company has been instrumental in creating a strong image among wholesalers and brand labels of China, Malaysia, the Philippines, and even Mauritius-made high-quality clothing, accessories, footwear, watches and jewelry. In particular, Esquel carefully exploits the China brand name worldwide. It was also successful in bringing modern manufacturing practices to distant locations such as Xinjiang province in northern China.

The inexpensive land, low-cost labor, quality work, a highly skilled and adaptable labor force, among other factors, put China in an enviable position. "On any day, Mainland China can match the best production in the world," claims Surinder Chhibber, the Asian chief executive officer of global clothing giant Esprit. "It has the manpower, skill and know-how to do it."[26] Even famous foreign brands, such as Esprit, Benetton and Calvin Klein, choose to manufacture their products in China not only because the labor is inexpensive, but the quality of the work is better as well. These days, the tags on many popular brand names read "Made in China," and for good reason.

Most Asian places have developed a strong export image. Japan is especially well-known for its high-quality car manufacturers, including Toyota Motors, Honda and Nissan. Toyota City is known as "automobile city"[27] because of its thriving automotive industry. Toyota Motors is also an example of a car manufacturer with a strong export strategy of manufacturing and selling cars in local markets. (See Exhibit 3.4)

Exhibit 3.4: EXPORTING EXPERTISE

Toyota is Japan's largest vehicle manufacturer and the third largest in the world. It owes much of its success to export strategy, including both cars and manufacturing capacity. The company has exported manufacturing capacity to major markets around the world and localized its operations, thus facilitating its exports. For example, Toyota produces more cars in ASEAN localities than any other manufacturer in the world.

Global manufacturing centers are chosen by Toyota on the basis of the size of the domestic market as well as the facilities and expertise available. These factors assist the distribution of the brand in the local markets and provide a foundation to build exports from new manufacturing centers.

For example, among the company's most important global manufacturing and export centers is Toyota Australia, with an annual turnover of A$4 billion (US$2.1 billion). It is "being developed as one of Toyota Japan's global manufacturing centers with a long-term commitment to the domestic market and a major, expanding export role."[1] Toyota Australia is responsible for major exports to the Middle East, Southeast Asia and the Oceania region. About 30% of Toyota cars manufactured in Australia are exported. In all, Toyota has invested A$1.8 billion (US$952 million) in the country over ten years.

Toyota's successful automobile export strategy has been instrumental in enhancing the image of Japan as a world-class manufacturing center. Its flexibility in exporting manufacturing capacity communicates the message that Japanese companies are flexible, innovative and responsive to new circumstances. The development of exports from exported manufacturing capacity also fosters a reputation for companies that are willing to transfer technology and foster growth in other economies.

Sources:

1 *http://www.investment2000.com.au/CaseStudiesToyota.htm*, viewed on September 28, 2000.

http://www.cartoday.com/livenews/99/09/0930.htm#Toyota Lists In Globalisation Strategy, viewed on September 28, 2000.

However, places and their businesses that implement export strategies must also avoid producing sub-standard products. The South Korean automobile industry has been hurt by the global expansion plans of conglomerates Daewoo and Hyundai, which have earned reputations — perhaps ill-deserved — for producing poor-quality products. When acquisition talks collapsed between Ford and South Korean auto manufacturer Daewoo Motors, it increased perceptions of problems with other South Korean auto producers.

The automotive and automotive-parts industries in Australia, Japan, South Korea and Thailand also illustrate the growing importance of nations and enterprises joining forces to add value to their own products or services. This is clear, too, in the case of the tourist industry where regions develop a unique character, such as for gastronomy (Shanghai-style Chinese cuisine); sunny beaches and other environments (the tropical image of Thailand and Malaysia); and a relaxing café culture (Manila). The expertise in serving tourists has contributed to new practices in other product and service areas.

To expand exports, places can employ a number of tools:

- Public- and private-sector actors can cooperate to develop strategies for strengthening export opportunities for local businesses.
- The local government can establish export advisory offices.
- The local government can provide financial incentives to stimulate export-oriented activities, such as participation in trade shows.
- The local government can assist export-interested businesses in recruiting personnel with relevant experience. Training in inter-cultural relations and languages are two increasingly important attributes.

HOW DO PLACE MARKETERS MARKET THEIR PLACES?

A place faces a number of important choices when it begins the task of place marketing. These are four broad strategies for attracting visitors, residents and employees, business and industry, and for increasing exports. These strategies are:

- Image marketing
- Attraction marketing
- Infrastructure marketing
- People marketing.

Image Marketing

Asia consists of 600,000 competing communities that need to attract potential place buyers by projecting a strong and relevant image. Without a unique and distinguishing image, a potentially attractive place may go unnoticed in the midst of the vast Asian place market. One of the goals in image marketing is to develop a clever slogan that is believable and demonstrable. For example, Singapore uses the slogan "Singapore — One of Asia's economic tigers." This slogan is not without foundation. A small country on the periphery of peninsular Malaysia, Singapore's central location makes it the natural regional center for trade, transport, banking, tourism and communication. Indeed, Singapore's initial success is due mainly to its ideal location on the busy sea routes between East and West.

Singapore also uses other messages. For example, the first message visitors see on arriving at Changi airport is: "Singapore — Lion City." Here, too, there are hard facts. Singapore has arguably the best worldwide communications network in Asia and direct dialing to all parts of the world is available at all hotels.

However, not all slogans work. Asia is saturated with many unfocused and easily copied slogans. While they may be catchy, slogans alone cannot do the job of image marketing, especially if they are not part of a larger marketing strategy. A place's image must be valid and communicated in many ways and through many channels if it is to take root and succeed.

A place may find itself in one of five image situations.

Overly Attractive Image

Some places suffer from having too attractive an image. Those who have visited Phuket in the peak season have experienced an overflow of people, noise, long waiting lines and high prices everywhere. Such a place needs little marketing and might even consider undertaking some de-marketing.

A similar situation marred Boracay's highly attractive image. Journalist Daffyd Roderick described the island paradise: "The island, renowned for its gorgeous white sand beaches and gin-blue seas is already fringed with a mossy-green shag-rug of algae growth that some say is due to a combination of high visitor numbers and a lack of sewage treatment. The moss felt nice and warm on my feet, but it also made me a bit nervous about the state of the water I was swimming in."[28] So Boracay finally decided to go after quality, not quantity. Instead of building more hotels, authorities are pressuring the least-desirable ones to upgrade or face sanctions. The still-popular destination is now pursuing a strategy of *sustainable tourism* based on a more targeted approach to development.

Several Asia reports such as *Emerging Asia: Changes and Challenges*[29] and *Asia's New Little Dragons: The Dynamic Emergence of Indonesia, Thailand, and Malaysia,*[30] point out the need to direct expansion, investment and population development to the so-called peripheral Asian areas. This shift in emphasis would have the favorable effect of reducing the problems of highly attractive areas and stimulating the growth of peripheral areas.

Positive Image

Xian, Hong Kong, Sumatra, Chiang Mai, Cebu City and Penang have positive images. Although these cities do not require an image change, the challenge is to amplify the positives and deliver them more effectively to desired target groups.

Businesses like to take advantage of places that are viewed positively. Commercial vehicles exploit their connection with Japan; producers of semiconductors emphasize their Japan, Korea, Singapore or Taiwan connection; and gem and jewelry manufacturers do the same with Thailand. Ironically, as the world market becomes more global, businesses increasingly want to identify with a local place that is viewed positively.

A sophisticated example of a business associating itself with cities that have positive images is the "San Miguel Around the World" campaign. San Miguel chose to associate itself with a host of highly visible destinations. The image is reflected in both text and visual form. Figure 3.7 shows an example of an Asian bank's attempt to associate with Asian countries and the Asian region. The Development Bank of Singaproe is leveraging its association with New Zealand, considered a progressive Asian economy. Figure 3.8 provides an example of a multinational's attempts to localize appeal and association. In its heyday, Asia Pulp and Paper was considered an Asian powerhouse, epitomizing Asian management expertise. Unfortunately for ABB, its attempt to communicate the company's contribution to the development of Asian corporations; and in turn the contribution of Asian corporations to Asia, backfired when Asia Pulp and Paper became one of Asia's biggest debacles soon after this advertisement appeared.

Weak Image

Many places have a weak image. They lack a marketing strategy with a clear message and leadership.

A weak image can also result from the place having a small population, being located in a peripheral area, lacking resources, and so on. These places have to be especially skillful in changing their image. They may have attractive features but fail to turn them into competitive advantages. Without effective images these places will remain anonymous. Many small places in Asia have simply disappeared behind the megastars of Tokyo, Seoul, Taipei, Hong Kong and Singapore. Despite improving facilities, their weak image has not brought them up to the hard-charging Asian standard. Some places are just awakening to their obscurity (see Exhibit 3.5).

Figure 3.7   The Development Bank of Singapore is an Asian player

Source: Development Bank of Singapore.

Figure 3.8   ABB is committed to the development of Asia

Source: *BusinessWeek*, October 16, 2000, p. 43.

Exhibit 3.5: THE KYUSHU REGION WANTS YOU!

As part of its effort to sustain trading relationships with neighboring economies, the Kyushu region — once the center of Japanese politics and culture but now overshadowed by the Kansai and Kanto regions — has had to devise new strategies to market itself in Asia and around the world as a business and industrial center. Strategically located on Japan's southernmost tip, the island region believes it is well situated to serve as a "trade gateway to Asia."

That means that Kyushu is trying to convince investors from within and outside Asia to locate their Asian headquarters, or significant operations, to the island. The city of Kitakyushu, for instance, is promoting itself as the "new international distribution center of the region." But what distinguishes Kyushu from Asia's other gateways, Hong Kong and Singapore?

In a bid to enhance the attractiveness of its services in trading, Kitakyushu City set up a Foreign Access Zone (FAZ), with financial backing from the central government, involving an impressive infrastructure development program. Projects include the Kitakyushu International Distribution (KID) Center — a world-class international distribution center — and the Asia-Pacific Import Mart (AIM), a business and exhibition complex.

Among other projects set up to promote economic development and attract more investors to Kyushu is the Technopolis project of the Ministry of International Trade and Industry (MITI), which aims to build technology hubs around several cities in the region. The "Brain Center" project, another MITI initiative, is intended to nurture the development of "brain industries" in the region by setting up science laboratories to support the software and IT sectors.

Oita Prefecture in northeastern Kyushu has been instrumental in promoting economic cooperation with Asian countries. It hosts the annual Kyushu Regional Exchange Summit, attracting representatives from throughout Asia. It is organized by local authorities in Kyushu and regional authorities in Asia, and is promoted as a venue for discussing strategies to revitalize Asian places, regions and countries.

Kyushu is also blessed with many attractions that are of interest to tourists — and expatriates. Among them is Beppu in Oita Prefecture, a resort town known for its hot springs. Mt Aso, in Kumamoto Prefecture, and Mt Sakurajima, in Kagoshima Prefecture, are also major tourist destinations. Kyushu is home to several theme parks and recreation developments such as Space World, Ocean Dome and Harmony Lane.

But Ocean Dome is also an example of how a major development project can go wrong. The complex, known as *Seagaia* in Japanese, is the world's largest all-weather indoor water park. The giant facility even features a fully retractable roof so that swimmers can enjoy the real sun, when the weather permits, while frolicking along the artificial beach. Built in grandiose style during the bubble economy, it has become a multi-million dollar drain for its developers and government backers. In 1999, the company had ¥262.8 billion (US$2.2 billion) in short- and long-term loans outstanding, an amount equal to 13.6 times the previous year's revenues of ¥19.3 billion (US$160.8 million), which is about how much it costs to operate the facility for a year. In 2001, management filed for bankruptcy protection.

The Miyazaki prefectural government provided ¥6 billion in soft financing for the facility, and prospects for recovering the investment — directly or indirectly — are long-term at best. Still, *Seagaia* — which has already gained a listing in the *Guinness Book of Records* — remains an attraction, as well as an example of over-exuberant optimism.

———

Sources:

http://jin.jcic.or.jp/access/regions/kyushu.html, viewed on September 18, 2000; *http://www.ics.com.au/jlgc/Globalisation2.htm*, viewed on September 12, 2000; *http://www.kyushu.miti.go.jp/invest/more/ mor_other3.htm*, viewed on October 4, 2000; *http://www.jef.or.jp/en/jti/ 200007_018.html*, viewed on October 5, 2000.

Contradictory Image

Many places have contradictory images because people hold opposite views about some features of the place. Seoul, for example, is perceived as both a hyper-modern, international city that works well, and as a sterile, congested and costly city, with sharp divisions between labor and business and big business and government. Hong Kong also conveys contradictions. While to some, it is a modern, well-developed place with many company headquarters, much of the world has seen TV programs describing the difficulty Hong Kong's once-admired bureaucracy has had in demonstrating its capacity to administer the Special Administrative Region efficiently and professionally.

Many places in developing Asia also carry contradictory images. However great these cities may have been before the economic crisis, the belief persists that they lack the work ethic, quality-consciousness and entrepreneurship.

The strategic challenge is to accentuate the positive image while simultaneously trying to change the realities that give rise to negative images. Image reversals are hard to accomplish because first impressions can be long lasting. Another is that media, especially local media, tend to accentuate the negative aspects of their place, focusing on such things as crime and corruption.

Negative Image

Many places are stuck with a negative image. On the place market, the Philippines is often referred to with negative characteristics. In the 1980s, for example, some publications referred to the country as "the sick man of Asia"[31] because of its poor economic performance. In an interview with former president Fidel Ramos, *Forbes.com* mentions that "The Philippines has been notorious for the scale of its corruption and for oligarchies with their concentrations of political and economic power."[32]

Located off the southeast coast of China is the former Portuguese colony of Macau. Over the years, the peninsula's historical importance has gradually faded. Once considered "one of the most important commercial centers in the Orient,"[33] and instrumental in the spread of Christianity, it is renowned today for its gangsters and triads. Entrenched in the public memory is the film *Macao* made by Josef Von Sternberg in 1952, which portrayed a corrupt, crime-ridden casino culture. *Time Asia* describes Macau as "...a shadowy blur of blackjack, roulette, poker and prostitution. Since 1996, bloody wars among the triads, or secret societies, have transformed Macau into a mini replica of 1920s Chicago, replete with machine gun assassinations outside casinos and gang leaders with nicknames like 'Fatti Pui' and 'Broken Tooth'. There have been 37 murders this year, up from 28 in 1998."[34]

There are other places in Asia that suffer from image problems. The town of Pagsanjan, three hours south of Manila, is famous for its

Pagsanjan Falls. Over the years, it has also come to be known as a "pedophile heaven."[35] Poverty has led the parents of young children to openly accept gifts and bribes from foreigners who, in turn, expect sexual favors from the children.[36] The media, by zeroing in on a place, can hurt its image. Although Singapore is a thriving city-state, it has been called "the most boring city" and been referred to as "the nanny state" because of the government's strict censorship measures.[37]

Places like this actually need less attention and some time to work out a new strategy for a more positive profile. In the case of Pagsanjan, the local government is eager to change its image. Organizations such as End Child Prostitution in Asian Tourism (ECPAT) and the Preda Foundation, Inc. (People's Recovery, Empowerment and Development Assistance Foundation Inc.)[38] are working to give children better lives and thus improve the image of the city. The government of Singapore likewise has allocated a budget to develop arts and culture in the country and thereby provide more leisure activities. The city is also slowly becoming a destination for international performers and entertainers.[39]

Yet images are not easy to develop or change. Image marketing is no quick fix. It can take years to create or transplant a new image effectively. Many political mandates are for only three to four years, making a substantial image change difficult. Image marketing requires research into how residents, visitors, and external and internal businesses currently perceive a place. Many places have no experience in initiating market analysis of this kind. Nor is it easy to get various individuals and groups to decide on the new image, let alone make the investments required to validate that image.

Attraction Marketing

Improving an image is not sufficient to increase a place's fundamental attractiveness. Places also need to invest in specific attractions.

Some places are fortunate to have natural attractions. One such place is Bali — often called "Island of Gods"[40] or "Dawn of the World."[41] The remarkable beaches, friendly people and its rich history make it a world-renowned tourist destination. Amritsar in India, whose name translates as "sweet lake", is known for its Golden Temple, the most sacred shrine of the Sikhs, with its holy tank called "the pool of immortality."[42] The Maldive Islands are unquestionably an ideal place to get away to. They offer an incomparable variety of attractions — golden beaches, crystal-clear lagoons and a varied underwater terrain.

Other places benefit from a remarkable legacy of historical buildings. Agra in India has its monument to love, the Taj Mahal, and northwestern

Cambodia is known for Angkor Wat, the largest ruins in Southeast Asia, whose buildings were constructed during the Khmer Dynasty in the 12th century. Hanoi, which markets itself as "One of the most beautiful cities in Asia,"[43] is another unique Asian place. It is a compact place, which makes it easy for tourists to enjoy the best parts of the city.

Other fortunate places which are home to world-renowned edifices include Kuala Lumpur which, in its Petronas Towers, has the world's tallest building, measuring 1,483 feet. Nagashima has the biggest roller coaster (97m), while the Imperial Palace in Beijing is the largest palace in Asia, covering 178 acres.[44] We call this type of attraction a "Guinness attraction" and to qualify for this accolade it must be the biggest (a city), highest (a building), longest (a bridge) or best in its class in some dimension.

Some places benefit from having beautiful landscaping or gardens. Examples include historic Asian gardens that are found at the Kinabalu Park in Sabah, Malaysia, which "represents over half the families of flowering plants in the world"; Meiji-Jingu-Gyoen Park located in the Harajuku district of Tokyo, labeled "best city park" by *Asiaweek* Magazine for the year 2000;[45] and the Royal Chitwan National Park, southwest of Kathmandu, renowned for being one of the best national parks in Asia.[46]

One very common strategy to enhance a place's attractiveness is to build giant convention and exhibition centers. Take Pusan, for instance. Strategically located at one of Korea's most advanced port cities is the Pusan Exhibition & Convention Center (PUEXCO), a world-class multi-purpose meeting facility. PUEXCO has three exhibition halls that can accommodate a total of 1,738 booths; a 2,800-seat grand convention hall; a year-round showroom; a restaurant mall; a shopping mall; and a parking lot, among other facilities. Perhaps best of all, it is situated on Haeundae Beach, among the country's top vacation destinations.

The convention and exhibition hall is expected to receive around 200,000 visitors annually, and better than US$1.2 billion in export contracts. In its first 15 months of operations, it held 39 international exhibitions and 59 international conventions, and employed 39,000 staff.[47] The role of the exhibition center in the value-added process is obvious from this example. Exhibit 3.6 illustrates the increasing stakes for success in the exhibition market.

Exhibit 3.6: HONG KONG & SHANGHAI: TRADE FAIR BATTLE

Hong Kong was little more than a fishing village at the turn of the century, while Shanghai was a sophisticated, international city and finance and trade center. All that is different now, and in many respects, the cities have reversed roles, much to Shanghai's chagrin. What makes it worse is that Shanghai people moving to Hong Kong in the 1940s and 1950s were largely responsible for building the former fishing village into a global powerhouse.

With over 80 trade fairs held each year in Hong Kong — most at the Hong Kong Convention and Exhibition Center — including some of the largest in the world, and over 420 conventions and corporate meetings, Hong Kong has firmly established itself as China's Trade Fair Capital, a position that by rights Shanghai would occupy if it weren't for the 40 years it was essentially closed to the world. But Shanghai intends to do more than just get even. Herman S.M. Hu — a prominent Hong Kong businessman whose family's roots are in Shanghai — says the once-forgotten city's residents are looking to surpass Hong Kong. And they've gone looking for help to do that.

Shanghai's approach to fast-tracking the upgrade of its trade fair facilities was to enlist the assistance of three world-class German exhibition companies in 1997: Deutsche Messe, Messe Dusseldorf and Messe Munich. Together with the Shanghai Pudong Land Development Corporation, the companies built The Shanghai New International Expo. The intention of the consortium was to present a major competitive force for attracting trade fairs to the resurgent financial and trade center. Construction took just four years.

In its first phase, the exhibition center was still dwarfed by the magnificent HKCEC, which boasts 248,000 square meters of exhibit space following a 1997 extension. The SNIE has just 45,000 square meters of indoor exhibit space but also offers another 20,000 square meters of outdoor exhibit space. Ultimately, the complex will offer approximately 200,000 square meters of indoor exhibit space and 50,000 square meters outdoors, making it larger than its Hong Kong rival.

But even in trade fair development, winning by a hair is good enough.

Sources:

http://tpwebapp.tdctrade.com/sp/pro000109.htm, viewed on September 28, 2000; *http://www.tdctrade.com/hktrader/9912/9912s11.htm*, viewed on September 28, 2000; *http://www.mdna.com/grounds.html#shanghai*, viewed on October 9, 2000; *http://www.hkcec.com.hk/*,viewed on October 9, 2000; *http://www.cematchina.com/media.htm*, viewed on October 5, 2000; *http:// www.mdna.com/ grounds.html#shanghai*, viewed on October 5, 2000; *http:/ /www.hkcec.com/english/whatsnew/press/press1.html*, viewed on October 10, 2000.

Among other types of attractions is the conversion of a downtown area into a pedestrian mall. Hay Street in Perth, Australia, is a remarkable artery for many visitors who seek a more leisurely shopping experience. Lan Kwai Fong in Hong Kong and the Yuyuan Market in Shanghai are today highly attractive walking streets. Business people enjoy a break when the rush of automobile traffic is replaced by more casual pedestrian traffic. Many mid-size Japanese cities will feature a covered central business district to attract fleeing suburbanites. Ayala Land, which developed the central business district of Makati in Metro Manila, built pedestrian bridges and cross-walks connecting buildings and main thoroughfares similar to those in Hong Kong in an attempt to increase the attractiveness of the district to pedestrians when a rival business district began development nearby.

A number of cities have capitalized on their major business streets. For example, Hanoi actively markets the streets of its Old Quarters, an area that has come to be known as a market of various local crafts and products. Known more popularly as "36 Old Streets," today the area has over 70 streets, the most popular of which include Han Gai for its silk clothing and silver products; Hang Quat for its religious objects and clothing; Hang Ma for its shiny paper products; and Lan Ong for its herbal medicinal products.[48]

Infrastructure Marketing

Clearly, neither image nor attractions can provide the complete answer to a place's development. Effective infrastructure is required at the base. In almost all place marketing the infrastructure plays a heavy role and throughout Asia investments in infrastructure now play a more central role. Infrastructure investments are not only desirable in themselves but they also help ease unemployment. Such investments have the strong support of multilateral investment institutions such as the World Bank and the Asian Development Bank.

Streets and highways, railways, airports and telecommunication networks are the most frequent infrastructure improvements. The World Bank estimates that Asia spends US$150–200 billion every year on infrastructure.[49] Place marketers are trying to differentiate their standings in IT. First, some places try to communicate that they offer excellent IT-knowledge and resources (for example, the MSC in Malaysia). Second, some places claim to have outstanding application experience (for example, Singapore — "The Customer Support Center for Asia/Pacific market" — or the Philippines as "Asia's Call Center".) Third, some places are claiming a niche application position (for example, Pacific Century Cyberworks in Hong Kong wants to become Asia's Internet content provider). And fourth, some places are marketing their comparatively low telecommunications tariffs (Hong Kong and Singapore).

Railways are also experiencing a renaissance in Asia. Taiwan is building a high-speed passenger transportation system connecting Taipei, in northern Taiwan, with Kaohsiung in the south, a distance of approximately 345 kilometers. The Taiwanese government estimates that the project will cost about NT$441.9 billion (over US$17.5 billion). Trains will travel at speeds of up to 300 kilometers per hour and will carry up to 300,000 passengers per day. Construction began in 1997 and operations will commence in July 2003.[50] China imported Japanese *Shinkansen* technology to build its high-speed Beijing-to-Shanghai railway early in this century. It has also imported German maglev technology. A 30-kilometer rail line connects Pudong's international airport to Shanghai. In 2003, China will decide whether to spend US$1 billion to build maglev links between Beijing and Tianjin, Shanghai and Hangzhou, and Shanghai and Beijing.[51] Meanwhile, in the early 1990s a group of Asian industrialists revived the fabled Orient Express. Malaysia, Thailand and the Philippines are all undertaking massive rail projects to connect commercial districts to suburbs.

These developments and investment plans will cause Asian places to compete for designation as highly attractive, high-speed station stops. This is a particularly important development for China, which has struggled to find ways to bring investment and prosperity inland. As urban areas become increasingly crowded and expensive, workers and their families will look at commuting as an attractive alternative to city living. Meanwhile, urban dwellers will have increasing access to outlying areas. In other words, the primary investment in infrastructure breeds *secondary investments* that are marketed in their turn.

The same phenomenon can be seen in Japan, a much smaller country, but which is, like the Philippines and Indonesia, an archipelago of distinct islands. Rail links between the islands are more efficient and faster than ships. The Seikan rail tunnel — completed in 1985 — is the world's longest. It extends 53.9 kilometers and connects the northern island of Hokkaido to Honshu.[52] While critics of the tunnel claim the jumbo jet makes the massive infrastructure project redundant, the tunnel makes possible an unbroken high-speed rail link between Tokyo and Sapporo that carries about 100 million passengers every year.

Science parks have appeared in many parts of Asia, and are another example of aggressive infrastructure marketing. Some of these parks — the Hong Kong Science Park, the Wuling Yuan Science Park in China, the Kanha National Science Park in India, and the Cibodas, Halimun and Yabshi Science Parks in Indonesia, for example — specialize in a particular niche. Other examples include the Singapore Science Park, the Hsinchu Science Based Industrial Park in Taiwan — sometimes called "Asia's most successful science park" — the Taedock Science Town in South Korea, the Kerala Science Park in India, and the Chinese National and Science Industry Parks in China. Many of these parks have

Figure 3.9 Excellent Infrastructure

Malaysia's massive Multimedia Super Corridor offers the promise of high-speed digital and air, rail and road transportation links.

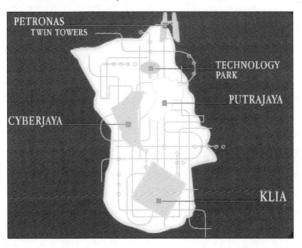

Source: *http://www.mdc.com.my/infra/index.html*, viewed on October 4, 2000.

developed retail stores, residential areas, recreational facilities and other city features.

Other worthwhile infrastructure investments include harbors, electricity and heating generation and distribution, facilities for water supply, availability of land, and housing and office space.

In Figure 3.9 we show a typical attraction message that emphasizes infrastructure.

People Marketing

The fourth marketing strategy is for a place to market its people. As far back as the 16th century, Niccolo Machiavelli concluded that the success or failure of an independent republic depended on the character of its citizens, the civic virtues they possess. The character theme has not lost impact, as it is a major focus in many place campaigns. A typical place market example is Ireland, whose message exclaims: "People are to Ireland as champagne is to France."

The same could be said of the Philippines, as we've already noted, in the context of its supply of intellectual resources. In its 2000 Global E-Economy Index, the U.S.-based Meta Group ranked the Philippines number one in the world in knowledge jobs — ahead of Australia, the U.S., Canada and France. That ranking confirmed what multinational technology executives have known for years: the Philippines is a bountiful source of scarce, world-class intellectual capital.[53]

With 800,000 IT jobs likely to go unfilled every year in the United States alone — and a projected two million shortfall in IT experts in India by 2006[54] — that makes the Philippines a strategic human resource for many of the world's top technology companies.

Cultural diversity in Asia is often used to communicate the excitement associated with visiting and working in the region. Singapore's Sentosa Island markets its Asian village as an attraction visitors will "never want to leave." Malaysia markets itself as a mixture of three distinct cultures.

People marketing may take on at least five forms:

1) Famous people

Asia is crowded with famous people participating in place-marketing promotions. Connecting a famous face with a place offers a fast and effective means for creating a positive association. Mongolia calls itself "The Land of Genghis Khan."[55] Calamba, Laguna in Southern Luzon positions itself as the "Home Town of National Hero, Jose Rizal." The northern Indian state of Gujarat reminds visitors that it is "The Birthplace of Mahatma Gandhi." The fishing village of Porbandar, where Gandhi was born, and the Sabarmati Ashram, which he founded, still draw tourists today. Famous martial arts star Jackie Chan has actively promoted his home country, Hong Kong.

Individual athletes and teams also give identity to many places in Asia. Sachin Tendulkar, India's most famous cricket player; Efren 'Bata' Reyes, the Philippines' outstanding pool player; and Fiji's Vijay Singh, champion professional golfer. Tiger Woods is a symbol of sportsmanship in Thailand, his mother's birthplace. In the Sydney Olympics 2000, several Asian countries took home gold medals, including South Korea, Japan, Indonesia and Thailand. China was the third-best performer overall, taking home a total of 28 gold medals in sports as diverse as badminton, tae kwon do and table tennis. These athletes are a source of pride and contribute significantly to national image, especially in an era when the Internet speeds success stories round the world in milliseconds.

2) Enthusiastic local leaders

Renown can spread fast for those places that have skillful business and political leaders. In a climate of high unemployment and low investments, it can be rewarding for leaders to step forward with a clear vision and enthusiasm. In the Philippines, when Jesse M. Robredo took office as mayor of Naga City, he introduced the Empowerment Ordinance that allows citizen to be part of city policies. He was quickly recognized for a style of governmental leadership which centred on his message that "effective city management is compatible with yielding power to the people."[56] Tang Fei, former president-elect, premier and head of government of Taiwan, is among Asia's notable leaders. Before his resignation, ostensibly for health reasons, in October 2000, Tang was known for having cleaned-up government, advancing ties with China and enhancing economic transparency.[57]

In Asia we find noticeably fewer examples of how different regions have marketed their local leaders. But there is a growing number. In the city of Taipei, James Soong became well recognized as "Taiwan's popular governor." A former provincial governor, Soong has been referred to as the "man of the people" and a "vote-getter."[58] He opened his city to the outside world and ushered in market economic reforms and innovative projects. He created new life in the region's administration and earned respect from potential place buyers.

Richard J. Gordon, the former mayor of Olangapo City in Northern Luzon, Philippines, had a dream to make the U.S. Naval facility in Subic Bay into a self-sustaining industrial, commercial, investment and tourist center. Gordon set his sights on making Subic Bay a dominant free-trade port that could compete with Hong Kong and help boost the Philippines' influence and position in Asia.

In 1980, as mayor of Olongapo City, he drafted a plan which provided for the cooperative use of Subic Bay by both the United States and Philippine governments, with commercial enterprises setting up operations as the U.S. Navy gradually pulled out. Gordon's visionary project formally began in 1992, when the U.S. Navy departed from its long-time deepwater port, leaving US$8 billion-worth of infrastructure behind.

Some tough times followed as Gordon sought to transform the former base into a high-tech industrial cluster. Because funds were scarce, former base employees worked as volunteers, maintaining the facilities as they waited for investors. The dedication paid off. Subic Bay fast became the Philippines' premier investment destination, attracting technology manufacturers and a leading logistics and rapid-shipment firm, Federal Express. Under Gordon's management, 70,000 jobs were created and almost US$3 billion in investments recorded. As a result, Gordon has received several awards for public service,[59] and was appointed tourism secretary inthe Arroyo government in 2001 with a similar mandate.

Asiaweek magazine named often-controversial Tokyo governor Ishihara Shintaro "best local administrator" for the year 2000. Ishihara made headlines with his cost-cutting initiatives, which included hitting Japan's large financial institutions in Tokyo — still on the mend from Asia's financial crisis — for an extra US$1 billion in taxes annually.[60] Ishihara's cutbacks included a reduction in his own salary and bonuses in an effort to trim the city's budget.

But Ishihara is best known for his outspoken views on the central government. "'He is one of the few Japanese leaders who can speak his mind clearly and openly to the public and take swift action on what he believes in,' says Matsui Kiyondo, editor-in-chief of the influential monthly magazine *Bungei Shunju*." At a time when the Japanese public has all but given up hope in the very idea of good government, Ishihara is showing it is possible.[61]

None of these figures, however, is without controversy. In some cases, and perhaps in all, their detractors and critics number as many as their admirers. But, on balance, they do two things for their places. First, there is genuine good accomplished that has impact and relevance to local communities. Second, this good work brings national, regional, and even international, attention to bear on their places, communities and countries.

3) Competent people

Local access to competent people is a strong attraction factor in Asian place marketing. When a place decides on its industry mix, it must attract the necessary competent people. China has attracted over 145,000 foreign-funded enterprises and has employed 17.5 million people. Foreign companies can take over a joint-venture partner's workforce, hire through a local labor bureau or job fair, or advertise in newspapers. However, the supply of competent people is a serious problem for China, one that imperils prospects for sustainable growth.

Former U.S. Secretary of Commerce William H. Daley said after his Multi-Agency Business Development Infrastructure Mission to China in March 1999, "Skilled workers are often in short supply. Shortages can be especially acute in south China, which has far fewer institutions for higher education than exist in the north." [62] He was particularly concerned about shortfalls in engineers and technicians, but also about the problem of attracting and retaining managers and marketing professionals.

China has acknowledged this problem and is, albeit nervously, encouraging investment in the strategic education sector. The problem is two-pronged. On the one hand, there is a shortage of skilled, productive labor for manufacturing. On the other, there is an acute shortage of executives with the education and experience required to professionally manage large operations, such as semiconductor plants, automobile manufacturing plants and consumer-products manufacturers.

Likewise, the approach to addressing the problem varies. Some companies choose to develop their own extensive in-house training facilities. Others adopt modern management technology that serves to involve employees in cross-functional teams tasked with increasing efficiency and productivity. To increase the supply of executives, multinational ventures send employees to degree and certificate courses offered by established and recently founded business and training institutions. But the point is that the lack of trained, qualified people is probably the most significant resource constraint on China's sustainable growth.

By contrast, the Philippines is among the most aggressive countries in training. Its 93.9% literacy rate [63] places it among the highest in Southeast Asia and the world. [64] Two cities in particular — Olongapo and Angeles — are known in part for their technical training centers created to promote foreign investment. These areas are home to big foreign names such as AOL, which is located in another former U.S. base, Clark Airbase, in Angeles City. And as we've already seen, the Subic Bay Industrial Park in Olongapo City, with its excellent location, infrastructure, transportation and living environment, and its skilled, dedicated workers, continues to attract significant investment (Figure 3.10).

Private enterprise is also supporting engineering and IT education, with major conglomerates — including Ayala Corporation, First Pacific, J.G. Summit, and the SM Group of Companies — investing in educational institutions to help ensure a steady supply of value-added intellectual resources. *The Asian Wall Street Journal* reporters G. Pascal Zachary and Robert Frank have noted that, "In a nation where a third of the people still farm coconuts and less than two percent of the population logs onto the Internet, the Philippines is home to a new wave of programmers who are drawing international attention."[65]

Meanwhile, Singapore is, to a significant degree, aggressively importing its intellectual talent. "We all agree that we must build an intellectually vibrant atmosphere so we can attract the best talents of the

Figure 3.10: Powered by People

Powered by People.

High Quality Human Resource

Subic Bay and the surrounding areas have a working population of about 170,000 including highly skilled workers from the former U.S. Naval Base as well as fres college graduates. The large pool of English speaking and well-educated workers and professionals guarantee a plentiful supply of manpower. The SBMA Labor Center has a large pool of registered applicants of various qualifications ready for immediate hiring by Subic Bay investors.

The two Training Centers inside Subic Bay and in the City of Olongapo are offering technical and specialized courses to meet the labor needs of existing and incoming investors.

Back to Top of Page

Source: http://www.subicbayindustrialpark.com/sbfz.html#humanresource, viewed on September 25, 2000.

region to come and contribute their intellectual assets for the good of Singapore," says Hum Sin Hoon, Dean of the National University of Singapore business school. He is so enthusiastic about talent building that he supports the government's decision to encourage Western business schools to open in Singapore — an outcome that creates new competition for his school. Hum believes that educational inducements are a necessary "part of the government drive to position Singapore as a knowledge-based economy."[66] Other countries are beginning to agree. In Malaysia, education is one of the country's fastest-growing sectors and, like China and the Philippines, is characterized by close private-sector/institutional partnerships. And in Hong Kong, education is the government's largest budget item.

4) People with an entrepreneurial profile

Entrepreneurial traditions vary quite a bit over the Asian landscape. Osaka, for example, is known as the "heart of entrepreneurial Japan."[67] The dense network of small and medium-sized firms influences the business climate there. Osaka actively uses its entrepreneurial character in its place marketing. Technology-intensive industry has steadily proved to be a major player in Taiwan's economy, with its output increasing in proportion to the total of industrial output from 26.8% in 1987 to 47.3% in 1999.[68] (The total industrial output of Taiwan for 1999 accounted for 33.2% of GDP).

Japan's Kansai region (in which Osaka is located), Taiwan and Hong Kong — "Asia's Business Supermarket"[69] — are all known for their entrepreneurial profiles. Stan Shih, founder of Acer and a Taiwan native, has become a spokesperson for Taiwan's globally minded entrepreneurs. Similarly, Richard Li, founder of Pacific Century Cyberworks, has become synonymous with high-tech deal-making. Li is the son of another chronically successful dealmaker, entrepreneur Li Ka-shing, also known as "Superman" in Hong Kong.

A place's entrepreneurial profile can be supported in many ways: sponsoring special educational programs for entrepreneurs, stimulating new entrepreneurial networks, and an active marketing of the place's entrepreneurial profile. Such marketing can strengthen a region's *internal* self-identity and simultaneously attract entrepreneurs and their companies.

5) People who have moved to the place

An approach that can best be described as the "follow-me phenomenon" is used in many cases. Profiling persons who have moved into a certain place can create appeal. We see at least three different profiling approaches. First, we can tell the story of an entire family that moved to the new place. The family members describe their experiences in their new home town, and the message often revolves around a heightened quality of life. The second approach is to focus on a special expert, scientist or businessperson who has chosen to move to a given place. These people are usually quoted, and a number of centrally attractive attributes are named. Third, personal statistics from an opinion survey can be presented regarding how people feel about living and working in the place. The attributes they appreciate most are then summarized.

A special case in this overall category is when a business owner provides a personal view of investing in a given place. Such a testimonial humanizes and puts a recognizable face on the place-choosing process. And there's no better example of that process at work than among Asia's overseas Chinese who returned to Mainland China in droves when the country opened significantly to foreign investment.

Overseas Chinese conglomerates in virtually every Southeast Asian country raced to set up shop in the homeland. Perhaps the most interesting example is of the present generation of Hong Kong businesspeople whose families fled Shanghai after Mao Zedong's communist government asserted control. The generation that left Shanghai played a massive role in transforming Hong Kong into a regional manufacturing, finance and services hub. And now their children are returning to Shanghai to do the same for the city of their forefathers.

But beyond marketing specific people, a place must encourage its citizens to be more friendly and considerate of visitors and new residents. Places must raise the level of their citizens' skills and attitudes so that they can meet the needs of the target markets. As an example, the Tourism Authority of Thailand (TAT), headed by its governor Pradech Phayakvichien, implemented two regulations intended to protect tourists in Thailand. One of these dealt with upgrading the standards of tour guides in the country and called for the employment of tour guides that hold a professional license issued by the TAT. Tour guides who have completed the regular two-year course are also required to attend an additional course to update their knowledge. To reduce the risk factor for tourists and to ensure quality service,[70] travel agents that fail to follow this regulation are fined.

WHO ARE THE MAJOR PLACE MARKETERS?

The marketers of a place can sometimes be difficult to identify. Place marketing is a continuous process that involves all citizens. However, the groups listed in Table 3.4 constitute the most active place marketers.

Table 3.4: Major actors in place marketing.

LOCAL ACTORS
Public-sector actors
1. Mayor and/or city manager
2. Business development department in the community
3. Urban planning department of the community (transport, education, sanitation, etc.)
4. Tourist bureau
5. Conventions bureau
6. Public information bureau

Private-sector actors
1. Individual citizens
2. Leading enterprises
3. Real-estate developers and agents
4. Financial institutions (banks and insurance companies)
5. Electricity and gas utilities, telecommunication companies
6. Chamber of commerce and other local business organizations
7. Hospitality and retail industries (hotels, restaurants, department stores, other retailers, exhibition and conventions centers)
8. Travel agencies
9. Labor market organizations
10. Architects
11. Transport companies (taxi, railway, airline)
12. Media (newspaper, radio, TV)

REGIONAL ACTORS
1. Regional economic development agencies
2. County and state government
3. Regional tourist boards

NATIONAL ACTORS
1. Political heads of government
2. Inward investment agencies
3. National tourist boards

INTERNATIONAL ACTORS
1. Embassies and consulates
2. Inward investment agencies
3. Economic development agencies with a specific link to a region or city
4. International enterprises with a place-bound link

Place-marketing strategy frequently emerges as a process in which the local actors provide the driving force: "Think globally with your local place-marketing strategy — but work it out locally." We will focus on the local actors and their development strategies.

Public-sector actors

In Asian countries where unemployment, underemployment and weak economic dynamism are perceived as primary problems, citizens often expect their elected officials to improve the climate for local growth. Unfortunately, public-sector actors often do not know what to do when taking office, in spite of their electioneering promises. They have a long tradition of focusing resources on *distributing* wealth. They often lack competence in *generating* wealth. Much of Asia's public sector enjoys a proud tradition of "social engineering," rather than "growth engineering." But the Asian financial crisis of 1997–98 now acts as a strong force driving public-sector actors to deal with growth engineering.

Nowhere is that process more apparent than in Singapore. Ironically, before the crisis, it was Singapore which sang the virtues of Asian values loudest. As the singing was led by its former Prime Minister and now Senior Minister Lee Kuan Yew, it is perhaps fitting that his son, Deputy Prime Minister Lee Hsien Loong, is now leading the charge in the opposite direction. The younger Lee is forcing Singapore to confront the new realities of globalization and liberalization, especially in the banking and financial sectors.

In November 1997, Lee, in his capacity as chairman of the Monetary Authority of Singapore (MAS), announced that foreign ownership of banks would no longer be limited to the traditional 40% ceiling. Concurrently, he directed MAS to begin issuing a new round of full and restricted bank licenses in a bid to increase competition and force local institutions to strengthen their management and business systems.

Despite those announcements, foreign institutions were not allowed to begin taking control of local banks immediately. But it was clear that this was one instance in which local companies had a finite window to prepare for a new way of doing business. As a consequence of Lee's re-engineering, Singapore's business community is reconsidering its traditional position in which large, state-backed firms dominated the economy and the business landscape. Given Singapore's historical reluctance to embrace Western business values and its position of leadership in that respect in Asia, the impact of this shift on the region should not be underestimated.

A similar driving force is also evident on the local level. Political leaders such as mayors and party members, as well as individual citizens, are pressing for a new approach. They have witnessed how new strategies implemented in regions and communities have produced impressive results. Asian media now widely distribute cross-border success stories. There is an *Asian benchmarking* of local strategies for growth. The members of one community will visit successful communities to learn how they did it. When a sufficient number of local public-sector actors adopt a growth orientation, a climate for change is felt nationally.

The climate for change is driven forward by leadership, talent and a capacity to work out long-term strategies, all necessary characteristics of effective public-sector actors. A city mayor, a city manager and other public executives can act as important catalysts for creating a new local business climate.

Private-sector actors

Without the consent and active participation of individual citizens not much growth engineering will be possible. In Pakistan, Central Asia and other parts of the world, for example, a group of active non-government organizations, the Aga Khan Development Network (AKDN), is actively engaged in economic, social and cultural development programs. The various agencies of the AKDN aim to improve living conditions and opportunities in these developing nations and assist the poor in reaching a level of self-reliance. Similar efforts are under way in Thailand, Indonesia and other Southeast Asian economies.

This type of collective effort is based on local pride. "Pride-building" is a primary element in a place-marketing strategy and it can apply to community involvement behind large events such as the Olympic Games, world championships, a city/regional celebration, a festival or an international exhibition. Those visiting Dubai for the shopping festival during March, or Sepang, Malaysia, during the Formula One Grand Prix in October, or the Hong Kong International Dragon Boat Festival, held annually on the fifth day of the fifth lunar month, or Japan's annual Equinox Festival understand what pride-building means in practice. Today, Asia is crowded with places where mega-events have unleashed collective energy.

But general pride among community members must go beyond the occasional mega-event. Pride must extend to a school with a unique profile; a science park with associated entrepreneurial companies; a new railway with an attractive high-speed connection; a profitable leading business with an exciting success story; or even low prices, tele-tariffs, housing costs, and lower income tax. This can be rephrased in a more fundamental way: *The place's marketable value proposition and theme must be widely known and accepted by its citizens.*

A place-bound pride is something that visitors quickly discover. Visit Shanghai and you will notice the pride associated with the city. Or travel to Cebu and you will notice the pride that the locals have for a city blessed with both natural and man-made resources. In both cases, citizens have a fundamental knowledge about the uniqueness of the place and they act, consciously or unconsciously, as place marketers.

The second important type of private-sector place marketer is *leading enterprises*. These enterprises recognize the advantage they will accrue by helping to improve the place's image. The enhanced image should create a valuable identity that can be used in the international arena. It could be the automotive or electronics industries of Japan, fine wines or environmental technology of Australia, or the high-technology products of Taiwan.

Banks, insurance companies, telecommunication companies, electricity utilities and real-estate agencies, in particular, recognize the importance of local identification for their future business growth. Even the most global of companies are considering their accountability to their places. The Hong Kong and Shanghai Banking Corporation (HSBC), although headquartered in England, participates actively in various place-market programs in Hong Kong. McDonald's is systematically making efforts to be integrated into the development of places. Nearly every global technology company has invested in local start-ups and joint ventures designed to develop local Asian economies. Their "good citizen" efforts have contributed to improving goodwill with their communities and consumers.

Asian real-estate developers and agents have played very critical roles. Real-estate developers in Shanghai, Hong Kong, Singapore, Kuala Lumpur, Bangalore and other Asian places are very active in economic development efforts and they will continue to play an important role in the future as place competition accelerates. Real-estate developers and agents not only sell and develop property but also participate in larger efforts to raise the profile of an entire city. Real-estate developers often have a good understanding of how potential place-buyers make their decisions based on the attractiveness of a given place.

Asian financial institutions (banks and insurance companies) also participate actively in local and regional economic development. Financial institutions are expected to serve the market for a long period of time. If these companies are to grow, the local market must grow as well. Therefore, an active presence becomes a natural aspect of business strategy for banks and insurance companies.

Telecommunication companies and electric and gas utilities provide another excellent example of active participation in development. With the deregulation of Asian markets, many of these infrastructure companies have been forced to compete with more subtle weapons than under previous monopoly conditions. Consequently, their interest and investment in place marketing is growing. A number of these companies, such as Singapore Telecom and the former Cable and Wireless Hong Kong Telecom, have set up special economic development departments or business location teams specifically to assist in place-marketing efforts.

Asian chambers of commerce and other local business organizations vary greatly in quality of skills and level of involvement. The Nepal Chamber of Commerce plays a big role in the economic development of that country by working with public and private sectors and promoting a positive national image.[71] The Philippine Chamber of Commerce & Industry plays a critical advisory role in the development of public policy in the Philippines. In Hong Kong, the Trade Development Council plays an instrumental role in promoting Hong Kong's role in Asia. These types of organizations offer considerable potential. Their influence depends on their vision and leadership. As a result of the Asian financial crisis during the late 1990s, there has been increased interest in the public sector to establish dialogue and partnership with local business organizations.

Hospitality and retail industries (hotels, restaurants, department stores, other retailers, exhibition and convention centers) are beginning to recognize that in many ways their success rests on the local image. A convention center may have excellent facilities, but if it is in an area with a bad image, it is seriously handicapped. There is increasing cooperation among convention centers and hospitality and retail enterprises in place marketing and destination development. Often, the personnel working in the hospitality and retail enterprises provide visitors with the first and last impressions of the place, and it is essential, therefore, that they have good communication skills and a friendly attitude.

Travel agencies fill a natural role in distributing information about a place. Their job is to make the place as attractive as possible without, of course, overstating and possibly disappointing. Many visitors are looking for something unusual, and travel agents must be increasingly prepared to respond with more specialized packages. One Thailand-based travel agency which specializes in tours to Thailand and Asia calls itself "Action Plus Holidays" (http://www.touristpackage.com). Another based in Singapore calls itself "Experience Tours Services" (http://web.singnet.com.sg/~ets0896/). New travel portals are appearing. ChinaZING markets itself as "a one-stop online travel exchange" for tourists planning a China trip.[72]

Labor market organizations have a potentially high impact on a place's attractiveness. There are individual cases where local and regional labor organizations have played a constructive role. Often, this follows a crisis which threatens to close a manufacturing plant or business. Only recently have local labor organizations begun to understand the wisdom of cooperating in building a pro-place alliance. Individual labor-leader circles have taken active roles in Singapore and Hong Kong. But, generally speaking, labor market organizations need to play a broader, more constructive role in place-marketing strategies.

Architects can also help create and promote a sense of place. Style and design reflect a place's prevailing attitudes. The skyscraping architecture of late 19th- and early 20th-century New York City communicated much of its attitude: powerful, ultramodern and dominant in industrial and financial aspirations. Hong Kong, with its internationally renowned skyline, communicates a similar attitude. Also, during the 20th century, architects in Europe created a number of trends that spread to many places. During the 20th century, several Asian architects have stood out not only in Asia but around the world. World-famous Chinese architect I.M. Pei, born in Canton, for example, has contributed significantly to architecture today, with modern creations that "illustrate his affinity for geometric shapes, silhouettes, and striking contrasts."[73] Among his most famous buildings are the Bank of China in Hong Kong; Fragrant Hill Hotel in Beijing; and the John F. Kennedy Library in Boston. Renowned Malaysian architect Ken Yeang, on the other hand, is known for his "Bio-climatic architecture", a concept he used in creating the Menara Mesiniaga, which is home to IBM in Selangor, Malaysia. His concept belongs to the 21st century as it takes into account the "ecological aftermath." More specifically, an ideal city for him would be "user-friendly, environmentally sustainable, community-sustainable, pedestrian-friendly, comfortable, and traffic-friendly."[74]

Standardized construction is being replaced by styles that emphasize *diversity* and *uniqueness*. Architects are filling a role as interpreters of the special character of a place. They are involved in city planning, introducing pedestrian malls, redesigning marketplaces, returning parks to their original glory, and so on. The common theme is that architecture and design should reflect the soul or heart of a place.

Transport companies (airline, taxi and railway) play an important role as place marketers. A nation's airlines are flying advertisements: Philippine Airlines (PAL), Japan Airlines (JAL), Singapore Airlines, Malaysian Airlines, Korean Air and Air India. More than 50% of the articles in in-flight magazines are special-interest pieces intended to sell a destination. The place-bound theme also emerges in airline souvenirs and meals that present items that are uniquely of the country or local, regional and national cuisine. In Figure 3.11, the young passenger is given a Vietnamese doll, reinforcing the airline's pride in maintaining traditional Vietnamese hospitality.

Flying with different airlines presents unavoidable comparisons of service orientations and personnel competence. For many travelers, the

Figure 3.11: Traditional Vietnamese Hospitality is Priceless

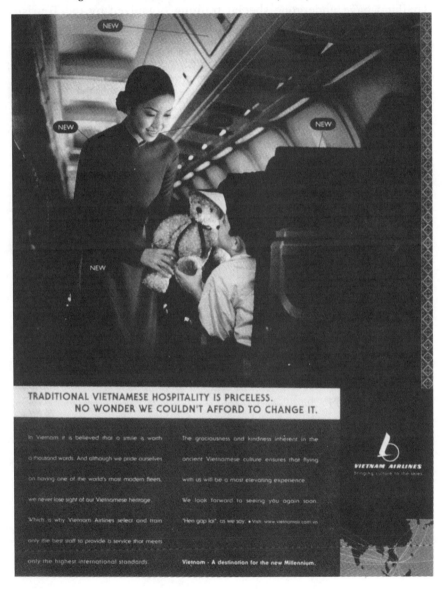

Source: Newsweek, June 19, 2000.

first encounter with a nation/place begins with the airline. The airport can also be used as an important gateway for place marketing.

Taxi trips, too, influence impressions of a place. The demeanor of taxi drivers often colors how visitors feel about a place. An aggressive place-marketing strategy should include training taxi drivers to be knowledgeable and good hosts. For example, almost 500 taxi drivers in Thailand have undergone special training organized by the Tourism Authority of Thailand as part of its plans to improve services for visitors. These drivers have been given the title "cultural ambassadors", and have had their role in promoting a positive image for the country fully explained to them.[75] Other cities in Asia could spend more time training cab drivers in courtesy, knowledge and safe driving.

Railways can also play an all-important role in place marketing. For example, India's luxury "Palace on Wheels" train, originally designed to transport the rulers of the princely states, was converted into a means to promote tourism in Rajasthan. Today, it prides itself on being rated "one of the ten best luxurious rail journeys in the world."[76]

Media (newspapers, radio, TV) have been developing a more local and regional focus since the 1990s. Local newspapers, radio and TV stations are bringing more local news, articles and analyses of local development. Media, of course, can help or hurt. If they focus on negative stories — crime, poor schools or pollution — they hurt a place's image. Therefore, place marketers must work closely with their local media to communicate their place-marketing strategy. In successful places, a regular dialogue takes place between the place marketers and the key journalists because they all have much to gain if the local area becomes more attractive.

CONCLUSION

In this chapter, we have identified four broad strategies to attract target markets: *image marketing; attraction marketing; infrastructure marketing;* and *people marketing.* Today Asian places are engaging more actively in these strategies. However, the approaches vary in professionalism and sophistication. Often, difficulties arise because decision-makers lack a useful structure for organizing place-marketing strategy and action. Another difficulty arises from a failure to understand how the target market — the potential buyers — really makes its choices. In the next chapter, we will focus on these problems.

1 http://www.i-philippines.ph/E-Services_Hub_of_Asia/e-services_hub_of_asia.html, viewed on June 4, 2001.
2 Deidre Sheehan, "Call of the Wired: The Philippines is plagued by economic and political woes. But a bright spot remains: hi-tech," *Far Eastern Economic Review*, June 28, 2001, p. 36.
3 Interview with Darcy Lalonde, September 12, 2000.
4 Julian Gearing, "Code Blues: Bureaucracy and poor infrastructure hamper Phuket's dreams of being a software paradise," *Asiaweek*, April 27, 2001, p. 32.
5 http://www.tbr.org/white.pdf, viewed on May 25, 2001.
6 http://www.wttc.org/ecres/pdfs/nea.pdf, viewed on May 25, 2001.
7 http://www.wttc.org/ecres/pdfs/sea.pdf, viewed on May 25, 2001.
8 "Asia Offers Opportunities for Growth," *Asiaweek*, August 4, 2000, (www.aseansec.org/tourism).
9 Michael Alan Hamlin, "Two Women & a Paradox", *Manila Bulletin*, July 5, 1999, p. C=2.
10 G. Pascal Zachary, "People Who Need People: With Skilled Workers in High Demand, Employers are Hunting Them Down No Matter Where They Live," *Asian Wall Street Journal*, October 2, 2000, p. S3.
11 Brook Larmer, "Home at Last: For a Group of Harvard MBAs, returning to China Means a Chance to Serve the Country — and Get Rich. The Tiananmen generation is back," *Newsweek*, July 31, 2000, p. 12.
12 Kathy Wilhelm and Dan Biers, "No Place Like Home," *Far Eastern Economic Review*, June 15, 2000, pp. 74–75.
13 Larmer, p. 12.
14 Leslie Pappas, "Promises, Promises: China's Talent Scouts Scramble to Win the Grads Back," *Newsweek*, July 31, 2000, p. 14.
15 Wilhelm and Biers, p. 74.
16 Brian Mertens and Angela Leary, "Asia's Boomerangs: Disillusioned with Corporate Life in the US, Asians are Returning Home to Find a New Economy that's Receptive to Their Ideas," *Asian Business*, July, 2000, p. 26.
17 Norman Crampton, *The Best Small Towns in America*, Englewood Cliffs, NJ: Prentice-Hall, 1993, p. 394.
18 http://www.chinainvestguide.org/index.htm, viewed on September 14, 2000.
19 Ang Wan May, "Revival by the River," *Business Times*, London, September 30, 1999, p. 32.
20 http://www.astbury.demon.co.uk/astprega.htm, viewed on September. 20, 2000.
21 http://dest.travelocity.com/DestGuides/0,1840,TRAVELOCITY|-5977|3|1|171756,00.html, viewed on November 10, 2000.
22 Tim Larimer, "Saigon Soars," *Time*, June 2, 1997.
23 http://www.arts.uwaterloo.ca/FINE/juhde/ghy-941.htm, viewed on October 2, 2000.
24 Supara Janchitfah, "Funding for the Future," *The Bangkok Post*, August 1, 1999, p. 6.
25 *Ibid.*
26 Internet: http://www.tdctrade.com/imn/imn168/feature1.htm, viewed on September 14, 2000.
27 Internet: http://www.city.toyota.aichi.jp/english/profile.html#3, viewed on October 2, 2000.
28 Daffyd Roderick, "Walkabout: Mass Impact — Tourism numbers for 2020 are scary to say the least," *Time Asia* (http://www.cnn.com/ASIANOW/time/asiabuzz/wa/2000/09/15/, viewed on October 9, 2000), September 15, 2000.

29 Asian Development Bank, *Emerging Asia: Changes and Challenges*, 1997.
30 Steven Schlossstein, *Asia's New Little Dragons The Dynamic Emergence of Indonesia, Thailand, and Malaysia*, Chicago: Contemporary Books, Inc., 1991.
31 http://www.asiasociety.org/publications/update_crisis_villegas.html, viewed on September 13, 2000.
32 http://www.forbes.com/forbes/97/0224/5904128a.htm, viewed on September 13, 2000.
33 http://www.cityguide.lsm.gov.mo/cg_english/macau.htm, viewed on October 9, 2000.
34 http://www.cnn.com/ASIANOW/time/magazine/99/1220/macau.-handover.html; Anthony, Spaeth, "Macau's Big Gamble," *Time*, 20 December, 1999, viewed on September 20, 2000.
35 http://www.jubileeaction.demon.co.uk/jubileeaction/reports/philipp.htm, viewed on September 13, 2000.
36 *Ibid.*
37 http://www.cnn.com/ASIANOW/asiaweek/96/1025/cs2.html, viewed on September 13, 2000.
38 http://www.preda.org/archives/r9102031.htm, viewed on September 13, 2000.
39 http://www.cnn.com/ASIANOW/asiaweek/96/1025/cs2.html, viewed on September 13, 2000.
40 http://www.balitravelguide.com/home.htm, viewed on September 13, 2000.
41 http://home.mira.net/~wreid/bali_p1a.html, viewed on September 11, 2000.
42 http://www.tsiindia.com/amritsar.html, viewed on October 10, 2000.
43 http://www.vietnamonline.com/travel/hanoi.htm, viewed on September 20, 2000.
44 "Asia's Best," *Asiaweek*, 18–25 August, 2000 p. 36–37.
45 *Ibid.* p. 89–90.
46 http://www.visitnepal.com/islandresort/introduction.htm, viewed on October 5, 2000.
47 http://www.puexco.com/eng/download.html, viewed on January 3, 2001.
48 http://www.destinationvietnam.com/dv/dv01/oldqtr.htm, viewed on September 28, 2000.
49 http://www.nrtee-trnee.ca/eng/programs/sustainable_cities/report_-complete.htm, viewed on October 2, 2000.
50 http://www.perkinscoie.com/Resource/intldocs/project_and_infra-structure_finan.htm, viewed on October 2, 2000.
51 http://www.bjreview.com.cn/bjreview/EN/China/China200211c.htm, viewed on August 16, 2001.
52 http://www.pref.aomori.jp/newline/sin-e08.html, viewed on October 9, 2000.
53 Michael Alan Hamlin, "Can Asia's New Economy Be Measured?" *The BridgeNews Forum*, July 20, 2000.
54 Cesar Bacani, "IT Crunch Time: Brace yourselves. Asia's IT crisis will not be solved by the death of dotcoms and the U.S. slowdown," *Asiaweek*, May 18, 2001, p. 25.
55 http://www.nationalgeographic.com/genghis/index.html, viewed on September 20, 2000
56 "Pride Restored," *Asiaweek*, August 4, 2000, p. 47.
57 http://th.gio.gov.tw/pi2000/pl003.htm, viewed on September 20, 2000.
58 http://www.antiwar.com/orig/chu2.html, viewed on September 20, 2000.
59 http://www.competitivecities.com/2000cities _speakers.htm, viewed on October 5, 2000.
60 "Mr No Says Yes to Tax," *The Asian Wall Street Journal*, February 24, 2000, p. 10.
61 "The Best Local Administrator," *Asiaweek,* August 18–25, 2000, p. 54.

62 http://www.doc.gov/asia-missions/ChinaDaley/china99_07.html, viewed on September 28, 2000.

63 http://www.census.gov.ph/data/sectordata/fl94-simplelit.html, viewed on November 10, 2000.

64 http://www.usaep.org/country/philipp.htm#1, viewed on October 2, 2000.

65 G. Pascal Zachary and Robert Frank, "High-Tech Hopes: Countries are pinning their economic dreams these days on a new truism: Innovation can — and does — happen anywhere," *The Asian Wall Street Journal*, October 2, 2000, p. S2.

66 Alistair Ingamells and Polly Chan Ching Sze, "The new e-realities of teaching: Business schools are making hasty changes to accommodate students hungry for e-commerce," *Asia-Inc.*, October, 2000, p. 16.

67 http://hotlineusa.com/osakafu/main.html, viewed on September, 21, 2000.

68 http://www.taiwanheadlines.gov.tw/20000317/2000031703.html, viewed on January 4, 2001.

69 http://www.tdctrade.com/beyond97/supermkt.htm, viewed on October 2, 2000.

70 http://www.travel-asia.com/07_21_00/stories/thais.htm, *TravelAsia*, 21 July, 2000, viewed on September 22, 2000.

71 http://www.nepalchamber.com/chamber/introduction/objective.html, viewed on September 21, 2000.

72 Edu H. Lopez, "Travel portal offers tourists customized travel to China," *Manila Bulletin* October 6, 2000, p. B-10.

73 http://www.ailf.org/heritage/chinese/essay02.htm, viewed on September 21, 2000.

74 http://www.jobpolitan.com/career_fair/architecture/ken_yeang.htm, viewed on September 20, 2000.

75 http://www.hotelthailand.com/ezine/issue1/zine1.html, *Thailand Travel E-Zine*, February 1999, viewed on September 21, 2000.

76 http://www.thepalaceonwheels.com/about.html, viewed on September 21, 2000.

C H A **4** T E R

How Place Buyers Make Their Choices

P lace buyers always have a number of high priorities influencing their choices. Their priorities and criteria are often complex and many factors influence their evaluation of a place. Furthermore, more than one person — each with his/her own personal criteria — often represents a place buyer. Some of these criteria are not expressed directly. To complicate matters further, the criteria undergo constant revision as business, industry, consumer and other circumstances change.

These unspoken criteria may be very private and yet of the highest priority. For example, a personal desire to guarantee continued good education for one's family might be critical in a place buyer's decision. Or local access to language training can be important. Such criteria can weigh more heavily in a place buyer's choice than more formal criteria. A skillful place seller appreciates, imagines, understands these matters and can essentially put him/herself in the mindset of a place buyer.

The absence of professional destination-marketing strategies in Asia has led naturally to an almost random handling of place buyers and, consequently, almost random results. Few places in Asia actually anticipate a place buyer's priorities and understand their decision processes. Instead, there is a rush to offer competitive incentives to reduce the costs of doing business for potential investors. This form of national discounting marginalizes the benefits of investment in many important respects.

This chapter addresses three questions:

1. What are the main factors influencing place-buyer decisions, and what are the steps in the decision-making process?
2. What additional factors influence investor, new resident or visitor decision-making?
3. How influential are published ratings of places in the place-buying process?

STEPS IN THE PLACE-BUYING PROCESS

Place buyers always go through a decision process irrespective of whether they are a company planning an investment, a family making a moving decision or visitors planning a vacation. Successful place sellers must anticipate the steps in that decision process, and develop a practical strategy to meet the needs and demands they represent. Firstly, we will examine the geographical dimension of the decision process and then the administrative dimension.

The Geographical Dimension

Consider a company going through a site-selection process. The potential steps in choosing a site are hypothetically illustrated in Figure 4.1.

Figure 4.1: Place buyers' steps in the Asian site-selection process

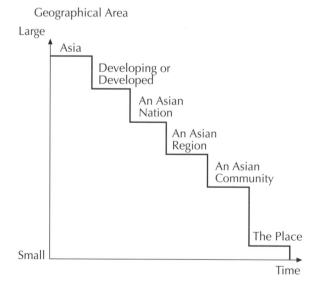

The **first step** addresses the question "Asia or not Asia?" Considering that 3.637 billion[1] inhabitants make Asia the biggest market in the world in terms of purchasing power, most place buyers cannot afford to stay outside Asia. Hundreds of places use "Asianized" messages in order to boost buyer interest.

In the **second step**, place buyers are seldom interested in claims such as "Best in Asia" and, instead, respond to a more functional argument that the place buyer will have access to the internal Asian market. Hong Kong, for example, continues to be known as "the major gateway to China and much of East Asia,"[2] despite Shanghai's determination to reclaim that status.

In the **third step**, in all of the Asian nations, place buyers are presented with a comprehensive basket of national offerings. Since all Asian countries today have established national agencies for inward investments and tourism promotion, this third step is crowded with offerings, some unique and many not. Place buyers will normally inform a number of Asian nations that a site-selection process has started, with the obvious intent to boost competition among the place sellers. The paradox, however, is that in an Asia struggling to move toward harmonization and free trade, place sellers are striving to provide more and more differentiated offerings.

The **fourth step**, which concentrates on Asian regions, is often the most competitive part of the selection process. Only 10 to 15 years ago, international competition was not as strong as it is today, regional platforms for business and tourism promotion were few and cooperation was uncommon. Today's Asia is witnessing a significant upheaval in regionally based activities to meet place buyers' expectations. Regions in China, India, South Korea, Japan, Malaysia and the Philippines, representing cooperative consortia of provinces and municipalities, have often found that working together enhances their attractiveness. Asia, in fact, has gone a step further and begun to form cooperative geographic regions representing more than one country. An example of this is the Indonesia-Malaysia-Singapore Growth Triangle or IMS-GT, established in 1996 between Riau Province and West Sumatra in Indonesia, the states of Johor, Melaka, Negeri Sembilan and Pahang in Malaysia, and Singapore. Also known as the "Southern Triangle," the group focuses "on transportation infrastructure (water, ports, new ferry services and roads), tourism, and industrial and agricultural projects."[3] Place buyers can quickly become spoiled by the service they receive at the regional level. In this fourth step, place buyers get concrete answers to their questions.

In the **fifth step**, where the complete basket of attraction factors is visible, the buyer encounters the potential of the 600,000 communities in

Asia. Here the place buyer meets the decision-makers. Precise hard and soft factors are evaluated. Many soft factors become highly relevant. Place buyers quickly discover if place sellers are living up to initial marketing messages and promises, and whether local representatives are acting in a professional manner. If the place buyer is from a foreign country, it helps if place sellers are able to communicate in the place buyer's language or the second most familiar language they speak. Basic intercultural differences should be known and understood in advance.

The **sixth** and last step is the place itself, where the buyer must choose from among the most attractive districts within a specific place. Because of the decentralized structure of places, new place sellers sometimes seem to emerge from nowhere. It is not unusual for contradictory and internally competing solutions to threaten the most carefully developed decisions. A climate of local confusion often surfaces at the 11th hour. Here it is necessary to keep the one-stop-shopping model intact. Steps five and six should therefore be coordinated to the fullest possible extent.

The knowledge that a place buyer has made a choice spreads fast among competing places. So does the place's reputation for being a good or bad partner. Places are wise to demonstrate after-care for their new arrivals to make sure that a good reputation is communicated to others. Exhibit 4.1 discusses the roles of information exchange.

Exhibit 4.1: EVERYONE'S A SELLER: EXCHANGING INFORMATION

For most places, information exchange is crucial to influencing a buyer. Once the company/locators have decided on places to consider for investment, the process of gathering information begins. It is crucial that everyone in a place be trained as a potential seller. That includes not only the obvious groups — water and traffic experts and human resource specialists — but also the university president and the taxi driver. The intelligent buyer will seek out all sources that provide clues to the breadth of services and quality of life.

What should a place do to prepare itself to become a good place seller?

1. A place needs accurate and thorough information. A place should routinely examine key areas such as schools, wages,

transport and labor resources for accuracy, and have up-to-date information responses immediately available. These requests can be anticipated and should be ready for sending on demand. Many places fail at this level and eliminate themselves from competition.

2. The place seller should convey the material in a clear, concise and audience-centered manner. In interviews, all place sellers should be well armed with information and be capable of answering questions. Training is essential and can range from a comprehensive videotaped simulation of an important interview to a one-day training session for all service employees.

3. Information needs to be returned quickly. Places need to see the search for information as a tight, competitive race. Information is usually sent via fax or email. If a place is decisive and responds efficiently, the investor will feel that future developments will also go smoothly.

Most of the above information follows good communication practice. An effective place seller will not only be thorough, clear and quick to respond, but will also set high standards and follow through on every detail.

▬▬▬▬
Source:

Interview with Bob Ady, managing partner of World Business Chicago, August 31, 1998.

The Administrative Dimension

When an organization finds itself with a place problem, need or opportunity, it must find a mechanism to retrieve information in order to make a decision. A company may feel that its present location is no longer favorable (a problem). A recruiter may attempt to interest a person in seeing the advantage of a move (a need). Or a visitor may be seeking a destination (an opportunity).

Although members of an organization may play a variety of place-buyer roles, the person who has the problem or need, or is exploring an opportunity, may not be the one who will make the ultimate decision. We can distinguish six place buyer roles:

Initiator: A person who has the responsibility to investigate the business climate of different markets and places may initiate the process. The impetus might be, for example, "Asia is the world's largest market, although it will take many years to reach its full potential. We cannot afford to be left behind and ought to consider entering the Asian market despite the obvious hurdles."

Influencer: Influencers could be colleagues of the initiator. They may provide support, reflection or ideas. It is important to be cognizant of who influences decision-makers. Making a major effort to identify and influence the influencers is a wise strategy in a large investment project.

Decision-maker: Here we meet the representatives who have the formal authority to make decisions. Lots of unnecessary work — and wishful thinking — can be avoided if the place seller tries to ascertain the real intentions of the decision-maker. To understand this one has to be sensitive to intercultural differences. For example, a refusal to say "no" may not mean an eventual "yes".

Approver: This is a person who can approve or reverse a decision. It can be, for example, a member or a number of members of a supervisory board. These people must be convinced that the decision is based on hard evidence in order to avoid backlashes later in the process. For example, a specific investment project backed by financial incentives from a place can experience problems later if, say, questionable incentive payments are discovered. It is important to get a sense of whether the individuals negotiating an arrangement have the confidence and support of the approver.

Buyer: The place buyer is the person who implements the final decision. This person or, in many cases, a team has an important role because he/she will share with others experiences from the implementation. If a buyer becomes dissatisfied with the implementation, a place can risk acquiring a negative image. Potential buyers will ask colleagues about the outcome. Negatively reported experiences are dangerous for a place's reputation.

User: The end-users of the place-buying process include employees, investors, visitors, delegates to conventions or exhibitions, experts and families moving to a new place. These users are undoubtedly the best marketing ambassadors for a place.

To illustrate, imagine that a Silicon Valley-based company specializing in Internet exchanges or marketplaces wants to enter the growing Asian market. The process began after an Asian conference on business-to-business (B2B) e-commerce in Singapore. One of the company's employees participated in a *BusinessWeek* forum for IT executives in Asia. She was so inspired by some of the seminars and promising forecasts that, on her way home, she wrote a memo to her colleagues (initiator). The market manager was interested and started to gather some general information on Asian market developments and the location of the most suitable places (influencer). The market manager prepared for the CEO a list of potential places: Seoul, Kuala Lumpur, Hong Kong, Singapore, Bangalore, Taipei, Shanghai, Miyazaki, Manila and Adelaide. The CEO and the marketing manager decide to conduct a fact-finding mission. They travel to three of the places: Hong Kong, Singapore and Manila (decision-maker). Returning to Silicon Valley, the CEO presents to the Board of Directors a plan for establishing the company's first Asian office in Singapore. The Board of Directors approves the plan (approver). To facilitate the implementation in Singapore, the CEO hires a well-known Singaporean, who is given complete responsibility to establish the Singapore office (buyer). After six months, the original initiator moves to Singapore, takes over as business manager and hires six additional employees (user).

In this place-buying process, different people played different buyer roles. In simpler cases, one or two people can play all six roles. For example, a person considering traveling to Asia for business purposes can complete the process after a 10-minute conversation with his/her travel agent. At the other extreme, a European telecommunications giant may spend three years and involve hundreds of people in different place-buying roles before deciding where to locate.

Place sellers need to understand the structure of the buyer's decision process. By understanding the different roles played by different people, destination marketers can implement a proactive strategy instead of responding reactively. In summary, a place seller must consider the following:

- Which people are involved in the place-buying decision and what are their roles?
- What exact factors, hard and soft, are used by the various decision-makers?
- What are the typical patterns of various target-market decisions in the place-buying process?

The answers to these basic questions help marketers choose effective messages, media and consultants to make the right decisions at the right time.

Information Search

Place buyers often look for different levels of information.

A minimum information search implies that the buyer already favors a place highly and needs confirmation. Basically, the buyer wants to make the best possible deal with the place, and the buyer may talk about alternative places in order to improve the negotiating position. The actual information search goes quickly and may not reveal the buyer's true intentions. The place seller's job is to find out what type of information search is actually taking place in each particular case.

A medium information search indicates a limited number of place options on the buyer's shopping list. An authentic situation of choice exists. The place buyer needs information to acquire an understanding of available opportunities and may already have a basic knowledge of the places being considered.

A maximum information search requires a total analysis of potential places. If the project is a large one, consultants are often invited to conduct the information search. With the increasing number of Asian places competing and, at the same time, frequently presenting similar offerings, there exists a need for maximum information searches.

Of key interest to the place seller are the major sources of information that the place buyer consults and the relative influence each has on the subsequent decision. Buyer information sources fall into four categories:

- Personal sources — family, friends, neighbors, acquaintances, work colleagues.
- Commercial sources — advertising, destination-marketing materials, place sellers, experts, travel agents, and the Internet.
- Public sources — mass media, place ratings, public reports.
- Experiential sources — visits to places.

The importance of these sources varies with the decision situation. Figure 4.2 describes the steps that a place buyer goes through in making a choice. In the first step (the total set), the place buyer recognizes that many eligible places may exist, including many of which he/she may not be aware. In the second step (the awareness set), he/she, having viewed public and commercial sources of information, becomes aware of certain potential information. In the third step, a further search narrows the field to a consideration set based on certain important criteria influenced by more personal and experiential sources of information. In the fourth step (the choice set), only the main competitors remain. Experiential sources now become crucial. The final choice set is often formed after intensive negotiations and is more or less guided by the exact fulfillment of the search criteria.

Figure 4.2: Successive sets involved in place-buyer decision-making

---

1. Total set

Most places that might be relevant for an IT company (could be hundreds)

⇓

2. Awareness set

Seoul, Kuala Lumpur, Hong Kong, Singapore, Bangalore, Taipei, Shanghai, Miyazaki, Manila and Adelaide

⇓

3. Consideration set

Singapore, Hong Kong, Shanghai

⇓

4. Choice set

Singapore, Hong Kong

⇓

5. Decision

Singapore

In the total set and the awareness set, various Asian place ratings may provide an initial picture of a place's business environment. *Lonely Planet* or *Business Traveler*, with their popular ratings of various Asian attractions, are two examples. Later in the choice process, the value of various place-rating guides decreases and more specific factors, hard and soft, become important.

The real value for the place seller comes from recognizing the stage of the place buyer. Knowing this, the place seller can undertake appropriate measures to meet the place buyer's needs. Once a decision is made, a place seller can learn quite a bit by following up with questions about why and how the choice was made. This feedback process is rarely exploited, even though it is essential that a place understands its market, its competitors and how potential place buyers make their choices. A place can then adapt its strategy to the current market environment. Exhibit 4.2 examines how the site selector gathers information.

Exhibit 4.2: HOW SITE SELECTORS CHOOSE

The decision to select a site has traditionally been surrounded by mystery and speculation and it is not unlike the selection of the Pope or the next site for the Summer Olympics. Andrew Levine, of Development Counselors International, polled 1,000 U.S. companies in an attempt to get into the site selector's head. The results are surprising and demonstrate that place sellers make investments that buyers consider low priority.

- The number one source of site-selector information was the corporate grapevine, followed by news stories and corporate travel.
- Direct mail, meetings with economic development agencies, and print advertising were seen as less valuable.
- Site selectors found that the most important support services were specific and not general. For example, help in getting permits, information about relocating, and accessing training programs were highly rated. Also important was the speed of response.
- Less important to site selectors was general site information, non-requested mailings, phone calls and lavish parties.
- The results are important. They imply that place sellers must listen carefully to what the client wants, be precise in answering requests, improve the various place sellers' and service providers' communication skills to meet the investor's needs, communicate clearly and effectively, and try not to confuse or dazzle the client.

While Levine only surveyed U.S. companies, these results have implications for investment practices in Asia.

Source:

Andrew T. Levine, "Getting Inside the Site Selector's Brain," *Commentary*, Fall, 1997, pp. 20–26.

Evaluation of Alternatives

The alternatives to the choice of a location are evaluated by combining subjective and objective factors. The role of subjective factors should not be underestimated, as shown by the examples in Exhibit 4.3.

Exhibit 4.3: SUBJECTIVE EVALUATION

Example 1

Buying a home has always been a big part of the Hong Kong dream for old and young alike. From an early age, children are taught that they should own property when they grow up. That's because real estate is seen as the only ultimately safe source of wealth. So with that lesson impressed upon Hong Kong's youth, the city's property market has always appreciated, and growth has sometimes been stratospheric. At least that was the climate until around the time of the 1997 handover, which coincided with the onset of the Asian financial crisis. Over the following year, property prices plummeted as much as 50%. A 420-square-foot apartment cost one Hong Kong resident US$192,000 in 1996, but by 1999 the value had decreased by 50%.

When it came to property prices, few people in Hong Kong spent much time worrying that prices might collapse. That misplaced confidence, together with a strong tradition of owning personal property in a climate of limited supply (owing to colonial-era government auction policies that controlled the amount of property offered for public sale), encouraged people to buy property no matter how high the price.

Example 2

When a place makes — or encourages — a massive investment in a poorly researched project that is driven by subjective factors, the effects are often costly. Take, for instance, BW Resources — primarily a leisure and gaming concern in the Philippines — whose principal shareholder, Dante Tan, was known to be a close associate of then president Joseph Estrada. The company's development plans looked like a sure thing in early 2000, especially with a $30-million investment from Macau casino tycoon Stanley Ho and the overt support of Estrada.

Projects on the drawing board included a new hotel complex, infrastructure development and low-cost housing for the poor — even transplanting Ho's famous floating Jumbo Palace Restaurant from Hong Kong to Manila Bay. According to Estrada, the advantage of bringing in foreign investors like Ho was the generation of new, badly needed jobs and increased economic activity. However, the former Philippine president underestimated the negative public reaction to the administration's support of gambling, and to the controversial Ho — often linked in published reports to mafia-like triad gangs. Conservative politicians, church leaders and academics were scathing in their criticism of the investment.

But the worst was yet to come. Alleged insider trading of the stock — focusing on key BW Resources officials including Tan and influential stock brokerages — caused the stock to plummet to less than 30% of its high, setting off investigations by government market regulators. After Estrada allegedly suggested to the commissioner of the Securities and Exchange Commission that he temper the investigation, public criticism increased to the point that both Estrada's and Ho's support of BW Resources proved to be more talk than walk. (Estrada was later accused during his impeachment trial of owning stock in BW Resources.)

Ho found himself locked in a bitter confrontation with the Catholic Church — vigorously opposed to gambling — as well as with anti-crime activists who publicly charged him with consorting with triads. As a result, Ho threatened to cancel his grand investment plans, saying he had become a victim of a vile smear campaign. Not long after, a fierce typhoon capsized the barge supporting his floating restaurant in Manila Bay, providing critics with a fitting metaphor for Ho's investment plans in the country.

But the implications were greatest for the Philippine economy. The stock market scandal resulted in a massive outflow of portfolio investments, establishing a trend that would make the market one of the worst-performing in Asia for the year. Newspaper reports and editorials suggested that new foreign investors were put off by the perception of cronyism and executive pressure on independent regulatory authorities, resulting in a near 40% drop in foreign direct investment.

———

Sources:

Todd Crowell, "Feeling the Squeeze in Hong Kong," *Asiaweek*, June 30, 2000, p. 59, http://www.asiaweek.com/asiaweek/magazine/2000/0630/

biz.property.html; Robin Ajello and Frederik Balfour, "Hong Kong: Home Sweet Home? Not These Days," *BusinessWeek*, July 10, 2000, p. 23, http://www.businessweek.com/2000/00_28/b3689201.htm; Jonathon Sprague and Antonio Lopez, "Many Losers, But Few Winners," *Asiaweek*, February 4, 2000, http://www.cnn.com/ASIANOW/asiaweek/magazine/2000/0204/nat.phil.ho.html; transcript of Itawag Mo Kay Erap, January 26, 2000, http://www.pia.ops.gov.ph/itawag/it2k0126.htm; *Tribune India* http://www.tribuneindia.com/20000705/biz.htm, photo caption in the July 5, 2000 issue of *Tribune India*; "Investments down 37%," *Philippine Daily Inquirer*, October 18, 2000, http://www.inquirer.net/issues/oct99/oct18/business/bus_4.htm.

In spite of subjective considerations, certain basic concepts can help us understand a place buyer's evaluation processes.

First, the buyer sees a given place as a collection of attraction factors. Such factors vary with the type of decision. For example:

- Vacation sites: unique attractions, recreation, climate, nature, travel costs.
- Places to live: job opportunities for family members, educational system, cost of living, quality of life.
- Production sites: relevant labor skills, labor relations, taxes, land costs, energy.
- Service sites: purchasing power on the local and regional market, relevant labor skills, IT standards and network of available competencies.
- Convention sites: service facilities, capacity, accessibility, service, costs.

Second, place buyers differ over which attractions they find salient and important. Some attractions are salient because the place buyer has been recently exposed to a highly relevant message, placing certain attraction factors at the top of the list. The buyer then decides which attraction factors are really important and attaches importance weights to the relevant factors.

Third, the place buyer is likely to develop a set of beliefs about where each place stands in regard to each attraction factor. The total set of beliefs that the place buyer holds about a particular place forms his/her image of the place. There may be a discrepancy between this image and the true standings of the place. A negative image of the Philippines — largely due to political scandal and controversy — does not necessarily reflect the true situation of investors or visitors in that country.

For example, in October 2000 a political controversy erupted. It centered on allegations that then president Joseph Estrada had taken kickbacks from operators of an illegal numbers game, which resulted in calls from influential sectors for his resignation. However, at the same time U.S. semiconductor firm Amkor Technology Inc. announced plans for additional investments amounting to $300 million, despite the political controversy. The company continued to view the Philippines as "a key strategic location." Factors such as manpower, educational facilities, infrastructure and the opportunity for expanding business opportunities in the global market contributed to Amkor's decision to increase its investment in the country.[4] While competition in the investment-attraction market is often a competition between perception and image, the Philippines example shows that perceptions among specific sectors may vary considerably from the general perception. For the technology sector, the perception of the Philippines is one of a source of intellectual talent.

Fourth, the place buyer is assumed to have a utility function for each attribute. The utility function describes how the place buyer expects value or satisfaction to vary with different levels of each attraction factor. Place sellers need to estimate the utility function of place buyers in order to adapt their offerings and arguments.

Fifth, the place buyer arrives at attitudes and judgments about choices of location through various evaluation procedures. Buyers may apply different evaluation procedures to make a choice between alternatives. For example, suppose that a Silicon Valley-based developer of electronic marketplaces for business-to-business e-commerce has narrowed its choice for an Asian development center to Manila, Bangalore and Hong Kong. Assume that the fast-growing company is primarily interested in four attributes: professional competencies, strategic location, productivity and costs. Table 4.1 shows how each city rates on the four attributes, as judged by this company.

Table 4.1: Place buyer's rating of three sites

	Attributes			
	Professional competence	Strategic location	Productivity	Costs
Manila	9	8	10	9
Bangalore	10	6	8	10
Hong Kong	7	10	7	5

Each attribute is rated from one to 10, with 10 representing the highest level for that attribute. Thus, Hong Kong is rated as having the best strategic location, Bangalore is the most professionally competent and has the best cost profile, and Manila has the most productivity.

The question is, which city is the Silicon Valley place buyer most likely to favor? If one city dominates the others on all criteria, we would predict that the planners would choose it. (Such a case is most uncommon). But the choice set consists of cities that vary in their appeal. If the planners rank costs above everything, Bangalore is the preferred choice. If the planners rate strategic location above everything, Hong Kong is the choice, and so on. For place buyers who care about only one attribute, we can easily predict their choices.

In the real evaluation process, place buyers consider several attributes and assign different weights. If the place sellers knew the respective weights that the Silicon Valley planners assigned to the four attributes, the place sellers could more reliably predict the preferred city.

Suppose the planners assigned 40% of the importance to competence, 30% to strategic location, 20% to productivity and 10% to costs. To find the planners' preference for each city, the values are multiplied by beliefs about each city. This leads to the following perceived overall values:

	Professional competence	Strategic location	Productivity	Costs	TOTAL
Manila	0.4 (9)	0.3 (8)	0.2 (10)	0.1 (9)	8.9
Bangalore	0.4 (10)	0.3 (6)	0.2 (8)	0.1 (10)	8.4
Hong Kong	0.4 (7)	0.3 (10)	0.2 (7)	0.1 (5)	7.7

We would predict that in this case the planners, given the weighting, would favor Manila. However, when differences are as small as between Manila and Bangalore, one should be careful about the outcome. An efficient place seller will add some other factors to the evaluation process, such as availability of IT workers, in this case.

This model, called the expectancy-value model of buyer choice, is one of several possible models describing how buyers in practice go about evaluating alternatives. Place sellers who understand this expectancy-value model have great opportunities to intervene. For example, Hong Kong's place marketers could improve Hong Kong's chances in six ways:

1. Improve the relevant attributes. Hong Kong could invest in improving professional competencies in the fields of software knowledge, such as in the Internet and electronic commerce. Hong Kong may already

have a fairly strong position in theoretical software knowledge. However, what Hong Kong needs is practical knowledge of Western-style commercial software development, something Manila has achieved in large part because of its distinctive colonial history. A plan to do this will result in real repositioning.

2. Alter beliefs about attributes. Because Hong Kong's actual competence in the area of software development is generally underestimated, it is important that its capabilities become better known. Attempting to alter beliefs about a place calls for psychological repositioning.

3. Alter beliefs about competitors' standings. Place sellers could try to change place buyers' beliefs about where competitive cities stand on each attribute. This makes sense when buyers mistakenly believe that a competitive place has more quality than it actually has. Such competitive de-positioning could be relevant where a "new" place like Hong Kong has emerged on the place market. Hong Kong should distribute well-targeted, comparative information to potential decision-makers.

4. Alter the importance weights. Place sellers could try to persuade place buyers to attach more importance to the attributes a place possesses. Hong Kong, for example, might emphasize the importance of low connectivity costs relative to the region for the Silicon Valley buyer. Investment in educational infrastructure — increasing the availability of IT workers and lowering costs — might also be addressed.

5. Call attention to neglected attributes. Hong Kong could draw the buyer's attention to neglected attributes. The huge investment in the Hong Kong Science Park and its rapid uptake are impressive. The place buyer could be invited to meet with board members of the Park and senior executives representing investors and locaters. The fact that almost all major IT multinationals have established operations in the Park is another attribute.

6. Shift the place buyer's ideals. Hong Kong can attempt to influence the Silicon Valley company's basic priorities, and could point out that its strategic location would permit better entry into the China marketplace of close to one billion people. By attempting to "reset" the place buyer's priorities, Hong Kong potentially creates a new set of criteria to be rated by the place buyer.

Purchase Decision

In the evaluation stage, the place buyer forms preferences among the places in the choice set and begins to lean towards a particular place. However, at least four factors can intervene between investment intention and the final decision.

One factor is the attitudes of others. Suppose that the CEO of the Silicon Valley-based company is warned by a colleague about Bangalore's relatively high energy costs and the erratic supply of electricity. Such attitudes can influence the ultimate purchase decision, as General Electric's former Chairman, Jack Welch, noted when opening an advanced US$53-million research facility in the city. Although GE had made an investment commitment, he warned that future investment would be negatively affected should the government fail to ensure a reliable, affordable supply of power.[5]

The second factor concerns the place buyer's perception of the credibility of the people involved in the purchase process. A place buyer's preference increases if he/she greatly respects the other person's opinion. As a result, it is very important for the place sellers to build credibility. One of the best ways to project credibility is to raise the public profile of local personalities by placing regular, well-written opinion pieces in major publications.

A third factor influencing a purchaser's intentions could be unanticipated situational factors that can emerge and alter the buyer's perception of costs and benefits. The Silicon Valley company's CEO, for example, may learn from news reports that Bangalore-based IT companies are having trouble finding enough IT workers and that the shortage is expected to grow as a result of the availability of more technical visas to the United States. That information could change his/ her assessment of Bangalore. This is especially the case when the evaluations of one or more cities are very close.

A fourth factor is that of perceived risk. New investment, especially if costly, involves risk. Place buyers cannot be certain about the investment outcome. This often produces anxiety and delay. The amount of perceived risk varies with the amount of money at stake, the amount of uncertainty about choice and the amount of the buyer's self-confidence. Different place buyers develop different routines for reducing risk, such as postponing a decision, gathering further information and establishing preferences for safe situations. Place sellers must understand the factors that create a feeling of risk and provide information and support to counter them. Being interested in Manila, our Silicon Valley company might feel uncertainty about political instability and the activity of rebel groups in the south. At the same time, place sellers in Manila are probably aware of this potential obstacle and must be prepared to lessen these concerns.

Place buyers throughout Asia face some degree of uncertainty. A new tax situation in Manila, labor market disputes in Bangalore, or overnight withdrawals of incentive packages in any country can occur suddenly. Consider the shake-up in investor confidence in Hong Kong following the Asian financial crisis. Frank Ching, senior editor of the *Far Eastern Economic Review*, said of the uncertainty: "Chief Executive Tung Chee-hwa and other senior officials of the Hong Kong SAR government, in particular Financial Secretary Donald Tsang, went to great lengths to reassure both the Hong Kong community and international investors of the basic soundness of Hong Kong's economic fundamentals. The financial crisis, however, together with a drop in real estate prices and projections of slower economic growth for the next year, have created a sense of unease among the people."[6] Most place buyers approach such turbulence with caution, and place sellers need to be realistic in countering the problems with real solutions and timely and clear arguments.

In general, there are five types of place buyers who are frequently encountered in Asia (see Exhibit 4.4).

Exhibit 4.4: FIVE TYPES OF PLACE-BUYERS' APPROACHES

Place buyers appear in many guises. The place marketer's challenge is to identify, as early as possible, which of five types of place buyers he/she is meeting.

The Shopper. A typical Shopper from outside Asia, eager to enter the Asian market, asks many general questions in an attempt to narrow options. The Shopper wants to have a general taste of Asia. In this case, the place marketer should help the buyer structure the decision alternatives and create trust in the place seller's judgment and helpfulness.

The Pawn. The Pawn is someone who represents the place buyer, whose identity might be open or hidden. The place seller should try to identify the real buyer and his/her true options and preferences.

The Quick-decider. The Quick-decider is eager to make a decision and seeks indicators that resolve the decision. The place seller should meet such an approach with firm, quantifiable benefits and by a willingness to close fast.

The Detailer. The Detailer needs to collect great detailed information prior to making a decision. Even if some of the Detailer's decisions could be questioned, the place seller must be prepared to deliver the specific data.

The Grinder. This place buyer focuses on costs and incentives. The Grinder, in the role of a visitor, wants to pay almost nothing and, at the same time, discover half of Asia. The Grinder, in the capacity of an investor, is sensitive towards precise economic bargaining results. The place seller should be prepared to quantify the economic benefits and avoid vagueness.

By distinguishing these different types of place buyers through systematic questioning, the place seller can increase his/her marketing effectiveness.

Post-purchase Behavior

After purchasing and operating in the chosen place, the place buyer will experience some level of satisfaction or dissatisfaction. The place seller's job, therefore, does not end when the purchase is made but continues into the post-purchase period. This phase can be called the after-care period. Indeed, in some Asian regions — Penang is a good example — such after-care has been used as one of the main attractions as well as one of the investment retention factors in the region. Hong Kong belatedly recognized the impact of after-care on reinvestment after years of neglect and the transfer of investors to more accommodating locales.

Post-investment Satisfaction

What determines whether the place buyer is highly satisfied, somewhat satisfied, or dissatisfied with a purchase? The place buyer's satisfaction is greatly influenced by how closely the place's perceived performance matches the buyer's prior expectations. Place buyers form their expectations on the basis of information received from the seller, colleagues, friends and other sources. If the seller exaggerated attraction factors, the buyer will experience *disconfirmed expectations*, leading to dissatisfaction. The larger the gap between expectations and performance, the greater the buyer's dissatisfaction. This suggests that the place seller must make claims that faithfully represent the place's likely performance levels so buyers are satisfied. A few place sellers might even understate performance so that buyers experience higher-than-expected satisfaction with the place.

The result of increased place competition is generally to overstate performance. Instead of giving in to this temptation, the place seller should stress what is unique about the place rather than exaggerate common factors. Furthermore, the seller should manage a strong after-care program. In too many cases, there is no marketing follow-through strategy behind advertised messages. This gap between messages and actual place performance should be avoided.

Post-investment Actions

The place buyer's level of satisfaction or dissatisfaction will influence his/her subsequent behavior. A satisfied place buyer is more likely to say good things about the place to others. Many places actively use their satisfied place buyers as ambassadors. We can see in Figure 4.3 that Greater Noida, located on the fringes of Delhi, by listing its major

Figure 4.3: Multinational place buyers already established in Greater Noida

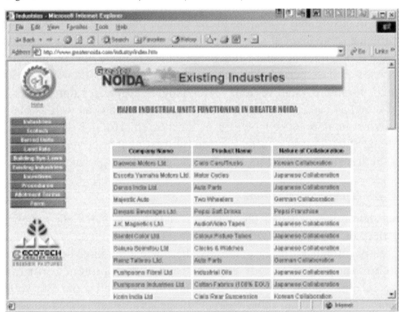

Source: http://www.greaternoida.com/industry/index.htm, viewed on October 5, 2000.

companies, products and collaborators on its website, suggests a high degree of interplay and cooperation to other potential investors.

Dissatisfied customers may resort to one of two courses of action. They may try to reduce dissonance by asking for some sort of compensation. Or they may do the opposite and seek information that might confirm the place's high value in spite of their experience. Between these two extremes, the place seller can act in several ways in order to minimize the amount of post-purchase dissatisfaction. In redressing customer grievances the main thing is to listen and to respond quickly. Responsive place sellers welcome feedback as a way to improve their performance continually. More and more Asian communities use various opinion polls and focused inquiries to gather feedback information to improve their performance.

Understanding the buyer's needs and buying processes is essential to building effective marketing strategies. By understanding how buyers go through the process of need recognition, information search, evaluation of alternatives, the purchase decision and post-purchase behavior, place marketers can continuously improve their effectiveness and attractiveness to top-line investors.

THE INFLUENCE OF PLACE-RATING INFORMATION

Place buyers typically search for comparative data on the attractiveness of different places. In the case of nations, the data usually includes Gross Domestic Product (GDP) per capita, adjusted to Purchasing Power Parity (PPP); inflation rate; interest rate; unemployment level; and so on. During the last decade, many new indicators have emerged, leaving almost no aspect of a nation, region or city untouched.

Place ratings, which have played an active role in the U.S., have now become a common tool in Asia as a result of the intensified competition between places. Consider the following examples of place ratings covering Asian places.

Magazines such as *Asiaweek*

The regional publication *Asiaweek* provides place buyers and place sellers with an Asian ranking covering Asian cities, as shown in Table 4.2. It points out where the most attractive cities are to be found. The indicators in this case are based on more than 20 criteria that include GDP growth, average monthly rental per square meter, university-educated people as a percentage of total population, annual urban inflation rate, and average income.

Table 4.2: Asia's best cities, 2000

2000 Rank	City	Country
1	Fukuoka	Japan
1	Tokyo	Japan
3	Singapore	Singapore
4	Osaka	Japan
4	Taipei	Taiwan
6	Hong Kong	China
7	Bandar Seri Begawan	Brunei
7	Kuala Lumpur	Malaysia
9	Georgetown	Malaysia
10	Pusan	Korea
10	Seoul	Korea
12	Kaohsiung	Taiwan
13	Chiangmai	Thailand
14	Macau	China
15	Shanghai	China
16	Beijing	China
17	Bangkok	Thailand
17	Davao City	Philippines
17	Hanoi	Vietnam
17	Ho Chi Minh	Vietnam
17	Kuching	Malaysia
22	Cebu City	Philippines
23	Guangzhou	China
24	Islamabad	Pakistan
25	Metro Manila	Philippines
26	Bandung	Indonesia
27	Bangalore	India
28	Jakarta	Indonesia
29	Colombo	Sri Lanka
29	Chongqing	China
29	Delhi	India
29	Phnom Penh	Cambodia
33	Bombay	India
34	Kathmandu	Nepal
35	Surabaya	Indonesia
36	Yangon	Myanmar
37	Chittagong	Bangladesh
37	Karachi	Pakistan
39	Dhaka	Bangladesh
40	Vientiane	Laos

Source: "The Asiaweek Quality of Life Index," Asiaweek, December 15, 2000, p. 47.

Immediately after these results are published the winners usually exploit their positions in their place-marketing promotions. For example, Fukuoka City in Japan was awarded the title "Best City in Asia" in 1997,1999 and 2000. Kyushu, where Fukuoka is located, uses this as a marketing strategy for potential investors in the region. The region's investment Web site reads: "*Asiaweek*, one of the world's top-ranking weeklies (published in Hong Kong), has again chosen Fukuoka as the best city in Asia in 1999 in its annual ranking event. You can now be assured that Fukuoka is the most livable city in Asia, enjoying a growing reputation as Japan's exciting cosmopolitan trendsetter. Visit Fukuoka and see for yourself."[7] The *Asiaweek* rating plays an important role in the city's efforts to project itself as an attractive investment destination.

Competition with Asia for foreign direct and other forms of investment is increasing competition among Asian countries for international recognition. Thus more emphasis is given to rankings and the conclusions demand more attention. A recent introduction to the *Asiaweek* survey on the best cities read, "In an increasingly complex world, cities need to be run more like corporations, with an emphasis on planning and competent management."[8]

The World Competitiveness Yearbook

The World Competitiveness Yearbook, produced by the Institute of Management Development (IMD) in Lausanne, Switzerland, has an impact that is difficult to overestimate. The yearbook analyzes 46 countries that are "all key nations on a world scale."

Each year, judgments of nation-attractiveness are announced. Some places welcome the judgments, while others try to forget or disparage the results (see Exhibit 4.5). Refer to Chapter 1, p. 20 for results.

Exhibit 4.5: ASIAN COUNTRIES COMPETING GLOBALLY

Thanks to globalization and liberalization — both resulting in increased competition for goods, services and investment — countries today are faced with the challenge of becoming technologically superior, more politically stable and more economically successful. Much of Asia, with its diverse mix of cultures and resources, is quickly developing in all three sectors to rival the developed Western world. According to *The World Competitiveness Yearbook 2000*, the economic performance of Asian countries and their recent global rankings in the aftermath of the Asian financial crisis are attributable to the "pace of their recoveries and the strength of their institutions."[1]

For the eighth year running, Singapore ranked highest among the Asian countries that were included in the year 2001 survey and number two globally as the second-most competitive economy, behind the United States. The Singaporean government takes this ranking seriously enough to include a special section on the Web site of the Singapore Economic Development Board, which archives and monitors Singapore's ranking in different global fields — investment, trading, aeronautics and telecommunications.

By contrast, Taiwan was ranked only 18th as a result of domestic political instability, increased tension with China and a consistent budget deficit. Some discount the importance of surveys on a country's competitiveness. For instance, Professor Tu Cheng-hua of the Graduate School of Sun-Yat-Sen Studies, National Taiwan University, said that while the government can consider the survey a reference to measure the pace of economic reform, it should not make international competitiveness — at least as determined by the survey — a priority. He based his conclusion principally on the work of business and marketing strategist Michael E. Porter. In his book *The Competitive Advantage of Nations*,[2] Porter argues that the concept of "national competitiveness" is insignificant, since every economy consists of different sectors, and every industrial sector needs a different environment featuring specific conditions that support enterprise growth in that sector.

Hong Kong moved from number 14 in the 2000 ranking to number six (where it also ranked in 1999) in the 2001 ranking. Unlike Professor Tu, Hong Kong's government officials and public-sector executives consider global competitiveness important. In fact, in 1998, officials from Hong Kong and the United States met to discuss the future competitiveness of Hong Kong in the global market. They came to the conclusion that, in spite of the handover, Hong Kong should be able to maintain its position as the "most entrepreneurial and open society in Asia."[3]

Sources:

1 Stephane Garelli, International Institute for Management Development Press Release, April 2000, viewed May 8, 2001 at http://www.imd.ch/wcy/pressrelease/pressrelease.cfm

2 Michael E. Porter, *The Competitive Advantager of Nations*, The Free Press (New York), 1990.

3 Group Discusses Hong Kong Report Card," Baker Institute Report — Internet Edition, Report 11, December 1998, viewed on May 8, 2001 at http://www.rice.edu/projects/baker/Pubs/reports/Pubs/bipp199812/bipp199812_10.html

Singapore Economic Development Board Website: http://www.sedb.com.sg/why/wh_wo.html;Tu Cheng-hua. Speech, "The Meaning of Competitiveness and the Past and Future of Chinese Taipei's Competitiveness," Competition Policy Information and Research Center — the *Fair Trade Commission Newsletter*, September 30, 1999 viewed on May 8, 2001 at http://www.apeccp.org.tw/doc/Taipei/Announce/news3-5.html; Doug Bereuter, "The Speaker's Task Force on the Hong Kong Transition, Fourth Report," July 23, 1998, viewed on May 8, 2001 at http://www.house.gov/international_relations/ap/hongkong4.htm; Mike Cinelli, "Hong Kong Leaders To Discuss Future Competitive Issues At Baker Institute Program," Rice University News Office Media Advisory, September 9, 1998, viewed on May 8, 2001 at http://riceinfo.rice.edu/projects/reno/Newsrel/1999/19980909_hongkong.html.

Singapore, Hong Kong and Australia were the top ranked countries in Asia on the World Competitiveness Scoreboard for 2001. Various place sellers in these countries promote these rankings. Positive IMD results tend to stimulate nations to further improve performance, in part as a result of negative attention that would be generated by a fall in ranking. Singapore's place sellers have a compellingly strong argument as to who is the overall winner in Asia. Among the winning Singapore attractiveness factors are growth in domestic savings, access to foreign capital markets, connections to the Internet, new information technology, technological cooperation, financial resources, strong institutional R&D, and basic research. It's worth noting that while the World Competitiveness Yearbook survey is probably the most popular indicator of national success and competitiveness, it's not the only one. For instance, The Heritage Foundation and *The Wall Street Journal* publish the Index of Economic Freedom each year.

Lonely Planet: A Readable Guide for Visitors

In sharp contrast to the hard statistical facts furnished by the *World Competitiveness Yearbook* and *AsiaWeek*, the anecdotal *Lonely Planet* emphasizes soft factors. *Lonely Planet Online*[9] presents a profile of each country in Asia — and around the world. The guide gives information on the destination of choice — the country's history, economy, attractions, events and other interesting facts. In addition, the guide includes a section that gives first-hand accounts of travelers' experiences and may help viewers decide whether the place is worth visiting. Other features include information on the best time to visit the country, as well as travel advisories issued by authorities. An introduction to Bangladesh reads:

> *"Reading the world's press you could be forgiven for thinking that Bangladesh is a disaster zone rather than a travel destination. But hiding behind these images of cyclones and floods is a strikingly lush and beautiful land with a rich history and a variety of attractions unusual for a country this size. For a start, you can visit archaeological sites dating back over 2000 years; check out the longest beach and the largest littoral mangrove forest in the world; and see decaying 'Gone With The Wind' mansions of 19th-century maharajas.*
>
> *"Despite being the world's most crowded country, rural Bangladesh feels relaxed, spacious and friendly: travelers from India have been agreeably surprised to find border officials offering them cups of tea rather than reams of forms to fill in. Facilities are limited but if you have an independent streak it's definitely worth avoiding the crowds heading to India and Nepal and following the old slogan of Bangladesh's tourist body: 'Come to Bangladesh before the tourists'."*[10]

Bangladeshi place sellers can exploit these soft and positive evaluations in their marketing strategies as they suggest a place of surprising beauty and customs.

As other regions and countries such as East Timor and Myanmar do not receive such an introduction, the implication is that *Lonely Planet* has not found anything of interest there. An obvious marketing goal for an excluded region, therefore, is to put more effort into a value-added process, to emerge with more attractions and receive better attention in subsequent editions of *Lonely Planet*.

Asian Profiles

Another source of information is the Asia Profiles section of the *Asia Source* Web site, which presents each Asian country in an identical format, providing information on geography, demographics, economies, communications, transportation, and the military. Another feature of the Web site is that it allows viewers to compare up to five different countries at once by placing all this information side by side.[11] This helps place buyers compare places and regions in a practical way. The *CIA World FactBook*, the World Bank, the International Monetary Fund, and the Asian Development Bank are other principal sources of data.

Asian Development Outlook

The Asian Development Bank's *Asian Development Outlook*, published annually, is another valuable source of information. Using data produced by the ADB, the World Bank, the International Monetary Fund and the United Nations, it provides information and forecasts in the form of text, charts, tables and statistics on developmental issues in individual countries and regions.

Other Ratings

Various consulting companies and publications in Asia produce ratings covering different aspects of business and markets. For example, *Asiaweek*'s Salary Survey 2000 shows respective earnings ranked according to country and position.[12] Human resource consultancy William M. Mercer provides useful information for multinational companies, specifically in their hiring of expatriate workers. Among the surveys that they have conducted are the Cost of Living Survey, which ranks 146 cities, and the Quality of Living Survey, which ranks 214 cities worldwide.[13] Other reliable sources of information are the results of research conducted by Korn/Ferry International[14] and Goldman Sachs.[15] Table 4.3 illustrates the destination-market share in the semiconductor sector of various Asian nations.

Table 4.3: Top five locations in Asia for semiconductors in 1994 and 2000

Others include Thailand, Indonesia and Philippines.

Source: http://www.atip.org/public/images/FIG3-96-036.GIF, viewed on October 6, 2000.

How are Place Ratings Compiled?

To understand how ratings may be compiled, we illustrate the IMD method of determining the most competitive nations. IMD defines eight different factors broken down into 244 criteria, which aggregate 40,000 data points over a five-year period. Less tangible aspects are measured via a worldwide survey of more than 2,500 leaders. The eight factors, which make up the competitive environment, are presented in Table 4.4.

Table 4.4: Factors of competitiveness (IMD methodology)

1. Domestic economy: macro-economic evaluation of the domestic economy, including GDP, investments, savings, consumption, production, cost of living, and forecast indicators (30 criteria).
2. Internationalization: extent to which the country participates in international trade and investment flows. Balance of trade, exports, imports, exchange rates, foreign investments, protectionism and openness (45 criteria).
3. Government: extent to which government policies are conducive to competitiveness. National debt, expenditures, fiscal policies, state involvement and efficiency, justice and security (46 criteria).
4. Finance: performance of capital markets and quality of financial services. Cost and availability of capital, stock market dynamism and banking sector efficiency (27 criteria).
5. Infrastructure: extent to which resources and systems are adequate to serve the basic needs of business. Basic and technological infrastructure, energy self-sufficiency and environmental constraints (37 criteria).
6. Management: extent to which enterprises are managed in an innovative, profitable and responsible manner. Productivity, labor costs, corporate performance and management efficiency (37 criteria).
7. Science and technology: scientific and technological capacity. R&D resources, technology management, scientific environment and intellectual property (25 criteria).
8. People: availability and qualifications of human resources. Population and labor-force characteristics, unemployment, education, quality of life, attitudes and values (43 criteria).

Source: *The World Competitive Yearbook 2000*, IMD, Lausanne, Switzerland, p. 40.

Most of these criteria can be measured by hard data supplied by various statistical sources. Other criteria of high relevance that are more qualitative are gathered by an annual survey sent to executives in top and middle management positions in all the countries covered by the Yearbook. The panel of experts includes 3,263 executives. Each respondent rates only the country he/she is working in to ensure that they possess a deep knowledge of the business environment of a specific place. The overall results are published in the annual yearbooks, which are sold and quoted extensively in the countries covered.[16]

How Reliable are Place Ratings?

Place ratings are seen to have at least four questionable characteristics. Firstly, different ratings services often produce inconsistent rankings for the same community, region or nation. Confusion may occur when a city receives the highest rating in one survey and then, a month later, another rating using similar criteria reveals that the same city has fallen into third position.

The second problem is that the same rating service can change the place's position in line with new definitions and methods of collecting data. This can generate frustration and, if methods undergo significant change, undermine general trust in the rating.

The third problem is the difficulty of rating over 600,000 communities and hundreds of officially recognized regions in Asia. There is so much data available that place buyers have difficulty extracting meaningful information. Two Asianstat source books, *Statistical Yearbook for Asia* and the *Pacific* and *Statistical Indicators for Asia and the Pacific* (monthly)[17] typify the abundance in statistics and comparisons. Aside from these reports, consulting firms, think tanks, investment analysts and multilateral lending agencies are all sources of large volumes of data.

A fourth problem is that, since most surveys are conducted in English, results may be skewed toward expatriate and highly educated local sectors of the Asian management community. For example, surveys by news and business magazines of top universities and business schools are seldom weighted to reflect significant contrasts in circulation around the region. For example, Singapore, Malaysia and the Philippines have much more influence on such surveys because of their English-language speaking populations than, say, Indonesia. That Indonesia has a population about twice as large as all three countries combined indicates that its perspectives are not well represented in the surveys.

How Useful are Place Ratings to Investors and Place Sellers?

In a world with so many new and competing "hot spots", ratings offer a quick and convenient picture. They require little effort to understand. Place sellers can easily exploit the results, especially in relation to media looking for quick and convenient headlines. A place marketer can use positive ratings in advertising activities as well. On the other hand, negative ratings are a stimulus to improve.

For a place buyer, ratings should basically be seen as a scanning tool supplying initial data. It would be foolish to rely on these alone. The place buyer needs additional facts and needs to put personal values on these attributes.

CONCLUSION

This chapter has described the steps in the place buyer's evaluation process. With more than 600,000 Asian communities and hundreds of regions, place buyers have much to consider. Many new and unknown places are emerging in the market and creating new opportunities for place buyers. As a consequence, the place-evaluation process is becoming increasingly complex. In order to discover the most attractive locations, place buyers are forced to be more systematic in their searches.

The model helps place marketers organize their understanding of what many place buyers go through in making a place decision. While being useful, the model may not account for how all place decisions are made and some place buyers may even shortcut the decision-making process for a variety of reasons. Still, anticipating buyer decision-making processes can aid in anticipating what place buyers think and do when making their place choices. The next chapter focuses on developing a strategic plan to market a place.

---

1 http://www.prb.org/pubs/wpds99/wpds99_asia.htm, viewed on October 5, 2000. *The World Development Report: Knowledge for Development* puts the total at 3.275 billion, as shown in Chapter One (1998/1999), pp. 190 and 191.

2 http://www.lonelyplanet.com/dest/nea/hong.htm, viewed on October 5, 2000.

3 http://www.usaep.org/policy/reportch4.htm, viewed on October 23, 2000. Development objectives have not been met as quickly as originally anticipated for a number of reasons. These reasons include the onset of the Asian financial crisis, but also the stresses of diverse national bureaucracies attempting to work together for the collective good.

4 "U.S. Semicon Firm to Invest P13.5 B, Employ 3,000 — Roxas," Department of Trade and Industry News Release, October 15, 2000.

5 Sadanand Dhume, "GE's India Dream," *Far Eastern Economic Review*, September 28, 2000, p. 13.

6 http://www.csis.org/html/hk4.html, viewed on October 6, 2000.

7 http://www.kyushu.miti.go.jp/invest/journalist/jou_asia2.htm, viewed on October 17, 2000.

8 http://www.cnn.com/ASIANOW/asiaweek/features/asiacities/ac1999/data/list.html, viewed on October 24, 2000.

9 http://www.lonelyplanet.com, viewed on September 8, 2000.

10 http://www.lonelyplanet.com/dest/ind/ban.htm, viewed on October 17, 2000.

11 http://www.asiasource.org/, viewed on September 8, 2000.
12 http://europe.cnn.com/ASIANOW/asiaweek/magazine/2000/0317/cs.3glossary.html, viewed on September 8, 2000.
13 http://www.wmmercer.com/uk/english/resource/resource_news_topic80.html, viewed on September 27, 2000.
14 http://www.kornferry.com/, viewed on October 17, 2000.
15 http://www.gs.com/, viewed on October 17, 2000.
16 *World Competitiveness Yearbook 2000*, http://www.imd.ch/wcy/methodology.cfm, viewed on May 7, 2001.
17 http://www.unescap.org/stat/statdata/statpub.htm, viewed on September 27, 2000.

C H A **5** T E R

The Auditing and Strategic Planning Process

Asian media are reporting the plight of many cities, communities, regions and nations. A sample of headlines is illustrative:

- "Is Japan Doomed? Reform and restructuring are just the first painful steps to recovery for Japan..."[1]
- "Hong Kong: Home Sweet Home? Not These Days: Property prices in Hong Kong have dropped and could affect the economy."[2]
- "Bracing for the Fallout: As Manila's Crisis deepens, a nightmare scenario looms: a new Asian Crisis."[3]

Why are these places in such a plight? Are they victims of powerful global and Asian forces that no amount of planning could have averted? Or have these places failed to plan for a better future?

The fact is that most troubled places are both victims and contributors to their own downfall. Significant changes are occurring in the location and investment patterns of the world's major industries. When Japan's property bubble burst, the financial sector came close to outright collapse, and mid-market enterprises found themselves exposed to pressures that threatened their profitable but inefficient distribution and retail channels. Large corporations faced the difficult prospect of increasing efficiency and productivity despite strict labor laws that made layoffs virtually impossible. No sector was left untouched. Yet failure by the government to address the country's structural and enterprise infirmities prolonged Japan's suffering for over a decade.

As Japan demonstrated, places share much of the blame when markets and opportunities sour. Many fail to anticipate changes, and many simply resist change (see Exhibit 5.1). They drift until shaken by some great crisis that causes a loss of companies, residents and visitors. Faced with an upheaval, concerned public officials and some business leaders hastily form commissions charged with saving their place. When the early warnings in areas such as the electronic-chip or automobile industries occur in many Asian places, it is puzzling to observe that so little is done to make a place more attractive to these companies.

Exhibit 5.1: MOVE OVER, OBUCHI

By early 2000, there was little doubt that fundamental change was taking place in Japan's big-business sector. Just as clear was that Japan's government was monumentally irrelevant to what was happening — at least in any positive sense.

There was reason for improved optimism within a broad spectrum of the economy, including consumers, small- and medium-sized industry, large corporations, and an emerging, dynamic class of entrepreneurs, many of whom had been laid off as a result of restructuring. However, not all the news was positive. Bankruptcies were at an all-time high, and unemployment was approaching three million.

Japan's hot-and-cold social and economic indicators demonstrated three things about its economy. First, traditional enterprises that faced up to restructuring were beginning to feel the benefits. Indeed, companies that restructured and focused on core businesses were leading their industries. Shin-Etsu Chemical Company, for instance, had been shedding unprofitable operations and breaking profit records for four years. Fuji Photo Film Company cut overhead and was sitting on a cash hoard of ¥380 billion (US$3.6 billion).

Non-traditional sectors were the primary engines of growth. The Japan Research Institute estimated that large manufacturers and banks were investing ¥12 trillion a year on IT systems to boost efficiency and productivity. As a result of the Internet boom, personal-computer manufacturers were complaining that they couldn't meet demand for cheaper, Internet-ready computers. In addition, technology and Internet stocks drove a 37% market surge the previous year.

Second, Japan's recession and restructuring produced a new breed of entrepreneurs. The growth of Japan's Jasdaq — the over-the-counter market — was largely attributable to new entrepreneurs, who were doing everything from rewriting the rules of competition in the entertainment industry to providing outplacement services for cost-conscious enterprises. Softbank's Masayoshi Son launched Nasdaq Japan, with the intent to further enhance high-tech entrepreneurship.

Third, government was not just a bystander in Japan's nascent recovery. Preoccupied with creating unnecessary projects, which had turned in vastly disappointing results, it had actually hindered recovery by impeding the pace of reform and restructuring. This practice helped produce a thunderously ominous debt — equivalent to 114% of gross domestic product — representing a deadly threat to recovery.

Still, the government refused to confront politically difficult decisions. It insisted on ploughing even more public money into failing organizations, announcing a ¥25 trillion infusion over three years into murky credit associations and struggling banks and credit unions to facilitate what it termed the "smooth realignment" of the financial sector. Despite record bankruptcies among small- and medium-sized firms that received controversial government-guaranteed loans, the public-money safety net was being expanded.

The government was lethargic in helping large firms restructure. It refused to revise notoriously outdated labor laws that made it almost impossible to reduce staff, especially for the larger firms. As a result, most of the restructuring that took place was in the small-company sector. In fact, small firms employed almost 50% of employees laid off in the previous three years owing to bankruptcy or restructuring. Firms with 500 employees or more employed only 14%.

Large companies intent on rapid restructuring were forced to pursue inefficient and unfair strategies to streamline their businesses. Such strategies included reassigning unwanted employees to small subsidiaries and then liquidating the subsidiaries under a "special" scheme that places a share of the liquidation burden on creditors. Such liquidations were up 120% in 1999. When that didn't work, farmed-out employees were often told that they had no chance of promotion and little or no work. To add insult to injury, they were deprived of standard corporate perks, even e-mail addresses, increasing the sense of isolation. The intent was to publicly humiliate the employee into retiring. It was ironic that the late Prime Minister Keizo Obuchi's kinder, gentler approach to restructuring translated into incredibly shabby treatment.

To complicate the situation, the government clung to unrealistic notions of what economic recovery entailed. On January 1, Obuchi said of the government's new budget: "One can't kill two birds with one stone. To achieve economic recovery and fiscal reform at the same time is difficult. It is only after the Japanese economy regains stable growth that we can make plans to improve fiscal conditions."

Without fiscal reform, there would be no sustained recovery, despite corporate efforts to restructure and the growth of non-traditional sectors. The lesson here is that the government continued to impede a recovery by placing barriers in the way of companies. The end result is that the two major forces of recovery — business and government — operate at cross-purposes.

Source:

Adapted from Michael Alan Hamlin, "Get Out of the Way, Obuchi," *Far Eastern Economic Review*, January 20, 2000, p. 41.

Too often, officials at this level do not do their job. There may be at least five reasons behind this problem:

1. The re-evaluation of incentives happens too infrequently. Officials are resistant to change owing to political considerations. In Japan's case, SMEs represented an important constituency for the ruling Liberal Democratic Party. Government was therefore loath to consider dramatic changes necessary to foster restructuring and reform. Instead, it continued to provide rescue packages that were increasingly ineffective.

2. There might be a lack of expertise in preparing and comprehending forecasts. The impact of globalization, which no one completely understands, compounds this difficulty.
3. Often, no constructive dialogue takes place between leading enterprises and public officials. In other cases, central bureaucracies are uninspired and resistant to change. As a result, no early warnings are communicated and discussed.
4. Weak leadership can undermine even the best attempts at forecasting and problem solving.
5. Plans are carefully constructed and there are high hopes of completion. But no one is able to implement the necessary actions and the plans collect dust.

These problems are compounded at the local community level, in large part because local government institutions lack the resources and the competencies to plan and lead development. However, places often have access to some apparatus — an economic commission, a development agency, a community business unit, a chamber of commerce — that is supposed to take responsibility for forecasting and planning for the future. Here we will address two questions that define such issues:

■ What planning approaches are places using today to guide their development?
■ How can strategic market planning help places improve planning outcomes?

FOUR APPROACHES TO PLACE DEVELOPMENT

There are four basic approaches to place development, namely:

■ community-service development
■ urban redesign and planning
■ economic development
■ strategic market planning.

While each approach follows a different philosophy for creating and maintaining viable communities, combinations of the different approaches are most common. We describe each approach below.

Community-service Development

The basic idea behind community-service development is to create a quality environment for two target markets: (a) citizens currently living and working in the community; and (b) potential citizens (external place buyers).

Community-service development supports good schools, adequate health facilities, day-care services, accessible bureaucracy, and so on, which all contribute to the quality of life in the community. At the same time, the cost of services is important to citizens and place buyers. A balance must be struck between adequate and attractive community services and the costs/fees associated with supplying them. Communities should search for innovative methods to provide good public services at a reasonable cost. Asia is full of community experiments in this area. For example, there is a clear trend in the increased use of information technology and inter-community service cooperation to cut costs and increase communication feedback. Singapore and Hong Kong, for example, have developed a new dimension to community services by using IT on a broad scale. Even in poor, developing, rural communities throughout Asia, Internet kiosks sponsored by local government and international funding agencies are being used for putting farmers in direct contact with wholesale and retail customers.

In some cases, again in part due to resource and capability constraints on local governments, the private sector leads these initiatives. For example, Internet cafés spring up around university and college towns. The result is that local places are not only in closer contact with the outside world, but in constant contact. The exchange of ideas and information over the Internet often stimulates local development.

Urban Redesign and Planning

Urban redesign and planning focuses on enhancing the design qualities of a place — its architecture, open spaces, land use, street layout, pedestrian areas, cleanliness and environmental quality. Larger Asian cities have, during the last two decades, invested huge resources in local redesign with both large and small projects. In Shanghai, for example, large investments — nearly US$400 million since 1996 — are being made to clean up the Huangpu River.[4] Similar, although smaller, investments — such as the development of Vietnam's waterways — are apparent throughout Asia. Some of the tallest buildings under construction today can be found in Asia. These include the Asia Plaza in Kaohsiung, Taiwan; the Fairwell International Center in Xiamen, China; and the Emirates Towers in Dubai, United Arab Emirates (UAE). Of course, the Petronas twin towers in Malaysia are among the world's tallest buildings. Almost all of the large Asian cities today are carrying on redesign programs to add value to their attractiveness as a destination.

   Smaller cities and communities have also been turning to urban redesign projects, often using a "back to our roots" theme. The Lahore Walled City in Pakistan exploits its cultural heritage in its historical structures and settings.[5] The historical city of Intramuros in Manila has also recently improved the facades of some of its landmarks, including Fort Santiago and Club Intramuros, a restaurant and golf club famous in earlier decades.[6] Macau provides another example of this kind of effort.[7]

   These projects often create a new sense of pride in local traditions. The successful urban designer should have the capacity to express the historical tradition and heritage of a place within a modern context. The presumption is that urban redesign is part of a well-thought-out and long-term strategic marketing plan that communicates the success of a place.

   Urban designers in recent years have begun incorporating greater ecological/environmental considerations in their planning. They are assessing the ecological consequences of greater population density, high-rise living, traffic and parking congestion, air pollution, city spaces, and so forth. Quality of life is linked to ecological concerns and has become a common driving force behind much redesign and planning. During the 1990s, most communities in Asia worked out some basic ecological plans, and those initiatives are picking up speed in the new century. These efforts are often used in marketing strategies. (See Exhibit 5.2).

Exhibit 5.2: HOI AN TURNS OFF THE LIGHTS AND PROSPERS

Hoi An is a classic case of turning conservation and preservation into a thriving tourist business. The Vietnamese town of 60,000 is a port that prospered as a multicultural trade center more than three centuries ago. During most of the 20th century, it was a forgotten place, with a hidden past and no future.

Today, tourist business has leaped from 16,000 in 1993 to 165,000 in 1999 and is still climbing. The town is now described as "glorious" and a "jewel."[1] How did it accomplish the turnaround? What lessons can be learned from such a dramatic change in fortune?

First, Hoi An was spared the destruction of the war years. Significantly, the town was blessed with a twelve-block district of historical buildings that formed the center of the old quarter.

Second, the town benefited from great vision and leadership. A Polish archaeologist, who urged local leaders to take action to restore the old quarter, initiated the project. By the mid 80s, Hoi An was recognized as a historically significant site by the government. Third, the Communist government, under the supervision of Nguyen Su, took firm steps to complete the transformation through such directives as extinguishing all the electric streetlights during special lunar months and dramatically lighting the ancient quarter with paper lanterns. All building codes are strictly enforced by teams of instructors who are charged with maintaining the age-old quarters in every detail. The result is a step back in time, which has brought many honors including designation as a world heritage site.

Hoi An serves as a model for places that have under-appreciated assets. Many towns and cities have historical towns and districts that can be created to be conservation-based tourist attractions or to encourage new business uses. What is missing for most communities is a commitment to leadership, government and private cooperation, and implementation. Hoi An is not simply a collection of old buildings in various colors and conditions. At some sacrifice to all the participants, it successfully marketed its past. In some ways it resembles the Disney discipline of creating the perfect environment. However, in this case, the product is the real thing.

Sources:

1 Geoffrey Hiller, "Vietnam Journal," www.hillerphoto.com/vietnam/ vj12.html, viewed on May 1, 2001.

Craig Tomas, "Preserved by Decree," December 15, 2000, www.asiaweek.com/asiaweek/f...s/asiacities2000/cities.hoian.html, viewed on May 1, 2000. Jacquelin Sanderling, "Visit to Hoi An," www.destinationvietnam.com/dv/dv14/dv14b.htm, viewed on May 1, 2001.

Economic Development

Poor growth performance in many Asian places has pushed communities to improve their economic-development services. Economic-development professionals, with the assistance of multilateral lending agencies such as the World Bank and the Asian Development Bank, focus largely on helping a place enhance its competitiveness. They analyze a place's strengths and weaknesses, opportunities and threats, and then propose various projects.

Many cities, communities and regions have established economic-development units or agencies. These are normally separate from urban community-planning units, which focus on infrastructure. There are at least three different ways of organizing economic-development activities.

First, there is the in-house model, which is completely under public control. The leading politicians and public officials are the decision-makers, while the unit's head and staff carry out the actual day-to-day work. The problem in this case is that the unit will have to listen to people from different parts of the community "who speak different languages" and have different agendas. The unit has to decide whose opinions should receive the most weight. Given its interest in potential votes, the unit may not always pursue the most rational course of action.

Second, there may be a mixed model where responsibility is shared between the public and private sectors (often the leading local companies). The advantage here is that the business community shares responsibility and may also share in the financial burden. The disadvantage is that the division of sharing work and responsibilities between the parties can be unclear.

Third, some communities and regions have chosen an outsourcing model that can be in the form of a company whose shares are bought by various local players. Commonly, there is 50% community ownership, with the rest owned by leading companies or local institutions. Another outsourcing model involves buying all place marketing and services from a specific consulting company.

Of these three models, the second and third are most common in Asia, reflecting the dramatic contrasts between authoritarian and democratic Asia. Frequently, the co-owned community company (the second model) outsources a marketing activity to existing consultants as in the third model.

Strategic Marketing

More and more communities have adopted a strategic market-planning approach in contrast to carrying out ad hoc planning. Strategic market planning, in the context of places, has passed through three generations (see Table 5.1).

The first generation consisted largely of chasing after heavy industry, a practice which has a long history and is still far from over. Generous incentive packages, concentrating on manufacturing industries, and low

Table 5.1: Three generations of strategic marketing planning

Generation	Objectives	Methodology	Underlying marketing rationale
First generation Smokestack chasing	• Manufacturing jobs	• Luring facilities from other locations	• Low operating costs • Government subsidies
Second-generation Targeting marketing	• Manufacturing and service jobs in target industries now enjoying profitable growth • Improving physical infrastructure	• Retention and expansion of existing firms • Improving vocational training • Public/private partnerships	• Competitive operating costs • Suitability of community for target industries • Good quality of life (emphasis on recreation and climate)
Third generation Product development	• Preparing the community for the jobs of the 1990s and beyond • Manufacturing and high-quality service jobs in target industries expected to enjoy continuing growth into the future • Selectivity and sophistication and key objectives	• Retention and expansion of existing firms • Spurring local entrepreneurship and investment • Selective recruiting of facilities from other locations • More intense public/private partnership • Developing technology resources • Improving commercial and technical education	• Prepare for growth in the contemporary world-wide economy • Competitive operating costs • Human and intellectual resources adaptable to the future change • Good quality of life (emphasis on cultural and intellectual development)

Source: Adapted from, but originally presented by, John T. Bailey, *Marketing Cities in the 1980s and Beyond* (Chicago American Economic Development Council, 1989). Used with the permission of the American Economic Development Council.

operating costs are some of the key ingredients in these destination-marketing messages. Cheap labor and land, combined with certain tax offerings, make up the more attractive local business climate. Many Asian communities are using these incentives.

In the 1970s and 1980s, places moved slowly to the second generation of strategic market planning. This generation is marked by the emergence of a number of new target groups in the planning efforts. Instead of a single goal, such as luring manufacturing jobs from other places, multiple goals appeared — retention, startups, tourism, export, promotion, and inward investment. Places changed their activities from using a hit-or-miss approach or a quick fix to more refined strategies based on competitive analysis and market positioning. Some places have started to segment markets and identify various types of investors. These places moved from mass marketing of diffuse products (typically financial incentives and pure subsidies) to specialized marketing, emphasizing a place's unique products that are tailored to specific customer needs. Places also put more emphasis on maintaining internal markets and resources, including existing businesses, industries, entrepreneurs, products and services, and collective resources (universities, research parks, financial institutions, and so on).

During this generation, more public/private partnerships grew. This was especially the case where some leading local companies were willing to participate actively in the process. However, a real broad spread of such partnerships did not occur in Asia during the second generation. Many Asian approaches remained quite centralized.

In the 1990s, with its increased unemployment rates, Asian places began moving into the third generation of product development and competitive niche thinking. In the global economy it is crucial to develop competitive positions that stand out in the marketplace. Places began to define themselves as being distinctive, with specific advantages for target industries. Niche products based on unique combinations were offered to target markets. Local clusters of related industries were stimulated. Each place wanted to combine its clusters with training facilities and infrastructure such as rail, roads, telecommunications and airports. Quality of life was now interpreted more broadly than in the second generation. The intellectual climate, the openness of the place and entrepreneurial encouragement became important attraction factors.

As the new century begins, place identity and image have become increasingly effective and prevalent in business positioning strategy. Companies are therefore more open to different types of local/regional cooperation. This is seen increasingly among banks, insurance companies, power utilities, telephone companies and transport providers.

These companies, in particular, have in common the simple fact that it is not easy to move away from the home market. One consequence is that a more intense public/private partnership is occurring in Asia.

These developments reflect the growth, development and sophistication of competition between places in a changing world economy. As a result of intensified competition, many places have become more business-like and market-oriented in their economic-development activities. Residents themselves have come to notice the lack of long-term and sustainable results of the "first generation" approach. What once was a question of lowering costs and attracting subsidies has today become a much more professional and sophisticated value-added planning process. These processes are anchored in long-term strategic plans.

The Asian financial crisis strengthened the "third generation" diffusion. The old "state-national model" characterized by large subsidies to local levels has been questioned and, in most instances, has failed. In other cases, surges in local influence and power are obvious, perhaps most so in the southern coastal areas of China. The old approaches are being replaced by a strong decentralization, in which places themselves take the initiative and responsibility for their future. In such a decentralized world, a strategy best described as "in search of excellence" emerges. This provides the nucleus or key for a more dynamic and developing Asia.

THE STRATEGIC MARKET PLANNING PROCESS

Places must begin to do what business organizations have been doing for many years; namely, strategic market planning. By "strategic market planning" we do not mean budgeting, which refers to when a community estimates its expected annual revenues and costs in order to achieve an appropriate balance. Nor do we mean project planning in reference to when a place decides to build a stadium, a new town hall or waterfront. Nor do we mean short-range planning, when a place makes certain decisions about finances, taxes and investments for the next year or two. Nor do we mean long-range planning, which consists of calculating a place's future population and resources and developing suitable infrastructure expansion, as may be found in capital budgets.

Strategic market planning assumes the future is largely uncertain and that it can be influenced by strategic actions and plans. The community's challenge is to design for itself a flexible system that can absorb shocks and adapt quickly and effectively to new developments and opportunities. This means that the community must establish information, planning, implementation and control systems that enable it to monitor the changing environment and respond constructively to opportunities and threats. The aim is to prepare plans and actions that integrate objectives and resources with changing opportunities. Through the strategic planning process, places can create a unique selling proposition. Certain attraction factors are encouraged while other factors may be de-emphasized.

Managing strategic market planning is more difficult for communities and regions than for individual companies. Companies typically have a clear line of authority and hierarchy as well as a balance sheet and a profit-and-loss statement to measure yearly progress. Communities, on the other hand, are chronic battlegrounds where interest groups battle for power and push their competing agendas and strategies. While the private-sector company is able to pursue a unifying goal of profit, community economic development runs the risk of being compromised by multiple interest groups and periodic elections. Where institutional arrangements fail to reconcile conflict and leadership fails to emerge, communities typically fail or stagnate. Strategic market planning is highly unlikely to succeed in sharply divided communities where consensus-building mechanisms fail to work. However, Asian practice shows that the strategic market-planning process can work in most communities where leadership, institutions and procedures exist that favor structured decision-making for the future. Sellers can promote "high intellectual capital" in such places.

But one should not underestimate a place's opportunity, just like that of business, to find objective and measurable performance criteria. For a community, success can be measured in terms of a strengthened tax base, group consensus, an increase in business startups, new residents, and so on. These factors may already exist. It is simply necessary to put them in a development context.

The strategic market-planning process moves through five stages that answer the following questions:

1. **Place audit.** What is the current state of the community, and how does it compare to places in similar situations? What are the community's major strengths/weaknesses, opportunities/threats? (This process is known as a SWOT analysis.)
2. **Vision and goals.** What do the community's businesses and residents want the community to be?
3. **Strategy formulation.** What broad strategies will help the community reach its goals?

4. Action plan. What specific actions must the community undertake to carry out its strategies?

5. Implementation and control. What must the community do to ensure successful implementation?

The following discussion describes the major concepts and tools used at each stage of the strategic market-planning process.

CONDUCTING THE PLACE AUDIT

The first task facing a team responsible for charting a community's future course is to understand accurately what the community is like and why. The tool for doing this systematically is called "a place audit." Hard and soft attraction factors must be scrutinized in a comparative context. The team must make an attempt to sort these factors into competitive strengths and weaknesses, and then follow up with an effort to relate them to opportunities and threats, thus providing the basis for visions and goals. An example of how a place audit can serve as a launching pad for success is Caloundra in Queensland, Australia (see Exhibit 5.2).

Exhibit 5.3: TRANSFORMING CALOUNDRA

It is hard to believe that the city of Caloundra on the Sunshine Coast of Queensland, Australia, was once a classic retirement town. Now it bustles with a rich mixture of young commuters, holidaymakers and retirees. The change follows the city council's implementation of its Vision in Action 1998–2003 plan. Already, Caloundra is seeing the fruits of that labor in the form of a diverse economic base featuring such industries as agriculture (500 enterprises), services (200), automotive (150), building/construction (120), manufacturing (70), tourism, and commerce. Agriculture, the city's primary industry (in number terms) generates A$100 million (US$51.6 million) annually. Over 200,000 tourists per annum generate A$150 million (US$77.4 million).

Caloundra, formerly Landsborough Shire, was proclaimed Caloundra City on December 19, 1987 as the first step to fulfillment of the community's vision for the city. Over the next 10 years the Council developed a community consultation process — formalized in October 1997 — for the development of a "corporate plan" for the city. The consultation process involved a self-audit process to identify the strengths, weaknesses, opportunities and threats to development. The Council and its constituents wanted to be far more than just a retirement enclave. They wanted to make their city an enterprise center. The result was Vision in Action.

The plan provided mid-term goals for the allocation of resources and the provision of services over five years. An Operations Plan consisted of 15 programs and 44 sub-programs involving 184 key initiatives to be accomplished within a year. To measure progress, 316 performance indicators were established for these initiatives and the results were monitored throughout the given year. The Operations Plan is released every year with the city's Annual Report, which publicly demonstrates the progress made toward achieving its goals each year.

Booming Caloundra has several other advantages. Its central business district is situated 45 minutes' drive north of Brisbane, the capital of Queensland — Australia's premier holiday state. The reinvented city's high population growth and easy access to Brisbane are important generators of new opportunities for growth and development. Thanks to superb strategic market planning, Caloundra is well positioned to capitalize on these opportunities.

Several important lessons can be learned from Caloundra. First, the importance of cooperative, goal-oriented planning cannot be stressed enough. It is owing to the hard work and committed interest of a diverse range of community and business leaders that the city has been able to attract new investors and industries. Second, the city's success illustrates the necessity of a long-term strategy. Caloundra's progress in creating a vibrant economy could not have been achieved without plans for an extended period of development. The third factor is a focused design. Caloundra is building a diversified economy and a positive living environment. These factors offered investors a clear set of benefits.

Sources:

http://www.caloundra.qld.gov.au/economic/pdf/city_of_opportunity.pdf, viewed on October 16, 2000; http://www.gonefishin.com.au/topspots/

Establishing a Place's Attraction Factors

A place audit must start with good information about the attraction factors.

Of course, economic and demographic features are basic. Every community must assess its population, purchasing power, competence, housing market, industry structure and labor market characteristics, health profile, natural resources, transportation facilities, quality of life, and education and research institutions. Many Asian communities publish this type of data annually, and its reliability has improved dramatically, thanks to new technology that makes tracking and storing information more efficient.

Unfortunately, simple data is not enough. New combinations of data are part of a winning market-planning effort. The team must therefore initiate fact-finding missions with an innovative ambition. If, for example, data show that senior city residents are seeking quieter, more affordable places to live, a small town may find it advantageous to package tranquil virtues and market them to this target audience. Suddenly this prospect reveals a whole new set of opportunities. The challenge is to find the winning combination.

Identifying Main Competitors

A place must do more than simply establish that it provides a good fit to the target market's needs. Every place needs to identify its competition. Thus Hong Kong, Singapore and Sydney are all competing for the status of "Asian Financial Center." On a much smaller scale, numerous tea-producing regions and places in Asia are competing with each other over which has the best brands, plantations and production resources. Almost every place wants to be a high-tech manufacturing and development center. Others want to be back-office support centers for multinationals.

A place needs to identify its main competitors in each specific niche or arena. This identification process extends beyond even regional borders. For example, Dubai calls itself "The Desert's Most Exciting City" and competes with other destinations by adding up its positive features. Its marketing message reads: "It has spectacular beaches but is not Australia; it is one of the world's most secure cities but is not Singapore; it has opulent city hotels and superb beachside resorts but is neither Jakarta nor Bali. It has world-class shopping but is not Hong Kong."[8]

In some areas there is the possibility that competitors could also be future partners. The "twin cities" concept — Hong Kong and Guangzhou, for example — is becoming more popular because partnerships can provide new resources in the global place market. Although not many Hong Kong and Guangzhou people are likely to think of themselves as residents of twin cities, that doesn't stop the synergy from happening.

Relative to other destinations, a place can be one of the following: a superior competitor, a peer competitor or a weak competitor.

1. A superior competitor. A place that is a superior competitor must protect its position. If it is extremely attractive, it might experience too much growth. This can result in traffic congestion, rising rents and labor costs, and damage to infrastructure. The place must also worry about the possible emergence of new competition. The decision to build the second Malaysia-Singapore Crossing (linking Kampung Landang at Tanjung Kupang in Johor to Jalan Ahmad Ibrahim at Tuas in Singapore), at a cost of US$1 billion, came about as a result of the increasing inadequacy of the first crossing (Johor Bahru in Malaysia to Woodlands in Singapore), which was built two-and-a-half decades ago. The new crossing is designed to handle four times the load of the first and avoid the congestion at the Johor Bahru city area.[9] As a result, Johor Bahru has had to think seriously about ways to continue to attract tourists.

2. A peer competitor. Here, two competing places might be equally attractive. Intense competition can stimulate each to develop better strategy. Cooperation is also an alternative. Consider, for example, the cooperative telecommunication agreements between SingTel in Singapore and Bharti Telecom Limited and Bharti Televentures Limited in India.[10] Such cross-border agreements can offer new stimulation to local business climates. However, SingTel's failed attempt to acquire Cable & Wireless Hong Kong Telecom also demonstrates that governments often resist cooperative initiatives in strategic sectors. Hong Kong Telecom went to local upstart Pacific Century CyberWorks instead.

3. A weak competitor. When a place is a weak competitor, short-term activities won't really solve its problems. The only solution is to make extraordinary efforts in the field of strategic market planning. Asia has already seen many examples of how such repositioning is possible, even in places with a heavy manufacturing image such as Chiba City

in Japan[11] and Shenyang in the industrial belt of China.[12]

The first challenge is to learn from good competitors what they have done to be successful. The second task is to learn how to do it better.

Identifying Major Trends and Developments

Since strategic market planning is a long-term process, it is vital to anticipate main trends and developments likely to affect places. These trends should be discussed not only on individual levels, but also more collectively within all kinds of community organizations in the search for new ideas.

Communities need to pay special attention to the following trends:

- In spite of current generous national and Asian Development Bank funding for regional and community programs, Asian communities in the future will have to rely more on their own capabilities to create a dynamic local climate.
- Places will be affected increasingly by Asian and global developments and changes. Therefore, they must actively monitor and anticipate developments in other parts of the world. So far, too few Asian communities appreciate the impact of globalization on their future.
- Places are often stuck in a dilemma. They are caught between the need to support public services — a need arising, in part, from high unemployment — and service decline attributable to tax-resistance on the part of voters. As a result, these places will need to make the most of diminishing financial resources. This means different and more innovative approaches to service delivery. Taxpayers in many developed Asian countries are on the verge of a tax revolt. In developing Asia, citizens must be shown that taxes will be used wisely and legally before they can be convinced to remit their tax obligations.
- Places will need to be more attentive to environmental forces and regulations in planning their future. A current Asian battle concerns which places are environmentally stronger. Stronger places can use this as part of their strategic market planning. Semarang in Indonesia, for example, was acclaimed "Cleanest City" and awarded the national Adipura Kencana Trophy for the years from 1992–1995.[13] The president of Indonesia gives the award and winning it often means the re-election of the city's mayor. Thus it is accorded great importance and taken very seriously.[14]
- Places are also competing in the growing area of information technology. Many communities see the advantage of becoming a pilot community for new IT applications, often with the support of an

ASEAN (e-ASEAN Task Force) program or the investment arms of multinational technology companies.

Additional large-scale developments (such as lifestyle changes, the dramatic increase in the elderly population, decentralization from national to local levels, integration between Southeast Asian nations, and so on) must be identified. The community must assess the impact of these developments and take steps to respond in a proactive way.

On a smaller scale, there are vital trends and developments influencing the business environment in specific industry sectors. Here are examples:

- Increases in funding available for Bangalore startup companies, brought about by the "international attention and credibility" earned by Indian technology concerns, have contributed to a shift in perspective. The city has become known as a center for "hired hands for Western firms." Now, it is developing into a value-added technology center and attempting to enter the "global market with its own hardware and software products."[15]
- The increasing number of Vietnamese-Americans working in Silicon Valley is creating a new dynamic that is benefiting the New Economy of Vietnam. Many have chosen to invest in opportunities in their homeland, setting up their own new technology companies. As a result, overseas Vietnamese workers, or *Viet Kieu*, are contributing to the country's economy not only in the form of remittances to relatives, but also by establishing domestic companies that generate new jobs. Their desire to help their homeland and other factors — such as the smart, low-cost workforce — are enticing more Vietnamese-Americans to return home.[16]
- A growing number of Hollywood film producers are discovering that Australia is one of the best places in the world to film their international motion pictures.[17] The excellent Australian producers, actors, crews, technicians and facilities have made the country a popular and cost-effective place for foreign, especially Hollywood-based, producers to film and produce their movies. The country also offers a diversity of outdoor settings — from deserts, beaches and snowfields to large, cosmopolitan cities.[18]

Analyzing Strengths and Weaknesses

It is one thing to catalog the characteristics of a place and another to classify them into major strengths and weaknesses, as well as opportunities and threats (SWOT analysis). Unfortunately, many communities publish great volumes of facts and figures without classifying their impact. The potential place buyer is left with the burden of sorting out the details to gain an accurate overall picture. The relevant message and the unique attraction factors are hidden in meaningless data. The city of Manila, for example, loses opportunities because it does not market itself effectively as the Southeast Asian headquarters of prominent organizations such as the Asian Development Bank and the World Health Organization (WHO).

A place needs to take an outsider-in approach and identify which of its characteristics represent a major strength, minor strength, neutral factor, minor weakness or major weakness in light of what specific investors are seeking. A place's competitive position reflects two sets of conditions: (1) outside forces that are generally beyond local/regional influence; and (2) location characteristics that specific location actions might influence. What is needed is a clear and sufficient long-term strategy where major strengths are leveraged to a maximum and where there is sufficient time to improve certain weaknesses.

Consider a hypothetical community that conducts an analysis on its strengths and weaknesses. The strategic market team assesses the 18 attraction factors discussed in Chapter 3, and the results are shown in Table 5.2.

Of course, all the attraction factors are not equally meaningful to different target groups. It is necessary to choose the factors of key importance to each target group and assign importance values to these individual factors. When combining performance ratings and importance levels, four possibilities emerge (see Table 5.3).

Cell A importance factors indicate that the place rates poorly and that critical improvements are needed; hence, "concentrate here." In Cell B, the importance factors show that the place is already strong; hence, "keep up the good work" and continue the value-adding process. In Cell C, low-importance factors indicate that the place is performing poorly; these factors consequently are of "low priority." In Cell D are unimportant factors where the place is performing strongly, indicating possible "overkill" or over-investing in these factors.

Even the concept of strength must be carefully interpreted. Although a place may have a major strength, that strength does not necessarily constitute a competitive advantage in relation to the selected target market. Competitors may have the same strength-level for that factor. What becomes important is for a place to have greater relative strength for factors important to the selected target group. Two competing places may both enjoy low manufacturing costs, but the one with the lower cost

Table 5.2: Strengths and weaknesses

	Major strength	Minor strength	Neutral	Minor weakness	Major weakness
Hard factors					
• Economic stability		x			
• Productivity				x	
• Costs	x				
• Property concept					x
• Local support services and networks				x	
• Communication infrastructure		x			
• Strategic location	x				
• Incentive schemes	x				
Soft factors					
• Niche development		x			
• Quality of life			x		
• Professional and workforce competencies			x		
• Culture		x			
• Personal		x			
• Management				x	
• Flexibility and dynamism		x			
• Professionalism in market contacts					x
• Entrepreneurship				x	

Table 5.3: Performance-importance matrix

Performance

		Low	High
	High	**A.** Concentrate here	**B.** Keep up the good work
Importance			
	Low	**B.** Low priority	**D.** Possible overkill

has a net competitive advantage. The other place may have to provide some extra inducements to compensate. In practice, it is often difficult to compare costs in two places, especially when the places are in different countries and a cross-border comparison must be made.

A place does not have to correct all its weaknesses or promote all its strengths, because factors vary in their importance to different target markets. The place must probe deeply into which strengths and weaknesses most affect the perceptions and behavior of target markets. The resulting analysis becomes a major basis for laying place-marketing plans.

Exhibit 5.4 describes how Pattaya executed a plan to change its image.

Exhibit 5.4: PATTAYA CLEANS UP ITS IMAGE

Anyone who knows anything about Pattaya will understand the enormity of the task of restoring or, rather, remaking the resort's image. At the height of its fame, it was known as the "Riviera of Thailand" and enjoyed a world-class reputation. Over the years, however, its "free-for-all" image and "anything-goes" attitude resulted in a dramatic decline in its reputation. The resort became Thailand's most notorious tourist trap, reflecting an extraordinary lack of concern for the environment and acquiring a sleazy image as a center for prostitution of every kind.

Concerned citizens and authorities are now working to regain the old glory of the world-famous resort. The Tourism Authority of Thailand, together with city leaders, has launched a US$3-million project to improve the city's international image and attract more families, sporting events and conventions. The development funds will be used to build a night market, a recreational park and other environment-friendly projects. A new water treatment plant at the old Naklua Market has also been built to handle the area's waste, previously dumped directly into the sea. The plant is expected to improve conditions for marine life and perhaps bring back the dolphins. The completion of the resort area's Beach Side Boulevard has restored and enhanced its beauty.

The effort to change negative perceptions of Pattaya includes a number of initiatives. Importantly, authorities have been even more vocal about newly enforced prohibitions on prostitution and under-age sex, and law enforcers are now aggressively punishing perpetrators, no matter what their nationality. The resort is emphasizing family-oriented forms of recreation such as festivals, zoos, museums, gardens and sports facilities (including 13 world-class golf courses). On the business side, Pattaya is trying to capitalize on its potential as a conference center. Government officials are also able to point to the increasing number of conventions held there annually, including some of the biggest in the region, as justification for their actions.

The effort to remake Pattaya is apparent in published reviews, which suggest that it "is about to experience a rebirth, rising like a phoenix out the fire"[1]; that it "offers a plethora of attractions;"[2] and that "the northern area provides a quiet, peaceful getaway, while the south presents an all-night kaleidoscope of sights and sounds."[3]

Pattaya has undergone an extensive image remake and has committed funds and plans. Its repositioning efforts demonstrate the importance of understanding weaknesses and applying a systematic plan.

Sources:

1 http://www.ttg.com.sg/current/archive/1996/1129-05/fe1119962906.html
2 http://www.ttg.com.sg/current/archive/1996/1129-05/fe1119962906.html
3 http://www.biztravelinthailand.com/tra99_04.html

http://www.hotelthailand.com/pattaya/patinfo.html, viewed on October 16, 2000; http://http0542.hosting.connect.com.au/scoop/asi/tha.htm, viewed on October 16; 2000; http://web3.asia1.com.sg/timesnet/data/ab/docs/ab0480.html, viewed on October 16, 2000.

Identifying Opportunities and Threats

The next step is to identify the opportunities and threats a place is facing. We define an opportunity as an arena for action in which a place has a fairly good chance to achieve a competitive advantage.

Consider the region of Bo Hai Rim[19] in China, which has the potential to become an important transshipment center. With the right value-added strategy, the Bo Hai Rim region could create an effective competitive advantage over other developing port areas. But if Bo Hai Rim were to market itself merely as a port area in itself, that would perhaps not be the most inspiring of driving forces for business, visitors and residents. Therefore, Bo Hai Rim must identify opportunities that combine the advantages of a port area with a number of additional attractions. To highlight the region's potential as a port and commerce center, it has integrated a *gateway–transport–telecommunications–science and technology–expansive–market* set of attractions into one comprehensive value proposition. This combination takes a number of forms. A recent report on Bo Hai Rim's port-development strategies for the 21st century cites the gateway advantage: "The Northeast Asian Economic Rim is the most important outlet enabling north, northeast and northwest China, as well as many parts of east China, to enter the Pacific and the world. The international community has attached ever-increasing importance to the development of the Northeast Asian Region, a fact which has added greater prominence to the favorable geographical location of Bo Hai Rim."[20]

The transport and telecommunications section of the report affirms that "the country's north-south trunk transportation and telecommunication lines pass through or originate in the area which shoulders one-third of the nation's transport volume."[21] The science and technology element claims that "scientific, technological and intellectual advantages come from the numerous institutes of higher learning and senior scientists in the area."[22] It supports its expansive market claim by pointing out that "with South Korea's rising interest in making investments in China in recent years, the prospect of developing this region, which shares the coastline of the Yellow Sea with South Korea, looks quite promising."[23] In combining these initiatives, the Bo Hai Rim region is working hard and effectively to define itself as a highly relevant opportunity for certain target groups.

In addition to opportunities, every place faces threats or challenges posed by an unfavorable trend or development in the environment that would lead, in the absence of purposeful action, to the erosion of the condition of the place. Planning teams need to identify various threats that can be classified according to their seriousness and probability of occurrence. Major threats are those that can seriously hurt the place and have a high probability of occurring. The place needs to prepare a contingency plan that spells out what steps to take before, during or after the occurrence of a major threat. If the Multimedia Super Corridor in Malaysia is running into big financial and other problems, the question is, what will happen to the surrounding communities? This could be a major threat. Minor threats are those with a low probability of occurring that would not hurt the place badly. Moderate threats are those with either high potential to harm a place or high-occurrence probability, but not both. They must be watched.

By assembling a picture of the major threats and opportunities facing a specific place, it is possible to characterize a place's overall attractiveness. An ideal place is one that is high in major opportunities and low in major threats. A speculative place is high in both major opportunities and threats. A mature place is low in major opportunities and threats. Finally, a troubled place is low in opportunities and high in threats.

Establishing the Main Issues

There might be as many opinions as there are citizens on the point of what constitutes a main issue. Every place must try to identify the main issues that it must address. Too common a response when establishing the main issues is to omit the most troublesome ones in order to avoid conflict, even though they may be crucial.

Another problem is created when the community treats all issues as equally important. We see many places in Asia that work on all fronts at once. All target groups and all market niches are treated equally. For example, Vietnam makes broad offers to all markets and niches. Under the umbrella of "hottest potential Asian Tiger,"[24] it markets itself to everyone. The question is — what are the priorities? Without making choices, a place has no way to choose between potential value-added investments.

Bandung in Indonesia is another place that must carefully re-plan its future. The past image of the city — a garrison town with military men as mayors — suggests that it doesn't prioritize social welfare or town planning. Corruption is also an issue that needs to be addressed. But with the fall of Suharto in 1998, decentralization is taking place, allowing citizens to voice their opinions and the city to raise its own revenue for infrastructure and other facilities. Bandung is establishing new main priorities and identifying new opportunities to sustain its prosperity.[25]

SETTING THE VISION AND OBJECTIVES

Carrying out a SWOT and issues analysis enables strategic planners to form a comprehensive picture of the community's situation. But it is not easy to choose among the many value-added projects that can be imagined. Divergent projects may not add up to coherent development plans and visions. Without a coherent vision, it is difficult to prioritize the various projects.

Vision development calls for planners to solicit input from the citizens as to what they want their community to be like in 10 or even 20 years' time. One helpful ploy in this process is to circulate two to four scenarios for comment. Since each place is a complex environment, the scenarios become tools for stimulating deeper thoughts about possible futures for the place.

Consider, for example, Johor Bahru in southern peninsular Malaysia[26] and its, in certain respects, attractive image. Johor Bahru presents a potential alternative to the high prices and crowded conditions of Singapore. But what are the possible scenarios for Johor Bahru 20 years from now? A number of reasonable scenarios can be distinguished:

1. **Uncurbed growth**. In this scenario, Johor Bahru encourages free and open growth. A 5% annual increase in retail and tourism activity occurs. Congestion and pollution may well follow. The image erodes as premium investors search for higher quality and more attractive environments.
2. **Managed quality growth.** In this scenario, Johor Bahru decision-makers choose to invest systematically in the development of more sophisticated services. Conferences with high-quality services become a niche. Total annual visits increase at the rate of 1%. More of the visitors come for business purposes. Business travelers spend more money and generate several new and unexpected networks of other investments for Johor Bahru. A more diversified Johor Bahru grows. The early years of this development are not free of conflict, however. The determination of promotions to advocate growth at any cost is a source of tension.
3. **Zero or negative growth.** Here Johor Bahru takes steps to reduce reliance on tourism and shoppers from Singapore. Environment and quality become the guiding criteria for local planning. The number of visitors decreases, and the proportion of business visitors grows. Johor Bahru commits to being a place of value-added enterprise activity. The new and complementing niches become banking, insurance and telemarketing. Johor Bahru nurtures the language skills of its residents and its intercultural experiences gained from decades of interaction with Singapore.

There is actually a fourth choice open to Johor Bahru, and that is to drift along, rather than to adopt any vision at all. Many places cannot agree on any scenario, and there is consequently no resulting vision. The leaders tend to believe that a vision limits their freedom to maneuver. There could also be a lack of knowledge regarding what strategies other successful places have used to develop a long-term vision. The vision step is critical because places without one are usually without direction and motivation. Exhibit 5.5 describes what a vision can do in practice.

Exhibit 5.5: THAILAND AS THE "DETROIT OF THE EAST"

Thailand wanted to be at the center of Southeast Asian production. In the midst of the Asian financial crisis, prospects for attaining this vision seemed bleak. But the Thai government at the time, with its free-market policies, welcomed foreign car manufacturers to the country with open arms, unlike some other Southeast Asian countries at the time (notably Malaysia with its own national car program). This important move, together with a government investment of US$1.5 billion to build the infrastructure (the Eastern Seaboard Development Project at Rayong Province) and the country's other strengths, helped reposition Thailand.

The country already had the potential to become a center for automotive manufacturing. Apart from its strategic location in Southeast Asia and its domestic market of around 61 million, labor in Thailand is relatively cheap. Also, as a result of the building of Japanese automotive and parts-manufacturing plants in the 1980s, there existed a significant pool of skilled labor. With this development in Rayong, additional automotive-parts suppliers were attracted to the region, and they provided a stable infrastructure that continues to attract investors.

A sign at the entrance of the Eastern Seaboard Industrial Estate reads, "Detroit of the East" — a comparison that now has some validity. Currently, over 40 automobile and parts manufacturers have established operations in Thailand, including big names that remain bullish about the country's potential — General Motors (US$500-million factory), BMW (US$32-million luxury car assembly line), Toyota (US$360-million plant), and a Mazda/Ford joint venture (US$472-million pickup plant).

Sources:

http://detnews.com/menu/stories/38247.htm, viewed on November 8, 2000; Julian Gearing, "The Detroit of Asia," Asiaweek, October 1, 1999; http://www.thaitrade.com/superth.html, viewed on November 8, 2000; http://www.industrialmag.com/events/singapore.htm, viewed on October 16, 2000; http://www.locationusa.com/industry/merge.html, viewed on October 16, 2000; Frederik Balfour, "Southeast Asia's Motor City," BusinessWeek, May 8, 2000, viewed on October 16, 2000 at http:/ www.business-week.com/2000/00_19/b3680166.htm.

The development of a vision goes further than simply distinguishing between potential growth paths. A vision should take a stand on such issues as:

- Which unique combinations of attraction factors should the community target?
- Which are the target markets of the community?
- Which are the long-term and short-term goals?
- Which are the operative prerequisites for the vision?

Given that a community can prepare different scenarios, how might it work out clear choices and a final vision? Certain observations can be made in this regard. First, the main actor is normally and formally the community. However, informally, it is always possible to trace some leading person, either employed by the community or with a strong tie to the community, who serves as a catalyst.

Second, a vision is normally born in a complex process involving citizens and relevant interest groups. One problem in Asia has been that, in many cases, the public sector is over-represented and favors short-term activities without future revenue-generating potential. However, unlike just a few years ago, it is now recognized that a successful vision must be created in a joint effort between the public and the private commercial sectors.

Third, it is not unusual for a community to seek external inspiration from different resource persons and consultants in developing future visions. Although external inspiration and perspectives are valuable, it is necessary that the primary motivations and actions are the responsibility of persons who have roots in the community. A vision needs a driver and this driver cannot — at least in the long run — be the consultant.

Fourth, the vision often spans a period of five to 10 years. Only a few years ago, conventional wisdom was to "set the sights" on the turn of the century. Now that we are there, the focus instead is on the years 2005 to 2010. Some Asian communities have taken a much longer-term perspective, focusing on 2025.

Fifth, the community council or its equivalent normally decides on the acceptance of the vision. A vision needs authoritative approval for credibility.

Once the community agrees on a vision, it is essential that it set specific objectives and goals. Objectives are clear statements about what a place wants to achieve; goals add specific magnitudes and timing to these objectives. For example, if a community vision states an objective to increase the number of jobs over the next several years, the vision can be more operational if the objective is turned into the following goal:

"Before the year 2005, at least seven new enterprises should be established which should create 400 jobs and bring in 800 new residents." Such statements make it easier to allocate the resources necessary to accomplish the goal and assign responsibilities. The Asian Development Bank has encouraged goal-setting by making it a prerequisite for receiving regional support.

FORMULATING THE STRATEGY

Once the community-planning team has defined the vision, goals and objectives, it can move into identifying and choosing strategies for accomplishing the goals. For example, when Suryadevra Ramchandra Rao was appointed head of the Surat Municipal Corporation (SMC) in 1995, he immediately took the first steps in transforming Surat into the second-cleanest city in India by identifying how the city would accomplish that goal, and how it would measure progress. At the time of his appointment, the city was notorious for its dirty streets and a deadly pneumonic plague in 1994. With the appointment of Rao, the city's image began to change almost immediately.

Rao's strategy was built on the premise of accountability. Before implementing waste-disposal programs to improve slum conditions in Surat, Rao realized that his demoralized people's faith in themselves and the city administration had to be restored. To accomplish that task, he initiated a program he dubbed "AC to DC: go from air-conditioned offices to daily chores."[27] The program was intended to make people responsible for their own environments, and thereby restore their confidence in their own capabilities and efforts. He then went on to punish violators of the city's hygiene standards, sparing no one — rich or poor. The result was a visible difference in the city's environment, which in turn received wide attention locally and internationally.

Today, the city's re-engineered municipal service is one that actually works, with roads and streets cleaned regularly, citizens' needs addressed, and violators of sanitation laws punished. Central to the city's success was Rao's restoration of the citizens' confidence in government. As a result, they signed up for Rao's program, and began working and contributing to the betterment of their city. Today, Surat is more attractive to investors, with most streets paved and garbage collected regularly. As a result, the city is poised to regain its reputation as a booming textile center and a key player in the diamond trade.[27]

For each potential strategy, the planning team must ask the following two questions:

1. What advantages do we possess that suggest that we can succeed with that strategy? In the case of the Thailand's Rayong Province, the liberal government policies form the basis of its strategy.
2. Do we have the resources required for a successful implementation of that strategy? The long-term strategy approach in Rayong made it easier to attract new resources.

Even communities lacking sufficient resources can sometimes develop a creative strategy solution. Until the 1980s, Rayong was known only as a tourist destination and for its fishing villages. With the creation of the Eastern Seaboard Industrial Estate in the province, however, Thailand came to be known as "a favorite hub for automotive manufacturing."[28] Two other cases where no other strengths were initially obvious are illustrated in Exhibit 5.6.

Exhibit 5.6: HOW VARANASI AND SEPANG DEVELOPED TOURIST ATTRACTIONS

What happens when a community lacks an obvious hook upon which to hang a strategy? The community may be small, isolated or unattractive. The answer may be to promote an event that is not widely known or to create some attraction that has media appeal. Varanasi and Sepang provide telling examples of how to create a market.

Varanasi
In between the Varunasa and Asi tributaries of the Ganges River lies one of the world's oldest continuously inhabited cities on earth, Varanasi, also known as Benares or Kashi. There are many similar places competing for tourists, but Varanasi has managed to create a distinctive, global value proposition. Being one of the oldest and most holy cities in India, Varanasi naturally attracts large numbers of domestic devotees. The 2000-year-old history of knowledge and culture is the main attraction. Sensing an increase in people's need for spiritual renewal and an increasing acceptance of things spiritual, the small "City of Light" has opened itself to foreign visitors, too. It has used advertisements, incentives and tour groups to market itself as a desirable tourist attraction.

As a result of these targeted efforts, millions of foreign visitors, pilgrims and non-pilgrims, come to the *ghats* (steps leading down to the Ganges) of Varanasi every year to participate in and view the annual bathing ritual that devout Hindus participate in to cleanse themselves spiritually. Special seminars on Hinduism and cultural festivities are aimed at bringing in visitors from overseas, and are supported with travel packages, train tours, and additional airline flights. Apart from the centuries-old cultural and spiritual attractions, it is the long series of *ghats* that draw visitors to Varanasi. Many Indians believe that anyone who dies on the banks of the Ganges in Varanasi attains instant *moksha* or enlightenment.

This event is now being used in a value-added process to market many more unusual offerings in the city and the region. For instance, while the age-old handicraft industries of Varanasi — such as silk (saris and brocades) and carpet weaving — have long been famous the world over, they have recently received substantially more attention as a result of the increasing number of visitors who go shopping in the city and market them by word of mouth. The City of Light now accounts for 50% of India's silk exports.

Varanasi has used its historical assets to both extend and broaden its market for tourist consumption and export of products. Too often, places fail to capitalize on their natural advantages and, as a result, become self-limited regional tourist attractions.

Sepang

Before the creation of its Formula One (F1) Circuit in March 1999, the small Malaysian city of Sepang was little known internationally. The area occupied by the Circuit was a humble palm-oil estate before serious investments were made in the sporting facility. While many of Malaysia's grandiose infrastructure investments are of doubtful utility or financial soundness, Sepang looks like an exception.

Despite receiving strong criticism over the building of this world-class facility, community leaders have succeeded in attracting international attention to Sepang. Detractors believed that the investment was too big (286 million ringgit or US$75 million, plus $8 million each time the track is used for the

Grand Prix), and that neither the country nor the region was ready for an advanced leisure attraction appealing to a specific target market. However, proponents insisted otherwise, and argued that the country had the profile and expertise required to showcase world-class racing events. They also pointed to the positive benefits the circuit would bring: increased tourism and foreign investment.

The track's advocates believed their persistence may have paid off. Crowds of racing aficionados — the site can accommodate 130,000 spectators — are attracted by arguably the best facilities in the world. It has the widest track on the circuit, which allows the drivers greater maneuverability. It is also the first track in Asia to be given the privilege of using the F1 logo. As a result, Sepang is the permanent venue for the FIA Formula One Championship and FIM 500cc World Motorcycle Grand Prix, two of the most prestigious sporting events in the world. The Formula One race captures the attention of over two billion people in 200 countries.

But the real prize is the spin-off potential. According to Malaysian Prime Minister Mahathir Mohamad, the building of this facility will usher in other opportunities for Sepang. Apart from complementing the development in the area, it creates a springboard for Sepang to become the center of motor-sports development in the region as well as a center for research and development for the automotive industry.

While Varanasi and Sepang do not have the attraction packages of Hong Kong, Bali or Sydney, they show that even small places without obvious strengths can capture attention in the global marketplace.

Sources:

Shubh Yatra Web site, http://www.shubhyatra.com/htm/uttarpradesh/varanasi.htm, viewed on October 18, 2000; Richard Ehrlich, "Benares Travel," http://members.tripod.com/ehrlich/2benares.htm, viewed on October 18, 2000; Rod Eason, "Indolink Travelog: An American in Varanasi," http://www.indialink.com/Travel/varanasi.htm, viewed on October 18, 2000; http://www.malaysiangp.com.my/history/index.htm, viewed on October 18, 2000; Frederick Balfour, "Spotlight on Malaysia," *BusinessWeek*, November 13, 2000; http://www.american.edu/projects/mandala/TED/formula1.htm, viewed on January 9, 2001.

DEVELOPING THE ACTION PLAN

In order to be meaningful, strategy must be elaborated into an action plan. This is particularly important in complex communities and regions where much strategic thinking runs the risk of falling through the cracks. Many of the positive results achieved by small communities derive from the fact that it is easier to assign responsibility and create simpler and quicker decision processes than in larger, more complex communities.

An action plan should list each action, plus four additional components for each action:

1. Who is responsible?
2. How is the action to be implemented?
3. How much will the action cost?
4. What is the expected completion date?

This level of detail provides several advantages. First, each person involved in the action plan knows what he/she must accomplish. Second, the marketer can easily discern whether the various actions are being satisfactorily implemented. Third, if towards the end of the period it is found that costs exceed the budget, the action detail permits canceling specific actions and their subsequent costs.

Some Asian communities have created long checklists of short- and long-term projects, which are also used as a marketing tool. The detailed lists are published to make clear the degree of implementation and, in some cases, to attract potential place buyers.

As Asian communities develop their local marketing strategies, it is critical to spell out concrete action plans identifying the actions of participants. A lack of clear goal-setting and detailed action planning is one of the most serious threats to successful community development.

IMPLEMENTING AND CONTROLLING THE MARKET PLAN

Visions, strategies and plans are useless until they are implemented effectively. The planning team needs to convene at regular intervals to review the community's progress toward its goals.

Most communities prepare some sort of annual summary which reflects hard facts such as number of citizens, economic results, jobs, income, taxes, and so on. We believe that facts and figures should be presented in relation to the vision, goals and strategies. We call this a place's annual report. Failures and concerns, as well as successes, should be included.

The community's annual report should receive broad public distribution. It could, for example, be included as an insert in the major local newspapers. Many communities have their own magazine that is sent directly to every household once or twice per year. During the last few years, more Asian communities are using the Internet to show citizens — as well as the general market — what they have accomplished. Their wish to reach the international place market is evidenced by offering to Internet users a choice of languages in which they can receive messages and information. For example, Figure 5.1 depicts Hong Kong's introductory pages on the Internet.

The Web site also includes facts on Hong Kong's policies and offerings, with relevant factors broken down in a systematic and readable way, enabling direct communication with citizens as well as the destination marketplace. Sections on publications and consultation papers allow citizens to both gauge the government's progress and participate in ongoing strategy review efforts.

Figure 5.1: A new way of distributing community performance

Source: http://www.info.gov.hk/eindex.htm, viewed on November 12, 2000.

TWO ABILITIES: STRATEGY AND IMPLEMENTATION

Every community in need of a real change and a positive spiral must develop its ability in two basic dimensions: strategy and implementation. Unfortunately, these two dimensions are seldom developed under the same leadership in the same place. Therefore, it is useful to differentiate between at least four basic environments in which strategy and implementation can take place. These environments are presented in Figure 5.2.

"Losers" include those communities and places that have no capacity to take actions along either dimension. Unfortunately, many communities fall into this category. Under crisis, they seek and demand heavy investments, subsidies or other compensatory actions. They argue on the basis of "justice" or "need."

"Frustrators" have the ability for strategic thinking but lack implementation skills. After some time, the planners become frustrated and then give up and quit the organization, or even leave the place.

"Gamblers" have a well-developed ability for implementation but their strategic ability is lacking. With luck and extremely hard work, gamblers may experience some success — at least in the short term. In time, the amount of extremely hard work required to succeed without effective strategic planning can lead to personnel burnout and turnover. Gamblers tend to work on all possible fronts and focused, targeted marketing rarely occurs.

"Expanders" are communities that are good at strategy and implementation. In almost all cases, there is leadership that is prepared to

Figure 5.2: Four abilities

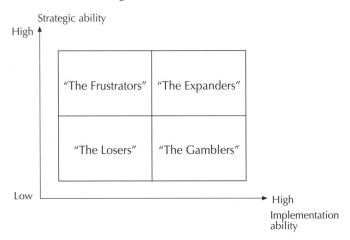

support a long-term strategy and stimulate sub-strategies and action plans. In this book we have mentioned several examples of the "best practice" communities.

CONCLUSION

Too many places fail to recognize threats before they become overwhelming, if not irreversible, and they consequently react rather than plan. Such passivity is not inevitable. Some Asian places have responded with active approaches such as community development, urban design and planning, and economic development. Strategic market planning represents an approach by which a place can design a better future. It calls for profiling the situation of the place: identifying the strengths/ weaknesses, opportunities/threats and main issues; setting a vision, objectives and goals; defining effective strategies for accomplishing these goals; developing appropriate actions; and implementing and controlling the plan.

In this process, even places with no obvious strengths can redefine their situation and find new combinations of attraction factors that should offer a unique value in the place market.

Although this version of strategic planning oversimplifies many of the problems of managing complex entities such as cities, communities and regions, it represents a more promising approach than any other alternative, including a trial-and-error approach, with its risk of haphazard outcomes. Many Asian communities have already put into practice important elements of strategic thinking and planning. The next chapter addresses the importance of evaluating and improving a place's assets.

1 Michael Alan Hamlin, "Is Japan Doomed?," *Far Eastern Economic Review*, June 3, 1999, p. 50.
2 Robin Ajello and Frederik Balfour, "Hong Kong: Home Sweet Home? Not These Days," *Businessweek*, July 10, 2000, p. 23.
3 Ricardo Saludo and Assif Shameen, "Bracing for the Fallout," *Asiaweek*, October 27, 2000, p. 23.
4 Alysha Webb, "Cleaning A River to Enhance A City," *Businessweek*, July 24, 2000, p. 4A2.
5 http://www.worldbank.org/html/fpd/urban/urb_age/culture/lahore.html, viewed on October 18, 2000.
6 "Re-inventing Club Intramuros," *Manila Bulletin*, August 13, 1999, viewed on October 9, 2000 at http://www.mb.com.ph/oldsite/scty/9908/13ac00a.asp.
7 http://www.macau99.org.mo/tdmrtp/varios/historical_e.htm, viewed on October 9, 2000.

8 http://www.datadubai.com/about.htm, viewed on October 18, 2000.

9 http://www.kiat.net/vision/index.html#landbridge, viewed on October 31, 2000.

10 SingTel press release, August 7, 2000, viewed on October 11, 2000 at http://home.singtel.com/news/default.asp?art_id={E84ACAD8-0632-8407-6FD9-5FB65088EB2A.

11 http://srd.yahoo.com/goo/smokestack+image+in+asia/4/*http://malaysia.cnet.com/Internet/Dispatches/Japan/981030/, viewed on October 11, 2000.

12 http://www.cnn.com/SPECIALS/1999/china.50/asian.superpower/middle.class/, viewed on October 13, 2000.

13 http://www.hsd.ait.ac.th/ump/Semarang.htm, viewed on October 11, 2000.

14 http://www.usaep.org/country/indonesa.htm, viewed on November 9, 2000.

15 Sadanand Dhume, "Wired Warriors," *Far Eastern Economic Review*, October 5, 2000, p. 34.

16 Dan Biers and Margot Cohen, "Return of the Prodigal Sons," *Far Eastern Economic Review*, September 21, 2000, p. 45.

17 Gary Maddox, "Lights, Camera, Sydney!," *Sydney Morning Herald*, June 10, 2000, viewed on May 7, 2001 at http://www.smh.com.au/travel/0006/10/travel1.html.

18 Australian Department of Foreign Affairs and Trade fact sheet on the Australian Film Industry, May 2000, viewed on May 7, 2001 at _industry.html" \t "_blank" http://www.dfat.gov.au/facts/film_industry.html.

19 Bo Hai Rim region includes Tianjin Municipality and Liaoning, Hebei and Shandong provinces. There are four Bo Hai ports: Tianjin, Dalian, Qinhuangdao, and Qingdao. http://depts.washington.edu/gttl/htdocs/conf99/seafin.html, viewed on November 8, 2000.

20 http://depts.washington.edu/gttl/htdocs/conf99/seafin.html, viewed on October 16, 2000.

21 *Ibid.*

22 *Ibid.*

23 *Ibid.*

24 http://www.cgtd.com/global/presviet.html, viewed on October 16, 2000.

25 Yasmin Ghahremani and Tom Mccawley, "Reformasi in Bandung," *Asiaweek,* Asia's Best Cities 1999, viewed on October 18, 2000 at http://www.cnn.com/ASIANOW/asiaweek/features/asiacities/ac1999/data/reform.bandung.html.

26 http://www.apsummit.org/overview_map_profiles.html, viewed on October 16, 2000.

27 Jagdish Rattanani, "Hearts and Minds," *Asiaweek,* Asia's Best Cities 1999, viewed on October 18, 2000 at http://www.cnn.com/ASIANOW/asiaweek/features/asiacities/ac1999/data/improved.surat.html.

28 http://www.thaitrade.com/superth.html, viewed on October 16, 2000.

CHAPTER 6

Strategies for Place Improvement

Many marketers believe that marketing a place means promoting it. Promotion is, ironically, one of the least important marketing tasks. Promotion alone does not help a troubled place. In fact it only helps place buyers to discover early on how troubled a place really is (see Exhibit 6.1).

Exhibit 6.1: BREATHTAKING NEPAL?

The government of Nepal attempted to enhance the country's tourism under its Visit Nepal 1998 program, which was grandly summarized by the slogan, "A World of its Own." Unfortunately, what arriving tourists discovered was a world of misadventure. Although Nepal is home to some of the most breathtaking sights in the world, the government's ambitions outweighed its planning expertise. Firstly, visitors had to cope with the inconveniences associated with inadequate infrastructure, including a lack of direct air access to the country, good hotels, tourist transport, trained guides, and maps. There was also an overwhelming waste-disposal problem and garbage lined the streets.

Secondly, appealing destinations were limited. Instead of building on potential, Nepal left many potential attractions underdeveloped. Every time tourists entered a town or municipality they had to pay an entry tax that officials claimed was for the maintenance of facilities and attractions. The tourists felt they were being taken advantage of and argued that they should be asked to pay these taxes at one single point rather than being asked for money at every stage throughout their trip.

As a result, disappointed visitors often cut short their visits. The potential long-term effect of Nepal's promotion campaign was a negative image sent around the world over the Internet by disillusioned visitors. Such instances of counterproductive word-of-mouth communications can set back the appeal of a place for years, even decades.

In most information campaigns, if the implicit promises of a tourist promotion are not delivered, there is a risk of severe backlash. When backlash does occur, a good reputation that may have taken years to build can be ruined overnight. Worse, rebuilding a reputation from a negative position requires far greater energy, resources and time than building from a neutral or unknown-brand position.

Nepal's campaign was a step backward for the country, its attractions and its people. While the government does seem aware of the problem and has tried to correct it, the results have been mixed. Although tourist arrivals increased in 1998, there was a marked dip in tourism revenues. At the same time, the government's annual report for 1998–99 announced that it had begun practicing regulated eco-tourism in order to protect the country's natural resources and to allow local residents to earn a reasonable living. This suggested that it still hadn't reconciled local development and conservation with seemingly arbitrary local tourism taxes.

There has been some progress. On a positive note, the government has conducted legitimate conservation-awareness lectures for residents, and initiated a number of infrastructure development projects.[1] In the Mt Everest region, the government has banned all bottled drinks, which are a source of much of the litter in the area. Today, the country is slowly working toward improving its tainted image. However, many still argue that the tourism budget is not used wisely and that more research should be conducted to determine the best investments. A good place to start would be a survey of tourists.

Sources:

1 http://www.south-asia.com/dnpwc/anual_report.html, viewed on January 18, 2001.

http://www.travel-nepal.com/vny98/, viewed on November 20, 2000;
http://www.nepalnews.com.np/contents/englishweekly/spotlight/2000/sep/sep29/coverstory.htm, viewed on November 20, 2000.

Place marketing means designing a place to satisfy the needs of its target markets. It succeeds when citizens and businesses are pleased with their communities, and the expectations of visitors and investors are met.

In this chapter, we examine various investments a place can make to improve livability, investibility and visitability. We see this as a process made up of four components. As we shall demonstrate, these components are not mutually exclusive.

1. The character of a place
   A place needs a sound design and development plan that will enhance its attractiveness and more fully develop its aesthetic qualities and values.
2. The fixed environment of a place
   A place needs to develop and maintain a basic infrastructure that is compatible with the natural environment.
3. The service provision of a place
   A place must provide basic services of sufficient quality to meet business and public needs.
4. The entertainment and recreation aspects of a place
   A place needs a range of attractions for citizens, residents and visitors.

While we cover more generic strategies for place improvement in later chapters, these strategies — design, infrastructure, services and attractions — can be viewed as the building blocks for establishing competitive strategies. Careful attention to these features and factors will create the foundation for setting an effective destination-attraction strategy.

It is usually assumed that these components form part of a place's competitive strategy. For the most part, attention to them is well within the range of a place's collective endeavors. They are preconditions that set the stage for a place's riskier and more opportunistic efforts to compete for economic advantages. They also lie squarely within the scope of legitimate public responsibility and provide real value for existing residents and business enterprises.

URBAN DESIGN

Place buyers often refer to the sense of a place or a place's specific character. Urban design reveals a great deal about the character of a place and redefines how that character is carried forward from one generation to the next. Interweaving a diverse array of physical structures into the overall fabric of a place is an art. Urban design makes a statement about a place because it reflects how values and decision-making combine on issues that affect development.

Historically, places have formed around natural harbors, near river connections, along canals and, later, by railroads that often paralleled water routes. Dirt paths turned to horse-and-wagon routes that later accommodated streetcars and automobiles. Transportation patterns shaped the contours of a place's development. Domestically, they connected commercial, industrial and residential growth. Externally, they created markets for raw materials and finished goods.

Older Asian cities followed a concentric form of expansion, pushing outward from a business hub or government district. From these centers of power, progress followed a nexus of key transportation routes that separated laborers, the middle-class and affluent residents. As manufacturing situated itself along transportation grids, more sectored forms of development appeared in which industrial, commercial and residential areas took on more random patterns. They grew out from the central city to the urban fringe and beyond. Within this patterned development, some cities formed a geometric grid pattern of streets with rectangular blocks, as in Taipei, Shanghai, Hong Kong and Melbourne. Others, like Tokyo, Seoul and New Delhi, followed a wheel-and-spoke pattern, where diagonal roads radiated from the center.[1] A third, more random, pattern combined several design formats, specifically in places of irregular terrain and annexed villages such as Kathmandu.[2]

The relationship between urban design and planning of places in Asia reflects geography, culture and the influence of private and public-sector leaders. Unfortunately, design and planning too often reflect the desire of Asian governments to project their success in transforming backward economies into emerging dragons, rather than an intent to provide the strategic infrastructure necessary to support place development. At other times, design and planning are actually hindered by the desire to protect and perpetuate economic models.

For example, although Kuala Lumpur has an impressive airport, the Multimedia Super Corridor and an impressive array of skyscrapers, its public transportation system serves the city and the airport poorly. None of the massive projects has yet demonstrated its financial benefit for the country. In Hong Kong, large developers have exerted considerable political influence in preventing the development of commuter transportation systems to serve neighboring Guangzhou. If residents were able to move conveniently and quickly in and out of Hong Kong, an exodus to cheaper Guangzhou might result. If an exodus did occur, real-estate prices in Hong Kong would depreciate.

Ironically, in the view of many investors, consumers and employees, that's just what Hong Kong needs. However, there are also examples (Nagoya, Sydney, Kuala Lumpur and Shanghai, for instance) of how strategic market planning has produced urban plans that have emerged from strong and visionary leadership, although the impact of that leadership is not always necessarily sustained (see Exhibit 6.2). Of these cities, Kuala Lumpur and Shanghai especially have seen periods of enlightened growth followed by a period of trouble brought on by political shifts and uncertainty.

Exhibit 6.2: FOUR ASIAN JEWELS

The redevelopment of Nagoya began just 45 days after the end of the Second World War, when the City Assembly voted to develop and implement an extensive Reconstruction Plan. U.S. bombing raids during the war had flattened the city. Half a century later, the city is reaping the benefits of an enlightened redevelopment plan that includes everything needed to create a modern city — from street and subway layouts to space allocated for public parks. Nagoya is a "meticulously planned modern city with wide, often tree-lined, boulevards arranged on a logical grid, a hidden core of timeless and reclusive back streets, and expansive parks and gardens."[1]

One of the most distinctive places in Asia is Sydney, with its stunning urban design and variety of architectural styles. That variety serves as an integral quality of Sydney's unique personality. The city's design flair can be traced back to the early 19th century. Since that time, Sydney has witnessed a multiplicity of urban design and architectural visions. Early on, the city fathers turned to the Greek Revival for inspiration. Victorian and American Revivalism were the themes in the mid and late 19th century. The Sydney Opera House, designed by Danish architect Jørn Utzon, and the Sydney Harbour Bridge, designed by Australian engineer J.J.C. Bradfield, best characterize the 20th century style.

Kuala Lumpur has an urban design that ranks as one of Asia's most atmospheric. It is the youngest capital city in Southeast Asia and plays host to a variety of periods and styles. Within the modest but bustling business center, the city's past is still apparent in the British colonial buildings of the Dataran Merdeka and the midnight lamps of the Petaling Street night market. That past coexists with constant reminders of the city's present and future. Buildings like the soaring Petronas Towers, designed by world-famous architect Cesar Pelli, have an ultramodern look that, while distinctly reflecting Malay culture, wouldn't be out of place in more cosmopolitan cities like Hong Kong or New York. Indeed, these contrasts in urban architecture reflect the multicultural heritage of Kuala Lumpur, a city that attracts the best of global business as well as tourists from all over the world.

Shanghai began as a small port at the entrance of the Yangtze and eventually developed into a great international city by the middle of the 19th century. Like Hong Kong years later, this was in large part the result of the presence and control of Europeans in specific sections of the city. A number of companies and architects from outside China designed and built the most outstanding buildings of the time within the boundaries of the International Settlement and the French Concession. The city became so excessive in its magnificence that it was considered the epitome of extravagance at the height of its development. The entire city was referred to as "the museum of architecture."

In the 1990s, Shanghai began another period of impressive architectural and infrastructure development to compete with Hong Kong and other regional cities for investment and opportunity. Shanghai was determined to regain its preeminence as a "glorious city." Its most famous business avenue, The Bund, is a study in contrasts between East and West, and such landmarks as the Wai Bai Du Bridge — originally called the Garden Bridge when it was built in 1907 — and the Shanghai Mansions — which was an upscale apartment complex in the 1930s and 1940s and is now a three-star hotel — characterize the aesthetic qualities of the place. The Peace Hotel, located in the commercial, cultural and financial center of the city, also reflects a variety of architectural influences and styles — from Eastern and Confucian elements to Western details.

These four places exemplify the rich variety of styles, cultures and moods that make up Asia and its cities. Visionary development has given these cities significant advantages in their ability to attract investment, residents and tourists by bestowing a unique character and allure.

Sources:

1 Jonathan Wall, "Getting to Know Nagoya," *Business Traveller Asia Pacific*, September 2000, pp. 18–23.

The Beaten Track Travel Guide Web site, http://thebeatentrack.com/sydney/architecture.shtml, viewed on January 19, 2001; http://www.wsu.edu:8080/~leep/project.html, viewed on January 19, 2001; *Rough Guide Travel* Web site, http://travel.roughguides.com/content/3401/, viewed on January 19, 2001; Jonathan Wall, "Shanghai's Great Leap Forward," *Business Traveller Asia Pacific*, July 2000, p. 36; Australia's Cultural Network Web site, http://www.acn.net.au/articles/1998/10/soh.htm, viewed on January 19, 2001; http://wwwcharlesbuntjer.com/xchina1a.html, viewed on January 19, 2001; Asia Travel Web site, http://asiatravel.com/china/shanghai/peacenorth, viewed on January 18, 2001; *China Guides* Web site, "Wai Bai Du Bridge," http://www.chinaguides.net/destination/shanghai/attractions/bund/waibaidu/waibaidu.html, viewed on January 18, 2001; Shanghai on the Internet Web site, http://www.sh.com/arch/archb01.htm, viewed on January 18, 2001.

Nagoya, Sydney, Kuala Lumpur and Shanghai represent four master plans conceived and implemented by visionary leaders. Historically, however, most places have never had the benefit of visionary leaders who create an attractive aesthetic and translate it into physical structures. The usual approach is that new transport technologies, economic changes and new consumer behavior slowly, step-by step, move urban design in one direction or another. This has resulted in urban decline, crime, vacant buildings, traffic congestion and loss of attractiveness in many Asian cities. A lack of local leadership and strategic thinking has led to a "more of the same" approach to development. This lack of innovative solutions is illustrated by the universal answer to traffic problems in the 1980s: building more roads.

During the 1990s, a noticeable change occurred in the strategies adopted to market places internationally. Urban planning increasingly incorporated a destination-marketing theme. As we saw earlier, quality of life and environment became more frequently emphasized as attraction factors. Tough competition between Asian places, in conjunction with the economic downturn of the late 1990s, encouraged forward thinking in urban planning. The underlying motivation was the need for places to offer a unique and exciting quality of life and an environment that was anchored in the history and traditions of a place. This conscious combination of the new and the old is illustrated in Exhibit 6.3.

Exhibit 6.3: SUNTEC, CITY OF THE FUTURE

How do we want to live? That's the question an influential group of Hong Kong and Singapore developers considered when they began "thinking for the future" as the first step towards a dramatically new approach to the development of conference centers. They decided the ideal place should include three key characteristics: quality, synergy between old and new, and integration between residential and working facilities. The place that emerged at the forefront of this new model of integrated urban living is Singapore's Suntec City.

This advanced urban design project was marketed as a world-class location for international business and financial markets and as a tourism magnet for the 21st century. It was designed to be internationally engaging and a showpiece for Singapore's economic future as a communications, networking and service economy. The central strategy for the project was to blend business, personal living, and recreation facilities to create "a city within a city" that would meet the challenges of a growing global metropolis. Today, the complex is a 24-hour city, reflecting the special and particular needs of its workers and residents.

The project began in 1988 and was completed in 1991. Suntec is strategically located on 11.7 hectares of land situated at the convergence of Singapore's business, financial, entertainment and tourist districts. According to the chief executive officer of Suntec City Development, Wong Ah Long, the reality of selling the complex to investors and tenants required the development of a different type of relationship with clients. "Our challenge was how to position Suntec, because this is a huge complex. We could not adopt the strategy of just renting like a normal landlord. We knew we had to do some out-of-the-box thinking and come up with something radical and creative to differentiate ourselves from the market."[1] And Wong and his associates did: they created Asia's Vertical Silicon Valley. [2]

Suntec City today is considered a premier information technology site, with over 100 IT companies in residence, including global leaders such as Oracle and Microsoft as well as Singapore's Infocomm Development Authority, the government arm specializing in developing the high-technology lifestyle of its people. In all, there are 700 companies and a working population of 15,000.

Suntec repositioned itself from a traditional landlord to a provider of professional-facilities services. The ultra-modern facilities and strategic location it offered to tenants were only two among many reasons why companies are drawn to the city. Wong said: "We are creating value with our tenants, working together and synergizing with them. Our tenants look at us not as a landlord but as a potential partner."[3] In fact, Suntec City has invested in a call center and an Internet incubator located in the facility, and is looking for more equity for rental deals. Wong is also actively recruiting U.S. start-ups to Suntec on the promise of world-class infrastructure and competitive operating costs.

All this attention is paying other dividends. Besides being a top choice for regional headquarters of IT multinationals and a harbor for local start-ups, Suntec is becoming a major player in Singapore's tourism industry. With the creation and launch of the Singapore Visitors Center within the complex, Suntec is attempting to make the center a one-stop information and resource bureau for travelers. Suntec's conference and exhibition facilities intend to attract visitors from all over the world, who shop in the facility's high-end retail mall. Wong believes that Suntec can "expect an increase in the number of visitors here, which will, in turn, emphasize Suntec as a key stop in Singapore for international visitors."[4]

That may very well happen. But the lesson to be drawn from Suntec City's development is the value of out-of-the-box thinking when it comes to marketing places.

Sources:

1 Kalpana Rashiwala, "All Aglow With Hi-Tech Buzz," *The Business Times*, May 11, 2000, p. 30.
2 *Ibid.*
3 *Ibid.*
4 *ibid.*
Sharon Hun, "Suntec City to be developed into Silicon Valley," *Channelnewsasia*, September 1, 2000, viewed on November 17, 2000 at http://www.channelnewsasia.com.sg/techbytes/techbytes_010900.htm.

Urban design is an important issue, not only in the big cities of Asia but also in small towns that are witnessing a renewed interest in small-scale urban design. The more clearly defined underlying force here is a move back to old values and attractions, nurturing and presenting them as a contrast to the problems of larger markets.

The city of Malacca is marketing itself as "the historic city of Malaysia."[3] Its rich past under the Portuguese, Dutch, British and Japanese has contributed significantly to the city's culture and architecture, which are among its main selling points. The Lycos travel guides say: "No other city in Malaysia is steeped in as old and as interesting a history as the city of Malacca."[4] There is good reason for such praise. The city's buildings are reflective of Portuguese architecture, while the streets show the Chinese influence. Other landmarks built during the Dutch occupation are still well preserved. Today, Malacca markets itself as a city with some of the best-preserved architecture in the country and the region.

A growing number of provinces, like Lampang in Thailand, are marketing their architecture with great confidence. Lanna, a distinctly Thai architectural style, is still very much evident in the province, with many buildings, bridges and homes constructed of wood, brick and stone in this unique tradition. Many of the province's temples are reflective of

Burmese architecture, while its use of horse-drawn carts as a mode of transportation provides another attraction. A similar example of small-town architectural character defining a place can be seen in the town of Luang Prabang in Laos, which represents a blend of Lao and French styles in well-conserved architecture and structures. In 1995, UNESCO declared it a World Heritage City.

Another growing Asian trend in urban design is the building of "greenfield" sites in the countryside. This is in contrast to inner city urban "brownfield" projects. Small communities within a convenient commuting distance of a big city tend to use various greenfield approaches. Examples can be seen in areas around northern Malaysia[5] and Indonesia.[6] Areas serving Hong Kong and southern China enterprise zones are likely to develop in a similar fashion, at least if the property barons eventually give way to reality.

The common thread in these cases is the effort to use urban design to enhance destination positioning. Current approaches to urban design emphasize what is environmentally compatible with physical, local, regional and national features, along with ways to resurrect the older character and history of places. Such thinking requires vision, a blending of the old with the new, and an appreciation that the character of a place is a valuable asset in retaining investors, residents and visitors.

INFRASTRUCTURE IMPROVEMENT

Where urban design gives character to a place, infrastructure makes the design possible. What message would Shanghai's spacious Bund boulevard provide if it were riddled with potholes? What would Japan be without its convenient railways? How could Manila compete internationally for back-office services without access to broadband technology? Countless examples illustrate the basic fact that much of a place's advantage stems from the infrastructure that either supports or undermines its attractions.

While excellent and well-maintained infrastructure cannot guarantee a community's growth, its absence is a serious liability. To sustain quality of life and to support economic productivity, a place requires that infrastructure be developed and maintained. China and other countries in East Asia that aspire to become market economies but are hampered by vastly under-developed infrastructure exemplify this challenge. Inadequate infrastructure inhibits the movement of people, goods and information and, therefore, economic development. This previous under-investment now requires governments, businesses, the World Bank and the Asian Development Bank to invest heavily to facilitate future growth. Far too often, residents take infrastructure for granted on the principle that out of sight is out of mind. What one generation put in place with great difficulty may be lost to the following generation that assumes that the water and sewer systems, bridges and tunnels, roads and waterways never need replacement. For older, more developed places, their in-place infrastructure can confer unique advantages in competition with new places that have to build entirely new systems from scratch just to accommodate growth. However, as many older places have allowed their infrastructures to deteriorate, they face the ever-growing liability of replacing and renewing their capital stock.

Every community must provide some basic standard of services to attract and retain people, businesses and visitors. Admittedly, no uniform standards exist except where set by law and health-and-safety regulations. The issue of who pays, who administers and who delivers services is blurred by complex systems of national governments, regional public organizations and communities. All places are subject to varying degrees of responsibility for transportation, roads, water and energy supply, and for meeting environmental standards.

Throughout Asia, places have gradually awakened to their infrastructure problems. It has been said that the 1990s was a decade of renewed Asian interest in infrastructure. This climate was influenced by four trends:

- Higher unemployment rates — in Japan's case, a prolonged recession — pushed politicians to improve competitiveness. Infrastructure projects became one answer in the battle to improve Asian competitiveness.

- Traffic congestion reached unacceptable levels throughout Asian cities. The Asian Development Bank concedes that traffic jams are among the biggest problems that large cities in Asia face. In Manila, for example, the urban poor spend, on average, over two hours commuting to work each day.[7]

- Increased competition from within and outside the region for Foreign Direct Investment (FDI) and new job creation forced a change in attitude in governments and enterprises. In the past, FDI was accepted; now, it is recruited, even seduced.

- A more critical environmental debate acts as a catalyst for a number of infrastructure projects.

Needs Assessment

All places require a needs assessment of their capital facilities by age, condition and scheduled repairs, as well as related five- to 20-year plans for rehabilitation and replacement. Years ago, city engineers and architects possessed a fairly good inventory of the relative condition, costs and schedules for maintenance of a place's infrastructure. In many cases that institutional knowledge and capacity has been lost because of shifting public and political responsibilities, the growth of separate authorities and systematic neglect. In other cases, places have been so committed to growth or development that they have underestimated or simply failed to anticipate the related infrastructure requirements and costs that accompany growth.

Many places in Asia have to work hard to reverse the rate of decline in their infrastructure. South Korea, for example, reduced spending to prevent inflation caused by the construction of major infrastructure projects. The reduction contributed to declining standards during the 1980s. To address this problem, the South Korean government encouraged the use of private capital to fund infrastructure projects beginning in 1997. Its "Five Year Plan called for investments of 50 to 60 trillion *won* through the year 2001,"[8] and it was hoped that the private financing of infrastructure would increase from 10% of total investment to 40% during that period.[9] Today, Korea often promotes its infrastructure standards in its destination marketing. Thailand, Malaysia and the Philippines have also introduced similar programs with varying success.

Unfortunately, during the miracle decades, many Asian countries systematically neglected their infrastructure. Now, the new trade patterns of Asia (China, Japan, South Korea, Singapore, Malaysia, Philippines, Hong Kong, Taiwan, Thailand and India) suggest that as much as US$515.4 billion is required annually for basic infrastructure investments in the early years of the 21st century.[10] Bangladesh is an example of how Asian governments, once they have acknowledged the role of infrastructure in national competitiveness, are addressing infrastructure inadequacy. Like South Korea, Bangladesh's government is opening infrastructure and other traditional services to the private sector and foreign investors, establishing the Infrastructure Investment Facilitation Centre in 1997 to stimulate investment by the private sector.[11] However, although the infrastructure component of the country's annual Development Program budget has been steadily increased — from 27% in 1990 to 35% in 1995 and 37% in 1997 — there is still a severe shortage of infrastructure.[12] Still, Bangladesh and other Asian countries with similar circumstances frequently and effectively market themselves on the basis of new and projected infrastructure projects.

While the exact costs of deterioration and neglect — as well as poor planning — can only be estimated, various studies have documented losses to governments, businesses and people that stem from under-investment or misplaced investment in infrastructure. Poor road conditions add considerably to the cost of operating motor vehicles. Bad communication links between South and Southeast Asia slow growth. The lack of efficient rail connections from the natural resources of the Mekong region in Indochina creates a serious bottleneck for that part of Asia and thus for investors. Deficient water and sewage facilities impede residential development and detract from business investment. Traffic congestion in the big Asian cities increases commuting time and consequent loss of productivity. Lack of energy availability and unreliability of services constitute a greater competitive disadvantage in the information age than high-energy costs. When housing stock is allowed to deteriorate beyond a certain point, replacement costs greatly exceed the expenses of rehabilitation. Today the lack of housing maintenance in Tokyo and Hong Kong generates enormous residential costs. Places learn the hard way that maintenance, repair and rehabilitation pay for themselves.

Infrastructure Management

A good assessment of infrastructure needs, periodically updated and systematically tracked, is essential for performance management — a new approach to infrastructure required by resource and environmental constraints. The mobility of jobs and people from cities to suburbs and beyond has created its own paradoxes. Cities have built costly new infrastructures on the expanding urban fringe while abandoning the already built, fixed urban environment in central cities and places. Simply building more and better roads to accommodate an expanding demand for road transportation often increases traffic congestion. The old idea of adding greater capacity to roads to handle more vehicles has gradually given way to the notion of moving more people with less fuel to generate less air pollution and less traffic congestion. A few Asian communities argue that they have elaborate air-pollution programs. Others claim to be eco-communities.

Increasingly, needs assessment and the management of infrastructure are linked by a new emphasis on performance, not simply construction. Places cannot replace everything. Formerly, capital budgeting and planning took on the character of wish lists; that is, everything a place would like to build, rehabilitate or replace if unlimited resources become available. However, resource constraints have compelled places and infrastructure authorities to think through various options that improve system-wide performance, provide the greatest return on investment and balance multiple needs. In spite of the many new infrastructure projects currently under way, in the aftermath of the 1997 financial crisis the majority of Asian local leaders would agree with Bruce McDowell of the U.S. Advisory Commission of Intergovernmental Relations. McDowell believes that "The future is more likely to focus on maintaining and getting the most out of existing facilities, keeping costs down, making public facilities fit more comfortably into the natural environment, and being more ingenious in meeting needs in the most efficient ways that science can devise."[13] Logically, the concept of "smart cities" or "smart regions" has become more common.

Each stage of the infrastructure-management process introduces new opportunities for doing things differently. Design now involves better materials, technologies and techniques. Construction is enhanced through improved materials and quality control. Operations and maintenance draw on new material, techniques, scheduling methods and management tools. Monitoring incorporates newer needs-assessment methods, better management systems and improved ways of estimating demand. In this integrated and multi-stage process, planning and programming use better forecasting, budgeting and project-development techniques.

Inter-governmental Planning

In the best traditions of architecture and engineering, everything is connected to everything else when it comes to infrastructure planning. Whether for historical reasons or owing to financial requirements, infrastructure systems and responsibilities are dispersed across separate public and sometimes private institutions and firms and are vertically regulated, funded or operated at several public levels.

In the past, when each community was responsible for its own city or village dump, places did not have to think about cooperating on non-polluting landfills, building expensive solid-waste incinerators, disposing of hazardous waste materials or developing waste-reduction recycling programs. They do now. Not cooperating horizontally and vertically puts communities in great peril.

Environmental, transportation and energy conservation programs were once governed by separate public policies. Gradually these programs are becoming linked in novel ways that, increasingly, affect everything that places do in the name of place development, including housing, zoning, land use, public health and education. Consequently, places may find themselves suffering from system overload — contrary and contradictory regulations imposed by higher government levels that can result in operating paralysis. Regulators and consumers now require utilities to scale back new construction and embrace conservation. NIMBYs (not-in-my-backyarders) and environmental groups have stymied the development of new landfills and the expansion of existing ones. Anti-noise groups and environmentalists have organized to block new airport construction and the expansion of existing facilities. These factors have contributed to urban sprawl by forcing the outward push of development. As both populations and economic activity disperse throughout and beyond metropolitan areas, public transport systems experience declining patronage and taxpayer resistance to subsidizing public transport in favor of private cars and more roads.

Forward thinking and planning across systems requires places to learn from one another through new technologies, innovations and experiments. For example, the *Shinkansen* trains in Japan started the Asian infrastructure program in high-speed trains. Three decades later, high-speed trains are part of the normal planning all over Japan. Other countries such as Taiwan, South Korea and China are also slowly adopting this technology. The Asian learning and adoption process could go more quickly.

As Asia becomes more interdependent, vast opportunities exist for infrastructure strategies that cross geo-political boundaries and involve inter-governmental cooperation.

The Environmental Imperative

To "think environmentally" is not simply a good maxim but an operating imperative of many places. Seoul's Ozone Alert System has inspired many national and regional decision-makers in Asia. The system's long-term effect in Asia cannot be overestimated. But that also goes for the annual Spring haze resulting from fires set in Indonesia's lush forests by slash-and-burn farmers. The haze has seriously imperiled environmental conditions in neighboring countries, especially Malaysia and Singapore.

Many cities in Asia are adopting ambitious systems for recycling and composting waste. New energy-efficient technologies are under way, combining heat-and-power systems and heat pumps. Education and poverty-alleviation programs are meant to address instances such as that in Indonesia where desperation results in activities that contribute to vast environmental degradation across large areas of Asia.

But the obstacles are enormous. In New Delhi, where existing infrastructure can no longer bear the heavy traffic loads, congested roadways are the cause of 70% of the environmental pollution.[14] According to the *China Environment Reporter*, "Some experts liken China's current motor vehicular pollution level to that of the United States in the 1970s. Antiquated coal-fired generation plants are another serious threat to southern coastal China and Hong Kong. Without projections for increased efficiency or improvements in technology, China's total emissions of nitrogen oxide and carbon monoxide were expected to reach 1.19 million and 14.12 million tons, respectively, in 2000, and 2.28 million and 24.76 million tons by 2010."[15] In spite of current know-how and acknowledgment by local and national governments of the seriousness of these issues, little is done in practice. One has to conclude that there are weaknesses in the strategic-planning process in China and much of the rest of Asia. To "think environmentally" is one thing; to "act environmentally" is, apparently, something else.

Most large cities and their immediate suburbs suffer from major traffic congestion. Transportation choices and travel times affect people's decisions on where to live in relation to work and schools, where they shop and dine, and where vacationers visit and stay. Millions of hours a year are lost as commuters find travel times — suburb-to-city or suburb-to-suburb — increasing because of congested roads. Obviously, this growing problem undermines productivity and quality of life.

Different places employ different solutions to ease the problem. One option is to use new information technology. For example, the so-called Intelligent Vehicle Highway Systems (IVHS) — radar, sensors, smart cars and a satellite-linked electronic navigation system — offer prospects for moving urban traffic more efficiently and safely. Certain places in South Korea and Japan are already using such traffic projects in their destination marketing. However, while new technologies may improve the flow of people and goods, they alone are unlikely to solve the people-moving problem.

A second line of defense that many places employ is to discourage the use of private vehicles by limiting parking options and increasing the costs of use. Places may raise fees for vehicle registration and licenses, increase parking-meter fees and fines, and stiffen penalties for traffic offenses. The war on the automobile extends to special permits for neighborhood residents and various restrictions on downtown parking. Asia uses gasoline taxes, although these are mostly lower than in Europe,[16] except in the case of Japan. Japan's gasoline taxes (48%) are higher than those in the U.S. (33.1%) and of many European countries, although not those of France (81.1%).[17] Generally, the cost of gasoline in Asia is considerably higher than in the United States. In Hong Kong, for example, (in March 2000) unleaded gasoline cost US$5.40 per gallon, compared to $1.50 per gallon in the United States.[18]

Car-pooling has been encouraged in cities such as Jakarta, Seoul[19] and Melbourne[20] through allotting special lanes or implementing a congestion charge for vehicles carrying only one passenger. Manila and Mumbai admit private cars into the city based on the number of their license plates, thus reducing traffic by 20% each day. In Singapore, which limits automobile ownership by auctioning off a limited number of Certificates of Entitlement that effectively double the cost of automobile acquisition, motorists must also pay a fee to enter the city center as a key component of an Area Licensing Scheme.[21]

Such environmental initiatives are frequently emerging in destination-marketing competitions. They were seen in the vigorous competition to host the Olympic Games in 2000,[22] as well as in China's winning bid for the 2008 games. The competing candidates for the games frequently used ecological progress as an argument for their selection over other competitors.

A third option is to improve collective transport systems. During the 1990s, Asia witnessed a revival of transport systems in city centers. Historical cities have damaged their "sense of the place" because of unrestrained automobile expansion. In an era where unique and attractive cities are favored more than ever, the pressure for collective transport systems is growing. New light-rail-transit systems in Bangkok and Manila are the direct result of their reputations as gridlocked cities. Unfortunately, these projects were at least a decade late in their implementation, delayed by lack of funding, bureaucratic infighting and chronic political instability. Inconvenient and inhospitable transportation grids reduced the attractiveness of these emerging economies as destinations for foreign direct investment.

Where governments are unable to meet infrastructure demand, initiatives by non-government organizations and private individuals are occurring around Asia. While parts of Japan, China, Thailand and South Korea, for example, celebrate an annual "car-free day," the concept is still not universally valued. With rapid development taking place in Asia, the notion of "car-free cities" seems unattainable at this stage. However, many places have decided to improve cycling routes and public transportation, clean up vehicle emissions and implement other measures. The idea driving these initiatives is one of "sustainable mobility."

When places seek to reduce automobile use in their inner cities, a corresponding pressure builds for them to improve their mass-transit systems. Metro areas experiencing no growth or even modest growth in population, however, face passenger losses with little adjustment in the supply of transit services. To operate effectively, mass-transit systems require certain population densities and demand levels. They are undermined by continuing population sprawl, which makes transit service less efficient to provide. Still, public demand for inter-suburb van service has increased, with the result that both public and private providers now offer this service.

A fourth option is to enforce auto-emission standards to discourage the purchase of larger cars. The Asian car industry is slowly trying to adopt such standards. Recently, the Crayon EV Commuter System was introduced by Toyota Motor Corporation in Tokyo. This diminutive vehicle, which uses electronic combustion ("e-com"), could well represent a new approach to the environmental challenges in Asian inner cities.[23] Other environment-friendly products include Toyota's Prius, which has been certified as a Super Ultra-Low Emission Vehicle (SULEV)[24] and Thailand's hybrid motorcycle prototype I or HMP-I, which switches from combustion power to electric power while stuck in heavy traffic.[25]

Synchronizing Place Development Needs with Infrastructure Development

Infrastructure development must meet multiple needs, but none is more important than adjusting to overall place-development priorities. Infrastructure is too important to be left simply to engineers, architects and the narrow confines of single-purpose infrastructure authorities (such as a toll-way authority). Various constituencies must be tapped so that public works are synchronized with broader place-development goals.

A new example of how planners are rethinking the interconnections of infrastructure systems, environmental imperatives and multipurpose inner-city design is found in Kobe, Japan. On January 17, 1995, the city of Kobe experienced an earthquake that registered 7.2 on the Richter scale. It was one of the most devastating and powerful earthquakes in Japan's history. Toshitama Kaihara, the governor of Hyogo Prefecture (which includes the city of Kobe), launched a US$170-billion rebuilding project called the Hyogo Phoenix Plan.[26] This plan included such mega-projects as a "New Eastern City" with international research institutes and 10,000 units of modern housing. Also envisioned in the plan was the expansion of port facilities, the construction of an airport on a man-made island five kilometers offshore, and the development of an enterprise zone that will offer preferential taxes for foreign and domestic high-tech industry players.

Governor Kaihara described the Phoenix Plan as one designed "not only to restore the region to its pre-quake condition but also to solve underlying problems faced by Japan, such as an increasingly aging population, the need for an open economy, and the concentration of problems associated with increased urbanization around the world."[27]

In many cases, infrastructure investments, whether in getting more out of existing facilities or in making new investments that meet multiple needs and priorities, may be the most critical decision that places make to improve their competitive position. Strategic market planning must deal intelligently and creatively with the choice of infrastructure proposals.

BASIC SERVICES: PROTECTION OF PEOPLE AND PROPERTY, SOCIAL SECURITY, AND EDUCATION

Successful places not only demand good design and infrastructure, they also require efficient public services. Poor public services, especially education and police protection, can create substantial positioning problems. High-quality public services, on the other hand, can be marketed as one of a place's primary attractions.

Consider the following questions for your place: Do tourists or visitors worry about their personal safety when coming to your community? How far from work must employees and executives live to obtain either the public services or the environment they desire? Are you pleased with sending your children to the local schools?

The ability of a place to attract and retain business activity is vastly diminished when its reputation for high crime or poor schools is foremost in people's minds. In the past, business often gravitated to places that had low taxes but few services. Now, with offshore locations providing such advantages, business is drawn to places that offer high-quality services that contribute to improved productivity and quality. Visitors increasingly factor security and safety considerations into their travel decisions. Parents' decisions on where to live and work often turn on the location of the best educational opportunities for their children. The U.S. practice of ranking the best schools and colleges has also been introduced in Asia.

All places should be concerned about their core public services: protection of people and property, basic social security and education. In Asia, these basic, visible, and high-citizen-contact services are often financed, administered and controlled locally. The overall decentralization in Asia has put more of these responsibilities into the hands of local communities. Local place marketers have the power to intervene and make the core public services more attractive.

Yet all places face resource constraints. Resources are affected by a place's fiscal capacity, tax limits and public willingness to spend. The relationship between spending and outcomes, and how outcome is measured, attracts a great deal of public debate. The quality of a place's public services depends on the level of resources and the degree to which they are used efficiently. Even with limited resources, places will realize some gains by using a different mix or allocation of resources.

Programs for Improving Security

The task of protecting people and property can be a formidable undertaking for a place. Bangkok, once known as one of Asia's least-violent cities, is at risk of becoming the "international crime capital of Asia." Thailand's hospitality and easygoing tolerance is certainly attractive to tourists but it has also proved attractive to less-savory clients. Gangsters from India, Pakistan, Macau, Korea, Nigeria, Russia and Europe descend upon the city to settle scores and evade law-enforcers by posing as investors and business people. Crime has reached an alarming level and has caused concern among local citizens as well as the National Security Council. Both are now working to save the city's declining reputation. Possible solutions to the problem include tightening up the country's tourist-friendly visa policy and improving coordination between local and foreign security agencies.[28]

In this sort of climate, places often put a higher priority on security than on other public-sector services. But new solutions are needed. Moving from a bureaucratic, top-down approach to one which encourages greater involvement from local citizens can deter certain types of criminal activity and behavior. This change can have a positive impact on how the public perceives police services.

Programs for Improving Education

Place sellers in Asia are competing today with claims of access to a highly qualified workforce. The accuracy of such claims, however, depends on how much the place invests in its educational system. Before investors make a location decision, they must be convinced that a suitable workforce really exists.

According to a report in the *Harvard Asia Quarterly* on foreign investment in China, the higher productivity and efficiency of labor in the coastal areas as compared to central and western areas is linked to the higher level of education of the workforce.[29] This is among the principal reasons foreign investors are attracted to the coastal areas of China. While the central and western areas may appear more attractive because of lower labor costs, the report notes that low labor costs in themselves do not ensure the productivity and efficiency of the laborers.

A place's response to educational needs requires three approaches: 1) local support of the educational sector; 2) action plans for improvement; and 3) integrated approaches to education.

Local support of the educational sector goes far beyond how parents and others rate the quality of their schools. The relevant issue here is the extent to which parents, public leaders, local and regional businesses and other organized interests are openly and actively involved in a place's education system. The trend towards decentralization in Asia is pushing responsibilities down to individual school districts and schools themselves. As a result, enlightened local groups may seize the opportunity to develop a unique school offering. For example, with the support of the South Australian government and local universities, Adelaide markets itself internationally as "the perfect education package." "Adelaide is a peaceful city in which to study, a safe place in which to live, and home to people from more than 100 different countries who live prosperously and peacefully. The safety, happiness and well-being of all international students are of paramount concern to Adelaide's universities, colleges and schools, and staff at each institution are dedicated to providing the best quality student support services available in Australia."[30]

Action plans for improving local educational systems are more common today now that the issue of education is increasingly linked to the attractiveness of a place. This new focus coincided with the rise of unemployment in Asia following the late 1990s financial crisis, and with the growing awareness of the role of education in nurturing Internet and IT enterprises. The public response, irrespective of party politics, was to present action plans, often with a local and regional profile, which aimed at improving the education system. Early in the 21st century, with even higher unemployment figures in developing and developed countries alike, and significant restructuring still in store for many of Asia's advanced economies, such action plans are emerging everywhere.

Integrated approaches to education link community colleges, local and regional businesses, research parks and state universities. The motive, again, is to foster local economic improvement in some type of cluster. In many places, science parks inspire the integration approach. In Asia, there are over 200 science parks, and these concentrations of qualified personnel, often with a specific knowledge-image, serve to fuel this bridge-building process. Japan, the pioneer of science parks in the continent, continues to lead with 111 science parks.[31] The integration of science parks has been compared to the medieval pattern, when each industry was concentrated in a single street of a town: clothes-makers, leather-workers, goldsmiths, and so on. The benefit of this concentration is that many different local partners can support specific education and training.

ATTRACTIONS

There is a difference between saying that a certain place works and saying that it is attractive. We use the term "attractions" to cover physical features and events that appeal to citizens, new residents, visitors, businesses and investors.

Places can be graded according to whether they have no attractions, a single attraction, a few attractions or many attractions. Many cities and communities fall into the first category: they lack any self-evident attractions that might draw new residents, visitors or businesses. Moving through Asia on the main motorways and air routes, you find city after city of "look-alikes." The residents may love their city, but to the traveler there is nothing noteworthy or unique. As these cities evolve, they increasingly resemble each other in featuring many of the same fast-food outlets, hotel chains and national merchandisers. They take on a quality of "placelessness," and may give the first-time visitor a sense of having been there before. The place has no sense of being different and special.

Even though a small city or community may lack attractions, it is possible to begin a value-adding process. Our experience tells us that the process can be even easier in smaller cities because of the closer contacts that exist between local interest groups. This implies that a place with few or no attractions can usually develop a new attraction. Throughout the countryside of Malaysia, the Philippines and Thailand, there are frequent signs announcing a special place attraction. Even the smallest place can make itself visible (see Figure 6.1).

Some cities and communities feature a few attractions, enough to entice travelers from reasonable distances, but not enough to hold them more than a day or two. Many of these places try to add new attractions to create a more competitive value package. For instance, in April 2000, Beijing began construction of its US$420-million National Theater, which will be the "city's biggest undertaking since Mao Zedong's mausoleum was built in 1977."[32] The theater is badly needed to compete with other cities in drawing international performers. In the current marketplace, venues such as Shanghai's Grand Theater dominate the

Figure 6.1: Making the most of a reputation or attraction

Driving through Calamba, Laguna, hometown of Philippine national hero Jose Rizal, visitors are greeted by signs welcoming them to this historic place.

artistic landscape.[33] There are many cases of similar recovery initiatives in modern-day Asia. The risks are high, but local and regional decision-makers are nevertheless prepared to invest in visionary attraction-building initiatives.

A number of Asian places possess a great number of attractions: Kuala Lumpur, Tokyo, Singapore, Sydney and Hong Kong. These places need not invent new attractions to add to their appeal. Their basic problem is maintaining the infrastructure and services to support the huge numbers of tourists and business visitors who continuously descend on them to enjoy their treasures. However, in practice, these large world-class cities continue to develop new attractions.

There are many places that need to create more attractions. A place cannot alter its climate, natural terrain or geographical position, but it can add new attractions to become more competitive. We shall comment here on 10 major types of attractions that places can consider:

1. Natural beauty and features
2. History and famous people
3. Shopping places

4. Cultural attractions
5. Recreation and entertainment
6. Sports arenas
7. Festivals and occasions
8. Buildings, monuments and sculptures
9. Museums
10. Other attractions.

Natural Beauty and Features

In the minds of most people, natural beauty consists of mountains, valleys, lakes, oceans and forests. A place with a spectacular sight or natural wonder, such as the Himalayas of Nepal, the Great Barrier Reef in Australia or Borneo's rainforests, has a competitive edge. Places resting on picturesque terrain and enjoying splendid vistas can capitalize on these features if they conscientiously protect and promote them.

Older Asian places have opportunities to make their cities more environmentally, physically and aesthetically attractive. Long-term urban redesign that focuses on aesthetic values can enhance natural attractions.

History and Famous People

Many places in Asia identify and promote themselves through their connection with an historic event or famous person. Lumbini, situated at the foothills of the Himalayas in Nepal, markets itself as the birthplace of the Gautama Buddha and as one of the four holy places of Buddhism.[34] With a target market ranging from 150 million to 300 million[35] believers worldwide, the region has recognized the great potential of this market.

Places that were the scene of historic events or retain the flavor of the past can perform well in the destination marketplace. Exhibit 6.4 provides an example of how this can be done.

Exhibit 6.4: "NO MORE HIROSHIMAS!"

The history of Asia — and the world — was altered tragically and, in many ways, permanently at Hiroshima as the Second World War came to an end. This city, located in Hiroshima Prefecture on Japan's main island, Honshu, is synonymous with the first-ever atomic bombing. The U.S. Airforce B-29 bomber Enola Gay dropped the bomb on the city on August 6,

1945. Three days later, a second atomic bomb was dropped on the city of Nagasaki, leading to the Japanese surrender on September 2, 1945. Despite the horrible suffering that resulted from this catastrophic event, the historic bombing has enabled Hiroshima to package its historical past to attract tourists from all over the world.

In leveraging its unfortunate history to capitalize on other tourist sites, Hiroshima is opportunistic. Every year, the catastrophic bombing is vividly commemorated for visitors on August 6, Hiroshima Day. The city uses a variety of communication channels, including the Internet, to promote its place in history and to invite potential visitors to a historically significant location. A great deal of tourist information — festival and event schedules, recommended tours, tourist facilities, weather information, sightseeing transportation and contact information — is offered on the Hiroshima Tourism Home Page on the Internet. Here's a typical tour:

ITINERARY OF THE MORI MOTINARI TOUR (using public transportation)
- Departure from any location
- Hiroshima Castle for one hour
- Departure from Hiroshima Castle
- Hiroshima City tour — A-bomb dome, Fudoin Temple, Art Museum, river cruise
- Travel by JR Train express liner (40 minutes)
- Miyajima — Itsukushima Shrine, Miyao Castle remains

This popular, one-day tour is much more than a visit to the A-bomb dome. It is full of majestic castles, historic sites and an array of shrines and temples. Hiroshima has become a complete and fully satisfying tourist destination, despite its tragic past.

Becoming prominent in the pop music industry has also enhanced Hiroshima's image. Hiroshima's name came to the forefront of public awareness with the release of Yoko Ono's song (recorded with Paul McCartney) "Hiroshima Sky is Always Blue" in Ron Destro's play, *Hiroshima*. The play and the song remind people of Hiroshima's historic background and the devastation experienced by so many Japanese families.

Hiroshima's singular public focus on the past has delivered a steady stream of visitors and has even attracted new residents to completely unrelated city features. With energy and focus, many places have historical attractions that could be similarly leveraged. What distinguishes Hiroshima is its recognition of the marketing value of one of history's most catastrophic events.

Sources:

Hiroshima Prefecture Web site, http://www.kankou.pref.hiroshima.jp/english/ profile.htm; Hiroshima Tourism Web site, http://www.tourism.city.hiroshima.jp/english/level2/h.html.

Qufu, in China's Shandong Province, is a place trying to enhance its value via its connection with a great philosopher and educator, Confucius. Since Qufu is competing with so many other more famous tourist destinations in China, it is important that it makes full use of the historical and cultural value of the birthplace of Confucius (see Figure 6.2). The province celebrates the Qufu International Confucius Culture Festival annually, with a memorial ceremony and re-creations of ancient music and dance. The famous philosopher's tomb, family mansion, temple and birthplace are opened to tourists. The World Heritage Committee has placed these sites on the World Heritage List.[36] The enterprising province also capitalizes on its history by promoting the famous Shandong cuisine and allowing tourists to attend local wedding ceremonies.[37]

While many places exploit their local personality and historical assets, others miss significant marketing opportunities. For most Japanese, Gunma Prefecture is simply countryside. But Gunma has produced three of Japan's best-known post-war prime ministers: Takeo Fukuda, Yasuhiro Nakasone and Keizo Obuchi. The area was the birthplace of one of Japan's most well-known poets, Sakutaro Hagiwara, and was also home to some of Japan's earliest inhabitants. Gunma's principal cities, Takasaki and Maebashi, should do more to capitalize on the prefecture's proclivity for producing major public figures and promote themselves as major centers of historical and contemporary significance. They could think about developing museums chronicling the lives and administrations of these leaders, documentaries for distribution to schools and other corporate communications initiatives that would create an image of Gunma as an important historical, cultural and political center.

Figure 6.2: Statue of Confucius in his family cemetery in Qufu

Source: ChinaStock

About 600 miles southeast of Shanghai lies Shaoshan, a place that markets itself as the birthplace of "a man who changed history", Chairman Mao Zedong. Not surprisingly, the city has built a 30-foot statue of Mao close to his ancestral farmhouse, which attracts over a million people during the annual commemoration of the Chinese revolution. The Museum of Comrade Mao, also in Shaoshan, was built to commemorate the triumphs of the legendary leader (see Figure 6.3).[58]

Another world-famous person is marketed by the small city of Rajkot in Gujarat, India. Mahatma Gandhi's ancestral home is found there and memories of his time are kept as if they were crown jewels. Today, people from all over the world, including presidents, authors and entertainers, go to Rajkot to share a glimpse of Gandhi's life.

Figure 6.3: The Shaoshan birthplace of Mao Zedong

Source: ChinaStock

Shopping Places

Every community has one or more shopping areas where people buy their food, clothing, appliances, furnishings and hundreds of other objects. Streets like Nathan Road in Kowloon, Hong Kong; Huaihai Lu in Shanghai; and Orchard Road in Singapore are famous examples of shopping places with global appeal. However, on a micro level most cities have natural marketplaces that can be improved in various ways.

Today, many street-oriented shopping areas, whether main street or neighborhood retailers, are fighting for survival against the growing appeal of regional and local shopping centers. Large shopping centers contain major department stores, dozens of franchised stores, medical and health services (including plastic surgery) and often movie theatres and other entertainment. They offer easy parking, concentrated and easily accessible stores, and, when enclosed, air-conditioning and protection against bad weather. Yet even these centers now suffer in many cases from overbuilding and intense competition, which leads to various adaptive reuses of once-prosperous malls.

In such a hotly competitive environment, comprehensive downtown development projects have been one answer to the decline. Collective traffic is improved, residential houses and condominiums are built in the inner cities, sidewalks are improved and trees are planted. Many larger street-oriented shopping areas have created a new attractiveness by opening the area for pedestrians only. Shanghai's famous walking street, Nanjing East Road, attracts visitors in search of something special.

Active communities throughout Asia are trying to improve the attractiveness of their natural marketplaces. Redesign programs are common, as places try to catch-up after decades of public neglect. Ho Chi Minh City is a prime example of what can be done. A building blitz in the inner city ignited the implementation of key economic reforms in 1986. These included the policy of *Doi Moi*, or "Restoration" (sometimes translated as "Renovation" or "New Life"), the legislation of a modern Law on Foreign Investment in 1987, and the lifting of the U.S. trade embargo in 1994.[39]

Collectively, these advances helped spur an increase of foreign investment in the tourism sector, which sparked a building boom through the development of new shopping areas and hotels. To further enhance its attractiveness, the Ho Chi Minh City marketplace aggressively promotes festivals and events, and organizes special outdoor markets year round. The strategy is to encourage citizens to move into the downtown area, and attractive city apartment buildings are being built to convert the new urban dwellers to permanent residents. Such multipurpose marketplaces are also being created in many smaller communities throughout Asia, as cities and towns revert to an age-old strategy — recreating the town center as the focus of commerce, entertainment and political life.

Cultural Attractions

Many communities are now sponsoring cultural programs in order to add new value to their place. Decentralization has accelerated the interest in local community culture.

In Asia, where culture is diverse, many places vie for the title of "cultural capital." In China, for example, competition between Beijing and Shanghai remains stiff. Because of its impressive infrastructure, Shanghai is more popular among world-class artists and performers. In the last two years, the city has opened a world-class art gallery, a museum and one of the largest libraries in the world. A science theater is also set to open in 2001. Beijing, however, remains more popular among younger, striving artists, as the city is more open to new styles and ideas than Shanghai.[40] Hong Kong and Singapore compete with both cities, and the rest of the region.

In Australia, Sydney is the cultural capital and home to many of Australia's leading arts and cultural organizations. Other, smaller, places such as Sarawak in Borneo and Tongyong in Korea also market their cultural heritage and facilities.

Cultural programs, however, are not important to all groups. The Organization for Economic Co-operation and Development (OECD) asked high-tech industries what factors are important in their place-buying decisions.[41] The cultural factor ranked number 10 on the list. Higher rankings were given to hard factors such as access to a qualified workforce, tax levels, cost of living, and so on. However, as we've seen in Asian place competition, when it comes to convincing expatriates to work in these communities, cultural attractions play a major role in determining the attractiveness of a place. If there is one factor that stands out as a magnet for attracting talent, it is the importance of an arts/culture presence.

Recreation and Entertainment

Every place needs to provide its citizens with areas for recreation and amusement — local restaurants, bars, cafés, clubs, discos, parks, community centers, performing arts companies, zoos and sports arenas. Now, however, more complex attractions and combinations are being developed.

One example of this can be seen in the emergence of theme parks. There are some giant examples: Disneyland in Tokyo; the Warner Brothers Movie World on Australia's Gold Coast; the Sunway Lagoon Park (housing the biggest artificial wave in the world) in Selangor; Everland (named the eighth-most attended amusement park in the world) in Korea; and Fantasy Island (Asia's largest theme park, home to one of Asia's most spectacular elevated water rides) on Singapore's Sentosa Island. Place buyers are attracted by the strong potential offered by a successful theme park. Place sellers are eagerly looking for an opportunity to put their place on the Asian place map and a theme park offers investment and visibility.

In the case of Hong Kong Disneyland, scheduled to open in the year 2005, the estimated total building cost is US$14.1 billion.[42] The park will cover 126 hectares of reclaimed land on Hong Kong's sparsely populated Lantau Island.[43] This huge investment was made possible by the formation of a joint venture between the Walt Disney Company and the Hong Kong Government, along with low-interest loans provided by the government. As the park attracts visitors, the likelihood is that investors and marketers will choose to locate on Lantau Island, previously known for its natural sights and monasteries.

In a relatively short time, theme parks, resort areas, national parks and entertainment districts have populated Asia. Japan's Sega Amusement

Theme Park chain offers virtual-reality games featuring interactive computer technology and games with exceptionally high-resolution graphics that allow players to feel that they are actually part of the scenario or in the game. There are currently seven of these parks in Japan and another in Sydney. In Figure 6.4, Singapore's top leisure destinations are shown in a map prepared by ASEAN as part of its tourism promotion campaign.

Smaller theme and amusement parks and other attractions have appeared throughout Asia. Japan, for example, has Osaka Expoland; Summarland and Korakuen Amusement Parks in Tokyo; Kobe Portopialand; Yokohama Dreamland; Shima Spain Village; Kijma Amusement Park (Beppu City); Gulliver's Kingdom; Mitsui Greenland (Iwamizawa); Sendai Hi-Land; Tojoko Land (Hyogo); Tedori Rivers (Ishikawa); and Athletic World (Aichi). To help families identify theme parks, a new Internet service has been set up through the Theme Parks Interest Group at http://pages.prodigy.com/alpha/themecoi.htm.

Some places integrate entertainment and theme parks as their main industry. Singapore's Sentosa Island again provides a good example.

Figure 6.4: Top Singapore attractions

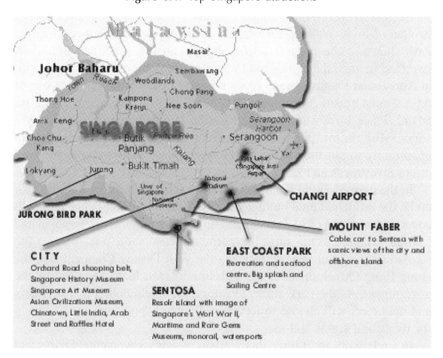

Source: http://www.aseansec.org/

However, the best overall Asian model is probably Macau. With its world-renowned casinos, horse-racing, historical attractions and the annual Formula One Grand Prix car race, the former Portuguese colony has become a giant theme park for Asia's prosperous citizens.

Sports Arenas

Almost all places feature some sport that has a strong local tradition. A winning team or an individual sports star can build civic pride and enthusiasm for a place. A major sports team can put a city or country's name on the map. South Korea's national soccer team is much more than a winning team. It provides a common theme of identification among its worldwide supporters. Cricket also plays this role for many Asian countries, including Australia, New Zealand, India, Pakistan, Sri Lanka and Bangladesh. The Cricket World Cup, held every four years, is one of the most widely viewed spectator sports in the world.

A sports arena — or an entire Olympic complex — requires a serious investment. Consider the massive investment Beijing made to win its bid to host the 2008 Olympic Games, after losing the Millennium Games. Poor environmental conditions contributed to the initial losing bid, so, for 2008, the city took no chances in its attempt to showcase China's capital. The project encompasses not just the renovation of 53 sporting facilities and the construction of an Olympic park — including the 405-hectare world-class Beijing International Exhibition and Sports Centre — but also involves improvements to the 760-hectare Wali Forest Park and the 50-hectare Chinese Nationalities Museum. In all, Beijing will invest around US$20 billion,[44] encompassing improvements to the city's infrastructure and other projects intended to contribute to the clean-up of the environment.[45]

Beijing's Asian competitor for the Games, the city of Osaka, proposed to invest just ¥169.5 billion (about US$1.5 billion),[46] in part because it has more developed infrastructure and better environmental conditions. But an Olympics is usually a one-time opportunity for a place. And while the Games in themselves are a huge focus of world attention, the prized return is when a place translates the event into a premier and sustainable global brand. That requires strategic vision, follow-through and persistence.

Many sports have a clear place-brand connection: Korea has tae kwon do; China has kung fu; Japan is known for aikido and a kung fu variant, karate. Japan also has a passion for baseball. Thailand is known for kickboxing and is considered by many to be the "capital of golf" in all of Southeast Asia with over 300 courses;[47] Sydney was the site of the Millennium Olympics; and India is often associated with cricket. In most of these places, it is possible to identify alliances between the community, some leading businesses and the local sports associations. The aim of the alliance can be to improve or open a new sports arena, promote the sport, organize sports events or attract new players.

With the constant expansion of pan-Asian broadcasting and other cross-border news coverage, and the significant increase in the popularity of pan-Asian games, places will invest even more in sports arenas in the future. The name of the place can easily be integrated into the local teams' names and hence distributed by the media, free of charge. Daily newspaper sports coverage and live television reports and summaries give cities and towns constant exposure and, in the case of winning teams, even more promotional benefits.

Festivals and Occasions

Most places sponsor public events to celebrate occasions and anniversaries. Perhaps the prototype of these events is the annual festival. Local festivals have always existed, but Asia, reflecting the interest in local specialties, has spawned a decade of festival innovation. The smallest city or community today organizes its own festival to celebrate its specific character.

One popular theme is to commemorate a celebrated person born in the city. Calcutta has put much effort into remembering its great poet, Rabindranath Tagore. As we saw earlier, Qufu has its annual International Confucius Culture Festival. Xu Ke, vice-mayor of Qufu has observed that "people in Qufu feel grateful to the master not only because he is the forefather of Chinese culture, but also because his fame helps promote local business."[48] Qufu understands the benefits óf a cultural icon.

Besides famous people, the theme can embrace classical or pop music (the Rainforest World Music Festival, the Asian Song Festival); theatre/dance (Bali Arts Festival); or movies (Sydney, Fukuoka, Singapore, New Zealand, Melbourne, Manila). Products with a place-bound link can be another theme with high commercial value. In this category are both wine celebrations and religious festivals. Thousands of small cities and communities in India, Nepal, Japan and China have local festivals that reflect their religious practices.

Among the unique festival themes is India's "Holi" Festival, a colorful and playful celebration that takes place every March. The millennium offered a unique opportunity for places to promote themselves and many took the opportunity to organize huge projects. For example, the Chinese government invested more than US$24 million in one such project (see Exhibit 6.5).

Exhibit 6.5: CHASING ATTRACTIONS

It has become a mantra among tourism planners that adding attractions is a key to success. Worldwide there has been a race to build the tallest building, the largest indoor garden or the biggest ice hotel. In Beijing, the government built the China Millennium Monument, a grandiose memorial landmark to the year 2000. It is one of the grandest structures in the world, and it celebrates the five-thousand-year history of Chinese civilization. Does such attraction-chasing make sense for places?

The answer is not always clear. In the case of the Millennium Monument, the objective was to produce numerous tourism benefits, ranging from hosting large numbers of visitors to increasing hotel and restaurant revenues. While those one-time objectives were largely achieved, after the millennium celebrations the Millennium Monument had an uncertain future and, therefore, uncertain revenue-generating prospects. Some believe it is in danger of becoming a forgotten souvenir of the year 2000 celebrations. Suggestions for what to do with it now include turning it into a film-production site. Whatever becomes of it, this is just one example where, despite less-than-compelling numbers, a place found a reason to build an extravagant new structure.

Most attractions can be evaluated on two criteria: Will they pay for themselves? What will they do for our image? In many cases, such as professional sports franchises and one-time attractions like the Millennium Monument, the payoff is not worth the effort. Any place considering such an investment needs to conduct a careful cost analysis of benefits. In many cases, the hard factor (building revenues) may be insufficient in itself, but the so-called slippery spin-offs (hotel, restaurant, visitor sales) tip the scales. However, attractions are often about image-making, prestige and self-esteem — the so-called soft factors. In studies of the impact of attractions, it is clear that residents of places with attractions feel better about their place as a place to live. The residents and city officials also feel that the attraction can bestow a big-league reputation to a city. And there is often a silver lining in even the gloomiest financial forecast. If the Millennium Monument can still be used to celebrate the year 2100, with inflation the US$1-billion price tag may well seem like a bargain.

■■■■■■
Sources:

Mid-Western Health Board Website, http://www.mwhb.ie/arc_nw24.htm; David Swindell and Mark Rosentaub, "Who Benefits from the Presence of Professional Sports Teams," *Public Administration Review*, January/February 1998, vol. 58, pp. 11–20.

Many places in Asia are also exploiting the expo trend. Bids for world-class expos and sporting events have come from various Asian countries in the hopes of gaining broad international recognition. Pusan's successful bid for the 2002 Asian Games, Beijing's bid for the 2008 Olympic Games and Manila's bid for World Expo 2002 are but three examples of this. Pusan's bid was built around the theme "One Asia, Global Pusan," indicating that the South Korean city is emerging as a player of note in the global economy. It underscores that message by promoting a particular "ideal" for the games — "New Vision, New Asia." The appeal is to investors. Beijing's 2008 Olympic Games will be billed as "New Beijing, Great Olympics," suggesting an exciting new Beijing for the new millennium. Here, the appeal is to public opinion in general, as Beijing seeks to shake off its dark, closed reputation. Before the Philippines' former president Joseph Estrada decided not to hold the 2002 World Expo in the Philippines — Manila's bid was championed by his predecessor — the expo was marketed under the theme "Ecotourism: Growing with Nature." This appeal was directed toward the preservation of the environment and recognition of global market opportunities for environmental goods and services. These examples show that even large international events must focus on certain unique, appealing themes to influence specific regional and target groups if they are to be successful.

Parallel to the rise of such large expos, Asian cities and communities are generating thousands of mini expos on all possible themes to reach many target groups. Places today are thinking creatively about developing events that, on a one-time or permanent basis, can bring higher visibility to a community.

Buildings, Monuments and Sculptures

Another pathway to place distinction is to add or preserve interesting local buildings, monuments and sculptures. An Asian "hot-spot map" can easily be drawn on the basis of unique and world-class buildings, monuments and sculptures (see Figure 6.5). Such a map could start in Cambodia, with its Angkor Wat — some parts of which are over 1,000 years old — and end in modern Kuala Lumpur, with its Petronas Twin Towers. Other popular Asian attractions include the Forbidden City in Beijing, and the Burj Al Arab in Dubai, an architectural icon symbolizing the very essence of the emirate. Everywhere on the map we find places where efforts have been made to use buildings as attractions for place marketing.

Because there are so many world-class monuments, a map of popular destinations in Asia would be comprehensive and useful. ASEAN has begun to provide maps of the most popular attractions of individual countries, as we saw in Singapore's map, and this effort should be enhanced to include other distribution channels.

One of the most famous monuments in Asia is the Great Wall of China. Built in 1791, it has long been regarded as the symbol of "China's greatness and the ability of man to achieve"[49] huge objectives, and as a dramatic symbol of the country's culture and civilization. Thus, a monument can be interpreted in various ways according to changing

Figure 6.5: ASEAN attractions

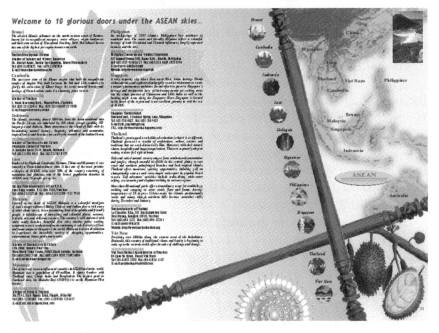

Source: ASEAN

historical events and values in the market. The Sydney Opera House is an example of a modern, world-class monument so universally recognized that it serves as a symbol of the city. The Golden Pavilion in Kyoto, representing the architecture of the Muromachi period, is yet another example.

Sculptures can evolve as symbols of a place. The Shwe Dagon Pagoda in Yangon, Myanmar, is the most notable sculpture in the city. The cone-shaped temple, 326 feet high, is completely covered in gold. Myanmar is home to other world-famous sculptures such as the Chaukhtatgyi Buddha, the largest reclining Buddha sculpture in the world, and the Mingun Bell in Sagaing City, the largest ringing bell.[50]

Museums

Asia kept better track of its heritage at the turn of the century than it did in the aftermath of the Second World War and the frenzied growth of the miracle years. The Prince of Wales Museum in western India, for instance, was built in 1902 and epitomizes Indo-Saracenic architecture, while the world-renowned Shanghai Museum (of ancient Chinese Art) has over 120,000 pieces of cultural relics in 12 categories.[51] Built in the 1930s using European architecture, it covers a total area of 18,000 square meters.[52] The National Museum of Bangkok is among the most comprehensive museums in Southeast Asia. The Ethnological Museum in Chittagong, Bangladesh, is one of the most specialized. Taiwan boasts the National Palace Museum.

As Asia looked into the 21st century, however, many began to recognize the importance of chronicling the varied heritage that accounts for Asia's unique place in the world. As a result, we can justifiably identify in developed Asia what might be termed the "museum mega-wave." The higher visibility and attraction of museums is a direct result of place competition and the determination to improve attractions. Most museums focus on historical heritage and the ethnicity of places. This is particularly true in Japan and South Korea. But Asia has also seen a surge in interest in its art and a dramatic appreciation in the prices it commands.

Today, Asia can provide the market with a museum for every taste and target group — even the most exclusive connoisseurs have something to explore. The US$64-million Hong Kong Heritage Museum features architectural design and state-of-the-art technology, while the Hong Kong Film Archive has an impressive collection of Hong Kong films and collateral. For the less culturally inclined, perhaps, there is the Hong Kong branch of the famous Madame Tussaud's Wax Museum, which features 90 life-size models of famous celebrities and world leaders. Also in Hong Kong is the Museum of Coastal Defense. Originally the Lei Yue Mun Fort, this museum showcases the country's rich heritage of coastal defense. Museums are scattered throughout Japan, including well-funded historical and cultural institutions such as the Gunma Prefecture Museum of Modern Art. For an out-of-this-world museum experience there is the Cosmo Isle Hakui in Hakui, Japan, a space and UFO museum which receives 70,000 visitors every year.[53] The Guangdong Museum of Art is on Ersha Island, "right in the middle of the Pearl River," and offers insights into contemporary Chinese art.[54]

A place without a museum is like a place without a festival or a sports team. A museum conveys a place's sense of culture and history and adds to its stature in the destination place market.

Other Attractions

There are many other types of attractions. Take for example the attraction potential of a concept such as "Top of Asia," which communicates excitement and adventure, natural beauty and cultural variety. The combination of attractions is actually the attraction.

Cape Canaveral, Florida, where the public can watch NASA rocket launches, represents a type of attraction that exists in the form of sites hosting modern and industrial activities. It can be the launching site of rockets or manufacturing plants producing cars, trains, steel, glass, fiber optics or watches. Such living sites can have an immediate attraction when they are opened in a carefully prepared way. The paradox is that, in Asia, such sites are often playing a role only when production has stopped. Then, the usual approach is to transform the place into some nostalgic industrial museum. An exception is the Cadbury Chocolate Factory in Dunedin, New Zealand, which is now a tourist destination as it offers free samples and cultivates younger chocolate lovers with its Cadbury Land Web site.

Popular attractions can also be connected to infrastructural systems and sites. It can be the *Shinkansen* trains in Japan, the meeting point of a huge airport (such as Dubai International Airport), a subway (Singapore or Hong Kong), a TV/radio tower (Menara, Kuala Lumpur) or even an impressive bridge (Penang Bridge or Akashi Kaikyo in Kobe). It is easy to see why the Akashi Kaikyo bridge, linking Kobe to Awaji, is considered among the attractions of Japan. The bridge, 3,911 meters long, is the world's longest suspension bridge.

PEOPLE

A place can possess fine infrastructure and many attractions and yet be unsuccessful because of the way visitors perceive its people. The hospitality of the residents of a place can affect that place's attractiveness in a number of ways.

Outsiders often carry an image of the people who live in a particular place. Some places inherit an unfortunate and often undeserved image that is hard to shake off. Such an image may have a strong effect on whether outsiders will deal with the community. Here are some widely shared images of the people living in certain places:

- Hong Kong — rudeness, language problems
- Japan — silent and reserved, language problems
- Macau — dangerous, criminal activity

Communities whose inhabitants are unfriendly to visitors spoil what might otherwise be a positive experience. Many tourists who visited Paris in the 1950s and 1960s admired the marvelous character of the city but left complaining about the shopkeepers. Hong Kong shopkeepers prior to the Asian financial crisis were often the targets of visitor complaints, despite the large selection of goods and clothing. The shopkeepers were haughty, rude and reluctant to wait on tourists.

Tough times forced a change in attitude. Hong Kong shopkeepers are now among the friendliest anywhere. That's because the crisis demonstrated in a very painful manner that Hong Kong had to work at keeping itself a viable retail destination and, with greater competition, place attractiveness depends on much more than the lowest prices. Singapore learned a similar lesson when its government carried out public-awareness campaigns encouraging people to be friendlier to tourists and other visitors.

The point is that a place's citizens are an important part of the specific target packages. Visitors to India complain about the aggressiveness of the motorists and the difficulty of getting help on the street when lost or looking for an address. This stands in contrast to the service-oriented attitudes often reported from Singapore and Australia. Probably no Asian country invests more in customer service, from cabs to hotels, than these two. Many places are finding an invaluable resource in using retired older citizens as paid service agents and unpaid volunteers in place promotion. Thus, places seeking to expand their tourist and attraction markets must invest in customer services from points of entry at airports or other transit facilities to points of delivery at hotels, restaurants and other attractions. To the extent that communities seek tourist and hospitality business, they must promote public understanding regarding the multiple jobs, spending and related opportunities that flow from satisfied visitors and investors.

CONCLUSION

Few places have, or can even pretend to have, it all: character, infrastructure, services and attractions. Great character in design and history may support tourism and visitors but may not draw other vital or new business opportunities unrelated to nostalgia and aesthetics. A city with top-flight attractions may be inundated with crime, pollution and poor public services. Great infrastructure without sufficient business investment does not buy much. Clean air, friendly people and an attractive environment may not help a place that lacks transportation, access to major markets and key attractions.

In focusing on four aspects of place development — urban design, infrastructure, basic services and attractions — we have presented readers with a series of options; namely, a practical appraisal concerning what improvements may be necessary and how such improvements can respond to more than one need (for example, infrastructure and the environment). We have offered illustrations and examples to emphasize the range of possibilities and opportunities. Table 6.1 is an audit instrument that a place can use to assess its infrastructure, attractions and people.

Table 6.1: Audit instrument for infrastructure, attractions and people

	Current status			
INFRASTRUCTURE	**Poor**	**Fair**	**Good**	**Excellent**
Housing				
Roads and transportation				
Water supply				
Power supply				
Environmental quality				
Basic social security				
Education				
Lodging and restaurant facilities				
Convention facilities				
Visitor services				
ATTRACTIONS				
Natural beauty and features				
History and famous people				
Shopping places				
Cultural attractions				
Recreation and entertainment				
Sports arenas				
Festivals and occasions				
Buildings, monuments, and sculptures				
Museums				
Other attractions				
PEOPLE				
Friendly and helpful				
Skilled				
Citizenship				

Potential Improvement

INFRASTRUCTURE	None	Modest	Major
Housing			
Roads and transportation			
Water supply			
Power supply			
Environmental quality			
Basic social security			
Education			
Lodging and restaurant facilities			
Convention facilities			
Visitor services			
ATTRACTIONS			
Natural beauty and features			
History and famous people			
Shopping places			
Cultural attractions			
Recreation and entertainment			
Sports arenas			
Festivals and occasions			
Buildings, monuments, and sculptures			
Museums			
Other attractions			
PEOPLE			
Friendly and helpful			
Skilled			
Citizenship			

Impact Potential

INFRASTRUCTURE	None	Modest	Major
Housing			
Roads and transportation			
Water supply			
Power supply			
Environmental quality			
Basic social security			
Education			
Lodging and restaurant facilities			
Convention facilities			
Visitor services			
ATTRACTIONS			
Natural beauty and features			
History and famous people			
Shopping places			
Cultural attractions			
Recreation and entertainment			
Sports arenas			
Festivals and occasions			
Buildings, monuments and sculptures			
Museums			
Other attractions			
PEOPLE			
Friendly and helpful			
Skilled			
Citizenship			

1 http://www.worldexecutive.com/cityguides/asia_pacific/index.html, viewed on November 23, 2000.

2 http://www.geocities.com/RainForest/5290/map-kat.htm, viewed on November 23, 2000.

3 http://www.melaka.gov.my/tourism/, viewed on November 22, 2000.

4 http://travel.lycos.com/Destinations/Asia/Malaysia/Malacca/, viewed on November 22, 2000.

5 http://www-irps.ucsd.edu/~sloan/papers/malaysiahdd.html, viewed on November 16, 2000.

6 http://www.usembassyjakarta.org/econ/investment2000-3.html, viewed on November 16, 2000.

7 http://www.adb.org/Documents/News/1997/nr1997026.asp, viewed on November 21, 2000.

8 http://www.cba.neu.edu/~mgt/koeras.htm, viewed on November 16, 2000.

9 http://www.imf.org/external/pubs/ft/fandd/1998/06/mody.htm, viewed on January 8, 2001.

10 http://www.hawaii.gov/dbedt/ert/stmad.html#profile, viewed on November 16, 2000.

11 "Hopes to Woo $1.5b in Private Capital," *The Daily Star*, September 9, 1997, viewed on January 8, 2001 at http://www.dailystarnews.com/199709/09/n7090905.htm.

12 http://wbln0018.worldbank.org/lo+web+sites/bangladesh+Web.nsf/0704a4348e105b2e462566720023975f/6053d9127ba777494625670c003830e1?-OpenDocument, viewed on November 16, 2000.

13 Bruce McDowell, "Public Works for Tomorrow," *Intergovernmental Perspective*, Summer, 1992, p. 23.

14 http://www.oneworld.org/cse/html/enres/news/oct99/dnoct21.htm, viewed on November 16, 2000.

15 http://www.chinaenvironment.net/cer/CER-9709.html, viewed on November 23, 2000.

16 http://www.newsweek-int.com/brc/archive/auto2000/s4.asp, viewed on November 21, 2000.

17 http://www.eia.doe.gov/emeu/env/japan.html.

18 "Aghast over gas prices? Don't fill up in Hong Kong," *The Detroit News*, March 10, 2000. http://detnews.com/2000/business/0003/10/B03-13236.htm, viewed on January 8, 2001.

19 http://www.geocities.com/sustrannet/newsflash/1997.htm, viewed on November 21, 2000.

20 http://www.flora.org/afo/afz/issue11.html, viewed on November 21, 2000.

21 http://www.geocities.com/sustrannet/newsflash/1996.htm, viewed on November 21, 2000.

22 http://www.about-australia.com/spgreen.htm, viewed on November 21, 2000.

23 http://www.electrifyingtimes.com/crayon.html, viewed on November 22, 2000.

24 http://prius.toyota.com/greener/index.html, viewed on November 22, 2000.

25 "Winning Ways," *Far Eastern Economic Review*, October 19, 2000, p. 60.

26 Irene M. Kunii and Satsuki Obe, "Kobe," Time, January 22, 1996, viewed on August 9, 2001 at http://www.time.com/time/international/1996/960122/japan.html

27 Michael J. Oakes, "Shaky Recovery," *Reason Magazine Online*, January 1998, viewed on November 23, 2000 at http://www.reason.com/9801/fe.oakes.html.

28 Anthony Davis, "Bangkok as Crime Central," *Asiaweek*, October 13, 2000, p. 34.

29 http://www.fas.harvard.edu/~asiactr/haq/200002/0002a008.htm, viewed on November 23, 2000.
30 http://www.educationadelaide.sa.gov.au/files/study/support.html, viewed on November 21, 2000.
31 http://www.atip.or.jp/ATIP/public/atip.reports.95/atip95.88r.html, viewed on November 20, 2000.
32 Hannah Beech, "Art Rivalry," *Time*, April 10, 2000, viewed on May 18, 2001 at http://www.cnn.com/ASIANOW/time/magazine/2000/0410/art.rivalry.html.
33 *Ibid.*
34 http://www.buddhanet.net/lumbini.htm, viewed on October 25, 2000.
35 http://www.connect.net/ron/buddhism.html, viewed on October 25, 2000.
36 http://www.unesco.org/whc/heritage.htm, viewed on October 25, 2000.
37 http://www.visit-china-97.com/4season/autumn.htm#9, viewed on October 25, 2000.
38 http://savvytraveler.com/Show/Features/2000/06.17/mao.html, viewed on October 25, 2000.
39 http://www.hotel-online.com/Neo/Trends/Andersen/VietnamEmergingHospitality-Market_Spring1996.htm,viewed on November 23, 2000.
40 http://www.cnn.com/ASIANOW/time/magazine/2000/0410/art.rivalry.html, viewed on November 23, 2000.
41 "High-Tech Industry and Localisation," OECD, Paris, 1989, p.21.
42 http://www.info.gov.hk/disneyland/finan_e.htm#3, viewed on November 24, 2000.
43 Yulanda Chung, "Making a Magic Kingdom," *Asiaweek*, November 12, 1999.
44 http://christianity.com/CC/article/1,1183,PTID1000%7CCHID74%7CCIID-192018,00.html, viewed on January 9, 2001.
45 http://www.dailystarnews.com/200009/27/n0092704.htm#BODY11, viewed on December 28, 2000.
46 http://www.t3.rim.or.jp/~sports/latest/2008.html, viewed on December 28, 2000.
47 http://www.golfinthailand.com/, viewed on October 26, 2000.
48 http://www.shanghai-daily.com/data/culture/9907m/culture990717.html, viewed on November 24, 2000.
49 http://zinnia.umfacad.maine.edu/~mshea/China/great.html, viewed on November 23, 2000.
50 http://www.myanmars.net/wonder/index.htm, viewed on November 21, 2000.
51 http://www.sh.com/travel/museum/museum.htm, viewed on November 20, 2000.
52 http://www.echinaart.com/GALLERY/ShanghaiArtMuseum.htm, viewed on November 20, 2000.
53 Cecelia Wong, "An Eastern Odyssey," *Time*, August 21–28 2000, p. 40.
54 Damian Harper, *The National Geographic Traveler: China*, p. 215.

C H A P T E R

7

Designing A Place's Image

W hat images come to mind when you hear the name Ho Chi Minh City? Are they of war, poverty, rebellion or enterprise? The business capital of Vietnam has a dramatic history. The French occupation in the mid 19th century, although the cause of much despair, struggle and strife, heavily influenced and enriched the country's culture and architecture. After the defeat of the French in 1954, Saigon, as the city was called then, became a bustling commercial center, famous for its unique blend of Eastern and Western traditions. In 1975, however, when the city fell to the communist government of what was then called North Vietnam, it closed its doors to the rest of the world. Saigon was renamed Ho Chi Minh City and its designation as the "Paris of the Orient" became a fading memory to residents and outsiders alike.

Now, early in the 21st century, the city is striving to develop a new and positive image. In 1986, the government of Vietnam implemented the economic reform policy of *Doi Moi*, or renovation. The announcement was meant to signal clearly the re-emergence of the country, especially Ho Chi Minh City, from a decade of near silence and economic decline. The policy and the new openness promised to pave the way for the rebirth of the once-thriving commercial hub. *Doi Moi* generated new opportunities for both local entrepreneurs and foreign investors and quickly stimulated an influx of visitors, including many from the Vietnamese diaspora, as well as new investors. The number of foreign visitors increased by 58%, from

669,990 in 1993 to more than 1.6 million in 1996. Business visitors accounted for 40% of the increase.[1] Likewise, foreign direct investment increased, from $366 million in 1988 to $4 billion in 1994.[2] Ho Chi Minh City was once again attracting people from all over the world, both for its beauty and its business opportunities.

Indeed, a number of famous French landmarks still standing today are among the chief tourist attractions that give the country its character. They include the Ben Thanh Market (formerly called Les Halles Centrale) and Nha Tho Duc Ba (or the Cathedral of Our Lady). The clock tower at the entrance to the Ben Thanh Market is closely identified with the city. Other famous monuments are a blend of Chinese, Muslim and Buddhist architecture. Meanwhile, the city is developing an export-manufacturing base and is already considered a fledgling center of information technology and software development because of the plentiful supply of intelligent, well-educated engineers. Although it has more than its fair share of challenges to overcome, Ho Chi Minh City has taken important strides towards being noticed and heard around the world.

What images come to mind when you hear a reference to China? For many, China's image is of a country that violates human rights and where social injustices are a part of daily life. Indeed, the United Nations and many of its individual member countries, government officials and human rights groups have regularly criticized China for its human-rights violations. Crackdowns on fledgling democratic institutions such as the China Democracy Party, suppression of the media, and the outlawing of spiritual movements such as the Falun Gong reinforce this negative image.[3]

Nevertheless, China works in a proactive way to rehabilitate and reposition its troubled image. For instance, a multi-million dollar media campaign sponsored by large state-owned enterprises was conducted in the United States with the aim of improving the country's image.[4] Other public relations efforts include radio infomercials and documentaries portraying the country in a positive light by spotlighting high-profile crackdowns on bureaucratic corruption.

Directed campaigns target specific sectors. China is employing a similar strategy to help bring the country closer to achieving its huge tourism potential. The China National Tourism Administration regularly implements "action tourism campaigns" focusing on the country's many historic attractions.[5] For example, it implemented the "China City and Country Tour 1998," followed by "China Ecotourism 1999" and "China New Millennium 2000." China continues to promote vacation destinations with a spectacular combination of year-round good weather and historical sites. However, a traveler looking for sun and beautiful sights is still more likely to think first of Australia, Malaysia and

Thailand, which have been branding these attributes for years. Because there are two competing messages — one intended, the other not — the image of China remains out of focus and under stress despite efforts to reverse broad negative perceptions.

Still, Ho Chi Minh City and China are examples of places where intense efforts are being undertaken to reposition country images. The goal is to attract new industries and to create new ways to compete for tourists. As we have seen in earlier chapters, other regional countries prominently conduct similar campaigns: Taiwan, South Korea, Hong Kong, Malaysia, Singapore and Thailand.

The image of a place is a critical determinant of the way citizens and businesses respond to the place. Therefore, a place must try to manage its image. Strategic image management requires the examination of the following five issues:

1. What determines a place's image?
2. How can a place's image be measured?
3. What guidelines exist for designing a place's image?
4. What tools are available for communicating an image?
5. How can a place correct a negative image?

WHAT DETERMINES A PLACE'S IMAGE?

We define a place's image as the sum of beliefs, ideas and impressions that people have of that place. Images represent a simplification of a large number of associations and pieces of information connected with a place. They are a product of the mind trying to process and frame huge amounts of data about a place. Note that if no data is available, no processing takes place. If no positive data is available, negative processing results.

An image is more than a simple belief. The belief that Macau is an island of triads and gangsters is just one element of a larger image of Macau; its other elements include a picturesque island, warm most of the year, and a unique culinary tradition. An image implies a whole set of beliefs about a place.

On the other hand, people's perceptions of a place do not necessarily reveal their attitudes towards that place. Two people may hold the same image of Macau's warm climate and yet have different feelings about it because they have different attitudes towards warm climates.

How does an image differ from a stereotype? A stereotype suggests a widely held image that is highly distorted and simplistic and that carries a favorable or unfavorable bias. For instance, the Asian continent,

Bangladesh, Mongolia and Tibet all generate a number of well-known stereotypes. An image, on the other hand, is a more personal perception of a place that can vary from person to person.

Different people can hold quite different images of the same place. One person may see a particular city as a childhood hometown while others may see it as a bustling city, an urban jungle or a great weekend-getaway destination. Therefore, a place wanting to build an attractive image should help investors, potential residents and visitors to discover this image. It is like the answers of the three stonecutters, who are asked what they are doing:

> *The first replies:* "I am cutting this stone into blocks."
> *The second replies:* "I am on a team that is building a cathedral."
> *The third replies:* "I am honoring God."

A place should have a strategy and the capacity to make visible not only blocks, but the cathedral or God to the marketers, to the investors and to visitors.

Image has always been of great interest and concern to marketers. What is our brand image? How do consumers perceive our product relative to the competition's product? How can we identify, measure and control our product's image to attract consumers and build market share? These questions must also be of concern to the place marketer. Today's marketer must look at a place's image as a major influence on investors, new residents and visitors. After all, once an investor chooses a location, that place then becomes a part of the investor's projected image to customers. For example, Sony of Japan and San Miguel of the Philippines are inseparably connected to their national homes in the public's mind.

Likewise, a vacationer is more likely to choose Australia over China if the image of Australia is more familiar and positive. Australia's winning the bid to host the 2000 Olympic Games further improved the country's image. At the same time, the winning position is in itself a good illustration of what world-class image management can achieve.

Strategic image management (SIM) is the ongoing process of researching a place's image among its various audiences, segmenting and targeting its specific audiences, positioning a place's attractions to support its desired image and communicating those attractions to target groups. The underlying premise of SIM is that, because a place's image is identifiable and changes over time, the marketer must be able to track and influence the image held by different target groups.

Normally, an image sticks in the public's mind for a long time, even after it loses its validity. Some people still think of Hiroshima as a place that was devastated by the atomic bomb, even though today's Hiroshima is very different. At other times, a place's image may change more rapidly as media and word-of-mouth spread vital news stories about it. Calcutta is often portrayed as a city of poverty and slums, characteristic of India's most pressing problems. The city attempts to veer away from this image by actively promoting its positive points, such as the friendly people and historical and natural sites. Kuala Lumpur is another place where image changes have happened quickly. Just a decade ago, Kuala Lumpur, next to its active neighbor, Thailand, was barely noticed as a destination for international travelers. Today's Kuala Lumpur is very different. Its image is of a rapidly developing city, a hub for information technology, sports and tourism, and a symbol of progress towards developed-nation status.

Image management is an ongoing process of researching image changes and trying to understand their dynamics.

HOW CAN A PLACE'S IMAGE BE MEASURED?

Planners follow a two-step process to assess a place's image. First, they select a target audience characterized by common traits, interests or perceptions. The second step requires planners to measure the target audience's perceptions of relevant attributes. We now examine these two steps.

Selecting an Audience

The first step in assessing a place's image is to select the audience segment whose perceptions are of interest. Seven broad audiences might be interested in living, visiting, working or investing in a place and they may hold different images of it. They are:

1. Residents: Most places want to attract new residents who can improve the tax base of the community. Understanding how potential residents are thinking is strategic information in destination marketing.
2. Visitors: Only a few highly popular places do not want to increase the number of visitors. Places need to know visitors' images of the specific place.
3. Managements: Places want to know what the prospective management target groups know and think about them.
4. Investors: Places may want to attract investors such as real-estate developers and other financiers who show confidence in a place's future by making generous loans and investments.

5. Entrepreneurs: Small businesses and entrepreneurs are important and places need to know how the prospects view a place as a community in which to live and work.
6. Foreign investors: Products and services — even on the global market — can be linked to a specific place. The image of this place can add value for foreign investors.
7. Location specialists: Various location specialists have important roles in the destination-attraction equation — representing both investor and marketer roles. A place must know what opinions these specialists hold.

Even within each broad audience, a large variation in the image of a place often exists. Tourists' perceptions differ depending on whether they are "sun worshippers" or "travelers." When looking at an organization or company, the perception of management differs depending on whether it is an "old economy" industrial player or a "new economy" software developer.

There are numerous ways of splitting a market into smaller segments (see Exhibit 7.1). Researchers should identify characteristics that maximize discrimination among groups holding different images. The characteristics include simple objective measures (demographic, geographical), complex objective measures (social class, family life cycle, lifestyle), behavioral measures (buying occasion, usage rate), or inferred measures (personality, needs, sought benefits).

Exhibit 7.1: AMANPULO: PEACEFUL ISLAND

Amanpulo, which is part of the Aman Group founded by Dutch-Indonesian journalist, publisher, and hotelier Adrian Zecha and investment banker Anil Thadani, is one of Asia's most well-defined places. The resort is located on the privately owned island of Pamalican in Cuyo, Palawan Province, in the Central Philippines. It is the smallest of the Quiniluban group of islands and has its own 1.2-km runway. The resort's target market is narrow: rich people who want to relax without stress, in a place that is "faultlessly discreet"[1] and where the entertainment is the founder's vision of pristine natural surroundings. Marketing an image of luxury amidst an environment of privacy and relaxation allows Amanpulo to target a specific audience and cater to its needs.

Marketing copy from Web sites promoting Amanpulo illustrates its focus on the wealthy seeking an escape from routine pressures:

"Amanpulo... was created for travelers seeking the idyllic beauty of a tropical island."[2]
"More than a beach resort, Amanpulo (peaceful island) is a splendid refuge from too much reality, a tropical island to lose yourself in."[3]
"Amanpulo is the most perfect place in the world for crashing out with books, music, or perhaps a watercolor sketch book, for it is 220 acres of island peace — a little bit of nature's haute couture range — with the purest white sand and the most cerulean sea."[4]

Hong Kong fashion-industry tycoon Joyce Ma says that Amanpulo, which is operated by Amanresorts, "is my way of regenerating. The total privacy, the impeccable service, the beauty and the silence — it is a dream world."[5] That formula has produced enviable financial returns. Although Zecha and Thandani used US$4 million of their own money to build the first resort, annual profit for the chain is US$75,000 per room. For comparison, Four Seasons, a luxury hotel chain, makes just US$4,000 per room.

Its longstanding reputation for affluence and confidentiality enables Amanpulo to cater exclusively to those who are wealthy and value their privacy. An awareness of social class, lifestyle, buying behavior and personal needs are all evident in products and services available to guests. The highly controlled resort resembles a film set, with its perfect surroundings, immaculate white sands and crystal-clear waters. There is a high-fashion boutique that carries the necessary beachwear, but also designer labels such as Natori, Silk Cocoon, and Prizmic & Brill bags. An art gallery epitomizes the exotic and expensive and the library is well stocked for leisurely reading. The super-efficient service staff are said to materialize whenever needed. Indeed, the staff-to-guest ratio is two to one, even during full occupancy. There is even an in-house doctor who is on call 24 hours a day. One thing guests won't find, however, is television sets.

It is no surprise that this protected, service-oriented place has attracted so many famous personalities, including Elizabeth Taylor, Robert de Niro and Claudia Schiffer. Attracted by the resort's well-maintained, discreet and exclusive reputation, other film and business celebrities are discovering Amanpulo and its sister resorts. Princess Diana was a guest of the group, and Robert Redford is said to have visited.

However, sustaining its competitive advantage in an increasingly demanding market is a challenge, even for Amanpulo. A key issue is the escalating number of exclusive beach resorts throughout Asia. But Zecha is confident that the Aman resorts, especially Amanpulo, will remain a major niche player in the resort-and-recreation industry. "We prefer to think small. Intimate. Involving. It's not that we are better than big hotels because we are small. We're different, that's all. Aman resorts responds to a contemporary lifestyle. That's what we offer — a lifestyle experience, one without limitations... The world is big. Our ambitions will continue to be small."[6]

Zecha's focus on an exclusive, narrow market is at the top end of the resort business. Nevertheless, he and the group's owners must constantly monitor the competition — and keep exquisitely high standards — to remain ahead in this high-end market. That was evident during a two-year stint without Zecha, who left when controlling shareholders began to meddle. Thadani says, "Had Zecha been away much longer, Amanresorts could have transformed into a mere chain."[7] In the world of small, exclusive resorts, even slight deviations can be fatal. Can Amanpulo be Amanpulo without Zecha?

Sources:

1 Tom Hilditch. "Paradise Regained," *Asiaweek*, July 15, 2001, p. 34.
2 http://www.travelsmart.net/ph/resorts/Palawan/Amanpulo, viewed on August 6, 2001.
3 http://www.guevent.com/travel/packagetours/amanpulo.html, viewed on May 7, 2001.
4 http://www.takler.co.uk/cunard_98/101 hotels/islands/hotel_indexman.html, viewed on November 21, 2000.
5 http://www.asiaweek.com/asiaweek/96/0419/aa3.html, viewed on May 7, 2001.
6 http://www.oalawan.com/amanpulo/amanpulo.html, viewed on August 6, 2001.
7 *Ibid. (Asiaweek)*

Alison Dakota Gee, "Camping Out in Style," *Asiaweek*, April 19, 1996, viewed on January 3, 2001 at http://www.asiaweek.com/asiaweek/96/0419/aa3.html. All Travel Network Web site, http://alltravelnetwork.com/philippines/Amanpulo_Pamalican_Island_Resort/, viewed on November 21, 2000; Antonio Lopez, "For Sale," *Asiaweek*, February 2, 1996, viewed on November 21, 2000 at http://europe.cnn.com/ASIANOW/asiaweek/96/0202/biz4.html; Paradise Islands of Palawan Web site, http://www.palawan.com/amanpulo/amanpulo.html, viewed on November 21, 2000.

The market segments are most useful when they have six characteristics:

1. Mutually exclusive: the various identified segments should not overlap.
2. Exhaustive: every potential target member should be included in some segment.
3. Measurable: the size, purchasing power and profile of the resulting segments can be readily measured.
4. Accessible: the resulting segments can be reached and served effectively.
5. Substantial: the resulting segments are large enough to be worth pursuing.
6. Differentially responsive: the segment is useful only if it responds differently from the other segments to various amounts, types and timing of marketing strategy.

To illustrate these criteria, suppose that some golf clubs in Chiang Mai — together with real-estate developers — want to advertise their offerings via direct mail to high-potential prospects for visits and/or investment. They would need to characterize the people interested in golf, know that they have the discretionary income to respond positively, access their addresses and languages, ascertain that there are many of them, and project that a sufficient number of them will open their mail and respond positively.

Once the overall audience is segmented by relevant criteria and groups of interest have been selected, the key task is to identify the attributes a particular target audience would use to evaluate a place. Only in a few cases has such segmentation been done by Asian places.

Measuring the Audience's Perception

Many methods have been proposed for measuring perceptions.
We describe three approaches.

Familiarity-favorability measurement

The first step is to establish how familiar the target audience is with a
place and how favorable members feel toward it. To establish familiarity,
respondents are asked to check one of the following:

Never heard of	Heard of a little bit	Know a little amount	Know a fair amount	Know very well

The results indicate the audience's awareness of a place. If most of the
respondents check the first two or three categories, a place has an
awareness problem. The respondents who have some familiarity with a
place are then asked to describe how favorable they feel toward it by
checking one of the following:

Very unfavorable	Somewhat unfavorable	Indifferent	Somewhat favorable	Very favorable

If most of the respondents check the first two of the five categories, a
place has a serious image problem.

Semantic Differential

The destination marketer must go further and research the content of a
place's image. One of the most popular tools for measuring images is the
semantic differential, which involves the following steps:

1. Developing a set of relevant dimensions. The researcher asks people
   to identify the dimensions they would use in thinking about a place.
   People could be asked: What things do you think of when you
   consider a vacation? Their reply might include weather, recreational
   opportunities, historical interest, cost, and so on. Each of these would
   be turned into a bipolar scale with extremes at each end. The scales
   can be rendered as five- or seven-point scales.
2. Reducing the set of relevant dimensions. The number of dimensions
   should be kept small to avoid respondent fatigue in having to rate
   several vacation sites. The researcher should remove redundant scales
   that add little information.

3. Administering the instrument to a sample of respondents. The respondents are asked to rate one place at a time. The bipolar adjectives should be arranged so as not to load all the negative adjectives on one side. After the results are in, the scales can be rearranged to display all the positive adjectives on one side for convenience of interpretation.
4. Averaging the results. The respondent's perceptions are averaged on each scale. When the averages are connected, they represent the average image that the audience has of a place.
5. Checking on the image variance. Because each image profile is a line of means, it does not reveal how variable the image actually is. If the variance is large, the image doesn't signify much and further audience segmentation is necessary.

Table 7.1 shows a set of bipolar scales used to measure the tourist image of Singapore.[6] The line connecting the means shows the image that a particular group of respondents had of Singapore. In this case, the respondents consisted of Western expatriate managers living in Asia (but not in Singapore).

Evaluation Maps

One way to measure how citizens view a place is to make an inventory of their visual impressions. This technique involves interviewing a city's residents and collecting their impressions and feelings about different areas of the city. Afterwards, words and responses are structured in a geographical form. Each part of the city, community, region or nation is given certain characteristics, such as "most liked" to "least liked."

Table 7.1: The image of Singapore

	1	2	3	4	5	6	7	
Innocent			x					Sinful
Feminine				x				Masculine
Friendly				x				Cold
Romantic					x			Boring
Old						x		New
Safe	x							Unsafe
Clean	x							Dirty
Interesting				x				Boring
Vibrant				x				Stagnant
Pretty			x					Ugly
Sophisticated			x					Simple
Natural					x			Artificial
Harmonious			x					Conflicting

Another way of gathering data, impressions and feelings about a place is to interview a panel of experts with a deep knowledge of the place. Figure 7.1 shows one such example: an evaluative map of economic freedom in Asia.

WHAT ARE THE GUIDELINES FOR DESIGNING A PLACE'S IMAGE?

Once planners understand a place's current image, they can deliberate on what image they can build. One challenge in doing this is to create an effective image for each target group. For an image to be effective, it must meet the following five criteria:

1. It must be valid. If a place promotes an image too far from reality, the chance of success is minimal. When the promotion agency of Andra Pradesh is marketing the state as "Andra Pradesh Unlimited," the image is stretched too far.
2. It must be believable. Even if the proposed image is valid, it may not be readily believable. When the Hong Kong Trade Development

Figure 7.1: An evaluation map of Asian countries and regions

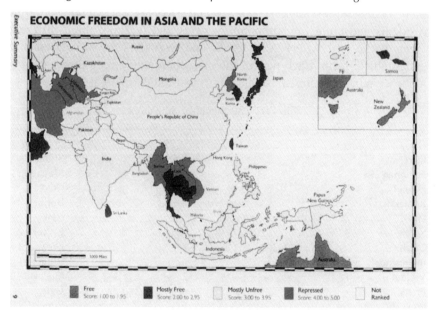

Source: *2001 Index of Economic Freedom*, "Economic Freedom in Asia and the Pacific," p. 9.

Council markets Hong Kong as "Asia's Business Super Market," this may be true. However, the problem is that investors might not be ready to believe it. Overselling is dangerous in the long run.

3. It must be simple. If a place disseminates too many images of itself, it leads to confusion. Since most places have not worked out any strategies, they often disseminate any image that seems vaguely positive. In this scenario there are no priorities and everything ends up being promoted. The result is confusion, at best.

4. It must have appeal. The image must suggest why people would want to live in, invest in, work in or visit a place. The link between Shanghai and international culture is exploited with its transformation into many different contexts that give Shanghai a compelling, permanent appeal.

5. It must be distinctive. The image works best when it is different from other common themes. There is overuse of phrases such as "A Friendly Place," or "In the Middle of Asia" (probably the most common approach at present) or "Best Business Climate". Other Asian cities and communities can find plenty of innovative space to exploit real and distinctive approaches. In Myanmar the problem is the name itself (see Exhibit 7.2).

Exhibit 7.2: WHAT'S IN A NAME?

Myanmar has a problem with its name: people inside and outside the country are confused by it. In June 1989, the State Law and Order Restoration Council (SLORC) abruptly announced that it was changing the country's official name from Burma to Myanmar. The move left citizens clamoring for a distinct social and political identity, and international investors scratching their heads. Despite the confusion, SLORC is sticking to its decision. According to Gustaaf Houtman, author of *Mental Culture in Burmese Crisis Politics: Aung San Suu Kyi and the National League for Democracy*, "though it [the name change] initially originated in response to containing Aung San Suu Kyi, [it] has turned into a program that fits snugly with a number of other military interests."[1] (Aung San Suu Kyi is a prominent international opponent of the military regime). As a result, the country's name has become a political tool rather than a descriptor of its inherent qualities, history and ethnicity — at least in this modern time.

Some places inherit great names. A name that is exciting (Hong Kong), romantic (Maldives or Bali) or stately (Japan) has an advantage in our image-conscious global economy. Others such as Myanmar are the victims of regional battles or ethnic controversies. The result is a name that satisfies very few, and is remembered by even fewer.

Myanmar and Yangon (formerly Rangoon) are not original names created by the SLORC. Rather, they were the names of the country and capital city, respectively, before the British Colonial Administration renamed them Burma and Rangoon. No Myanmar administration ever took the trouble — or saw SLORC's perceived need — to restore their old names until strongman and General/President Saw Maung's decided to bring back the pre-colonial names.

SLORC made the change for three major reasons: to compensate for the loss of support to popular Burmese Socialist Program Party leader Aung San Suu Kyi; to disassociate the country from its sad history with its British colonizers; and to create a sense of national unity for a country previously divided by political and ethnic convictions. As Houtman puts it, "There was no better statement of its authority over the country than demonstration that it had the power to take back from the British all the names that symbolized their rule so divisive to ethnic harmony."[2] In reality, it was probably more a case of "back to the past". And the story doesn't end there. Ethnic groups are still in dispute over the appropriate and true name of the country, and their arguments are likewise based on history and ethnicity as well as opposition to the military dictatorship.

In the entertainment business, actors routinely change their names for a number of audience-related reasons, and, unlike places, there is no need for a consensus. Places that do not like their name and feel the need for an image change have many possibilities: Sydney to Beautiful Harbor, Brisbane to Beachtown, Japan to Electronics Country, Mongolia to Genghisland, and so on. If this seems ridiculous, consider that in the United States the state of North Dakota considered dropping the word North because it sounded so cold, or that after the Second World War companies in Usa, Japan, labeled their exports, "Made in U.S.A." so that they would be better appreciated by U.S. consumers.

Indeed, what a place calls itself is often determined by history, political pressures, products or leaders' names. After the Vietnam War, Saigon was renamed in honor of communist revolutionary and leader Ho Chi Minh. After the 1949 revolution, the People's Republic of China emerged. In the new age of unions, crowded maps and the search for distinction, names are likely to undergo more surgery. In reality, nations are most unlikely to replace their brand names, but emerging regions and regional aggregations formed on the basis of cross-border relationships, new product development or tourism are candidates for change. In these cases, accuracy, attraction potential and differentiation concepts are crucial.

Sources:

1 Gustaaf Houtman, *Mental Culture in Burmese Crisis Politics: Aung San Suu Kyi and the National League for Democracy*, Chapter 2, viewed on November 22, 2000 at (http://homepages.tesco.net/~ghoutman/chapter_02.htm).
2 *Ibid.*

http://college.antioch.edu/~iabrams/nobelprizeannual.1991.html, viewed on November 22, 2000; http://www.vietfederation.ca/30-4-00/TonThatThien.htm, viewed on November 22, 2000; http://www3.itu.int/MISSIONS/Myanmar/psmrr04.htm, viewed on November 22, 2000.

WHAT TOOLS ARE AVAILABLE FOR COMMUNICATING AN IMAGE?

Destination image-makers can draw on three tools to implement an effective image of a place: 1) slogans, themes and positions; 2) visual symbols; and 3) events and deeds. Each medium has its own rules and possibilities.

Slogans, Themes and Positions

Typically, image-makers develop a slogan to unify a specific campaign and the slogan, if successful, is carried through many campaigns. A slogan is a short, encompassing phrase that embodies an overall vision of a place. Table 7.2 lists such slogans. When integrated into a strategic marketing plan, slogans can be useful in generating enthusiasm, momentum and fresh ideas.

Table 7.2: Place campaign slogans

Place	Slogan
South Australia	Relax, indulge, discover, enjoy[9]
Thailand	Amazing Thailand[10]
Vietnam	A Destination for the New Millennium[11] or Enchantment for the Next Thousand Years[12]
Australia	Australia 2000 Fun and Games[13]
Nepal	Mt Everest and More[14]
Macau	Macau Welcomes You[15]
Maldives	The Sunny Side of Life[16]
Singapore	Live it Up in Singapore![17]
Hong Kong	City of Life[18]
Perth	Best on Earth in Perth[19]

A good slogan provides a platform from which a place's image can be further amplified. Thus, a slogan such as the Maldive Islands' "The Sunny Side of Life" teases the public as to what the island can offer; it can also be used by various individual travel agents in their marketing.

A variation from using a catchall slogan is to spell out themes to drive specific marketing programs addressed to defined target groups. The most effective themes are versatile and flexible yet grounded in reality. The Department of Tourism of the Indian province of Kerala has developed a platform from the theme "The Green Gateway of India." The state has backed the theme with real performance as various travel agents actively promote Kerala as "God's Own Country" with its lush forests and fields and famous life-extending Ayurvedic[20] treatments. The theme in this case is the underlying assumption for all action and change.

Another tool is image positioning, where a place positions itself in regional, national and international terms as a place for a certain type of activity or as a viable alternative location/attraction to another place that may have a stronger or more well-established position. The challenge of image positioning is to develop an image that communicates benefits and

Table 7.3: Image-positioning statements

Siargao	Surfing Capital of Asia[21]
Hong Kong	Asia's World City[22]
West Bengal	Gateway to the East[23]
Singapore	Tourism Capital[24]
Sydney	Cultural Capital[25]
Osaka	Sports Paradise[26]

unique attributes that make a place stand out among other places. A number of image-positioning statements are shown in Table 7.3.

Visual Symbols

Visual symbols have figured prominently in destination marketing. Many landmark sites are permanently etched in the public's mind:

Opera House	Sydney
Great Wall of China	Beijing
Taj Mahal	Agra
Gold Souq or Burj Al-Arab	Dubai
Magellan's Cross	Cebu

When used in a systematic way, these visual symbols appear on official stationery, brochures, billboards, pins and dozens of other places.

To be successful, a visual image needs to reinforce an image argument. If the visual is inconsistent with the slogan, theme or position, it undermines a place's credibility. Such inconsistent situations are common where there is a non-existent or incoherent marketing strategy. This is a big challenge, particularly for small places where a focused approach is even more necessary in order to reach the market.

Here are four commonly used visual image strategies:

1. The diverse visual. In the diverse strategy, viewers are treated to a wide range of visual images about a place. The aim is to dispel the notion that a place has a single character. Many big Asian cities have a diverse visual strategy. At the same time, there are different levels of visual images. Two or three world-class images usually have a top priority. A whole range of "minor" images, creating an overall complete and diverse strategy, often supplements these images. Malaysia is marketing its mix of three of the world's oldest cultures — Chinese, Malay and Indian — with its "Malaysia: Truly Asia" campaign. The marketing message showcases diverse attractions such as the country's varied Asian history, culture, festivals, music and food. The overall visual effect is one of versatility and completeness.
2. The consistent visual. This is the opposite of the diverse visual. When a place possesses a clear and positive image, it is easier to assemble a consistent visual. On the other hand, problems may occur if quite different target groups are approached with one and the same consistent visual. For example, one visual, the kangaroo of Australia,

may be of little relevance for certain target groups, such as international businesses.

3. The humorous visual. In the humorous strategy, the visual portrays a place in a witty style. This can be especially useful when dealing with a negative aspect. To promote their country to Europeans travelers, the Australian Tourist Commission launched "Discover the other side of yourself."[27] This humorous campaign was aimed at overcoming barriers of distance and cost by convincing European travelers they were in for an unforgettable, perhaps transformational, experience in the country. It promised visitors the discovery of a true but unknown side of themselves. Television ads humorously illustrated the transformation of extreme personality types while holidaying in Australia. For example, one portrayed a workaholic enjoying the sun and sand on one of Australia's many beautiful beaches. Another showed a "control freak" transformed into a free spirit, running around trying to catch sheep. While it might seem an overly provocative positioning, the campaign worked. The visual told the entire story: Australia is a holiday destination for anyone around the world because it offers world-class facilities, beautiful sights and a variety of activities guaranteed to cure any personality disorder.

4. The denying visual. Another way to handle a negative image about a place is to overwhelm the target audience with positive images, some of which subtly deny the negative aspects. Many places use a denying visual, but there are risks. The denied negative aspects may turn up when visitors confront the realities. The message of the visual image may be that of a romantic and picturesque inner city with medieval traditions, whereas in reality it is a place with modern traffic congestion, characterized by an almost complete lack of urban planning to support the visual image. That's the case in Bangkok, where many visitors complain about the chronic traffic congestion and obvious lack of urban planning. A standard question about Bangkok is: How can this rapidly developing city be destroyed like this? However, Bangkok persists in marketing itself as a picturesque, ancient city. The Grand Palace is now a world-class icon and when it is depicted there are no cars to be seen. It can do this because the country is a rich repository of beautiful cultural buildings, historical sites and artifacts. But denying initial visual impressions can cause frustration among visitors when high expectations are challenged on arrival, and further undermined during the process of moving from attraction to attraction.

Events and Deeds

Most image campaigns take the form of catchy slogans, advertisements, brochures, pamphlets and videos. But images can also be communicated through events and deeds. A successful effort can brand a place and its image permanently. The events can be bold, or they can be on the quiet side, subtly influencing an audience over time. For years, China showcased its athletes as other Cold War communist countries once did, as a symbol of national strength and resolve. Japan celebrated its automobile and electrical appliances, and soon South Korea followed. Taiwan is busy building a national brand based on original, value-added products of all kinds. The aim is to build up a quality image abroad and at home. Many places are doing this but the difference is that China, Japan and other Asian countries have systematically used branding as a national tool for political and economic reasons.

The fair and festival business is a constant in Asia. Such established festivals as the Dragon Boat Festival in China and the Gion Festival in Kyoto are sure sell-outs every year. When Chiba's city fathers decided to make their city a destination, they launched a festival devoted to the city and its products. And Malaysia's Borneo, by re-establishing quality and introducing innovation to its Rainforest World Music Festival, has reaped enormous positive publicity.

HOW CAN A PLACE CORRECT A NEGATIVE IMAGE?

Many external forces beyond a place's control shape its image. When Taiwan suffers an earthquake, or Korea experiences an oil spill, or Mumbai has another bomb explosion, there can be a tremendous wave of negative publicity. This can also happen as a consequence of a chronically poor economy and bad local leadership. Under such circumstances, a place has to address the problem of its negative image. Exhibit 7.3 discusses strategies for reversing the impact of negative publicity surrounding the kidnapping of tourists from a Malaysian resort.

Exhibit 7.3: BEATING AN IMAGE

Violence presents a real threat to a country's image. The kidnapping of 21 tourists in a high-end diving resort in Sipadan forced a review of how Malaysia and its domestic security are viewed worldwide. A typical observation is found in a newspaper article ominously entitled "Malaysia Takes a Dive," which reported the kidnappings. The writer observed that "perhaps too busy with their own dinner, the police didn't notice [the kidnapping], and the thugs coolly made off with three fresh hostages. It gets worse. When some resort staff who managed to avoid capture by fleeing into the bush emerged hours later, they took their own boat over to Mataking to see why the police had not come to their rescue. There they found the police boats mired in low-tide mud."[1] The damage to a place's image can be swift in such cases, and controlling the problem is essential.

The kidnappings in Malaysia were an offshoot of the Muslim insurgency in the southern Philippines. On April 23, 2000, nine Malaysians and 12 foreigners were taken hostage from the Sipadan resort by gunmen of the Abu Sayyaf, a ragtag group of military rebels seeking independence for Mindanao, a large island in the southern Philippines. On September 10, three more Malaysians were abducted by Abu Sayyaf bandits from the Pasir Resort on Pandanan Island off Sabah's east coast. After the first kidnapping incident, the Malaysian government insisted that it had increased the vigilance of its coastal security. But the second kidnapping badly undermined that assertion.

The rules of a place's response to such an attack on its image should be automatic:

1. A clear, early and forceful verbal or written response to the attack is often effective.
2. Any confusion in the media regarding events or remedies should be quickly and comprehensively addressed whenever possible.
3. Any advertisements or announcements that affect the negative image should be withheld until resolution.
4. A set of solutions should be offered as quickly as possible. Whenever the remedies are in place, the promotion should be thorough and evident in all the channels of communication — TV, radio, print and the Internet.

The kidnappings in Malaysia are not as persistent a problem as inner-city crime or longstanding environmental image issues for many other cities. However, a relatively minor image problem can imply lack of control or deep-seated hostility. In the competitive battle for destination positioning, travel agents may redirect their individual and corporate clients to more peaceful and reliable locations; foreign investors may opt for the more stable political image offered by Singapore; and political allies may begin to wonder what price they are paying for their support.

Sources:

1   Ken Stier, "Malaysia Takes a Dive," *Time Asia*, September 21, 2000, viewed on January 11, 2001 at http://www.time.com/time/asia/features/news/2000/09/21/malaysia.kidnap.html.

Edd K. Usman, "$1M for Each Jolo Hostage of Abu Sayyaf?," *Manila Bulletin*, June 3, 2000, viewed on January 11, 2001 at http://www.mb.com.ph/MAIN/2000-06/MN060311.asp.

Making a Positive Out of a Negative

One obvious option is to admit to a problem and turn the negative into a positive. For years, many places in Central Asia have complained about their lack of tourist potential in the dark and cold climate that starts in October and persists until April. This extreme climate can be used as an opportunity and aggressively promoted as such. Indeed, Turkmenistan, Uzbekistan, Kazakhstan and Mongolia are trying to transform negative elements into positive attributes. An appropriate marketing slogan, such as "Top of Asia," could indicate not only a geographical position but also top performance in many other dimensions. Hence, we expect to see these various countries increasingly using the climate as a positive argument in relation to various target groups.

In fact, in the year 2000, Kazakhstan introduced the first international Khan Tengri Festival. The snow-sport festival brought together 520 sportsmen from 30 countries, including some top international climbers.[28] Other cold-climate destinations in Asia turn this to their advantage by hosting similar festivals. Cheju Island in Korea actively promotes its annual snow festival in the hopes of having it recognized as the biggest in Northeast Asia.[29] The Sapporo Snow Festival in Hokkaido, Japan, attracts two million people annually and is considered to be among the top international snow festivals in the world.[30]

Together, these northern examples show how, in an international economy, a region can change a number of traditionally interpreted weaknesses into world-class opportunities.

Another image-building technique is the transformation of a place that was originally viewed negatively into something positive. After the Second World War, Asia was a continent characterized by the aftermath of foreign invasions and unwelcome colonization. Ironically, that unfortunate history has given several places a position on the tourist map. In Singapore, the Changi Prison Chapel and Museum and the Kranji War Memorial serve as reminders of the tragic war. In 1937, the Japanese left Nanjing Province in China burnt out, with 300,000[31] people dead after the infamous Nanjing Massacre (sometimes called "the other holocaust")[32]. Today, the Nanjing Massacre Memorial, built in 1985 and featuring often horrific exhibits and artifacts, draws visitors to the province and serves as a lesson from the past. Such negative events have put these places in a highly visible historical perspective, and Asians easily recognize them as significant to their past and their heritage. Museums and other monuments, which have been built in order to keep history living for new generations, attract large numbers of visitors. In many cases, companies are involved in restoration and other activities to make history more vivid. For instance, a number of corporate sponsors make possible Fort Siloso, Sentosa Island's war memorial. Australia has formed the Australian War Memorial Foundation, which raises funds from the private sector to preserve its war memorials and galleries, and to acquire artifacts.

Marketing Icons

Another strategy for correcting a negative image is icon marketing. Consider the image of Shanghai, which, during most of the second half of the 20th century, struck visitors as a sadly closed city. Its image evoked smuggled pictures of protestors and violent demonstrations; repression of government opposition; underdeveloped transportation and communication infrastructure; and taciturn, secretive Chinese leaders determined to bring the once-proud city and its people to their knees. The overall impression of darkness and iron-fisted control portrayed Shanghai as a place that few people would want to visit.

The entrance of Zhu Rongji, current Chinese premier and new-style international icon signaled a dramatic new direction. In a winning demonstration of impression management, the former mayor of Shanghai used a distinctly "no nonsense" style to help reshape the public's image of the city and his country. Slowly, the stern Cold War communist image faded and revealed a new Shanghai and China (see Exhibit 7.4, which profiles a new Chinese icon).

Exhibit 7.4: A CHINESE ICON

Zhu Rongji, a no-nonsense political leader with a by-the-rules engineering background, is a living icon who symbolizes the vast Renaissance-like improvements in Shanghai and much of China in the late 20th century. Zhu first came to prominence as mayor of Shanghai from 1987 to 1991. He took responsibility for the city, a dimly lit, unpainted financial wreck, at a time when China would soon be reeling from the international backlash that followed the bloody Tiananmen crackdown.

A leader by example, Zhu adopted the style and image of a non-stop doer — building on a gigantic scale, investing government money and power in private enterprise and promoting local stock market listings. He also wooed venture capitalists to encourage funding for start-up companies. At the same time, he convinced state-owned companies to accept his then radical market-reform initiatives.

In March 1998, Zhu became the fifth premier of the State Council. Since then, "one-chop Zhu" — the nickname he earned as mayor of Shanghai for cutting through red tape — has been at the forefront of economic and political change in China and often on the receiving end of sharp criticism from conservatives. As in Shanghai, one of his first priorities as premier was to streamline the national government's bloated bureaucracy. In the meantime, Zhu has championed an ambitious privatization program covering housing, education and banking-sector reform.

After his inauguration, Zhu set a three-year goal to pull the state-owned sector out of debt through extensive dismissals of redundant employees and debt-for-equity swaps. This ambitious task was complicated by the Asian financial crisis and the cost and difficulty of retraining workers. In January 2001, Zhu and his administration declared that the debt-ridden state-owned sector had shown significant signs of turnaround, although not everyone agreed. While competition for efficiency and profits was real, critics feared that real results did not depend on competition. Improvements, critics argued, were frequently the result of external factors and state intervention; for example, large oil companies benefited from higher oil prices while other state-owned enterprises found relief in a generous debt-relief program led by the government. Zhu ignored criticisms and continued to press for change.

However, that pressure was more a function of Zhu's role as China's chief supporter of reforms necessary to gain membership into the World Trade Organization (WTO) than of the critics' worries. Despite frequent setbacks at home and abroad, the determined reformer pushed difficult agreements with the United States and the European Union, necessary precursors to WTO entry. As a result, in 2000, after seven straight years of decline, China's growth accelerated on the strength of renewed investor confidence and greater openness to China's exports. Today, despite consistent criticism from conservatives, Zhu continues to push aggressively for the continued development of his country into a more open, prosperous place. And, importantly, his style and character are inseparable from his agenda and deeds.

Sources

Karby Leggett, "China Touts Reform of State Enterprises," *Asian Wall Street Journal*, January 9, 2000, p. 1.
"Biographies of Prominent Chinese Leaders," *Inside China Today* Web site, http://www.insidechina.com/bio/biolead.php3, viewed on May 7, 2001; "Zhu Rongji: Premier, State Council — Biographical Profile," *China Online*, January 13, 2000, viewed on January 8, 2001 at http://www.chinaonline.com/refer/biographies/secure/BB-REV-ZhuRongji3-3.asp. Peter Wonacott, "China, U.S. Accelerate WTO Push: Fears That Delays May Thwart Economic Growth Heighten Urgency of Talks," *The Asian Wall Street Journal*, January 12–14, 2000, p.1.; Zhu Rongji, "Report on the Work of the Government," speech delivered at the Third Session of the Ninth National People's Congress, http://www.chinaonline.com/commentary_analysis/economics/currentnews/secure/C00031020.asp, viewed on January 11, 2001; Michael Panizza, "China's Emerging Private Business Sector," viewed on January 12, 2001 at http://www.hfni.gsehd.gwu.edu/~ylowrey/Mpanizza.htm.

Removing the Negative

Image improvement, rather than real improvement, is too often used as a panacea or a quick fix for a place's problems. Place leaders besieged by failing businesses or a drop in tourism are usually quick to demand a new image. Yet, in most instances, it does not work if a place has not started to correct its more deep-rooted problems.

Consider the case of the port city of Dalian. If, in the early 1990s, Asians had been asked to prepare a list of deeply troubled urban cities, the city of Dalian would undoubtedly have been included. A place with major environmental problems — petrochemical and fuel plants polluting the city's air and water — Dalian deserved its reputation as the center of China's industrial rust belt. Dalian today, while it still has problems, is an improving city that is considered the "bright pearl of northern China."[33] What steps did it take to achieve this transformation?

Firstly, stricter emission controls were implemented and polluting companies shut down. As the city's reformist mayor, Bo Xilai, explained, Dalian's "expenditure for environmental protection was substantial, but we were aware that [the] benefits are great. Once a city is clean, people feel better and foreigners are attracted to invest more. The city gains value this way."[34] The Dalian Environmental Protection Bureau also sponsored a radio program, "Voice of Green," to promote environmental awareness among the local population.[35] When Dalian citizens began to witness the cleaning up of their city and the new jobs created, their attitudes started to improve. They began to police themselves, encourage innovation and change, and monitor their own political, economic and educational institutions. As a result, the city's port is the third-largest in China and the country's largest export harbor. Its workforce is considered to be among the most skilled in the country.[36]

Secondly, the city's image-makers began to work together to communicate the changing reality of Dalian. The local government launched international promotional campaigns to attract foreign investment and initiated a civic beautification campaign at home. These campaigns demonstrated the city's transformation economically and visually. As a result, articles in newspapers and magazines heralded the arrival of a new giant in port facilities. Indeed, image met reality in Dalian. Visitors to the city saw the changes and experienced the revival of the environment. The mayor's dream of transforming the city into the Hong Kong of northeastern China was becoming a reality.

CONCLUSION

The creation of a powerful image is part of the entire marketing process. It demands a good strategic-marketing audit, a determined improvement of the product and a creative invention of the symbols. Once a place has taken these steps, its next task is to disseminate its new image to its target groups.

The next chapter examines how place marketers can distribute messages and images effectively.

1 http://www.vietnamtourism.com/e_pages/tourist/general/t_statistic.htm, viewed on January 21, 2001.
2 http://www.tradeport.org/ts/countries/vietnam/isa/isar0024.html, viewed on January 2, 2001.
3 Chien-min Chung, "The Ghosts of Tiananmen," *Asiaweek*, January 19, 2001, p. 20.
4 http://www.cnn.com/US/9806/20/china.infomercials/, viewed on December 4, 2000.
5 http://www.cnta.com/HTMLE/theme98/zhici/zhici.htm, viewed on December 5, 2000.
6 Results are based on a survey of Western expatriates and Asian executives working in Asia with knowledge of Singapore, December 2000.
7 http://www.aptourism.com/html/invaptpforeword.htm, viewed on December 4, 2000.
8 http://www.tdctrade.com/beyond97/supermkt.htm, viewed on December 4, 2000.
9 http://www.visit-southaustralia.com.au/, viewed on January 29, 2000.
10 http://www.amazingthailand.th/amazing2000/index.html, viewed on November 27, 2000.
11 http://www.adb.org/GMS/wgt10.asp, viewed on November 27, 2000.
12 http://www.biztravelinthailand.com/tat.html, viewed on November 27, 2000.
13 http://www.2000.australia.com/, viewed on December 5, 2000.
14 http://www.nepalnews.com.np/contents/englishweekly/independent/11-03/tourism.htm, viewed on November 27, 2000.
15 http://www.macautourism.gov.mo/index.htm, viewed on June 27, 2001.
16 http://www.visitmaldives.com/, viewed on November 29, 2000.
17 http://www.newasia-singapore.com/, viewed on November 29, 2000.
18 http://www.hkta.org/usa/pr/kaleidoscope.html, viewed on November 29, 2000.
19 http://www.eventscorp.com.au, viewed on December 5, 2000.
20 *Ayurveda* (def.): "a holistic alternative medical system, originating in India, whose goal is to prevent disease with the balance of three elements believed to be present and at work in the body," Yahoo! Health Web site, http://health.yahoo.com/health/Alternative_Medicine/Alternative_Therapies/Ayurvedic_Medicine/, viewed on January 29, 2001.
21 http://www.siargao.com/, viewed on December 5, 2000.
22 http://www.hkta.org/usa/pr/kaleidoscope.html, viewed on November 29, 2000.
23 http://www.wbidc.com/overview/gateway.htm, viewed on November 27, 2000.
24 http://www.stb.com.sg/t21/index.stm, viewed on November 29, 2000.
25 http://www.cityofsydney.nsw.gov.au/catz_scfaf_city_culture.asp#Cultural_capital, viewed on December 5, 2000.
26 http://www.city.osaka.jp/english/newsen.html, viewed on December 5, 2000.
27 http://www.atc.net.au/brand/campaigns/brand/brand.htm, viewed on December 4, 2000.
28 http://www.danskbjergklub.dk/dsf/emailsICC/FKT2000.html, viewed on December 4, 2000.
29 http://korea.insights.co.kr/english/festival/fes_37.html, viewed on December 4, 2000.
30 http://jin.jcic.or.jp/atlas/festivals/fes01.html, viewed on January 29, 2001.
31 http://www.chinanow.com/english/nanjing/travel/sights/massacre.html, viewed on December 5, 2000.
32 http://www.skycitygallery.com/japan/japan.html, viewed on December 5, 2000.
33 http://www.asi.fr/~lfarget/dalian.htm, viewed on December 4, 2000.
34 David Hsieh, "The Green Revolution," *Asiaweek*, December 17, 1999.

35 Wen Bo, "Greening the Chinese Media," China Environment News, Summer 1998, viewed on December 5, 2000 at http://www.ecsp.si.edu/ecsplib.nsf/451f9216fa25558f852564a30080384a/c9129ec7433d4a6d8525664b007574ad?-OpenDocument.
36 http://www.china-dalian.com/about.asp, viewed on December 5, 2000.

8

Distributing a Place's Image and Message

E very place needs to develop a story about itself and to tell it consistently and well. Yet, the sheer number of markets and media channels creates a high risk for sending contrary and confusing messages. If, say, the tourist commission in Pusan promotes the booming tourism sector and the chamber of commerce promotes the same area as a site for its port facilities and production companies, confusion could easily arise.

This chapter examines the challenges involved in distributing a strong and coherent image of a place. Those in charge of distributing the place's image must address the following questions:

1. Who is the target audience?
2. What broad tools of influence are available?
3. What major advertising-media channels are available and what are their respective characteristics?
4. What criteria should be used in choosing specific advertising-media vehicles?
5. How should the advertising messages be timed?
6. How can the media mix be developed?
7. How can the communication outcomes be evaluated?
8. How can conflicting media sources and messages be handled?

CLARIFYING THE TARGET AUDIENCE AND DESIRED BEHAVIOR

The first step before choosing messages and media is to clarify the target audience. For example, how should Madhya Pradesh, the largest state of the Indian Union, clarify its target audiences with so many diverse attractions? Called the "Heart of India," Madhya Pradesh was the inspiration for Rudyard Kipling's *Jungle Books*. Kipling's vivid descriptions immortalized the Kanha National Park, now called "Kipling Country." With a glorious past, a geographical gateway location and a border shared with seven other states, Madhya Pradesh could target many tourist audiences. The state is already a leader in attracting Foreign Direct Investment (FDI), and ranked number three among Indian states in approved FDI from 1991–1997.[1] It is highly regarded among investors. However, this fact, along with the tourist profile, makes it difficult to clarify and prioritize target audiences. Each potential target market calls for different messages and media. Should the government of Madhya Pradesh rely on advertisements or feature articles? Should it place messages in local and international business newspapers or in Air India's in-flight magazines?

A second step calls for visualizing the target behavior that the marketers want to elicit from the target audience. That behavior may be to spend three days in the mountains, buy a condominium or visit in the summer rather than in the winter.

Beyond these steps, it is necessary to determine the target visitor or investor's stage of readiness to undertake the target behavior. A tourist seeking a romantic vacation in Kanha may hold one of several preconceptions regarding Kanha as a destination: knows nothing about Kanha and Madhya Pradesh; has some awareness of Kanha; knows a lot about Kanha; would like to go to Kanha; intends to go to Kanha. A media strategy for those who want to go might be to mail them discount coupons to provide an incentive to act. Another strategy is to communicate some additional information on "unknown" attractions. In this case, it could be an invitation to witness some of the region's colorful religious festivals.

The same issue of the buyer's readiness arises with business targets. In marketing a factory site, place sellers need to distinguish between suspects, prospects, hot prospects and customers (see Exhibit 4.4). Each place-buyer group warrants a different media-mix strategy. Advertisements in trade journals offering a free booklet describing the factory site and its advantages might ferret out suspects. Prospects might receive phone calls followed by sales calls. Hot prospects might be personally invited and driven to the site, and introduced to the community leaders and some relevant businesses.

CHOOSING BROAD TOOLS OF INFLUENCE

Place sellers can use several broad tools of influence to promote a place to target groups. The major promotional tools are advertising, direct marketing, sales promotion, public relations and personal selling. Descriptions of their characteristics, effectiveness, use and costs follow.

Advertising

Advertising is the use of any paid form of non-personal presentation and promotion of ideas, goods or services by an identified sponsor. Thus, the purchase by a community, region or nation — or even an individual company promoting its place — of printed space (magazines, newspapers, billboards) or broadcast time (television, radio, Internet) constitutes advertising.

Because of the many forms and uses of advertising, it is difficult to generalize about its distinctive qualities as a component of the promotional mix. Yet the following qualities can be noted:

1. **Public.** Advertising is a highly public form of communication. Its public nature confers a kind of legitimacy on a place and its products and also suggests a standardized offering. Because many people receive the same message, place buyers, new residents or visitors know that their motives for choosing a destination will be publicly understood. Thus, if a person takes a vacation in Kanha, he/she will expect others to interpret the natural splendor of Kanha in the same way it is presented in the travel advertisements.
2. **Pervasive.** Advertising is a pervasive medium that permits the place seller multiple repetitions of a message. It also allows the place buyer to receive and compare the messages of various Asian places. A seller's large-scale advertising suggests, at least, that a place has certain resources behind it.
3. **Dramatic.** Advertising provides opportunities for dramatizing a place and its attractions through the artful use of print, sound and color. However, sometimes the tool's very success at expressiveness may dilute or detract from the message.
4. **Impersonal.** Advertising is often less compelling than personal presentation. The target group feels no obligation to pay attention or respond. Advertising is able to carry on only a monologue, not a dialogue, with the audience.[2]

Advertising can be used to build up a long-term image for a place or, on the other hand, to trigger quick sales, such as an ad offering a special low-price airfare to Sri Lanka or Bali.

Advertising is an efficient way to reach numerous geographically dispersed investors or visitors at a low cost per exposure. Certain forms of advertising, such as television and video productions, require a large budget, while other forms can be done on a smaller budget.

During the last two decades, Asian newspapers and magazines have experienced a sharp increase in the scope of destination-marketing advertisements. Likewise, television commercials are on the rise, on both regional and domestic networks. An increasingly borderless Asia — in part brought about by the advent of the Internet as well as excellent air links — has helped to develop the market. *The Asian Wall Street Journal* and *International Herald Tribune* are two of the leading regional newspapers. Major regional publications — including international magazines with regional editions — include the *Far Eastern Economic Review, Asiaweek, Time, Newsweek, BusinessWeek* and *Fortune.* An analysis of Asia's destination-marketing advertisements leads to three conclusions:

1. A lack of uniqueness in the advertisements.
2. The Asian (especially Chinese) dimension is turning up in virtually all the advertisements.
3. The most compelling and innovative messages are often those of communities or cities, and not nations or regions.

Direct Marketing

Direct marketing encompasses the use of communication media to reach individuals in the audience where the effect is measurable. The two traditional tools of direct marketing are direct mail and the telephone. Individuals on a place's database can be sent appropriate newsletters, brochures, postcards or videos about a place. Lately, it has even become fashionable to send Christmas cards to potential place buyers. Fax and e-mail communications are increasingly popular direct-marketing distribution channels.

The direct marketer is able to measure the response rate of direct mail in terms of inquiries, intention to buy, or sales. This feature contrasts with advertising, which usually does not contain any response mechanism, such as a mail-back coupon or the sponsor's telephone number. Although direct-marketing advertising costs more per person reached, its superior targeting and response features often more than make up for the extra cost.

In addition to fax and e-mail communications, direct-marketing media have taken on other new forms in recent years, including direct-response radio and television, where a product is offered and the customer can immediately call a toll-free number to place an order using a credit card. Logically, the personal sales call is another example of direct marketing, since the salesperson knows the response at the end of the visit. However, we will treat personal selling as a separate influence channel later.

Direct marketing has a number of distinctive characteristics:

1. **Targeting efficiency.** The marketer can be selective as to who should receive the message.
2. **Message customization.** The marketer can customize the message for each inquiry, based on what is known about that prospect.
3. **Interactive quality.** The prospect or customer who receives the message can interact and communicate with the marketer regarding questions, suggestions, complaints and orders.
4. **Response measurement.** The marketer can measure the response rate to evaluate the success of the marketing program.
5. **Relationship building.** The marketer can build and enhance the relationship with a particular prospect through sending thoughtful messages on special occasions (such as birthdays and anniversaries) or giving patronage awards.

These characteristics of direct marketing offer interesting possibilities for destination marketers. Direct marketing is an efficient way to acquire leads on prospective enterprises, potential residents, vacation seekers and other place buyers. Once the leads are collected, direct marketing can further present offers, test interest and measure readiness to buy. For these reasons, we expect direct marketing to occupy a growing part of the marketer's budgets in the coming years.

Sales Promotion

Sales promotion encompasses the use of short-term incentives to encourage buyers to purchase a product or service. Where advertising offers a reason to buy, sales promotion offers an incentive to buy. Not surprisingly, sales promotion yields a faster purchase response than advertising.

Sales promotion includes such devices as free samples, coupons, cash rebates, discounts, premiums, prizes, patronage rewards, free trials, warranties, demonstrations and contests. Marketers have developed a whole set of such tools in their bidding wars for corporate and factory relocation: inducements include tax concessions, subsidized housing and job retraining, special financing, infrastructure improvements and cheap land. Sales promotion of this kind has increased in Asia during the last decade.

Although sales promotion tools — coupons, contests, premiums, and the like — are highly diverse, they have three distinctive characteristics:

1. **Communication.** They gain attention and usually provide information that may lead the target audience to show more interest in a place.
2. **Incentive.** They incorporate some concession, inducement or contribution that gives specific target packages to the audiences.
3. **Invitation.** They include a distinct invitation to engage in an immediate transaction.

Sales-promotion tools create a stronger and quicker response than any other influence channel. Sales promotion can dramatize product offers and boost sagging sales. Promotion effects, however, are usually short term, and do not build lasting place preferences.

Public Relations

Public relations is the effort to build good relations with an organization's publics by obtaining favorable publicity, building up a good public image and handling or heading off unfavorable rumors, stories and events. Major public relations tools include press relations, event publicity and lobbying. The appeal of public relations is based on its three distinctive qualities:

1. **Highly credible.** News stories and features written by independent journalists seem more authentic and credible than advertisements.
2. **Indirect.** Public relations can reach many prospects who might otherwise avoid salespeople and advertisements. The message gets to the place buyers as news rather than as a sales-directed communication.
3. **Dramatic.** Like advertising, public relations has a potential for dramatizing a place.

Marketers tend to under-use public relations or use it as an afterthought. Yet, a well-thought-out public relations program, coordinated with other promotion-mix elements, can be extremely effective (see Exhibit 8.1).

Exhibit 8.1: RESTORING ECONOMIC CONFIDENCE
IN KOREA

By mid December 1997, Asia's financial crisis was at its height in South Korea. Considered one of Asia's dragon economies for nearly three decades, this proud country was struggling to meet short-term foreign currency obligations of US$25 million following a 40% drop in the value of its currency. Worse, critical sources of foreign exchange had dried up, along with investor confidence. The value of portfolio investment declined by 50%.

South Korea's first democratically elected president, Kim Dae Jung, sharing his advisors' belief that the country had suffered a debilitating loss of confidence among international investors, assembled a group of senior economic advisors to "assess the situation, produce an International Monetary Fund (IMF)-supported reform plan, and restore investor confidence."[1] Indeed, they had their task cut out for them. In international media, South Korea was portrayed as a nationalistic, hostile environment for international investors, a militant labor-groups minefield, and an economy characterized by hugely inefficient conglomerates run by corrupt and incompetent first- and second-generation founders. As a result, Kim's crisis team proved largely ineffectual in selling the "New Korea."

In February 1998, South Korea's Ministry of Finance and Economy retained international public relations firm Burson-Marsteller (BM) to help the country take charge of the global crisis dialogue. BM contracted an outside research company to identify or verify critical perceived threats to recovery among the international investment and financial communities. The results showed that respondents "(1) viewed the economic crisis as caused by structural defects in the economy and not simply a loss of confidence; (2) viewed the Korean government as reacting to events rather than implementing a plan for recovery; and (3) did not believe there was a broad consensus supporting reform."[2]

The BM plan identified international and domestic financial institutions, international media, and international economic and political policy communities as its chief target audiences.

Four key messages were to be communicated: 1) South Korea had developed an effective plan to restore economic growth; 2) a strong financial team was in place to implement the plan; 3) Kim's administration was consistently pro-business, transparent and fair; and 4) the country was committed to providing timely and reliable access to economic information.

Implementation took several forms. First, communications counsel was provided to senior ministry officials. A number of seminars were conducted to help these officials acquire the skills to interact effectively with credit-rating agencies, investors and purveyors of economic information. Second, the economic team appointed by the president was given communication training that emphasized delivering presentations to the financial and economic communities.

Third, a third-party network of allies and spokespeople to support the ministry's message was developed. These allies participated in road shows and signed opinion pieces developed for publication in influential media. Fourth, BM worked closely with the media, arranging interviews, providing background information and submitting opinion pieces. There were also regular briefings for the foreign press. Fifth, speaking opportunities were arranged for ranking ministry officials, with speeches written by BM to ensure consistency of communication. Sixth, a regular, investment newsletter-type publication was developed and sent to key publics.

In the meantime, BM also implemented tactical initiatives that enabled the government to respond rapidly to, and keep track of, emerging issues, and to keep the investment audience engaged in anticipation of the country's first bond offering since the onset of the crisis.

As a result of the comprehensive communications program with the international media, there was a dramatic shift in the tone of international reports. In November 1998, *The Los Angeles Times* reported that "More than any other country in the region, and certainly more than Japan, South Korea has been a model from the U.S. perspective. It has accepted International Monetary Fund medicine even when the prescription was questionable, moved to reform and re-capitalize its outdated banking system, and taken steps to expand democracy, open markets, and begin dismantling bloated companies and crony capitalism."[3]

Sources:

1 Jerry A. Hendrix, "Restoring Economic Confidence in Korea during the Asian Financial Crisis," *Public Relations Cases*, 5th edition (Wadsworth/ Thomson Learning, 2001), pp.349–353, case 9.b.
2 Burson-Marsteller, "Sovereign Financial Communications Program Provided to the Government of Korea," Case Study, 1998.
3 Hendrix, p. 353.

Within Asia, there are thousands of small, medium and large public relations companies, and hundreds of established firms. They range from one-person outfits to multinational firms. But one thing is certain: the proliferating number of media and the public relations practices of multinational firms are making professional public relations practice in Asia both respected and sought after.

The craft of public relations is segmented and specialized. There are financial public relations, employee public relations, government public relations, and so on. The branch we are interested in is marketing public relations (MPR).[3] In the hands of a place marketer, MPR can contribute in the following ways:

1. **Assist in the launch of new products.** Each time McDonald's or Jollibee establish a new restaurant, they launch a public relations campaign with special events, press releases, and so on. Other industries such as consumer products companies, multinational technology concerns, telecommunications companies and electronic marketplaces follow the same practice.
2. **Assist in repositioning a mature product.** Singapore, with its mature tourist image, is ambitiously using public relations to reposition itself as a regional business and financial center. The long-term goal is to build up and enhance the city's service sectors and investment in them.
3. **Create interest in a product category.** The Asian telecommunications industry is struggling to survive in a newly liberalized and highly competitive global market. These companies have sponsored public relations campaigns in conjunction with places — especially those targeting business travelers — to attract attention to this industry. This effort is particularly pronounced in Singapore and Hong Kong.
4. **Influence specific target groups.** The Philippines, in an effort to build up tourism, implements its special "Rediscovery Philippines"[4]

campaigns directed towards Filipino communities in the United States. India does the same to promote investment to its non-resident Indians (NRI) around the world. Malaysian resorts, in part because of their colonial past, target European rather than North American markets.

5. **Defend places that have encountered public problems.** In the aftermath of the Asian financial crisis, many Asian places have undergone severe political upheaval. These places are initiating public relations programs aimed at convincing investors that they are stable and growing. With the level of new FDI down across the region, this is a high-stakes effort. Because substance must follow style, it is not surprising that many of these efforts fall short.

6. **Build a place's image in a way that reflects favorably on its products.** The reorientation in Taiwan towards the manufacture of original, value-added products — especially technology products — creates a new place for image initiatives. For example, the government has initiated deft campaigns that communicate the diversity and originality of products designed and produced in Taiwan — from bicycles to scanners to sophisticated software. As Fiji shifts from a tourism-oriented economy to a more business-oriented approach, the country's Trade and Investment Bureau introduced the annual Exporter of the Year Awards to encourage exporters to make a greater contribution to export earnings. Awards categories incorporate small, medium and large exporters, as well as special awards for the indigenous exporters. The top prize is the prestigious Prime Minister's Exporter of the Year Award. The awards have gained momentum over the years and are used by winning companies to promote their products. Fiji is also active in promotional missions as well as in organizing investment seminars to promote its business image.[7]

As the power of mass advertising weakens as a result of rising media costs, increasing clutter and fragmented audiences, marketing managers are turning more to public relations. Often public relations can create a memorable impact on public awareness at a fraction of the cost of advertising. The place seller does not pay for the space or time obtained in the media. Instead, it pays for specialist staff to develop and place stories and to manage certain events. Sometimes the community pays the public relations company only when a story is actually accepted in a newspaper. If a place develops a story with an interesting angle, it might be picked up by all the news media and be worth millions of dollars in equivalent advertising. Furthermore, this would have more credibility than advertising. Some experts claim that an audience is five times more likely to be influenced by editorial copy than by advertising.

Personal Selling

Personal selling is the most effective tool at certain stages of the process of choosing a destination, particularly in building up an investor's or visitor's preference and conviction toward an action. The reason is that personal selling has three distinct advantages over advertising.

1. **Personal confrontation.** Personal selling involves a live, immediate and interactive relationship between two or more people. Each party is able to observe firsthand the other's needs and characteristics and make immediate adjustments.
2. **Cultivation.** Personal selling permits all kinds of relationships to spring up, ranging from a matter-of-fact selling relationship to a deep personal friendship. Effective sales representatives keep their customers' interests at heart if they want long-term relationships.
3. **Response.** Personal selling makes the buyer feel under some obligation to respond after listening to the sales talk. The buyer feels a responsibility to be attentive and to respond, even if only with a polite "Thank you."

These advantages come at a cost. A sales force represents a fixed financial commitment. Advertising can be turned on and off, but the size of a sales force is more difficult to alter.

Other Tools

Additional image and promotion tools — not all under a place's control — can help or hurt a place. Here are some examples:

Television

TV broadcasting has at least two routes that can influence the marketing context. First, a place can suddenly become popular in the Asian or world arena because of a television appearance. For example, the long-running Australian television program "Home and Away,"[6] filmed in Sydney's high-rent Palm Beach, made the whole area well known to a broad international audience. "Survivor" popularized Malaysian beaches in millions of homes worldwide. Second, there is often a place battle when a broadcasting company is announcing its plan to open a new TV studio/TV team. Marketers know from experience that close connections to such a media center — irrespective of its size — makes a place much more visible. Third, with the advent of regional television broadcasting, many countries and places in Asia have shifted significant resources to capitalize on the extended reach that CNN and CNBC, especially, provide. There is also considerable prestige associated with advertising on these networks. As a result, the rates for buying an advertising spot on CNBC India, for example, increased five times in the year 2000.[7] The willingness of advertisers to pay these rates suggests that they are realizing a reasonable return on their investment.

However, considering the 300 million television-watching households in the continent, Asia's television-advertising market remains small and the figures low. For the year 2000, television advertising amounted to only US$13.5 billion in Asia (excluding Japan), with China and India combined spending only US$5 billion a year. On the other hand, the Americas, with 100 million television-watching households, spent US$50 billion in television advertising for the same year.[8]

Song

Marketing places through music can add value to a place's image and brand. The score and the location of the classic film *A Passage to India* gave sound and visual appeal to an Indian region. The song "A Land Down Under" pays tribute to a legendary place. And who visits South Asia without listening to the music produced by its unique musical instruments, or travels to East Asia without hearing its distinctive sounds? In 1997, the Association of South East Asian Nations adopted as its anthem a composition by Filipino composer Ryan Cayabyab and lyricist Nicanor G. Tiongson, which later became the ASEAN Song of Unity.

The annual Voice of Asia International Music and Song Festival held in Almaty, Kazakhstan, has helped boost the city's image as an international destination. Participants come from all over the world and hundreds of journalists cover the event, which takes place in the open in the Medeu Gorge. This is an example of a unique opportunity for participants to market their home countries through their music. Participants are asked to perform songs that reflect their countries' melodies and national features, and to use indigenous instruments.

Another major opportunity can arise when a song's theme reflects the image of a place. The Yoko Ono song on Hiroshima, discussed in Chapter 6, is an example of how a song can contribute to place recognition. Yet another opportunity occurs when a singer or band achieves recognition outside their home country. Examples include Taiwan's Coco Lee, Indonesia's Anggun, and Australia's Kylie Minogue, Natalie Imbruglia and the band Silverchair, who are recognized all over the world. Rudyard Kipling's poem "On the Road to Mandalay," which was put to music by Frank Sinatra and Noel Coward, has also been used productively (*The Road to Mandalay* is the name of a luxury cruise liner operated by Orient Express that navigates between Bagan City and Mandalay). Other art forms can also influence public perception of a place, as shown in Exhibit 8.2.

Exhibit 8.2: GETTING THE BIG PICTURE

In the film *The Beach*, the spectacular location holds its own against the film's popular star, Leonardo DiCaprio. Shot on the uninhabited island of Phi Phi Le, near the city of Phuket in Thailand, the film provides what amounts to a free promotional package, despite much local opposition to the filming. Environmentalists were concerned that the filming — involving large numbers of people and a great deal of equipment — would have a negative impact on the natural beauty of the beach. They were also worried that popularizing the pristine beach would likewise cause a stampede to this and similar islands whose natural beauty had gone untouched by modern development.

A film such as *The Beach* can reach millions of people and has the potential to celebrate, define, vilify or even destroy a place. While it's important to build a consensus among all stakeholders for marketing a place, places that are looking for a marketing edge will find that the practice of encouraging local filmmakers and enticing film companies to shoot in their communities will raise their profile.

Asia is fast becoming a choice location for directors and producers alike. In fact, in 1998, some 20,000 jobs and US$10.3 billion in revenues in the U.S. film industry were lost to foreign production workers, according to the 1998 U.S. Runaway Film and Television Production Study Report commissioned by the Directors' Guild of America and the Screen Actors' Guild. Asia is often Hollywood's alternative back lot, largely because of the lower production costs and the expertise that resides within the region. The region also offers diverse and unconventional settings to filmmakers. Thailand, China, Malaysia, Fiji, the Philippines and Australia are just some of the countries that have been used as backdrops for blockbusters such as the James Bond film *Tomorrow Never Dies; The Last Emperor; Anna and the King; Castaway; Mission Impossible II;* and *Platoon*.

And while U.S. blockbusters still dominate the industry, Asia is finding ways to stimulate the film market. In many countries, such as Australia, state organizations have been created to provide free assistance with location scouting and advice on local production and post-production facilities. There is also an increase in the number of large-scale, multi-screen cinemas that can show a wider variety of films. Films such as *The Seven Samurai, Nowhere to Hide, The Piano, Farewell To My Concubine* and *Crouching Tiger, Hidden Dragon* are winning awards and making significant inroads into the world market.

Still, Asia can do more to promote its image as a film producer. Recent disagreements between film production groups and government agencies regarding the appropriateness of shooting particular films in a country have slowed the destination-promotion process. Also affecting distribution is the continuing practice of using subtitles, which, before *Crouching Tiger, Hidden Dragon*, limited a worldwide market. Despite these reservations, Asian-based films are going to grow and places that are eager to accommodate film production groups and to cut red tape are most likely to benefit from a film's inherent promotion of their destination to millions, almost free of charge.

Sources:

The Far East, February 1998, CineWeb Reel News Web site, viewed on December 7, 2000 at http://www.cineweb.com/reelnews/update/1998/feb/fareast.htm; Fact Sheets — Australian Department of Foreign Affairs and Trade, May 2000, viewed on December 7, 2000 at http://www.dfat.gov.au/facts/film_industry.html; "DGA/SAG Commissioned Study Shows Total Economic Impact of U.S. Economic Runaway Production Reached $10.3 Billion in 1998," Film and Television Action Committee Web site, viewed on February 12, 2001 at http://www.ftac.net/dga_sag_report/index.html.

Sports

Places often compete to host sporting events because of their ability to attract visitors, increase visitor spending and improve a destination's positioning. A championship season often serves as a catalyst to launching more effective and broader place-distribution campaigns. A water-sports festival or competition at a small beach in the Pacific can quickly elevate that destination's image into the mass-market league. The

Rainforest Cup in Sarawak[9] and Le Tour de Langkawi are actually place-tours. And sports teams can encompass all the dimensions of a place's ambitions and image. Among the reasons Melbourne is considered to be Australia's sports capital is that it is home to many of the country's most successful athletes and sports teams.[10]

Novelty Icons

The media occasionally shines a sudden spotlight on an icon that causes tourists to become determined to visit a place. For example, millions of people have made the pilgrimage to Tibet and Nepal to search the Himalayas in hopes of sighting "the Abominable Snowman" or Yeti. This unlikely iconic attribute has created a tourist industry which features attractions such as submarine rides and a multimedia tourist center that disseminates the latest news on the Yeti.

Even an individual landmark can be refocused via a literary icon. The Chinese legend of Fa Mulan, the girl who disguised herself as a man so that she could become a warrior, has been the inspiration of many poems, essays, paintings and operas and has significantly shaped the image of the Great Wall of China. In a more recent example, Disney's worldwide release of *Mulan* implanted the image of the Great Wall in the minds of many children. The Khajuraho temples in Madhya Pradesh are closely linked to the Indian book of love, *The Kama Sutra*. Each year, tourists from all over the world visit the temples, buy postcards and souvenirs, eat meals and boost the local economy.

SELECTING ADVERTISING MEDIA CHANNELS

The selection of effective media channels and vehicles is a formidable task. Choices are more complex than ever. For instance, Asia and the Pacific have witnessed an explosion in the entertainment and media industry. According to a projection by PricewaterhouseCoopers, the industry will show 7.2% growth in 2001.[11] Cable television is now almost an Asia-wide phenomenon. In China alone, there are 80 million subscribers to cable television networks.[12] Today, there are "generalist" channels — such as Zee TV (India), ABS-CBN (Philippines) and TV 7 Thailand — and "thematic" channels — CNBC Asia, Discovery, ESPN Asia and National Geographic.

The first step in selection calls for allocating the advertising budget to the major media channels. These channels must be examined for their capacity to deliver reach, frequency and impact. They include television, radio, the Internet, telephone, newspapers, magazines, newsletters, brochures, direct mail and billboards. Table 8.1 summarizes the respective advantages and limitations of these media.

Television

Television is the most effective medium for dramatizing the look and sound of a place. Television placement can range from 15- to 60-second network commercials to full programs produced in cooperation with a

Table 8.1: Profiles of major media types

Medium	Advantages	Limitations
1. Television	Combines sight, sound and motion. Appealing to the senses, high attention, high reach.	High absolute cost, high clutter, fleeting exposure, less audience selectivity.
2. Radio	Mass use, high geographic and demographic selectivity, low cost.	Lower attention than television, non-standardized rate structures; fleeting exposure.
3. Internet	High selectivity, interactive possibilities, relatively low cost.	A relatively new medium with a low number of users in some countries.
4. Telephone	Many users, opportunity to give a personal touch.	Too little local coordination in telecommunications services.
5. Newspapers	Flexibility, timeliness, good local market coverage, broad acceptance.	Short life, poor reproduction quality.
6. Magazines	High geographic and demographic selectivity, credibility and prestige.	Long advertisement purchase lead-time; some wasted circulation.
7. Newsletters	Very high selectivity, full control, interactive opportunities, relatively low costs.	Costs could run away.
8. Brochures	Flexibility, full control, can dramatize messages.	Brochure production can be a goal in itself; costs could run away.
9. Direct mail	Very high selectivity, measurable.	Relatively high costs, "junk mail" image.
10. Billboards	Flexibility, high repeat exposure, low cost, low competition.	No audience selectivity.

broadcasting company. Various place themes are common and popular and are often integrated in news programs. Compared with the situation in the United States, place marketing on television commercials is not yet common in Asia.

On the other hand, air travelers — and now some train travelers — are more often confronted with marketing messages which are distributed within a terminal, an aircraft, a railway station or onboard some Asian trains. Also, regional television stations such as CNN International, CNBC and the Star television network are having a profound effect on how investors and tourists receive information and on how marketers communicate with target constituencies.

Radio

Radio can be used in a number of ways to promote a place. Spot radio advertisements can advertise vacations, land availability or job availability. Different radio stations deliver different audiences and therefore must be selected carefully.

Radio stations can also serve as effective channels to build up a local identity. Transmitting a feeling of belonging and expressing a "sense of a place" are common goals of local radio stations. Thus, the local radio station can play a natural part in the marketing strategy.

Internet

The Internet channel is an increasingly important place-selling tool. Even the smallest Asian place has a Web site that can be found within seconds. However, a major problem is that place marketing via the Internet is often generic. Differentiated messages and concepts should be a priority when addressing the global marketplace. Surfing the Internet in search of Asian places reveals the following:

- The content of messages often takes the same form, irrespective of the character of a place.
- Places on the Internet often lack a marketing strategy. In the absence of a strategy, many messages list descriptive details instead of promoting a selective theme.
- Target marketing and specific packages delivered to selected audiences are still lacking.
- The interactive potential of the Internet has not yet been fully exploited.

In the future, the Internet may become the most important channel through which to advertise and communicate with place buyers. Indeed, research for this book reflects both the growing popularity and accessibility of marketing information provided over the Internet. For such potentially broad market coverage, initial costs are relatively low. On the other hand, there are long-term costs involved in keeping the Web site current and interesting to viewers. Obsolete information can convey a negative image for a place that is unwilling to support reinvestment in the site, or which fails to make it a top marketing-communications priority.

An impressive example of how the Internet is used effectively to promote investment is the Trade Tie-up Promotion Program, or TTPP, of the Japan External Trade Organization (JETRO). This Internet-based solutions system operates as a middle party by matching business proposals and requests from registered Japanese and overseas companies. The TTPP also offers free registration and browsing, a simple search function to find companies in 14 different business categories and easy contact with Japanese companies (see Figure 8.1).

Telephone

Telemarketing is a fast-growing sales tool. It has all the virtues of direct mail plus the ability to add a personal touch. The telephone can be used to gather leads, qualify them, sell to the leads and arrange personal meetings.

A major problem for many places, communities and regions is coordinating the rapid proliferation of their telephone services. New technologies are now opening for places to provide visitors with 24-hour call-center services. Hong Kong and Singapore are leading Europe and much of the United States in this respect. They have expanded their tourist services by employing 24-hour toll-free numbers and offering potential visitors a professional information and reservation service in relevant languages. This is certainly only the beginning. In the future, visitors will be able to book reservations and meet all their travel needs with a one-call service.

Newspapers

Newspapers offer a quick way to communicate messages about a place, such as news about festivals, exhibitions and various new projects. The weekly travel section of newspapers provides an opportunity to promote editorial material as well as place advertisements. Stories and advertisements about business opportunities can be placed in the business sections. Newspapers generally do not provide the same quality of artwork as magazines, but they are able to offer lower costs to reach selective geographical audiences and can do so in a timelier manner.

Figure 8.1: Trade Tie-up Promotion Program

Source: Japan External Trade Organization (JETRO), Manila office.

A marketer must also establish a strong relationship with key editors. Many mayors and civic leaders complain bitterly about a lack of understanding by local journalists of the problems of their place. But when officials are asked what they have done to improve a place's economic climate, all too often the answer is "I'll get back to you." Keeping the reporting community well informed with prompt and accurate information is a key link in the destination-marketing process.

Magazines

The virtue of magazines is that so many are available that the advertiser can reach almost any target group by knowing a group's reading habits. Public relations people often attempt to place long, favorable stories about a place in magazines, especially prestigious regional magazines that have greater credibility and reach than domestic publications. In-flight magazines are also popular vehicles for communicating destination-marketing messages.

A place advertisement must have some credibility if it is to be effective. For instance, if the place-selling message basically focuses on tax incentives and various subsidies — although these may be packaged in an attractive way — the place runs the risk of implying that financial incentives are offered as a compensation for negative factors. Such risks are apparent in the case of InvestHK in Figure 8.2. Among the seven advantages being marketed, two have a clear compensatory dimension: low taxes and no "red tape." What's missing, of course, is the high cost of real estate and tight unemployment. The other advantages are also subject to debate, except perhaps for "Pro-business Government," which is not a competitive trait but an expected one.

Newsletters

One way of building up long-term relations is to send highly selective newsletters to potential investors. This tool has grown in usage in recent years. The newsletters often have a simple layout, yet they can have an impact because they provide fresh news that cannot be read elsewhere. Furthermore, the information is very specialized and concentrates on narrow audiences.

Newsletters also have the advantage of focus and low cost. The Internet has emerged as a means of publishing newsletters electronically, leaving the cost of printing to the discretion of the reader.

Figure 8.2: Incentives — too good to be true

Competitive, efficient, and fast. Boldly cutting to the chase and surging ahead - that's the Spirit of Hong Kong! Coming aboard?

Hong Kong is Asia's world-class business hub. For the seventh consecutive year, we have been declared the freest economy in the world by the U.S.-based Heritage Foundation.

In the New Economy, global business is fast-moving, ever-changing, and highly-competitive. Companies need every advantage in the search for lucrative markets, and new investment opportunities. Coming to Asia? Then Hong Kong is the place to be!

- China's vast market on your doorstep
- Pro-business Government
- Established rule of law
- Low taxes - corporate and individual
- Leading-edge infrastructure
- No "red tape"
- Freedom of the press and information

InvestHK warmly congratulates the "Spirit of Hong Kong", which recently won Silver in the Boston to Buenos Aires leg of the "BT Global Challenge" - the gruelling 48,000 kilometre around-the-world yacht race. The 72-foot yacht, made in Mainland China by a Hong Kong company, symbolizes our vibrance as a world-class business centre. Follow our progress at **www.btchallenge.com**.

The Government of the Hong Kong Special Administrative Region (SAR)

Come and see what we're all about at www.InvestHK.gov.hk

15th Floor, One Pacific Place, Queensway, Hong Kong
Telephone: (852) 3107-1000   Facsimile: (852) 3107-9007   E-mail: enq@InvestHK.gov.hk

Source: *Fortune*, January 19, 2001, inside-back cover.

Brochures

The advantages of brochures are their low cost, their flexibility and their portability. Marketers can use brochures to tell the story of a place in a complete, and sometimes dramatic, manner. Brochures are staples of the tourism industry, as they can be displayed in many highly visible outlets in hotels, shops and restaurants. A tourist who is looking for information or something to do for a one-day or weekend visit often finds the brochure to be the clearest and timeliest of sources. Yet managers in charge of site selection often complain about the massive number of place-marketing brochures that come from various parts of Asia and the stereotypical impression they give. Brochures are often distributed without any target strategy and therefore entail a great deal of waste. When places neglect a target strategy, the brochures are often superfluous.

On the other hand, brochures designed for a specific target market can be very effective in getting a message across. Those prepared by the JETRO Business Support Centers are notable examples. These are distributed through JETRO offices around the world. For example, the brochure for Fukuoka (see Figure 8.3) provides basic information on Fukuoka and its Business Support Center, as well as an application form for interested companies.

Direct Mail

Direct mail has the capacity to reach a highly focused target audience. The message can be standard or completely customized for each recipient. Direct mail can describe an offer, serve as a reminder, make a suggestion or issue a request. It may consist of a long letter with personal greetings or it may include four-color graphics to jump-start interest in a place. The medium permits experimentation with different headlines, copy, envelopes, offers or prices to produce the most effective advertisement. Also, direct mail, in contrast to mass advertising, is a measurable-response medium.

Billboards

Billboards represent a geographically fixed medium seen only by those who drive past them. Like brochures, billboards can create a long-term impression and encourage people to make spontaneous decisions, prompting travelers to visit nearby attractions ("Visit Penang's Kek Lok Si Temple"). Billboards are also used in air terminals, railway stations and other public meeting places to greet visitors. Increasingly, the billboard message is much more than a simple "Welcome!." A higher

Figure 8.3: Fukuoka Business Support Center

Source: Japan External Trade Organization, Manila office.

value is communicated if the billboard states specific attributes — "Welcome to the Lion City" or "Welcome to Asia's Meeting Place." Both messages are found at Changi Airport in Singapore. Unfortunately, the main airport-messages in Asia cover "standardized" international products such as Diners Card, Visa or MasterCard, Nokia, Toyota, and so on. The traveler could be anywhere in the world and not know it from the signage; but that is changing. The localization of messages has increased dramatically in recent years. In some countries, such as Malaysia, it's required. In other places, marketers are acknowledging market forces.

Alternative Media

The media planner needs to consider an additional range of flexible and sometimes less-conventional media channels, such as audiocassettes, videotapes, faxes, trade missions, CDs, postcards, welcome centers, consulates and sponsorships.

Here are examples of how these channels have been used to promote a place:

- An audiocassette featuring typical local music or a famous local artist is sometimes given as a gift to the guest of the community.
- Videotapes are conventional tools today. The content of the tape can be flexible and effective as a vehicle for marketing a place. In many ways the videotape is the most vivid and dramatic tool in the destination-marketing arsenal.
- Faxes are used as an ad hoc tool to communicate with specific audiences.
- Place-destination CDs are beginning to replace both audio and videocassettes, since they enable the prospect to interact with the place's message.
- The once-simple picture postcard has become an important weapon in communicating a place's individuality. Unconventional layouts have yet to be explored, leaving considerable room for creative expression.
- Welcome centers, consulates and embassies are meeting places where media impact can be achieved (see Exhibit 8.3).
- Sponsoring car stickers and other products that promote a place is potentially effective. Some destinations invest in "trinket marketing," which is the marketing of a collection of items — pins, jackets, commemorative plates — that can add value to a place's image and brand, particularly during an event such as a world expo. The Sydney 2000 Olympics-related campaign is a good example of this.

There is also huge potential for a place to integrate local companies into its marketing efforts to increase visibility and coverage. Unconventional and creative ideas can originate from joint efforts for producing destination-enhancing company products, trade shows and advertising.

Exhibit 8.3: CALL THE CONSULATE: IS ANYONE HOME?

A good test for a place's ability to handle inquiries is the responsiveness of its representative consulate in overseas markets. On Monday, December 18, 2000, at 3:00 pm, the Hong Kong-based consuls of a number of countries were called to see how they respond to inquiries about locating a business in their respective countries. The results are described below.

- Thailand: no answer or phone message. Thailand will have to wait for another day.
- New Zealand: the caller received a voice message giving the telephone and fax numbers and the address of the Trade Development Board. The caller reached a person at the Trade Development Board, who suggested viewing the official Web site for information.
- Malaysia: a person asked the caller to call back the next day. Monday must have been an unscheduled national holiday.
- South Korea: the caller reached a person who suggested calling the Career Trade Center. The caller reached the Career Trade Center and was not given information over the phone but was asked to leave her fax number.
- India: the caller was transferred to another department and then asked to fax a list of information needed.
- The Philippines: the caller was transferred to the Trade and Investment Development Office, where she was interrupted before she finished her queries. She was then asked to fax all the information she needed.
- Australia: the caller reached a person who suggested another number for trade inquiries. After reaching that number the caller was requested to leave her contact number so a representative could get back to her.

- Singapore: a voice message gave the phone number of the Economic Development Board in Hong Kong for trade inquiries. When the caller reached that number, she was offered information but was requested to view the Web site first.
- Vietnam: the caller was offered a choice of only two languages — Mandarin or English — and no Cantonese. Then the caller was requested to telephone another department for trade inquiries. The caller reached a person at that number who asked her to visit the office so that she could be given more information.
- Japan: the caller reached a person and was transferred to a representative. The caller was asked to search the official Web site and was immediately faxed information on the country's labor laws.

Consuls, besides answering inquiries about tourism and business, serve as the natural communication link between the country and their constituents. It is important that inattentiveness or unreasonable barriers do not detour or waste inquiries and valuable leads.

1. If a consulate is listed in the telephone book, it should make sure it meets the expectations of people who need their questions answered.
2. A live human voice is best; one who is well trained, has good communication skills, and has the support and material to follow a precious lead.
3. An answering machine message should be clear, loud and informative.
4. Too many consuls use the answering message to either pre-screen callers or set up hurdles for information-seekers. High scores are given to consuls that keep reasonable hours, are quick to respond and have simple instructions on how to get information.

Choosing from the Categories

Marketers choose from among the various media channels outlined above by considering the following variables:

1. Target audience media habits. For example, direct mail and telemarketing are among the most effective media for reaching location decision-makers.
2. Product or service. Media categories have varying potential for demonstration, visualization, explanation, believability and color. Television, for example, is the most effective medium for describing a place or for creating an emotional effect, while magazines are ideal for presenting a single four-color image of a place.
3. Message. A message containing a great deal of technical data might require specialized magazines, the Internet or direct mailings.
4. Cost. What should count, of course, is the cost-per-thousand high-quality exposures, rather than the total cost.

Many marketers employ a variety of media because they recognize that different audiences pay attention to different media. Using several media extends the message's reach and re-emphasizes the content but may avoid repeating the message to the same audience. It is a difficult task to choose the right media mix since the product — i.e. a specific place — has so many complex offerings and, thus, possible target groups. The best way to judge the options is to base the media mix on a systematic marketing strategy in which basic offerings and target groups are well defined. Much remains to be done in Asia on this point.

SELECTING THE SPECIFIC MEDIA VEHICLES

The planner's second step is to choose the specific media vehicles within each media category that will produce the desired response in the most cost-effective way. Establishing how and why places mix costs and choose products is a major marketing decision (see Exhibit 8.4).

Exhibit 8.4: SINGAPORE TARGETS TWO AUDIENCES

Singapore, determined to become Asia's and, ultimately, the world's first choice for conventions and tourism, decided to advertise its new image for two types of place buyers: exhibition/convention organizers and visitors. For the exhibition/convention organizers, they chose to promote the new image and a number of venues and facilities in the November 2, 2000 issue of *The International Herald Tribune*. A special supplement lauded the attractiveness of Singapore as a business and financial center. It included the article "A Top Conference Location: Home to 3,000 Events a Year," which provided details of key events organized and conducted in Singapore. Another article — "Business Travel: Singapore Begins to Sizzle" — was concerned with the current status of business travel and facilities.

At the same time, Singapore marketed itself to foreign, regional and domestic tourists. It advertised the city's rich multicultural diversity, high-end facilities and attractions to Asian and foreign audiences via a massive multimedia marketing campaign with the theme "New Asia — Singapore." Advertisements were published in travel and weekly news magazines, and attention-grabbing spots were run on major television networks. A number of travel Web sites designed for specific segments of the market (such as www.meet-in-singapore.com.sg) were set up. The main message emphasized the city's cultural heritage: "Welcome to New Asia — Singapore, where East meets West, and Asian heritage blends with modernity and sophistication."[1] As a supplementary channel, Singapore marketers participated in Asian tourism exhibitions.

Each of these communication vehicles, which form a critical part of the Singapore media mix, has a targeted audience and specific channel characteristics. Frequency, impact and a greater reach are important for attracting potential tourists, and it is the advertisements in the various magazines and TV networks and the colorful Web sites that aim to accomplish this objective.

Sources

1 New Asia — Singapore Web site, www.newasia-singapore.com, viewed on January 17, 2001.

"Taking Initiatives: A New Spirit in Singapore," sponsored section in *The International Herald Tribune*, November 2, 2000, viewed on January 16, 2001 at http://www.iht.com/sponsored/sps_6.html.

To coordinate marketing efforts similar to Singapore's, media planners use data published by *Standard Rate and Data* that provide circulation and cost information for different sizes, color options, positions and quantities of advertisements. Beyond this, the media planner evaluates the different magazines on qualitative characteristics such as credibility, prestige, the availability of geographical or occupational editions, reproduction quality, editorial climate, lead-time and psychological impact. Marketers in Asia must be aware, however, that determining circulation and readership for domestic media is often very difficult because they are frequently not subject to independent audit, as most regional and international publications are. For example, claimed circulation is frequently a fraction of the actual circulation of daily newspapers.

The media planner makes a final judgment as to which specific vehicles will deliver the best reach, frequency and impact for the money available. The first variable, reach, is a measure of how many people are normally exposed to a single message carried by that medium. When the objective is to deliver the message to a large audience, mass media — particularly national television — are recommended.

By advertising in *The International Herald Tribune*, the Singapore government reached out to a target audience — exhibition/convention organizers and possible convention attendees. Singapore's two-pronged strategy has the flexibility to home in on exhibition/convention organizers who are a small, but critical, audience.

Some messages are effective only if they result in multiple exposures to the same individuals: this second variable is frequency. Some frequency of exposure is necessary if places are to avoid fading into oblivion. One or two Hollywood films shot in Port Moresby in Papua New Guinea does not guarantee any lasting impression of this place. Follow-up support is necessary in order to provide frequency.

The third variable, impact, describes how effective a particular medium is with the type of message and the target audience. Thus, *The International Herald Tribune* has more impact carrying the new Singaporean image than the magazine *ELLE*; the latter reaches the wrong audience. Usually, media that customize the message (such as direct mail and newsletters) or allow personal contact (such as conventions, exhibitions, trade missions and personal selling) achieve greater impact.

Media planners normally calculate the cost-per-thousand-people a particular vehicle reaches. Suppose that Sydney wants to market its new capital image to Asia and is considering advertising in either the *Far Eastern Economic Review* or in *Asiaweek*. In 2000, a one-page, four-color advertisement in the *Far Eastern Economic Review* cost US$15,580 and provided guaranteed circulation to over 95,000 readers.[13] *Asiaweek* cost US$21,970 and provided guaranteed regional circulation of 128,500.[14] Thus, the cost per reader in the *Far Eastern Economic Review* was US$164 and for *Asiaweek* US$171, suggesting that the *Far*

Eastern Economic Review would be the better buy. On the other hand, this cost advantage must be evaluated by considering the different readership profiles. For instance, the readers of *Asiaweek,* on average, have taken 10 air trips in the past year, while readers of the *Far Eastern Economic Review* are among the most influential business and political leaders of the region. Costs for other potential vehicles, including television and radio, can be calculated and compared in the same way.

Communication objectives and costs guide what planners want to do, but budget determines realistically what they can do. Budget heavily shapes media choices. Many methods have been proposed for setting communication budgets. The budget can be set by arbitrarily allocating a certain amount of money or a percentage of sales. It is also important to decide what a place can afford based on previous experience; to establish a percentage of the financial return expected to result from the campaign; and to observe what competitors have done.

The budget is also influenced by the amount of information and persuasion that is necessary to market a place. How much should a place spend to attract visitors? Singapore, Hong Kong, Thailand, Malaysia and Australia are international destinations and are included in tourist itineraries. However, if Marovo Lagoon in the Solomon Islands wants to attract tourists, it needs to launch a wide range of promotional tools to persuade prospects. A budget for Marovo Lagoon has to be large enough to overcome its off-the-beaten-path image. To have a chance, it must also find innovative resources through regional place-marketing cooperation.

Finally, planners should know that communication investments and returns are not necessarily linear. To invest too little money can be worse than investing no money. A certain minimum level of investment is required to create initial interest in a place. Higher levels of investment produce a higher level of audience response. However, above a certain level, still further investment may not be cost-effective. In fact, if the message is seen too frequently, many people stop noticing it or become irritated.

DECIDING ON MEDIA TIMING

The third step in media selection is timing, which breaks down into a macro problem and a micro problem. The macro problem is that of cyclical or seasonal timing. Audience size and interest vary at different times of the year. Most marketers do not advertise when there is little interest but spend the bulk of their advertising budgets when natural interest in a place increases and peaks. Counter-seasonal or counter-cyclical advertising is rare. On the other hand, it can prove to be of great economic value to market a destination such as the Himalayas in the off-season. For this to be effective, the attraction must have real value; it cannot simply offer visitors incentives of inferior value. The Himalayas could be marketed as being more beautiful and less crowded during the off-season. Visitors are offered more space, a peaceful setting and different activities, such as hiking.

A micro problem is the short-run timing of advertising. How should advertising be spaced during a short period of, say, one week? Consider three contrasting patterns:

- The first is "burst" advertising and consists of concentrating all the exposures in a very short period of time, such as all in one day. Presumably, this burst will attract maximum attention and interest and, if recall is good, the effect may last for a while.
- The second pattern is continuous advertising, in which the exposures appear evenly throughout the period. This pattern may be most effective when the audience buys or uses the product frequently and needs to be continuously reminded.
- The third pattern is intermittent advertising, in which intermittent small bursts of advertising appear with no advertising in between. This pattern creates somewhat more attention than continuous advertising and also has some of its reminder advantage.

Timing decisions should take three factors into consideration. *Audience turnover* is the rate at which the target audience changes between two periods. The greater the turnover, the more continuous the advertising should be. *Behavior frequency* is the number of times during the year that the target audience makes the decision that the marketer is trying to influence. The more frequent the behavior, the more advertising should be continuous. *The forgetting rate* is the rate at which a given message is forgotten or a given behavior-change is extinguished. Again, the shorter the audience's memory, the more continuous the advertising should be.

EVALUATING MEDIA RESULTS

Measuring the results that media campaigns produce is not an easy task. To measure place-marketing results is even more difficult since there are so many interconnecting variables.

Nevertheless, evaluation research helps media planners locate possible weaknesses in the communication or implementation process.

Did the place-message communication reach the right people? Did they understand the message and find it credible and persuasive? Did it reach them frequently enough or at the right times? Should more have been spent? The marketer should regularly evaluate the communication and sales effects of advertising.

Measuring the communication effect tells whether an advertisement is communicating well. Copy testing can be done before or after an advertisement is printed or broadcast. There are three major methods of pre-testing advertising. The first is through direct rating, in which the advertiser exposes a panel of consumers to alternative advertisements and asks them to rate the advertisements. These direct ratings are meant to show how well the advertisements attract attention and how they affect consumers. Although an imperfect measure of an advertisement's actual impact, a high rating indicates a potentially more effective advertisement. In portfolio tests, consumers, taking as much time as they need, view or listen to a portfolio of advertisements. Then, aided or unaided by the interviewer, they are asked to recall all the advertisements and their content. Their recall level indicates the ability of an advertisement to stand out and its message to be understood and remembered. Laboratory tests use equipment to measure consumers' physiological reactions to an advertisement — heartbeat, blood pressure, pupil dilation and perspiration. These tests measure an advertisement's attention-getting power but reveal little about its impact on beliefs, attitudes or intentions.

There are three popular methods of post-testing advertisements. Using a recall test, the advertiser asks people who have been exposed to magazines or television programs to recall everything they can about the advertising message. Recall scores indicate the advertisement's power to be noticed and retained. In recognition tests, the researcher asks readers of a given issue of a magazine to point out what they recognize from having seen before. Recognition scores can be used to assess the advertisement's impact in different market segments and to compare the company's advertisements with those of its competitors. In persuasion tests, people are asked whether the advertisement has caused them to be more favorably disposed towards a place and by how much.

The sales effect of advertising is often harder to measure. Many factors besides advertising affect sales — place features, price and availability. One way to measure the sales effect of advertising is to compare past sales with past advertising expenditures. Another way is through experiments where similar territories receive different advertising intensities to see whether this leads to different sales levels.

Advertising's communication impact is most easily measured where direct-response measurements can be obtained. Mail or phone orders, requests for catalogues, or sales calls all help the marketer measure response. They allow the marketer to determine how many inquiries the mail pieces generated and how many purchases came from the inquiries.

In general, measurement efforts are designed to answer three basic questions·

1. What was the response obtained?
2. Were the objectives met?
3. What changes are recommended?

A well-designed set of evaluation procedures enables the message and the media to be constantly improved.

MANAGING CONFLICTING MEDIA SOURCES AND MESSAGES

A place can spend millions of dollars advertising for visitors, residents or investors only to find that uncontrolled communications are overwhelming the formal messages. The uncontrolled international attention caused by the pedophile cases in Phnom Penh, Cambodia, is a case in point. This negative communication contrasts sharply with the official messages about Phnom Penh's attraction for investors, visitors and residents. Many places have experienced such conflicting attention from media: drug problems in Myanmar, terrorist attacks in East Timor, high unemployment in Bangladesh (35.2% in 1996)[15] leading to high crime rates, or charges against a mayor for child molestation and rape in the Philippines. Long and serious image-building efforts can quickly be destroyed in a world with global news coverage.

The best of all possible worlds occurs when informal and formal impressions merge to reinforce the image. When the government of Taiwan allowed limited but direct links with Mainland China through the islands of Quemoy and Matsu, it signaled an important step towards reconciliation, or at least peaceful co-existence. Early in 2001, the passenger ferry *Taiwu* set off from the heavily fortified Quemoy, Taiwan's front line of defense against a possible Chinese invasion, for Xiamen on the Fujian coast to the sounds of school children singing "Happy, Happy, Happy New Year", a song that celebrates reunions.[16]

While China's response to the new, and very small, link was somewhat cool, this journey symbolized the increasing economic and social interconnectedness of China and Taiwan and the desperate need to "normalize" relations. As a result, this small step was covered in virtually every major international publication, despite China's refusal to reciprocate by taking the trip in the other direction. Nevertheless, the next step was for Taiwan to allow Mainland tourists to visit for the first time by 2002. This would represent not only a further warming of relationships, but, potentially, a dramatic boost in tourism revenues for Taiwan.

Ideally, a place would like to showcase only its positive features. It would like to hide from view the slums, the homeless people, the indelicate treatment of minorities, the unemployment and other unflattering impressions. However, this degree of media control is impossible. More typically, a place finds itself driven by unplanned and often unwelcome events.

What should places do about such negative impressions? There are three possibilities. The first is to ignore them — "act as if it doesn't exist and it will go away." The second is to counter-attack by quickly sending out a countering message. The third is to solve the problem that has given rise to the negative impressions.

None of these responses is the best under all circumstances. Much depends on how serious the negative impression is, how widespread it is and how remediable it is. If the damage is not serious, if public knowledge is very limited, and if it is easily remedied, it is best to ignore the negative impression. If the damage is not serious but is widely known and easily remedied, it may pay to counter-attack. If the situation is very serious and widely known and not easily remedied, it is best to work toward a long-term response.

The case of Mitsubishi Motors Corp. provides an example of a serious negative situation that was at first ignored, counter-attacked, and ultimately solved at huge expense to the company. The practice of labeling customer complaints about vehicle defects with the letter "h", the first letter of the Japanese word for secret (*himitsu*), began as early as 1977. The systematic cover-up was intended to keep information from the Transport Ministry in order to avoid embarrassing recalls. Defects were quietly addressed on a case-by-case basis. In 2000, following a government inspection, the company acknowledged that, for decades, it had covered up auto defects, including failing brakes and fuel leaks.[17] The Japanese government then began examining its options for punishing the company's cover-up and for endangering the safety of customers.[18] As the year drew to a close, the company had spent ¥10 billion (US$83 million) in recalling cars worldwide.[19]

The consequences for the Mitsubishi image go far beyond the costs of rectifying the problems with the automobiles. The impression of incompetence that emerged from this affair implied a lack of skill on the part of the entire Japanese automobile industry. All the manufacturers have invested heavily in the global perception of Japanese quality and this cover-up was a threat to an image developed painstakingly over most of the second half of the 20th century. The threats to the industry were compounded by the company adopting the wrong approach when the negative publicity first appeared. Parallel cases can be traced in Asian cities where obvious drug-abuse problems have been consistently ignored and even denied. Such situations can quickly develop into negative images that not only relate to the original problem, but may also create distrust of a place and its civic decision-making processes.

CONCLUSION

The number of places that compete for the attention of investors, new residents and visitors is overwhelming. A casual reading of the travel sections in the Sunday newspapers of Asia's major cities reveals advertisements for every place on the globe. Trade journals for business sites are full of promises of cooperation and offers of brochures, videotapes, newsletters, and so on.

In this crowded media environment, a systematic approach is most likely to convert prospects into buyers. Place marketing has the best chance for success when the message is matched to the media, all players are pushing in the same direction and informal impressions reinforce the paid efforts.

In the next three chapters we apply marketing thinking to the four major sources of place enrichment: tourism and business hospitality, business attraction and development, export promotion, and new residents.

---

1 http://www.indiainfoline.com/econ/andb/capm/capm13.html, viewed on February 12, 2001.

2 Sidney Levy, *Promotional Behavior*, Glenview, Illinois: Scott Foresman, 1971 (See Chapter 4 for more characteristics of advertising, personal selling and sales promotion.

3 Thomas L. Harris, *The Marketers Guide to Public Relations*, New York: John Wiley and Sons, 1991.

4 http://www.tourism.gov.ph/rediscovery/rediscov.htm, viewed on December 13, 2000.

5 http://www.ftib.org.fj/events.htm#Exporter, viewed on December 14, 2000.

6 http://www.missouri.demon.co.uk/faq/faq2.htm, viewed on December 13, 2000.

7 http://www.kagan.com/archive/kagan/2000/12/08/cnbc.shtml, viewed on February 12, 2001.

8 Alkman Granitsas, "Black Hole," *Far Eastern Economic Review*, July 27, 2000, viewed on February 13, 2001 at http://www.feer.com/_0007_27/p34innov.html.

9 http://www.rainforestcup.com/, viewed on December 14, 2000.

10 http://www.sport.vic.gov.au/dir017/srvsite.nsf/pages/wcs_melbsports, viewed on December 18, 2000.

11 http://www.pwcglobal.com/extweb/newcolth.nsf/docid/397F61C8AC47094-18525697A00657DEC?OpenDocument, viewed on December 19, 2000.

12 http://www.chinaonline.com/industry/telecom/NewsArchive/Secure/2000/january/B200012605-SS.asp, viewed on January 2, 2001.

13 http://www.media.com.hk/kits/feer.htm#6, viewed on January 2, 2001.

14 http://www.media.com.hk/kits/asiaweek.htm#6, viewed on December 19, 2000.

15 http://www.bartleby.com/151/a69.html, viewed on December 18, 2000.

16 http://www.msnbc.com/news/512687.asp#BODY, viewed on May 18, 2001.

17 http://detnews.com/2000/autos/0008/23/b03-109584.htm, viewed on December 18, 2000.

18 http://www.jca.ax.apc.org/web-news/corpwatch-jp/83.html, viewed on December 18, 2000.

19 http://www.theage.com.au/bus/20001114/A47718-2000Nov13.html, viewed on January 15, 2000.

9

Attracting the Tourism and Hospitality Business Markets

T he travel section of the Asian edition of *Time* magazine is called Travel Watch. It introduces readers to various Asian destinations.

1. Perth: "...from an Asian perspective, Perth can hardly be considered remote — or uninviting. Board a nonstop flight in Singapore and you're there in less than five hours."[1]

2. Laos: "It has a freshness — the first tourists didn't visit until 1989 — and a devoutly Buddhist population that give the country a quiet feel unlike anywhere else in the region."[2]

3. Jaipur: "Nicknamed the Pink City, Jaipur is a rose-tinted wonder, from the walls of its enormous castle to the houses that climb pell-mell up the hills."[3]

Notice how each destination is distinctively described. Each destination provides something real and different. Travel links are also both convenient and frequent. Perth, for instance, can be reached through nonstop services from Singapore, Bangkok, Kuala Lumpur and Denpasar. Laos is accessible by air or rail from Thailand, a major waypoint between Europe, Asia and Vietnam. Jaipur is accessible from any major city in India via train or bus. As these examples show, any place that is able to clearly communicate its distinctiveness can compete in the tourism and hospitality markets as long as it consistently offers something attractive and remains accessible.

This chapter presents an analysis of two markets: tourism and the hospitality business (conventions, trade shows and business meetings). Although the two overlap somewhat, they are distinctive enough in markets, needs, facilities and competition to warrant separate treatment. They are also fundamental components of Asia's most successful economies.

THE TOURISM MARKET

When the Association of South East Asian Nations (ASEAN) announced plans to host Visit ASEAN Millennium Year 2002, this promotional initiative demonstrated the importance of tourism for Southeast Asian nations. For the year 2000, tourism and travel accounted for 7.9% of total employment — or an estimated 17 million jobs — and 3.3% of GDP for the region.[4] Tourism is expected to grow even more in the early decades of the 21st century. This interest in tourism revenues is not surprising. Over 24 million people in East Asia alone (1998)[5] are unemployed and public leaders know that tourism can be increased more rapidly than many other areas of the economy.

In marketing tourism we will want to consider the following questions:

- How important is tourism to a place's economy?
- How can the tourist market be segmented and monitored for shifting trends, lifestyles, needs and preferences?
- What kinds of strategies and investments must places and businesses make to be competitive in the tourist industry?
- How can a place establish a niche in the tourist business, and what are the risks and opportunities?
- What kinds of messages and media are effective in attracting and retaining tourists?
- How should a place's tourism activities be organized and managed?

How Important is Tourism?

Most Asian communities and places are actively seeking to increase their share in the tourism industry. Tourism not only produces jobs and income, it also generates spin-off decisions regarding business locations or new residents. Such secondary effects are seldom calculated when tourism is discussed.

Fiji, already a major Asian tourist destination, has enormous potential to develop additional place-selling programs and offerings to business, investors and potential residents. Indeed, investment exploded in the late 1990s. Foreign Direct Investment increased from $27 and $34 million in 1996 and 1997, to $91 million in 1998.[6] The city of Qingdao, on China's Shandong Peninsula, combines tourism with trade and technology in its annual International Beer Festival. Originally celebrated in the early 1990s as a local holiday, the festival has developed into one of national importance, attracting over one million tourists to the town annually.[7] Along with the recreational and sporting activities, the festival incorporates the International Beer & Beverages Fair, which draws brewers from Holland, South Africa, U.S.A., U.K., Singapore, Japan and Hong Kong. This event is a unique opportunity for Qingdao to showcase both its unique German-Chinese culture and its ability to host an international event.

The Fiji and Qingdao examples illustrate the direct and indirect importance of tourism. The complex links to other target groups illustrate the difficulties in calculating the exact value of tourism. The various place sellers and place buyers are so closely interlinked that tourism and business are two sides of one product. Exhibit 9.1 shows how two cities leveraged a once-in-a-lifetime opportunity.

Exhibit 9.1: AFTER THE DANCE: SYDNEY AND MELBOURNE

Playing host to an international event can be a coup for any city. The potential gain from infrastructure investment and a surge in tourism can — if carefully managed — stimulate a turnaround of even the most beleaguered city economy. However, playing host to such an event is no guarantee of long-term or even short-term success, as the stories of Sydney and Melbourne demonstrate. The secret is leveraging the event to generate follow-up business, and consistently working to enhance competitiveness.

The year 2000 was a big year for Australia. Seeking to increase tourist arrivals and enhance their worldwide images, both Sydney and Melbourne would host major international events — the summer Olympics in Sydney and the Grand Prix in Melbourne. Both cities made substantial investments in facilities and both benefited from increased tourist inflows and considerable international media coverage; yet following the two giant international events, Sydney is booming while Melbourne is slowly drifting into Sydney's shadow. What accounts for this development?

Garry Grimmer, head of the Melbourne Convention and Marketing Bureau, is responsible for marketing Sydney, formerly known for little more than being the home of the Sydney Opera House and the Sydney Harbour Bridge. He put the city firmly on the international awareness-map by promoting it as the as the site of the 2000 Olympic Games. As a result, the city increasingly competes with other Asian mega-event destinations, such as Hong Kong and Singapore, for investment and convention-and-exhibition business.

Although the 2000 Olympics was leveraged to promote Sydney, according to the New South Wales premier, Bob Carr, the Olympics represented only a small fraction of state investment. "The Olympics are the icing on the cake. They are working for us because everything else is working for us, but they are only $1 in every $300 invested in the state."[1] The relative modesty of the investment, however, belies the physical transformation it catalyzed.

Sprucing up Sydney's municipal infrastructure was the natural first step taken by the city council in developing the Olympic city. Construction and development of new infrastructure started in September 1993. When Sydney's visitors arrived, new railways, new highways, new hotels, new parks, expanded facilities at the airport, and inner-city and CBD retail-renewal projects awaited them.

Keeping such attractions humming requires a strategic, intense effort to attract tourists. Careful research and effective strategies ensured that this effort did not end with the Olympic Games, at either the local or national level. Immediately following the Games, the Australian Tourist Commission (ATC) announced a strategy for increasing tourism to Sydney and other Australian destinations. The strategy included over 90 joint, tactical advertising campaigns promoting holiday packages by more than 200 industry partners. These joint campaigns were estimated to be worth more than US$45 million. A hard-hitting A$6-million (US$3 million) direct-marketing campaign was set in motion, including the redevelopment of the ATC's Internet site, www.australia.com.

Research is a major component of the initiative. Its purpose is to identify how the Olympic exposure shifted Australia's image internationally, and to leverage that awareness. According to *CEI Asia Pacific*, a conventions, exhibitions and incentives trade publication, Sydney is perceived as a destination that offers world-class infrastructure and attractions at values more expensive destinations can't hope to match. Sydney's strategy is to continuously develop the meetings, incentives, conventions and exhibitions (MICE) sectors to help position the city as the key Australian tourist destination. The statistics agree: of the 4.6 million people who visited Australia in the 12 months to June 2000, almost two million visited Sydney.

Unlike Sydney, Melbourne's time in the Australian limelight — and its reputation as a thriving global city long considered the nation's financial and cultural center — is gradually diminishing. But like Sydney, Melbourne is an Olympic city, having hosted the 1956 Games. As in Sydney's case, the international attention catapulted the city to international awareness — for a time. But during the 1970s, worldwide recession hit the city's principal employment and revenue generators — the garment and automotive sectors — especially hard. Melbourne enjoyed only a brief recovery before financial crises in the '80s and '90s resulted in further setbacks in the city's economy. Although the city's circumstances improved with Australia's resurgence late in the decade, its role as Australia's leading city appears to be over, at least for some time.

An aging population with a declining growth rate — it has the second-lowest fertility rate in the country — is both a reflector and an indicator of the city's diminished importance. Sydney, by contrast, is growing, due principally to the migration of young adults from outlying regions into the city, and has 500,000 more people than Melbourne. More than two-thirds of all international businesses with operations in the country chose Sydney over Melbourne for their Australian headquarters. While Melbourne has managed to hold on to its reputation as Australia's financial and cultural center, the city and its 2000 Qantas Australian Grand Prix just could not compete with the sheer scope of the Olympic Games and the tourism marketing frenzy they generated. While Grand Prix aficionados may be committed, the Olympics appeal to a much broader worldwide constituency. In fact, the 2000 Grand Prix provides a good example of why Melbourne isn't doing better: short-sighted vision, and the failure to make the commitment necessary to build consensus among key sectors.

A long-brewing, but largely unaddressed, controversy marred the 2000 Grand Prix. The racetrack was built on the site of the Albert Park Reserve adjacent to the popular Albert Park. Many believe that the circuit endangers the historic park by attracting large and potentially unruly crowds. As a result, activists determined to save the park have protested against the Grand Prix since its transfer from Adelaide in 1996. According to activists, the city has concealed and downplayed the likely impact of the circuit on the park.

Indeed, city counselors argue for the very real benefits the Grand Prix provides: 300,000 visitors who spend A$95 million (US$48.9 million) in just four days and another 440 million television viewers — and potential visitors — in 120 countries. And they warn of the number of jobs at risk if the event were cancelled, suggesting that the environmental tradeoff, if real, is necessary. Not surprisingly, these arguments failed to satisfy activists intent on saving a symbol of their heritage, and many were arrested in protests before the 2000 race. The threat of a major international incident was real. Although the protests never reached that level, the event's organizers continue to have to deal with protestors every time the event is held.

Clearly, the city is suffering, when it should be celebrating, as a result of the failure of its government to address legitimate perceived environmental concerns before the circuit was built. As a consequence, the city is distracted by the necessity of having to defend its actions, instead of focusing on the more important task of marketing its attractions in a highly competitive environment. While the Olympics also brought protestors out in Sydney, the Games are a one-off event and don't attract continuing protest. Meanwhile, Melbourne keeps shrinking.

Ironically, it was the Olympics that originally brought international attention to bear on Melbourne four decades earlier. Did the city take its good fortune for granted, or has it tried hard but ineffectively to sustain its international prestige? Whichever, sports writer John Henderson neatly summed up the difference between Sydney and Melbourne. Referring to the speed by which Sydney was overtaking Melbourne, Henderson said, "It's as if Melbourne is choking on the exhaust fumes of Sydney's speeding Maserati."[2] The test for Sydney is not to run out of high-test gasoline.

Sources:

1 Turi Condon, "After the Party," *BRW Magazine* Web site, http://www.brw.com.au/newsadmin/stories/brw/20000324/5129.htm, viewed on January 26, 2001.
2 John Henderson, "Melbourne in Sydney's Shadow," *Denver Post* Web site, http://www.denverpost.com/olympics/oly0924c.htm, September 24, 2000, viewed on January 25, 2001.

Shane Nugent, "Why Sydney Keeps Growing — Trends In Population Distribution In New South Wales — 1991 to 1996," http://elecpress.monash.edu.au/pnp/pnpv6n4/nugent3.html, viewed February 26, 2001; Darren Gray, "National Birth Rate Plunging," *The Age* Web site, http://www.theage.com.au/news/19991117/A47561-1999Nov16.html, November 17, 1999, viewed February 29, 2001; "2000 Grand Prix Set-up the Works," *Save Albert Park Newsletter* Issue 71, http://home.vicnet.net.au/~sapark/sapweb/nl71.html, March 2000, viewed on January 26, 2001; Laurence Hilmond Chalip, "Leveraging the Sydney Olympics for Tourism," http://blues.uab.es/olympic.studies/papers/chalip00-3.html,viewed on January 26, 2001; Tourism NSW Web site, www.tourism.nsw.gov.au/corporate/downloads/01FactNSW.pdf; Miles Clarke, "Sydney aims to profit from games," *CEI Asia Pacific*, January/February 2001, pp. 28–33; "Victorian Major Events Co.," http://www.vmec.com.au/ach/content.htm, viewed April 19, 2001.

Asian tourism still lags behind Europe and the Americas in international tourism (see Figure 9.1). But East Asia and the Pacific's share of world tourism is now increasing. Growth appears steady for the region — 11.1% from 1998 to 1999, compared with Europe's 2.7%. Tourism in the Middle East and South Asia also increased by 8.3% in 1999. The improving position of East Asia and the Pacific should be defended. One way of doing this is to improve local and regional place-marketing strategies. The opening of Central Asia is another important factor that can draw increased tourism to the Asian region.

Figure 9.1: International Tourism 1960–1998

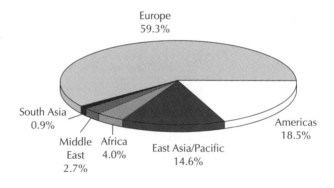

International Tourist Arrivals
Share of World Total (%) — 1999

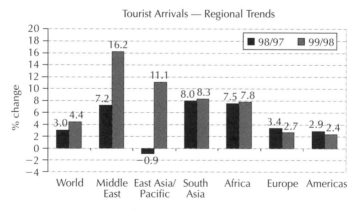

Sources: Compendium of Tourist Statistics, World Tourist Organization (WTO), Madrid, 1998; WTO, Web site: http://www.world-tourism.org/main/frameset/frame_market_data.htm, viewed on March 19, 2001.

Segmenting the Tourism Market

Places must decide not only how many tourists they want and how to balance tourism with other industries, but also what kinds of tourists they want. Of course, choices will be constrained by the place's climate, natural topography and resources, history, culture and facilities. As with any other business, tourist marketers must distinguish between the actual and potential customers, know their needs and wants, determine which target markets to serve, and decide on appropriate products, services and programs to serve these markets.

Not every tourist will be interested in a particular place. A place would waste its money trying to attract everyone who travels. Instead of taking a shotgun approach, a place must adopt a rifle approach and sharply define its target groups. Exhibit 9.2 explains how modern technology helps tourists find the markets they seek.

Exhibit 9.2: ELECTRONIC BUYING

The highly trained, full-service travel agents of yesterday are rapidly disappearing. Downward pressure on margins has made the sector less attractive as a career. As a result, their replacements often have less firsthand knowledge and tend to leave the place buyer frustrated in his/her efforts to plan a trip. The travel industry is in a major transition and is trying to develop solutions to this problem.

There are three main avenues that represent the wave of the future for travel agencies. The first is better training of current agents. Governments in countries like Singapore are offering full-time training programs for future travel agents. The second is using the Internet to link customers to animated and interactive sites that provide airline fares and hotel rates. Most sites now allow visitors to book reservations and to make payment online. In many Asian countries, this method is already widely used by regular travelers.

Third, there is a gradual move toward sophisticated customer-profiling that promises an extensive customer database. Visitors may well expect their most exotic wishes — pre-ordered concert tickets or an individualized tour of modern art galleries, for example — to be anticipated by potential hosts. These innovations come in the face of increased competition from many companies seeking the visitor's patronage.

Who — or what — will emerge as the principal source of information for tourists planning vacations? The results are mixed. There is increasing use of the Internet by travelers who are seeking place awareness and great deals. The frequency and execution of purchasing a trip, however, varies greatly from country to country. Still, while most Asians continue to rely heavily on personal, hands-on travel agencies, despite the disadvantages, the increased competition that online travel agencies provide will be beneficial to the customer, and usage is certain to grow. But the proliferation of sites also means that places will have to be increasingly proactive if they are to gain the attention of the travel industry and, more importantly, individual tourists.

To be effective, place sellers need to encourage online travel agencies to package their destination competitively and in a way that stands out amidst the cyberspace glut. Moreover, place sellers will find it necessary to co-brand their festivals and events with travel agencies for maximum impact. It will be competitively advantageous for places to market an identifiable image that is consistent, targeted and distinctive from competing places.

Source:

Conrad de Souza and Lim Boon Kwee, "Future of the Travel Agent in the Asia Pacific," http://gonzales.com.sg/tagent.html, 1997, viewed on January 10, 2001.

Place marketing can use two methods to identify natural target groups. The first approach is to collect information about current tourists. Where do they come from? Why do they come to this place? What are their demographic characteristics? How satisfied are they? How many are repeat tourists? How much do they spend? By examining these and other questions, the place can determine which tourists are worth attracting.

The second approach is to audit the place's attractions and then conjecture about the types of tourists who would have a natural interest in these attractions. The aim is to identify new sources of tourists. One cannot assume that the current tourists reflect all the potentially interested target groups. For example, if Western Tien-Shan in Uzbekistan only promoted skiing, the region would miss other target groups interested in summer hiking, camel-riding trips, hunting and rafting.

Different place features attract different tourists. The local tourist board or other units must ask questions keyed to the segmentation variables in Table 9.1. These variables — attractions sought, market areas or locations, customer characteristics, and/or benefits sought — can help to define the best tourist prospects to attract.

Table 9.1: Segmentation variables for the tourist market

Attractions sought	Market areas/Customer locations	Characteristics	Benefits
• Sea, sun, ski	• Non-Asian	• Age	• Price
• Natural beauty/ wilderness	• European	• Income	• Convenience
	• Domestic	• Family	• Quality
• Recreation	• Regional	• Single	• Food
• Gaming	• Local	• Professionals	• Service
• Culture/history/ people	• Seasonal/ year around	• Lifestyles	• Facilities
		• Ethnic group	• Transportation
• Events/sports	• Language		
• Theme parks			
• Facilities/hotels/ restaurants			
• Unique products: wine, beer, perfume, clothes, watches			

After a place identifies a natural target market, the tourist board must research where these tourists are found. Which countries, non-Asian and Asian, contain a large number of citizens who have the means and motivation to enjoy the particular place? For example, religious tourism involves the movement of about 100 million people per year. Among the countries that lead in this target market are India, Tibet and China, which offer a variety of religious tours. It is important to know where the various target markets are for Buddhism, Hinduism and Islam.

An analysis may uncover too many or too few potential target markets. If too many are identified, the tourist board must calculate the potential profit from attracting each segment. The potential profit of a target tourist segment is the difference between the amount that the tourist segment would spend and the cost of attracting and serving this segment. The attraction cost depends on the marketing plan. The serving cost depends on the infrastructure requirements. Ultimately, the tourist board ranks the potential tourist segments in order of their profitability and concentrates on attracting those segments highest on its list (see Exhibit 9.3).

Exhibit 9.3: NEPAL IDENTIFIES THE SOUTH INDIAN TOURISM MARKET

In May 2000, the Nepal Tourism Board (NTB) launched an aggressive tourism campaign for the months of June and July. Its purpose was to market the country as the perfect destination for tourists from neighboring India. The campaign objective was to re-emphasize the many advantages that only Indians have when visiting Nepal — visas are unnecessary; Hindi, India's major language, is widely spoken in Nepal; and Indian currency is readily accepted. Other than these obvious benefits, the NTB also wanted to highlight the other attractions that the country offers Indian visitors, such as easy accessibility and pleasant weather, in contrast to India's monsoon-ridden climate.

One of the key components of the campaign was the opportunity given to Indian journalists to travel to Nepal. Building on the campaign slogan "Mt Everest and More," the Nepal Tourism Board organized media visits to generate excitement and publicity. They provided the journalists with a firsthand experience of visits to the attractions Nepal has to offer, including the Heritage Sites of Kathmandu Valley and the scenic city of Pokhara. With limited resources for traditional advertising channels, the NTB hopes that these visits will help build the momentum necessary to make the campaign a success for Nepal's tourism industry.

Sources:

"Once again Indian tourists flock to Nepal," NepalNews.com Web site, http://www.nepalnews.com.np/contents/englishweekly/independent/11-03/ tourism.htm, viewed January 23, 2001; Preeti Mehra, "Nepal drive to win back Indian tourists," The Hindu Business Line: Internet Edition Web site, http://www.hindubusinessline.com/2000/05/22/stories/142272g1.htm, May 22, 2000, viewed on January 23, 2001.

If the analysis identifies too few natural tourist segments, the tourist board must undertake investment marketing. The existing features of the place attract a natural market; new features that might be added attract an investment market. Investment marketing consists of allocating money towards infrastructure improvements (hotels, transportation, and so on) and attractions that can potentially bring new types of tourists. The payoff from investment marketing comes some years later, but this investment is necessary if the place cannot identify a sufficient number of natural tourist segments. Exhibit 9.4 illustrates how a new attraction can broaden the appeal of a mature market.

Exhibit 9.4: EAST MEETS WEST IN THE MAGIC KINGDOM

Unlike the initial reception given to EuroDisney in Paris, Tokyo Disneyland has been acknowledged as a successful culture transfer and "the most important cultural event in the eighties in Japan."[1] In its first 10 years, Tokyo Disneyland played host to 125 million domestic and foreign visitors. Since its opening in 1983, the theme park has been the most popular entertainment destination in Japan. The park's annual visitor attendance has exceeded every other amusement park in the world, even its two U.S. counterparts.

Despite suggestions to incorporate Japanese culture into the development of the park, the Japanese owners stayed firm in implementing a traditional Disney-style image and staying faithful to the fundamental investment philosophy of Disney. For example, retail stores, armed with an aggressive sales force to capitalize on tourists' susceptibility to souvenir offers, are scattered all over the park. Also, Disney emphasizes an environment that is clean-cut, which appeals to a country traditionally concerned with cleanliness.

The huge success of the Tokyo park may also be attributed to a strong Japanese appetite for American popular entertainment and to the increasing Japanese focus on leisure. One American journalist observed, "The Japanese are obsessed with American pop culture. Teens pay exorbitant prices for vintage Levis and Nikes, American records fill the music shops, and Western characters are used frequently, often without any apparent understanding of what they mean (for example, an elderly woman wearing a T-shirt that says 'BITCH' across the front, or a club that boasts music 'Live on Everyday')."[2]

However, for competing place marketers, the Disney model presents a major challenge. First, Disney sets very high standards for the fundamentals — design, service, cleanliness and safety.

Any place in Asia that wishes to attract the visiting public needs to benchmark its project against the Disney standard. Second, Disney has the ability to take real-life situations and convert them into virtual reality. For example, park attractions such as It's A Small World, Space Mountain, and the Western River Railroad are believable illusions that can even make real-life events pale by comparison. The place marketer with an historical or natural attraction needs to find communication mechanisms to make the project interactive and meaningful to the public — a way to make Donald Duck blink.

Sources:

1 Harbour Fraser Fodder, "Pop culture imperialism? Tokyo Disneyland," *Harvard Magazine* Web site, http://www.harvard-magazine.com/issues/ja97/right.disney.html, January 1997, viewed on January 23, 2001.
2 Travis Higdon, "Interview with Michie Nakatani of Shonen Knife," http://www.monsterbit.com/pcp/shonen.html, viewed on March 13, 2001.

Yoonwoi Choi, "Tokyo and Euro Disneyland: Successes and failures in the light of cultural feasibility," http://nimbus.ocis.temple.edu/~ychoi/disney.html, viewed on January 23, 2001.

Consider Nepal, which continues to attract many tourists from Asia, as well as many Europeans and Americans. The Nepal Tourism Board has observed that although an increasing number of young backpackers and campers were visiting the breathtaking sights of Mt Everest to enjoy its natural beauty, they spent little. A serious question for Nepal was whether the Board's tourism scorecard should be based on the number of tourists attracted (the current standard) or the spending quality of the tourists. Many critics believe that Nepal would be better off attracting fewer but higher-income tourists who would stay longer and spend more.

In an attempt to attract high-income tourists, the Nepal Tourism Board has set relatively high visa fees for certain areas. It is also slowly improving tourist facilities as an act of investment marketing. However, the upscale strategy is threatened by the persistent problem of litter in Kathmandu that dissuades tourists from enjoying the city. The litter problem is an issue so intense that, at one point, it seemed to defy solution.

Whatever tourist segment a place aims at, it needs to be very specific. True, a ski area attracts skiers; swimming and natural reefs attract snorklers and divers; art attracts the culture seekers; gambling attracts gaming tourists. Yet, even with such givens, places must segment tourists according to additional characteristics. Tourists to Fiji, for example, are offered very specific target packages. Although Fiji offers mainly sun and sand, there is a wide variety of resorts that specialize in activities such as diving, surfing, golfing, camping and backpacking. Some specialize in weddings and honeymoons. There are resorts to fit the lifestyle and budget of any tourist — family, eco-friendly, villas, inexpensive apartments or out-of-the-way island retreats. Many exclusive and luxury resorts are concentrated on the Northern Islands, which offer high-level tourism. But segmentation will go much further in the future. The Fijian region is composed of 300 islands, each of which can offer unique characteristics. Thus, various places can distinguish themselves by marketing bicycle-riding, horse-riding, health spas, theme parks, and so on.

Markets and attractions change over time. However, some places manage to keep the same tourist image for decades. One such example is the Island of Tahiti in French Polynesia, which many people visit repeatedly, decade after decade. Tahiti markets itself through its connection with famous people who have lived on or visited the island. Among them is French painter Paul Gaugin, who captured the beauty of the island in his work. He is a household name, and a cruise around the island and a museum have been named after him. Other celebrities include Meg Ryan, Rod Stewart and Marlon Brando. Writer Somerset Maugham described Tahiti in his book *The Moon and Sixpence*: "I looked up and I saw the outline of the island. And I knew right away that there was the place I'd been looking for all of my life." The Tahitians' *joie de vivre* is famous worldwide and is the underlying reason for the many festivals conducted throughout the year. The most famous of these is the month-long Heiva I Tahiti, which involves music, dance and sports competitions. Tahiti exemplifies a certain degree of stability in a place market subject to intensifying competition, but it must maintain its hard-won turf by continuing to appeal to its varied markets. Festivals and special events are popularly marketed on all types of themes: musical instruments, canoe-racing, carnival, flowers, golf and island tours. Tourists can pick and choose.

Asian cities can be compared on a number of tourist performance indicators (see Table 9.2).

The first thing to note is the strength of China, which is in a class by itself. As a center of international conferences, Hong Kong combines all the most important attractions: high-quality accommodation, effective transport infrastructures and a huge variety of cultural offerings. The second observation concerns the huge differences in average stay. Japan offers a special combination of tourist attractions such as historical sites,

Table 9.2: Top destinations in Asia-Pacific, 1998 (in thousands)

Country	Arrivals	Nights spent	Average stay (days)
1. China	25,073	57,925	
2. Hong Kong	9,575		3.38
3. Thailand	7,843	65,232	8.4
4. Singapore	5,631		
5. Malaysia	5,551	16,124	5.5
6. Indonesia	4,606		
7. Korea, Rep. of	4,250		4.9
8. Australia	4,167	17,300	
9. Japan	4,106		8.8
10. Macau	4,044	2,753	

Source: *Compendium of Tourist Statistics*, World Tourist Organization, Madrid, 2000.

museums and theater in many forms. These advantages work to lengthen the average stay.

Places must be ready to respond to changing demographics and lifestyles. The smaller the place or city, the more vulnerable it is. What new chances could the aging Asian population give to places like Kerala, with its Ayurvedic spas, or the medical springs in Tuva or Azerbaijan? Which new strategies should a place work out in response to increased ecological interest among tourists? How can a place exploit the trend toward shorter visits by two-career families who have less time to spend away from home? And what can be done to exploit the opportunity that occurs when a place is suddenly connected to, or bypassed by, a new high-speed railway?

Changing demographics and lifestyles also present a continuous challenge to the tourism industry. The high-living baby-boomers of yesterday are today's older and increasingly retired baby-boomers. Where they once opted for status destinations and elaborate accommodations, they now opt for all-inclusive resorts and package tours that promise comfort, consistency and cost-effectiveness.

Tourist Strategies and Investments
In the face of growing tourist competition, places must be prepared to maintain and, indeed, upgrade their place investments. A major trend today is heritage development, the task of preserving the history of places, their buildings, their people and customs, and other artifacts that capture their traditions. Typical examples can be found in the town of

Vigan, in Ilocos Sur, Philippines, and Bukhara in Uzbekistan. In Vigan, a careful restoration is taking place to portray its proud historical traditions. The city, which is on the UNESCO World Heritage List, has one of the greatest collections of Filipino-Chinese-Spanish-Mexican architectural styles anywhere. The city of Bukhara has also come to life again since Uzbekistan gained independence from the Soviet Union in 1991. Restoration programs are ambitious. Aging buildings are being brought back to their former glory using mud bricks similar to those of the medieval times. Among them are the city's main landmark, the 150-foot Kalyan Minaret, and the Abdel Aziz Khan Islamic School, listed among UNESCO's 100 most-endangered heritage sites. The city's former chief architect, Nasim Hakimovich Sharipov, has said that "the goal of all of the people of Bukhara is to see how it looked in the past."[9]

Countless examples exist of places rediscovering their pasts, capitalizing on the birthplace of a famous person, an event, a battle or other "hidden gems." Places rely on various associations for identification: Mongolia is The Land of Genghis Khan; Malacca is The Historic City of Malaysia; Bhutan is The Last Shangri-La; and Bagerhat is The Historic Mosque City of Bangladesh. But there are other examples where opportunities have been lost. Exhibit 9.5 describes how environmentalists were unsuccessful in their bid to save one of China's greatest historical sites and tourist destinations.

Exhibit 9.5: THE END OF THE THREE GORGES CANYONS

For hundreds of years, China's Three Gorges Canyons have provided shelter for millions of townspeople, farmland for countless Chinese families, hundreds of sites for historical and archaeological digs, and spectacular locations for tourists to appreciate, and have inspired popular Chinese legends. Despite this rich history and the cultural importance of the majestic canyons, in 1992 the government decided to build what would become one of the world's largest hydroelectric dams at the mouth of the Three Gorges, a project that would result in the Gorges being submerged. The decision generated sustained international controversy regarding the ecological and social consequences of the dam's construction.

Despite the intense criticism, the Chinese government showed little enthusiasm for preserving the physical legacy and beauty of the Three Gorges. Deputy Director of the Three Gorges Project Commission under the State Council, Guo Shuyan, responded to criticism by saying that the project was "environmentally sound, on the whole."[1] In fact, the Beijing leadership has demonstrated little patience for critics who, they say, disregard the kind of urgent development priorities that face China and that developed countries themselves faced during their own early struggles to develop.

Critics have another view. Dr John Byrne, director of the University of Delaware's Center for Energy and Environmental Policy, said of the dam, "Unfortunately, China has decided to launch the project — then solve the problems along the way."[2] A character in *Soul Mountain* by Gao Xingjian, the first Chinese writer to win the Nobel Prize for Literature, warns, "When people assault nature like this, nature inevitably takes revenge."[3] But the environment is only one of the many victims of the massive undertaking. For instance, toxic materials and other potential pollutants have accumulated in the area as a result of the construction. Because no effort has been made to clean the mess up, they could very well become a genuinely serious health hazard. They also threaten the river currents, producing increased pollution from industrial and residential users.

As a result of the construction, the number of overseas visitors declined from a peak of 100,000 in 1994 to less than 50,000 in 1999. Many tourists bypass the Three Gorges entirely because of the uncertainty surrounding the development. Others assume that the dam has already irreversibly damaged the river's scenic views. Yet the area still boasts countless historical sites such as the Qu Yuan Temple, Yon Yang County's Temple of Zhang Fei, the ancient Ghost City of Fengdu, the aptly named Tower of Last Chance to Glance Home, and the carvings on Moya Cliff. But once the dam is completed in 2009, these relics and sites, together with perhaps a thousand more, will be submerged. There are not many chances left to view these centuries-old treasures, although Chinese officials have vowed to move, rebuild or duplicate the artifacts or place them in museums.

Conversely, of course, increased marketing of the Three Gorges as a tourist destination would likely backfire on the government, and intensify demands that the project be halted.

Still, most of the grand scenery will remain untouched until Phase 2, which ends in 2003. When that phase is complete, the waters of the Yangtze River begin rising — and continue doing so until completion — to form a narrow reservoir, covering the first of hundreds of towns, orchards and historical artifacts. While the power generated by the dam will no doubt contribute to building China's economy, many will always wonder if progress in one area must be accompanied by such huge losses in another. In the intense global competition for tourism, places with such scenic beauty and historical sites will eventually regret the loss of irreplaceable assets.

Sources:

1   Bruce Kennedy, "China's biggest construction project since the Great Wall generates controversy at home and abroad," *CNN Interactive* Web site, http://www.cnn.com/SPECIALS/1999/china.50/asian.superpower/three.gorges, viewed on January 24, 2001.
2   Marcia Kunstel and Joseph Albright, "China's Controversial Three Gorges Dam Looks Unstoppable," http://www.coxnews.com/washington/GORGES.HTM, viewed on January 24, 2001.
3   Todd Shaper, "Ghosts of The Yangtze: For travelers, time is running out before the Three Gorges Dam permanently alters the face of China's great Yangtze River," *Far Eastern Economic Review*, March 29, 2001, p. 67.

"Three Gorges tourism drying up," *South China Morning Post*, http://www.probeinternational.org/pi/3g/index.cfm?DSP=content&ContentID=664, December 9, 1999, viewed on January 24, 2001; "TED Case Studies: Three Gorges Dam," Trade and Environment Database Web site, http://www.american.edu/ted/THREEDAM.htm, viewed on January 24, 2001.

Investors in cross-border tourist projects may apply for financial support from multilateral development organizations and financial institutions, such as the International Finance Corporation, The World Bank and the Asian Development Bank. But the real potential for cross-border tourism in the region has yet to be capitalized on. Countries such as Singapore, Malaysia, Indonesia and the Philippines are attempting to develop cross-border enterprise zones, which may involve some subsidiary interest in tourism. But there is great rivalry for visitors in Asia (see Exhibit 9.6), so it's not surprising that cross-border tourism investment is more common in Europe. "The European Vineyard Routes," where six member states have joined forces to develop tourism in the European wine region, is one such example. This tour is further promoted through multilingual guides, press briefings, training missions, permanent liaison offices and the creation of a quality chart and labels. Other examples include the cross-border cycling tours around Europe, the cross-border sport fishing in the Hautes-Pyrenees, and the specialized "Asparagus Tour" project in the Dutch-Belgian border region.

Exhibit 9.6: PETTY RIVALRY?

Cross-border tourism and sports events ideally serve to promote destinations and strengthen the ties of participating places. Sometimes, however, national rivalries can be a cause for conflict even in very large cross-border events. Such was the case during the preparations for football's 2002 World Cup.

Historical rivalry between the co-hosts, South Korea and Japan, is said to have been the principal reason precipitating a heated controversy over communications and promotion that detracted from the spirit of the championship. Japan's move to have its own name appear on the tickets and other game-related items before that of its co-host was said to have angered South Korea, which was particularly sensitive because the showpiece final game was to be held in Tokyo. By reversing the order of the names, South Korea argued, Japan was acting in bad faith and undermining South Korea's role. The International Football Federation (FIFA), world soccer's governing body, agreed. FIFA ruled that the event's official title, 2002 FIFA World Cup Korea/Japan, should appear without revisions in all materials bearing the name of the championship.

The rivalry began as early as the bidding, with the two countries engaged in a tight competition for the championship. However, FIFA had its own internal problems — the chairman and the committee were split — that made it impossible to award the bid to just one of the contenders. Instead, it proposed that South Korea and Japan co-host the world cup. Rather than suffer the humiliation of losing the bid, the two countries agreed. FIFA believed that, aside from the usual advantages of hosting the World Cup, co-hosting might help South Korea and Japan patch up their historical rivalry. But because football is an issue of national pride, many believed that it would cause even more problems, such as disagreements over sponsors, revenue sharing, visas for guests and travel arrangements. As a result, many believe that FIFA's decision was unfortunate and might wind up killing the essence of the World Cup, rather than promoting it.

Sources:

http://www.timesofindia.com/210101/21foot2.htm, viewed on February 26, 2001; http://www.asiaweek.com/asiaweek/96/0621/ed1.html, viewed on February 26, 2001.

With the current international trend towards shorter but more frequent vacations, many places within two hours' travel of major metropolitan areas have found new opportunities to access the tourist market. The renewed growth of the family-vacation market also has redirected some places towards a "family-friendly" image. Many Asian theme parks, hotels and vacation facilities are within easy reach of Asian travelers. For example, Guam and Palau market themselves as weekend destinations to near-by places such as Japan, the Philippines and Taiwan. A place with such a location can exploit its strategic position, even if it is an international destination.

Another dimension in tourist attraction is how much language and intercultural understanding a place can provide. The Americans and English, who tend to be generally more adventurous when choosing holiday destinations, find their native tongue understood almost anywhere in Asia. The tendency for large groups of Japanese, South Koreans and Taiwanese to holiday in the same resort and to create a "national cluster" is well known. The majority of these tourists prefer to eat in restaurants where the menu is in their language or English and to stay in hotels where the staff speaks, or has some knowledge of, their language. The majority of tourists in destinations such as Guam, Palau and Hawaii are Japanese. Vietnam has become a popular destination for Japan's "salary girls," who generally live with parents and enjoy fairly substantial disposable incomes. Tourist-related industries in these places now recognize the importance of learning the Japanese language for the convenience and comfort of their guests, many of whom travel in a group and do not speak English. Many schools in Palau also offer courses in Japanese to train those that work in the hospitality industry.

Such intercultural initiatives can be actively used by places trying to attract certain foreign target groups to their place. Certain places in Asia that need an increased visitor market have consciously invested in improving the language skills not only of their hospitality staff but also of other important players such as school superintendents and civic leaders.

The environmental movement has compelled the travel industry to adapt more earth-friendly approaches, and places are seeking to develop a "green" image. Tourist places have become more sensitive to zoning, density, land use and the problems of overbuilding. In some places, regional and local tourist agencies, airlines, railways and hotel chains are all talking about green issues and how best to accommodate growth while respecting environmental values. Tourism awards in some Asian countries and places such as New Zealand and Thailand now have a special category for outstanding environmental practices. Unfortunately, a "green" image is more common in Australia and some South Pacific islands where tourism — at least mass tourism — is less well developed. In South and Central Asia and some Southeast Asian countries, we find fewer cases of green consciousness, but they are on the upswing.

Event-based tourism has become a vital component of tourist attraction programs. Small or rural places typically begin with a festival or event to establish their identity. Urban newspapers typically publish a listing of events, festivals and celebrations that occur within a few hours' drive. Local and regional tourism offices make sure that travel agents, restaurants, hotels, airports, and railway and bus stations have event-based calendars to display. Some Asian cities have an events agency as a division of the local government. EventsCorp, the events agency of the West Australian Government,[10] for example, handles the promotion of major events. Other places, such as the Celebration Singapore Web site, devote a section of their official tourism Web sites[11] to list upcoming events and festivals.

Tourism investment ranges from relatively low-cost market entry for festivals or events to multimillion-dollar infrastructure costs for stadiums, transit systems, airports, railway stations and convention centers. Today, urban-renewal planners seek to build tourism into the heart of their city's revitalization. The Varanasi Redevelopment Project and the West End Strategy in Adelaide[12] are examples of urban renewal where the old and new are merged to create attractions for residents, businesses and tourists. These examples also illustrate the advantage of having projects developed jointly by the public and private sectors. The public sector can be the overall catalyst, with the private sector acting as the actual operator.

The ADB, UNDP and other multilateral financial institutions and agencies can also support investments in various tourism projects. The structural funds provided by these organizations are frequently a major contributor to tourism development. Aid tends to go to "underdeveloped" regions, those affected by the decline of industry and those concerned with rural development. Actions are also taken under certain community initiatives such as in the case of Pattaya and Cebu, where citizens are actively involved in promoting tourism.

Opportunities for tourism to implement joint measures, set up networks and try out new actions are planned under the community's programs. The governments of many Asian countries, including Hong Kong, Thailand, Australia and New Zealand, have increased tourism funding to bring in more income and provide more employment. In the Philippines, a nation whose tourism industry has suffered as a result of terrorism, natural disasters and political instability, financial institutions are encouraged to fund investors with tourism-related projects. Philippines tourism investments amounted to US$6.27 billion from 1994–1997, but that figure is inadequate given the competition and fundamental problems.[13] Many Asian countries spend far more, and for good reason. According to the World Travel and Tourism Council, the Asia Pacific region requires US$553 billion in capital investments in infrastructure and superstructure to reach its forecast growth in the region.[14]

Positioning and Niching in the Tourist Market
To attract tourists, places must respond to the travel basics of cost, convenience and timeliness. Tourists, like other consumers, weigh the costs against the benefits of specific destinations — and their investment of time, effort and resources against a reasonable return in education, experience, fun, relaxation and prospective memories. Convenience takes on various meanings in travel decisions: time involved in travel, the distance from airport to lodgings, language barriers, cleanliness and sanitary concerns, access to interests (beaches, attractions and amenities), and special needs (elderly, disabled, children, dietary, medical care, fax and telecommunication, auto rental). Timeliness embraces those factors that introduce risk to travel: wars, terrorism, civil disturbances and political instability, currency fluctuations and convertibility, airline and transit safety, and health conditions.

As a general rule, all places and tourist businesses seek to be competitive in costs, minimized risks, and maximized conveniences and amenities. Tourist packages range from total hour-by-hour planning to multiple options and choices. To accommodate multiple tourist needs, packages range from no-frills destination-to-destination to site-and-event based full-frills luxury. Beyond the basics, travelers make comparisons about the relative advantages and disadvantages of competing destinations: geographical (local, regional, national, Asian or non-Asian), special interests (hiking, snorkeling, mountaineering), and amenities (music, art, entertainment, and so on). Should I dive in Palau or in Palawan? Should we go to some of the "new" places in Central Asia or continue our return trips to India? Tourists, like other consumers, constantly make trade-offs between cost and convenience, quality and reliability, service and beauty, and so on. Depreciation of a country's currency, for example, can immediately attract tourists from another country.

Places must market not only their destination in general, but also their specific attractions. Places must provide easy access to their attractions by bus (as in Singapore or Hong Kong), tram (as in Hong Kong, Melbourne or Bendigo), subway (as in Hong Kong, Singapore, Seoul or Pusan), boat (as in Hong Kong), and plane (as in the Hong Kong International Airport, with over 31 million passengers in 1999). Places can distribute brochures, audiotapes and videotapes, postcards and Internet pages. All major hotels now provide in-home video packages to assist visitors in planning local tours, booking events, or in seeing various sites. City bus or boat companies offer half-day, full-day and evening tours to highlight the place's major attractions. There are various ways to get around in a city, but sometimes an authentic experience of the place includes the many unique local modes of transportation each country can offer (see Exhibit 9.7).

Exhibit 9.7: RICKSHAW, TUK-TUK, JUNK AND JEEPNEY

In a developing region like Asia, it is hard not to notice the dramatically increasing volume of new cars, trucks and vans on every new street and highway. For public transportation, there are bullet and commuter trains, subways, taxis and countless buses. With so many choices, most tourists have no trouble at all getting to their chosen destination. But a trip to any Asian country is not complete without soaking up the scenery while taking a native mode of transport, like a rickshaw, tuk-tuk, junk or jeepney.

The rickshaw was originally invented in Japan in 1869, and from there it spread to China and to many other countries in the region. Its original name was the *jinrikshaw*, meaning "man-powered cart," and it consisted of a two-wheeled cart with two long handles by which the operator pulled the cart forward. The once-ubiquitous rickshaw has become virtually extinct in modern Asia, only hanging on because of its attraction for tourists. Interestingly, many tourists only want their pictures taken while posing in one of the old carts, but don't take a ride.

While there's not much demand for the original rickshaws today, this form of transport has evolved into more modern forms. In the Philippines, for example, there are carts with bicycles and motorcycles attached. These "modern" pedicabs can justifiably be called "tricycle-rickshaws," and they are still widely used in many Asian countries.

"Tuk-tuk, tuk-tuk." That's the sound another odd-looking vehicle makes when maneuvering through Asia's crowded streets. At least that's the sound it made when they were still running on diesel. The tuk-tuk is basically a motorized rickshaw with three wheels and now that they use LPG, they make less noise but still prove to be a colorful experience for travelers to Thailand or New Zealand.

The jeepney is the most popular way to get around the major cities of the Philippines. It was designed after the jeeps used by the Americans in the Second World War. The jeepneys of today are decorated and colored to suit the whims of the owner, and give the roads a festive, if chaotic, feel. Some owners have even gone to the extreme of putting in full-size stereo systems and lights to make them look like the cockpits of airplanes.

If the traffic-laden streets are too much to deal with, there is always the option of traveling by water. Many major Asian cities offer a variety of ways to get to favored destinations via ferry, boat or junk. In Bangkok, it is still possible to see ferries rushing along the city's canals (*klongs*), transporting schoolchildren, shoppers, workers and tourists alike. Chinese junks and sampans continue to dot Hong Kong's busy harbor alongside the famous Star Ferry.

Journalist Harold Stephens describes the transportation situation in Asia this way: "The question remains, who needs a taxi in Asia anyway? The tuk-tuk may be around for a long time."[1]

Sources:

1 Harold Stephens, "Traveling In and Around Thailand: Getting Around Without A Taxi," *Bangkok Post* Web site, http://www.bangkokpost.net/travel/taxi.html, viewed on January 26, 2001.

Thailand Passport Web site, www.thaipassport.com/main/infodesk/tuktuk.asp, viewed on January 26, 2001; *GoAbroad* Web site; http://www.goabroad.com/guides/guidesp3.cfm ?pkguides=490&fkcountry=69&weight=55, viewed on January 26, 2001.

Places need to closely monitor the relative popularity of their various attractions by determining the number and type of tourists attracted to each location. The popularity of Pattaya as the "Riviera of Asia," Bangkok as the "City of Angels," Auckland as the "City of Sails," or even landmarks such as the Borubudur Temple in Java City can suddenly or gradually change. Places must therefore continually seek to deepen the quality of their attractions, rather than take them for granted. The value-added process should never stop.

Macau, the "City of Casinos," and Pattaya must develop new attractions. In the case of Pattaya, for instance, it is of great importance to exploit the opportunities generated as a result of its campaign to clean up the resort city's sleazy image, and to market business-related conferences and conventions (see Exhibit 5.3 on p. 170). Officials can work to bring back the resort city's former glory as well by adding new concepts and attractions. Hong Kong, for example, lives up to its "Asia's world city" slogan by continuously developing new attractions for tourists and visitors (Hong Kong Disneyland and the Hong Kong Convention and Exhibition Centre, for example) and developing and encouraging private-sector development of new areas in the New Territories as well as established sectors of the Special Administrative Region. Among these are the New Town Plaza shopping mall, the Hong Kong Railway Museum, the Wong Shek Pier for windsurfers, Kau Sai Chau Golf Courses, the Clear Water Bay Golf and Country Club, and the Sha Tin Racecourse (horse-racing). It is marketed as the city that "offers tourists more sights and attractions per square kilometer than anywhere else in the world."[16] There will be more. "Hong Kong is developing a second convention and exhibition center, a new major performing arts venue, and a multipurpose stadium able to hold more than 40,000 people."[17]

However, concepts alone do not attract tourists. Places must seek to deepen the travel experience by providing greater value and making the experience more significant and rewarding. Such appeals may be couched in terms of culture, tradition and people. A city can develop itself in a more visitor-friendly direction. This can be done by creating tours that emphasize nationality interests, designing brochures in a variety of languages, and providing hassle-free currency exchanges. To provide such value-adding elements a place can deepen cultural bonds and ties. A recent trend in Asia is to establish so called partner-city ties across Asian borders, and conferences and associations have been created to support these initiatives. Examples of this include the Sister Cities Programme of the Asia Pacific Cities Summit,[18] the Sister Cities New Zealand,[19] and the Australian Sister Cities Association Inc.[20]

Competition for place advantage in tourism extends to restaurants, facilities, sports, cultural amenities and entertainment. There is a permanent struggle between Asian places to have the most five-star hotels; the best wine and drink; the best chefs; the best and most museums and theatres; or best native, cultural or ethnic flair. The popularity of the *Lonely Planet Guide* series is a reflection of this struggle. Almost every corner of Asia is ranked by travel guides and magazines according to best hotels, restaurants, and so on. These testimonials and rankings, where favorable, are then incorporated into travel brochures, place advertising and travel guides.

Communicating with the Tourist Market

Tourist competition, like business attraction and retention, involves image making. Place images are heavily influenced by artistic creations of the place, including movies, television, postcards, music and popular entertainers. Decades later, these place images still persist. India exploits Sir Richard Attenborough's film *Gandhi* as an idealized image of the Indian, while Indonesia still benefits from Hollywood's version of *The Year of Living Dangerously*. More recently, Beijing's Forbidden Palace has become associated with legendary Chinese heroine Mulan, at least by children who have viewed the Disney film of that name. Hong Kong features the martial arts films of Bruce Lee and Jackie Chan, and Japan focuses on its world-renowned Kabuki theater, Sumo wrestling, and ancient temples and shrines. Many Asian countries are also associated with their colorful national dress — the Kimono of Japan; the sari, bindi, mendhi and turbans of South Asia; the Barong Tagalog of the Philippines; the "Nehru suit" of India; and the chong sam of China.

Places often discover hidden assets that have large tourist potential. Such assets can sometimes be communicated with humor and brilliance and even develop into cult objects. A strategy used by some places is to market themselves by means of an icon original to the place. As an example, Australia actively markets itself via its national animal, the kangaroo. This animal is found in virtually all Australian tourism promotional and travel-related materials: ads, t-shirts, chocolates, souvenirs, and so on. Most tourism packages include a visit to a kangaroo farm, where tourists are allowed to pet and feed the animals. The Australian state of Tasmania has its own icon — the Tasmanian Devil — and New Zealand likewise markets itself by incorporating its national emblem, the kiwi, in promotional materials. Hong Kong incorporates a mythical Chinese icon, a red dragon (see Figure 9.2), to create a unique "brand."

Figure 9.2: Hong Kong incorporates a mythical icon in its "brand."

Source: http://www.brandhk.gov.hk/brandhk/eindex.ht, viewed on July 9, 2001.

Finally, effective place imaging requires a congruence between the place as it actually exists and the way that it is advertised. Glossy photographs of sunsets, beaches, buildings and events need to have some relationship to what tourists actually experience; otherwise places run the risk of losing tourist goodwill and generating bad word of mouth. Travel agents are extremely responsive to place feedback from customers, and they are not likely to recommend a destination that distorts reality. Places should survey travel agents about the feedback they get from their customers.

Organizing and Managing Tourism Marketing
The task of many place sellers is to make their particular place a tourist-friendly destination. For this to be effective, there needs to be a model for

organizing and managing tourism marketing. Table 9.3 outlines the Singapore Tourism Board's model. Singapore is among the top tourist destinations in Asia and their plan is clear and thorough.

Table 9.3: Singapore Tourism Board Organization Structure

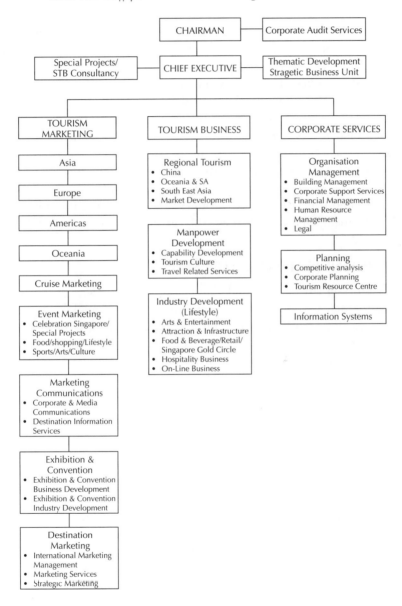

Even though the national structure seems dominant in many place-marketing models in Asia, the main promotion usually takes place at the regional and local level, where public and private institutions have joined forces to a great extent. In some parts of Asia, local chambers of commerce are heavily involved in tourism strategies and promotion. Several major Asian cities have significantly more economic resources for tourism marketing than the regional and national tourist-promotion agencies.

It is evident that the public and private sectors have improved their collaboration in tourism — especially during the last decade, when the competitive climate in Asia has pushed the sectors closer together in many places. More commercial considerations are being recognized as important. The American strategy of joining forces, especially on local and regional levels, has spread to Asia. Bridge-building between the sectors is occurring. The ASEAN Tourism Association[21] (ASEANTA — a division of ASEAN) is an organization that is composed of the private and public sectors from ASEAN countries. The APEC Tourism Working Group (comprising 21 officials from APEC economies) formulated the APEC Tourism Charter, which actively involves the private sector.[22]

THE BUSINESS HOSPITALITY MARKET

Although Asia still lags behind Europe and the Americas in tourism, it has witnessed a significant increase in business travel in two main categories. First, millions of small and regular business meetings are increasingly taking place in a cross-border context. Second, there is a growing market for trade shows, conventions, assemblies, conferences and consumer shows. In each case the key revenue factors are the size of the group, the length of the stay, and service demands.

Table 9.4 shows the top 20 countries of the world with the most business and professional visitors. Seven of these are Asian countries. However, the leisure-market share in all Asian countries except Taiwan is much higher than that of the business market.

Thailand is unique in attracting large numbers of holiday tourists for extended stays because of its spectacular beaches and resorts. Hong Kong, Indonesia and Singapore benefit greatly from business travelers apart from leisure tourists. It must be remembered that business travelers who stay overnight expect leisure-type offerings such as entertainment, historical attractions or natural beauty. This means that each place must be able to offer comprehensive and specific target packages (STP) incorporating both business and leisure offerings.

Table 9.4: Business and leisure tourism in selected countries, 1998
(in thousands)

		Nights of inbound tourism in hotels	Business and professional	Leisure, recreation and holidays
Italy	Europe	87,192	8,922	49,577
United Kingdom	Europe		7,589	10,475
Poland	Europe	5,480	5,180	7,900
United States	Americas		4,728	22,342
Spain	Europe	111,819	3,485	41,973
Hong Kong	Asia		3,093	4,688
Canada	Americas		3,045	10,556
Russian Fed.	Europe		3,011	2,885
Belgium	Europe	9,483	2,278	3,611
Turkey	Europe	30,159	1,973	6,825
Indonesia	Asia		1,599	2,395
Ukraine	Europe	1,140	1,478	853
Ireland	Europe	15,033	1,455	2,365
Singapore	Asia		1,385	2,829
Brazil	Americas	35,170	1,286	3,459
Finland	Europe	3,226	1,165	1,291
Japan	Asia		1,105	2,358
Taiwan	Asia		825	762
Thailand	Asia	65,232	772	6,833
Macau	Asia	2,753	771	4,044

Source: *Compendium of Tourist Statistics*, World Tourist Organization, Madrid, 2000.

Developing Competitive Meeting Facilities

As the meetings market has grown, so have the number of places and facilities competing for the business. Asian places are boosting their capacity to handle huge meetings. The Elecrama Exhibitions at the Bombay Exhibition Center in Mumbai attracted a total of 110,000 visitors in 1999. A profile of the visitors showed that the majority were directors (44%) and senior and middle management (33%).[23] This contribution to Mumbai was significant since many of the visitors purchased local services and products from the local market.

Apart from Hong Kong or Singapore, which are leading and classic meeting places, convention facilities in other parts of Asia improved immensely in the 1990s. Many other places also offer attractive world-class packages: Shanghai, Tokyo, Bangkok, Sydney, Jakarta, Taipei, Osaka, Kuala Lumpur, Manila, Beijing, Guangzhou and Melbourne.

Many others are lining up to join them: New Delhi, Cebu, Shenzhen, Ho Chi Minh, Mumbai, Karachi, Seoul, Hanoi, Guangdong, Kobe, Shandong, Tianjin, Brisbane and Chengdu.

A successful convention place doesn't just offer an attractive price. A world-class package must also contain a unique combination of physical meeting facilities and a number of exciting value-added offerings. As a consequence, Asian places are specializing in certain types of conventions, congresses and exhibitions. The competitive climate and specialization is now heightened as more Asian players are entering the convention market. For instance, Langkawi, Malaysia, has managed to attract a convention for the maritime and aerospace industry, while the Chinese city of Wuhan has focused on a metalworking technology and equipment fair.

The Asian market also includes thousands of small places competing with their very specific packages. The Hunter Valley wine country, a two-hour drive from Sydney, promotes its natural setting of vineyards for business meetings and conferences. Other small places with easily identifiable positions are Bali, Pattaya, Penang, Phuket and Dubai. They are all meeting places with a very special flavor, and competing with them demands more amenities and benefits. Dubai, with its geographical advantage, hosts over 70 exhibitions and conventions every year and offers the novel setting of a desert oasis. Bali is also blessed with a good geographical location within easy reach of Jakarta, Singapore, Perth and Hong Kong, and can provide attractive combinations of business and leisure facilities.

The competition for hospitality business breeds a certain spiraling "space race" between competing cities, in which internal and external dynamics play a part. The internal dynamic stems largely from hotel and hospitality business expansion, which builds or overbuilds to meet prospective demands from conventions and trade shows. When hotel occupancy rates fall below a profit level — roughly 60% occupancy — pressure mounts to expand exhibition and meeting space to increase these rates.

The external dynamic comes from the competitors' space-expansion plans. Several Asian cities have recently expanded their exhibition space and there are many new projects in the planning stage. The Asian dimension is becoming more important as a result of increasing interest within the region for a move towards a single market, although it will be many years yet before Asia merges into an E.U.-type market. Still, exhibitions, trade fairs, conventions and conferences are increasingly being organized for the larger Asian market, and serve to unify perspectives and goals.

Strategies for Winning in the Business Hospitality Market

Conventions, conferences and the trade-show business, in contrast to tourist attractions, involve dealing with dedicated specialists such as trade-association directors, site-selection committees and convention specialists who make site-selection recommendations based on price, facilities and various other amenities. Facilities are critical to accommodating an association's needs — which often means that a place will need the capacity to run multiple shows concurrently — and provide first-class space at reasonable rates. Discounted hotel, restaurant, theater, airline, auto rental, transit and other amenities are all part of competitive packaging. Such packaging requires considerable cooperation between the place sellers in a specific place.

Facilities must also be upgraded to meet aesthetic and convenience needs — restaurants, shops, restrooms, greater cleanliness, speed of set-ups and take-downs, security, and proximity to central shopping areas and restaurants. Central and convenient communication is not so easily managed within Asian cities of the old urban design. Since these urban traditions — and bottlenecks — are part of the unique product, they often cannot be easily changed.

Kuala Lumpur, with its Multimedia Super Corridor and excellent international airport which combines futuristic technology, Malaysian culture and natural beauty, is a prime example of how much a place is willing to invest in attracting visitors and investors, and in advancing its position as one of Asia's emerging meeting places and technological hubs. However, with the airport located an hour away from the main city and with transportation links still incomplete, there has been criticism directed at its location and the timing of the opening. The Asian financial crisis of 1997 also sparked further criticism when the government chose to continue with the projects — and their massive capital outlay — despite a severe downturn in economic fortunes and depreciation of the currency. However, the government persisted, in the belief that the projects would help push the country to the forefront of Asian technology and business. Time will tell.

Each convention center has its competitive advantages and disadvantages. Some convention places in Central Asia have bad weather during autumn and spring, while others in South Asia and the United Arab Emirates (New Delhi or Dubai, for example) are too hot in the summer to be competitive. In places such as Tokyo and Mumbai, hotel prices are too high to attract convention-place buyers. The dream of all places is to attract customers during unfavorable periods and offer inducements including cut-rate prices and free services.

The Asian convention business is hotly competitive and requires places to benchmark against the top global locations. There is no sign of a pull-back in expansion or ambitions, despite unstable market conditions. In periods of recession, organizers cut back on travel for professional development, trade shows and even sales contacts, preferring to use videoconferences, teleconferences and fax machines instead. Like tourism, the meetings market experienced some difficult years in the late 1990s. Yet, despite the impact of the financial crisis, more investments in professional meeting facilities were planned than ever before. This commitment to development reflects the belief that the Asian market will expand in the long run.

CONCLUSION

Tourism and the business-hospitality market have emerged as viable place-development opportunities on an equal footing with business retention and business attraction. In service-driven economies with aging populations, these two businesses are generally expected to grow at rates ahead of the national economy.

There are several tourism/travel-related trends worth noting:

- The economic development plans of places will increasingly emphasize the contribution of the tourism and travel industry.
- Greater market segmentation will follow from better marketing information, and the strategic marketing and management of tourism will receive increased emphasis.
- Travelers will combine business and personal travel more often, with an emphasis on cultural and recreation activities that will require places to adapt to cross-marketing.
- Greater interest in sports and recreation will require places to invest more in open space and recreational facilities, and to develop lower-key, environmentally sensitive experiences.
- The opening of Central Asia will create a boom in Asian tourism.
- Shorter working weeks in Asia will increase short-break tourism. Smaller places — within a convenient travel distance of the big cities — can be real winners if they adopt a proactive marketing strategy.

Smaller places can promote tourism and business meetings at relatively little cost. However, as they seek access to broader markets, the cost for public and private investments rises rapidly. At the upper end of the scale, large capital investments are required for airports, convention centers, basic infrastructure and public services. Private-sector investment in hotels, shopping areas and restaurants needs to be carefully coordinated and planned with public investments so that one does not proceed without the other. Physical assets must be continually upgraded, and new products and concepts developed.

Exhibit 9.8 offers a test that places can use to assess their visitor-friendliness.

Exhibit 9.8: A VISITOR-FRIENDLINESS TEST

While no exact test exists to measure a place's friendliness to its visitors, the following 10 questions provide a rough estimate. With 10 points for each favorable answer, a passing score is 60. Anything lower probably spells trouble.

1. Are the central access points to your community/place (road, rail, plane) equipped with visitor-information centers or do they at least provide instructions on where to find information easily?
2. If the primary access point is an airport or a railway station, does it provide a full range of visitor-information services (for example, accommodations, tourist booth, visuals on sites, listing of events and what to do, specialized information for the elderly, foreigners, families, and so on)?
3. Do facilitators for visitors — cab, bus, airline/railway personnel, airport/railway security operators, reservation personnel — receive any formal training, and does a system exist to monitor the quality of these services?
4. Do hotels/motels offer in-house television channels providing visitors with access to information on events, attractions, restaurants and things to do?
5. Is a single organization/agency responsible for visitor business and are public funds provided for its activities?
6. Does that organization/agency have a marketing profile of visitors and is this profile used in its marketing activities?
7. Does the place's hospitality industry accommodate foreign visitors' needs (language, directions, special interests, and so on)?
8. Does a range of accommodations exist to meet the actual or expected needs of visitors (by price range, size, facilities, access to sites, and so on)?

9. Is access to sites, attractions and amenities (events, recreational, central location) easily available at reasonable cost?
10. Does the place welcome visitors and accommodate their needs (commercial hours, credit cards, language, signage, traffic, parking, public services, and so on)?

1 Morris Dye, "Pleasant Perth is Just a Kangaroo Hop Away," *Time*, August 7, 2000, p. 5.
2 David Atkinson, "Laos Unplugged: Living Life in the Slow Lane," *Time*, May 22, 2000, p. 7.
3 Ron Gluckman, "Live Like a King in the Castles of Rajasthan," *Time*, January 15, 2001, p. 5.
4 http://www.wttc.org/TSA/pdfs/sea.pdf, viewed on January 22, 2001.
5 http://riceinfo.rice.edu/projects/baker/Pubs/BakerPub/publications/claes/ecca/ecca.html, viewed on January 27, 2001.
6 *Asian Development Outlook 2000*, Asian Development Bank, Manila, 2000, p. 258.
7 http://www.asiannet.com/china/qingdao/, viewed on January 25, 2001.
8 http://www.casinosnepal.com/traveller/2000/aug/loma.htm, viewed on January 25, 2001.
9 http://europe.cnn.com/2000/STYLE/design/07/10/restoring.bukhara.ap, viewed on January 25, 2001.
10 http://www.eventscorp.com.au, viewed on June 28, 2001.
11 http://www.celebrationsingapore.com.sg, viewed on June 28, 2001.
12 http://www.adelaide.sa.gov.au/WestEnd/, viewed on January 25, 2001.
13 http://www.hotel-online.com/Neo/Trends/AsiaPacificJournal/AsiaPacific-TourismOutlook_1997.html, viewed on February 16, 2001.
14 *Ibid.*
15 "Hong Kong Airport Sets New Highs in April," *People's Daily*, May 15, 2000. Internet: http://english.peopledaily.com.cn/200005/15/eng20000515_40817.html, viewed on January 26, 2001.
16 http://asiatravel.com/hknut2.html, viewed on January 26, 2001.
17 "Tourism: New Challenges, New Directions," http://www.brandhk.gov.hk/brandhk/e_pdf/efact10.pdf, viewed on July 9, 2001.
18 http://www.apsummit.org/overview_secretariat_int_relations_sister_-city_kobe.html, viewed on February 21, 2001.
19 http://www.pie.co.nz/sistercities/, viewed on February 21, 2001.
20 http://www.asca.asn.au/, viewed on February 21, 2001.
21 http://www.aseanta.org/, viewed on February 26, 2001.
22 http://www.apecsec.org.sg/whatsnew/announce/twgcharter.html, viewed on February 26, 2001.
23 http://www.ieema.org/ELECRAMA/elecrama99.htm, viewed on January 25, 2000.
24 http://www.winecountry.com.au, viewed on February 13, 2001.

C H A P T E R

10

Attracting, Retaining
and Expanding Business

very place performs particular economic functions. Some places
have diversified economies, while others are dominated by a
single industry. Some are service centers, and others are
agricultural communities. However, a place's economic activities are not
necessarily constrained by its surrounding economic boundaries. The
Internet and agreements between Asian nations to transform the region
into a free-trade zone present unparalleled opportunity for places of any
size and virtually any stage of development. Indeed, with the enormous
Asian market around the corner — the 40 Asia-Pacific countries and
their 3.275 billion inhabitants — the smallest place can expand its
business in the regional and international market with fewer and fewer
administrative obstacles. Viewing a place through a cross-border Asian
lens can lead to a better understanding of how a place functions in an
international context.

A place's ability to compete changes over time. At one time, Malacca
and Samarkand were thriving as dynamic hubs for international trade.
Some centuries later, they had become minor players in the trade world.
Once again they have come to prominence, this time as leaders in the
tourist market. Like corporate giants and entire industries, places may
rise and fall with new technologies, new competitors, new political
realities and shifting consumer preferences.

Over the last half century, a general pattern can be identified in Asian place strategy. During Asian industrialization after the Second World War, places (with the exception of Japan) used specific raw materials and other competitive factors as an incentive for industrialists to establish new manufacturing plants. Asian countries focused on rebuilding, modernizing and expanding non-existent or diminished industrial capacities, in most cases with support from former colonizers who often became military allies. The north Asia states of South Korea, Taiwan and Singapore led this expansion, following Japan's lead. By the 1970s, the rest of Southeast Asia was, for the most part, aggressively following their lead and helped account for an historic expansion that the World Bank would eventually call "the East Asian miracle." During this period growth was largely driven by an increase in the number of people of productive age willing to work cheaply in manufacturing and export-assembly jobs. As a result, most of Asia benefited substantially from the plentiful supply of people of productive age.

In the late 1980s and the 1990s, many Asian places began to think about making the transition from relatively low value-added exports — mostly dominated by garments, electrical appliances and electronics — to higher value-added development and production. At the same time, excess capacity, securities and real-estate speculation, driven by increasingly global fund-flows, and weak regulatory institutions collectively conspired to set the stage for the 1997 financial crisis — which changed fundamental assumptions in places all over Asia. When the crisis hit, Japan had already been suffering from the unregulated excesses of speculative growth for the better part of the decade. As a result of the crisis, many Asian corporations reluctantly opened their arms to foreign investors interested in mergers and acquisitions in previously protected sectors. The underlying assumption was that new investors could revitalize otherwise declining businesses. The crisis demonstrated that even the most foreign sources of capital could be welcomed under the "right" circumstances as many proud conglomerates were forced to sell prized assets.

Now in the first decade of the 21st century, many places have started to focus on encouraging new business start-ups, investment in research and development that will bring greater added value to their exports, and the development of their service sectors. Inspired by the high growth figures in American high-tech centers, research parks and clusters, Asian places have worked out their own "silicon strategies."

Today, places can use one or more of six generic strategies to improve their competitive positions:

1. Attracting tourist and business visitors.
2. Attracting business from elsewhere.
3. Retaining and expanding existing business.
4. Promoting small business and fostering new business start-ups.
5 Expanding exports and outside investments.
6. Expanding the population or changing the mix of residents.

We have already examined the first strategy in Chapter 9. We will examine the last two strategies, expanding exports and investments and altering the residential population base, in Chapters 11 and 12. Here, though, we will focus on place strategies for attracting, retaining, expanding and starting new businesses.

ATTRACTING BUSINESSES FROM ELSEWHERE

Asian places have a remarkable history of attracting businesses from elsewhere. Attracting new business and new kinds of businesses became even more important after the 1997 financial crisis when many places experienced the negative consequences from low rankings and bad images in the place market. Suddenly international competition became intense. The specter of mass unemployment again haunted Asian citizens and politicians.

How Businesses Select Locations

Places should begin their business-attraction planning with an assessment of their economy and an audit of their locational characteristics (their local business climate). Accurate and frequent updating of operating conditions, cost factors and quality-of-life features provides an understanding of how well one place compares to others. Table 3.3 (Chapter 3) offered a list of "hard" and "soft" attraction factors which businesses consider important in most site designations. These attraction factors change over time and from project to project. During the last three decades, the competitive advantages, strengths and weaknesses of places changed. As Table 10.1 indicates, new non-economic factors — or soft factors — have become increasingly important in location-expansion decisions.

Various soft factors have gained prominence and assumed multiple forms: quality of public education; skilled labor force in the relevant niche; political stability; a trusting local business climate; modern telecommunications; local access to support services such as marketing and banking; recreational activities and sports teams; shopping facilities, cultural institutions and other general quality-of-life considerations.

Table 10.1: Locational characteristics: Old and new

Characteristics	Old	New
Labor	Low cost, unskilled	Quality, highly skilled
Tax climate	Low taxes, low service	Modest taxes, high services
Incentives	Least-cost production, cheap land and labor	Value-added adaptable labor force, professionals
Amenities	Housing and transportation	Culture, recreation, museums, shopping, airport
Schools	Availability	Quality schools
Higher education	Not key	Quality schools and research facilities
Regulation	Minimum	Compatible quality of life and business flexibility
Energy	Cost/Availability	Dependability/reliability
Communication	Assumed	Technology access
Business	Aggressive chamber of commerce	Partnerships

Environmental considerations — stronger air, water, and chemical and waste disposal regulations, for example — also grew in importance.

In a market characterized by many place sellers and few place buyers, place sellers primarily compete on place inducements. However, place inducements are not always the crucial determinant. In increasing numbers, buyers are shifting their interest toward places that offer firm-specific and, especially, non-cost factors. Places with universities, relevant research facilities and good quality-of-life factors have an advantage over places that lack these features.

In competing for factories and other investments, place sellers seek (in addition to direct and indirect job creation) to expand the local and regional tax base. Normally, an Asian community or region can measure its performance in terms of changes to the tax base. Professional place buyers must keep this carefully in mind in selecting their site (see Exhibit 10.1).

Exhibit 10.1: MARKETING CLUSTERS: A COMPETITIVE MODEL

Places that have a number of similar industries are more likely to attract companies in comparable businesses. Michael Porter argues that these competing or complementary companies form clusters of excellence that build productivity through rivalries and asset sharing. In Porter's view, places should encourage competition because it forces companies to innovate in order to stay ahead and also attracts world-class talent. What do Porter's insights mean to the thousands of Asian communities that are seeking to expand their workforces and create a higher standard of living?

- The place that already has a cluster needs to expand its financial and skills base. The task here is to anticipate the needs of clusters — for example, in the areas of communication, human resources and transportation — and deliver higher-quality support. In some places, such as Taiwan, the cluster is being expanded to surrounding communities. This can improve competitiveness and secure a critical mass.

- Many Asian places are in what can be termed the "pre-cluster stage." These places might consider targeting promising industries in order to create fully-fledged clusters. The place may have only a few companies or a number of companies without any real similarities. In this case, its task is to inventory the marketplace, its assets and its workforce to determine the right combination of companies to locate in the area. Success stories abound. For instance, Bangalore has achieved genuine cluster development in the software industry, albeit at the lower value-added end of the sector. Zhong-Guan Village in northwestern Beijing, Cebu in the Philippines, and Ho Chi Minh City are likewise at various stages of software-cluster development. Hong Kong, too, is building an Internet/software cluster, as are Malaysia and Singapore. Singapore is also trying to create a niche for itself as the regional leader in financial services. To be successful, these places must derive the benefits that technology, an educated workforce and targeted development provide.

- For some places in the very early stage of development, a practical approach might involve practicing strong attraction strategies and casting a wider net. The Hunter region of New South Wales, an old industrial region famous for its wineries, is a good example of a town practicing a strategy that concentrates on making deals. The Hunter Economic Development Corporation constructed a strategic model that combines an aggressive use of grants, incentives and subsidies with first-rate execution. It has attracted an eclectic array of new businesses to its industrial parks, including steel, food and automotive companies. This cluster is not product-specific, for example, shoes or glass, but its aggressive development approach should be viewed as entrepreneurial. The Hunter's focus is buttressed with a careful attention to promotion, a willingness to cut through red tape and a willingness to take risks.

In the cases described above, the common denominator — irrespective of whether the place is a cluster, pre-cluster, or early-development model — is that strategic market planning is crucial.

___

Sources:

Michael E. Porter, "Cluster and the New Economics of Competition," *Harvard Business Review*, November/December 1998, pp. 77–90. See also Porter's *"On Competition,"* Harvard Business School Press, Boston, 1998; Hunter Economic Development Corporation Web site, http://www.hedc.nsw.gov.au/, viewed on February 7, 2001.

The Race for High-tech Industries

Following the Second World War, Asian communities focused almost solely on attracting basic heavy-manufacturing industries. Today, they seek "clean" factories. The race is to build an attractive local climate to attract high-tech industries. This "Silicon strategy" is symbolized by places like Hong Kong's Cyberport, Singapore, Malaysia's Multimedia Super Corridor, Cebu, and Beijing's Zhong-Guan Village. India's high-tech star, Bangalore, developed — like so many of its North American counterparts — because it is a combination of excellent educational institutions, an entrepreneurial culture, and at least reasonable access to capital. Thousands of small places are also establishing their own high-tech strategies. They are struggling to keep a critical mass and to support "their" knowledge-based firms. Both small and big Silicon Valley clones are promoting science and/or business parks, research centers and buildings designed to house two or more knowledge-based companies.

Yet today, many companies using the Silicon strategy are in trouble. During the financial crisis, most of Asia's high-tech centers remained underdeveloped, and many continue as highly subsidized research parks and incubators. A major problem facing such places is to achieve a critical mass that gives the place a sufficient quality image or niche-leadership position. Many places suffer from "brain drain" and need to develop education and quality-of-life incentives to deep clusters of talent. In South Korea, for example, up to 21,000 people were expected to emigrate in 2001 out of frustration over poor schools.[1] Indeed, during Asia's miracle years, investments in educational infrastructure were badly neglected in most countries. And because of global competition for technical and IT graduates, Asia has a hard time retaining the intellectual resources it needs (Exhibit 10.2). Yet for many Asian nations, technology exports play an increasingly fundamental economic role (Figure 10.1).

Exhibit 10.2: COMPETITION FOR SCARCE INTELLECTUAL RESOURCES IMPERILS THE NEW ASIAN ECONOMY

The estimates of global demand for knowledge workers vary, but none of them are very encouraging. For instance, in 2000 the U.S. alone was expected to need 1.6 million information-technology workers according to the Information Technology Association of America (ITAA), but only half of those jobs were likely to be filled. That gap was a serious concern for the Federal Reserve chairman and chief architect of The New Economy, Alan Greenspan.

So serious, in fact, that he called on the U.S. Congress to increase the number of high-technology visas issued each year to lessen upward pressure on wages and other incentives. Although Congress doubled the number of visas issued to technology investors in 1998, the Immigration and Nationalization Service filled the quota in just six months — and issued another 10,000 to 20,000 visas by mistake.

Congress heeded Greenspan's call — and that of the U.S. IT sector — and, despite some pronounced grumbling by the labor sector, increased the quota again by about half, to approximately 195,000 for the next six years, starting in the year 2001. This was done because few doubt claims — overtly endorsed by Greenspan — that the IT sector fueled U.S. growth during the high-flying 1990s by consistently increasing productivity.

There is little doubt, too, that IT growth itself has been substantially fueled by the sector's capacity to attract the world's brightest minds. From 1985 to 1996, foreign students who received their basic education at home but planned to work in the U.S. after graduation accounted for two-thirds of the increase in science and engineering doctorates. Although overall demand for IT workers in the U.S. cooled in 2001 when the economy slowed and just 900,000 new jobs opened, 425,000 remain unfilled. "Our 2001 numbers suggest that hiring has by no means halted for IT workers," said ITAA president Harris N. Miller. "Rather, demand still far exceeds supply in this market."[1]

And this is the crucial point for Asia's budding IT economies. While increasing U.S. immigration quotas for technology workers to 200,000 won't leave Asia without any high-tech workers — India alone produces about 122,000 every year and China graduates a similar number of engineers — it is likely to attract Asia's very best minds anxious to avail themselves of the very best opportunities available. Just as important, increasing domestic demand for technology workers will give rise to a worrying increase in the number of IT-related jobs that go unfilled. Malaysia will need twice as many workers in 2010 than it had in 2001. There are 100 jobs in China for every IT-related graduate, and India will be short two million technology workers by 2006.

This puts Asia's less-developed economies like India, China, and the Philippines in the odd position of subsidizing U.S. growth. While that investment is paid back in part by historic levels of imports into the U.S. economy these workers are helping to expand, the rate at which Asia emerges from its crisis will be restricted by the loss — even temporarily — of a large "consignment" of its best intellectual resources.

That's not all. Since the U.S. and other developed-economy technology firms can't import all the workers they need, they will make up for the shortfall by recruiting the minds and expertise — directly and by outsourcing — that remain in Asia. Few people are aware, for instance, that the Philippines has been the fastest-growing importer of U.S. advanced technology for the last decade. Much of that is going to offshore operations that, at the low end, provide call-center services and semiconductor assembly, and, at the high end, are engaged in software-solution and other new technology development.

But why complain about all those jobs being generated? While those jobs are important, the demand for technology workers will be especially tough for two key sectors of Asian economies. First, although large companies remaking themselves into Internet players dominate news reports, most demand for technology workers will come from traditional, medium-sized firms that must race to integrate into global Web-based supply chains.

In the U.S., companies with just 50–99 employees account for 70% of the demand for technology workers. In the New Asian Economy, growth will likewise be driven predominantly by medium-sized firms, which already account for most employment. Limiting their access to workers means restraining growth overall.

Second, demand for technology workers will severely limit the capacity of Asian technology and Internet start-ups to attract the intellectual capital they need to transform bright ideas into viable enterprises. And indeed, although The New Asian Economy is just emerging, it is plagued by a desperate shortage of knowledge workers. Perhaps this is not really surprising, considering that Hong Kong produces just 4,000 IT graduates a year when it requires at least 5,000. Singapore educates just 25% of the 10,000 new technology workers it needs every year. As a result, Singapore, Malaysia and other Asian countries are desperately recruiting workers from as far as Russia, Eastern Europe and the Middle East, as well as poaching from the Philippines and India.

Tight supply has one other drawback for Asian economies: the Greenspan effect, or upward pressure on wages. The result can be a technology worker's dream and a technology entrepreneur's worst nightmare: workers casually migrating from offer to offer as stock options or other inducements move progressively higher, making life that much more difficult for medium-sized firms short on intellectual capital and stock options alike.

Meanwhile, Hong Kong, Malaysia and Singapore have all established billion-dollar start-up funds to encourage local technopreneurs to set up shop. But with the competition for intellectual capital — along with bureaucratic inefficiency and aversion to risk — that money would probably be better spent training knowledge workers. Singapore officials seem to agree. Although Hong Kong and Malaysia have increased spending on education, Singapore has set a high standard, with generous scholarship schemes and investment in faculty education. It has also welcomed foreign institutions such as Insead and the University of Chicago. Wharton is assisting the new Singapore Management University to develop its curriculum.

At the end of the day, it's not public-sector capital that Asia needs to grow technopreneurship. Private-sector incubators and venture capitalists abound. And in the next two years, infrastructure — as wireless and broadband networks expand — will likewise be eclipsed as a potential impediment to growth. Ironically, the one real impediment to growth — the capacity to produce and keep the right kind of people — can't be solved as easily. This problem is only now getting the attention from the sector best positioned to do something about it: government.

Unless something massive is done to address the critical shortage of intellectual resources, Asian countries will fail to live up to the promise of The New Asian Economy.[2]

Source:

1   "US Demand for information technology workers down," Associated Press report in *The Philippine Star*, April 4, 2001, p. B-3.

2   Case adapted from Michael Alan Hamlin "Brain Drain," *Far Eastern Economic Review*, May 4, 2000, p. 40;

http://www.cs.ucf.edu/csdept/info/it/ITStudentInfo.pdf, viewed on April 2, 2001; Yasmin Ghahremani and Maureen Tkacik, "Show Me The Stock Options," *Asiaweek*, February 25, 2000, http://www.asiaweek.com/asiaweek/technology/2000/0225/tech.cover1.html, viewed on April 2, 2001; Kim S. Nash, "H-1B counting snafu may slash '00 quota," *ComputerWorld*, October 1999, http://www.indolink.com/NRINews/Community/errorH1.html, viewed April 3, 2001; Larry E. Gee, "Legislation Will Help Ease Shortage of High-Tech Workers," http://sanantonio.bcentral.com/sanantonio/stories/2000/10/30/focus2.html, October 27, 2000, viewed April 3, 2001; "Executive Summary: Bridging the Gap: Information Technology Skills for a New Millennium," http://www.itaa.org/workforce/studies/hw00execsumm.htm, viewed on April 3, 2001; Cesar Bacani, "IT Crunch Time: Brace Yourselves. Asia's IT Crisis will not be solved by the death of the dotcoms and the U.S. Slowdown," *Asiaweek*, May 18, 2001, pp. 25–30.

Figure 10.1: Leading high-tech exporters

Source: *The Asian Wall Street Journal,* October 2, 2000, p. S4.

As can also be seen in Figure 10.1, Asian countries are among the top three exporters of high-technology products. The Philippines has the biggest percentage of manufactured exports, while Japan leads in computer-generated manufacturing, electronics, telecoms and opto-electronics. From a place-selling perspective, Asian sites must continue developing more competitive strategies and offerings. Asian high-tech offerings must be of a long-term character in order to inspire enough confidence to compete not just with U.S. and European place markets, but with other Asian nations competing for intellectual resources and investment.

Attracting Service Industries and Corporate Headquarters

The impact of Asian service industries fluctuates dramatically between nations, regions and, especially, communities. Hong Kong's service sector accounts for a very high 85% of its GDP. In Table 10.2, we can contrast several Asian countries with the highest and the lowest percentage of GDP in the service sector.

Table 10.2: Development of the service sector

Percentage of GDP in the service sector for 1999

Highest		Lowest	
Singapore	67.7%	Laos	25.9
Maldives	65.3	Kyrgyz Republic	27.8
Taiwan	62.9	China	27.9

Source: Asian Development Outlook 2000, Oxford University Press, p. 247.

Differences are actually much larger if we examine specific communities. Bank services in Hong Kong and Singapore largely withstood the effects of the Asian financial crisis that decimated the banking sectors in Japan, South Korea, Taiwan, Thailand and Indonesia. The financial sector in both countries is rapidly liberalizing to become globally competitive. As a result, they represent a whole service world forming in a competitive cluster to become Asia's financial center, with Shanghai threatening to join the competition. Many other places in Asia have realized the contribution of the financial-services sector to development and are actively working to strengthen it, especially through foreign investment.

The conventional pre-crisis Asian view saw service-sector employment as providing low-paying, low-skilled work, exporting little, and having a low economic-multiplier effect. However, this attitude is being re-examined as Asians confront high unemployment, overcapacity in the manufacturing sector and the need to increase the value-added component in other sectors as cost pressures increase as a result of globalization and liberalization. The old view that "real jobs" are available only in the manufacturing sector is quickly disappearing, along with the notion that something without physical dimensions cannot be associated with "value."

Places today recognize that services account for well over 50% of the world's economic output and that it is the value-added relationship between services and manufacturing (and vice versa) that is critical to job creation. These places have also noted how the service sector within East Asia and the Pacific grew from 46% of GDP in 1990 to 54% in 1999. In Europe and Central Asia, the service sector grew from 40% of GDP in 1990 to 58% in 1999.[2] Naturally, such dramatic figures push places into a healthy increased interest in service industries. Places are also developing new strategies to develop and attract entrepreneurs and retain strong managers in service sectors.[3] *BusinessWeek* has analyzed a number of Asian entrepreneurs and financiers (see Table 10.3) and

Table 10.3: Top Asian entrepreneurs and financiers

Entrepreneur	Business	Starting Company	Nation
ENTREPRENEURS			
Joichi Ito	Web commerce and venture capital	Neoteny	Japan
Li Ka-Shing	Telecommunications	Hutchinson Whampoa and Cheung Kong	Hong Kong
Richard Li	Internet holding	Pacific Century Cyberworks	Hong Kong
Liu Yonghao	Feed/food processing/private enterprise promotion	New Hope Group	China
Hiroshi Mikitani	E-commerce	Rakuten Inc.	Japan
Michael Mou	Telecommunications equipment	DBTel	Taiwan
N.R. Narayana Murthy	Internet software	Infosys Technologies	India
Kumi Sato	Internet counselling	womenjapan.com	Japan
Masayoshi Son	Internet holding	Softbank Corp.	Japan
Jaime Augusto Zobel de Ayala II	Group of companies	Ayala Corp.	Philippines
FINANCIERS			
Banthoon Lamsam	Banking	Thai Farmers Bank	Thailand
Masaru Hayami	Banking	Bank of Japan	Japan
Toshiharu Kojima	Investment bank	Nikko Salomon Smith Barney	Japan
Lee Min Hwa	Venture capitalist	Korea Venture Business Assn.	South Korea
Oki Matsumoto	Online brokerage	Monex Inc.	Japan
Yoshihiko Miyauchi	Leasing company	Orix Corp.	Japan
Kenichi Ohmae	Education	Attacker's Business School	Japan
Yoshiki Otake	Insurance	AFLAC Japan	Japan
Kanwal Rekhi	Venture capitalist	Angel Investor	India
Muhammad Yunus	Investment bank	Grameen Bank	Bangladesh

Source: "The Stars of Asia", *BusinessWeek*, July 3, 2000, pp. 36A2–36A3.

observed that they have been at the forefront of change and recovery since the financial crisis in Asia.

A place can attract service industries and new service entrepreneurs such as those listed in Table 10.3. Growth potential can be especially significant if the place is on the market early in the entrepreneurial process. Being an early host for EF (the world's largest private institute for language education), Club Med or Reuters can bring a positive place image and new job opportunities and networks. These networks open unexpected contacts and create positive spirals. But place sellers need a systematic approach. In most Asian countries, service-business associations have a comprehensive knowledge of service structures, individual actors and where new businesses will emerge. Place sellers need to establish contacts with such associations and networks.

Many urban redesign projects are planned from the very beginning to suit certain service businesses. Such projects can include a city district specifically designed to attract insurance companies, a pedestrian street where travel agencies can gather or a shopping area with a certain service profile. They can be connected with the implementation of many conversion programs — a closed hospital, a downsized industry or a former military campus converted into various service-related clusters. A project may take the form of an incubator for small service companies or a full-scale service center, specifically loaded with information technology and other built-in attractions.

A primary target for many larger places is to attract company headquarters. It should be noted, though, that headquarters relocations are infrequent. Places cannot lure or entice a move if the company is not looking to move. Relocation is most likely to occur if the company is under pressure (from, say, takeovers, mergers, breakups, reorganizations) or when the local business climate has become burdensome (from higher operating costs, heavy taxes that cause recruiting problems, declining quality of life, or a bad place image in general). Yet Asia witnessed a number of headquarters being established during the 1990s, primarily by non-Asian companies wanting to establish a presence within Asia — Caltex's move from Dallas, Texas, to Singapore is a case in point. And thanks to the Internet and new technologies, many companies locate executive offices in developed business centers, such as Singapore and Hong Kong, but locate back-office functions in less-developed countries with lower costs, such as the Philippines (as in the case of Caltex) and China. Exhibit 10.3 describes a search process for an Asian headquarters.

**Exhibit 10.3: ASIAN HEADQUARTERS —
A PLACE-BUYING CASE**

In 2000, Germany's largest Internet incubator and private equity-investment company, InternetMediaHouse (IMH), decided to establish an Asian headquarters. In determining where to settle the company's business, Franklin Lavin, IMH CEO, observed that "The key to success in Asia is in managing cross-border operations and aggregating several small countries; unlike in Europe where businesses are mostly contained within countries."[1] IMH believed it had two choices: Hong Kong and Singapore. Having worked in both locations, Lavin believed he was well informed of the advantages and disadvantages of each location.

Lavin was unhappy, for example, with the tough Hong Kong immigration procedures and requirements, which made it impossible for his partner to join him. In contrast, Singapore generally welcomes immigrants who are able to demonstrate professional credentials and a credible work history. Lavin also felt that declining English standards in Hong Kong, and the orientation of local business practices more towards process than people, were less than ideal for a firm that relies heavily on the innovation and creativity of its staff. Again, by contrast, Singapore has invested heavily in education in recent years, and the government has encouraged the development of "people skills."

Lavin decided to locate the company's regional headquarters in Hong Kong, he said, largely because "Hong Kong has the most vibrant business environment and a high degree of 'entrepreneurialism.' There's a level of 'entrepreneurialism' here that I have never see anywhere else."[2] The relatively large pool of entrepreneurial talent available there — despite overall tight labor conditions — was a critical factor in the company's ability to make a profit. Moreover, many view Singapore as more regulated than Hong Kong, and it does not offer the access to China that Hong Kong can still provide. Hong Kong's aggressive business climate, in addition to two critical areas in which Singapore couldn't compete with Hong Kong — proximity to China's market and its millions of potential "netpreneurs" — are what tipped the balance in its favor. Hong Kong was also able to fuel its growth with lower corporate taxes.

Ultimately, a unique combination of hard and soft attraction factors made Hong Kong Lavin's choice. Conventional wisdom says that hard factors, such as costs and financial incentives, are always decisive. In this case, the company managed to visualize certain value-added effects such as the entrepreneurial spirit and the pro-business perspective of the city and its people. Professor Michael Enright characterizes Hong Kong's future capacity to attract regional headquarters this way: "Hong Kong is likely to remain unsurpassed as a foothold onto the Mainland. In the words of one Western executive, 'If your game is China, you have no alternative to Hong Kong.'"[3] While Hong Kong faces uncertainties, Enright believes that "these uncertainties can be influenced or managed by Hong Kong people. This has been the case in the past and there is no reason to believe it will not be the case in the future."[4]

Like Enright and Lavin, many investors believe that the entrepreneurial, can-do attitude of Hong Kong people is a key component of Hong Kong's competitiveness. It is often such intangibles that determine whether a place will lead its competitors in attracting investors. Place buyers have a variety of needs and make decisions, like Lavin, on the basis of varying circumstances. The effective place seller will have an arsenal of benefits and solutions to address buyers' needs. Enright's latest research into attractiveness attributes shows that Hong Kong is, and will probably continue to be, a winner for a number of reasons. Of more than 1,000 companies that responded to Enright's survey, 35% preferred Hong Kong as their regional headquarters. Singapore, with 30%, came in a close second, while Shanghai — often said to be on the road to overtaking Hong Kong — came far behind, with just 3%. He concludes that Hong Kong is "the only true Asia-Pacific Center."[5]

Sources:

1 "Case Study — InternetMediaHouseAsia (IMHA)", *Corporate Location Magazine* Web site, http://www.corporatelocation.com/default.asp?-Page=112&SID=15&Country=5, viewed on February 13, 2001.

2   *Ibid.*
3   Michael Enright, David Dodwell (contrib.), and Edith Scott (contrib.), *The Hong Kong Advantage,* Oxford University Press, May 1997, p. 322.
4   *Ibid.,* p. 3.
5   Gren Manuel, "Hong Kong Leads Rivals in Regional Headquarters," *The Asian Wall Street Journal,* January 9, 2001, p. 3.

"The RHQ Question: How are multinational companies organizing themselves in the Asia-Pacific, and why do they choose to site their regional headquarters the way they do?," *Business Asia,* December 11, 2000, pp. 1–4. This study was conducted in conjunction with research undertaken by Enright and his contributors to be published in a forthcoming book to be titled, *Multinational Strategies and the City Centers of the Asia-Pacific.*

As suggested in Exhibit 10.3, Singapore and Hong Kong are two major players in attracting foreign investment into Asia. This means that places in and around Hong Kong must provide enough attractions to compensate for hard factors such as higher real-estate costs and higher salaries. Perceptions that would help in positioning Hong Kong as the premier location for foreign investment include the view that Hong Kong is a secure, long-term place to run a business. In addition, it has the huge, immeasurable advantage of being the world's most open economy. (For the third year in a row,[4] Hong Kong was identified as being the world's freest economy by the U.S. Heritage Foundation's 2001 Index of Economic Freedom).

In a world characterized by increasing opportunities and shifting resources, places need to provide regional barometers that reflect different housing costs, salaries, taxes, energy costs, and so on. In the first stages of a search process, place buyers in the service sector rely heavily on such regional barometers.

Attracting Shopping Malls, Retailers and Wholesalers

Probably the most influential business-location phenomena in transforming a place's landscape and economy have been changing retail and wholesale forces. This has been an evolutionary process that has seen horseback peddlers replaced by department stores, which then gave rise to large retail-anchored suburban malls, anchorless malls and mini-malls of specialty stores. The current trend is towards factory-outlet malls and discount-warehouses. These changing retailing patterns have radically transformed many places, and will continue to do so.

For the first 11 months of the year 2000, the retail sales value of consumer goods in China rose 9.8%.[5] Australia's retail trade turnover increased 7.7% in 2000.[6] Hong Kong's retail sales struggled because of high overheads, but still managed to grow 2.5% that year.[7] In the Philippines, the 1999 sales of a leading credit-card company rose by 50% over the previous year. The number of cardholders also increased by 39% and the number of transactions by 34.7% in the same period.[8] And growth seemed unstoppable. Diners Club expected to grow 20% in 2001,[9] despite political uneasiness, a downturn in exports and investment, and the prospect of global recession.

The sector can be separated into two major categories: *wholesale business* (defined as units engaged in the resale of goods to manufacturers and others for further processing) and *retail business* (defined as distribution to final consumers). Some places have allocated vast resources to place-selling efforts that focus on wholesale and/or retail businesses. Urban redesign is directed towards attracting these place buyers. The potential contribution of the distribution business makes it worthwhile — from a place-selling point of view — to understand the following current trends in the Asian distribution sector:

- A reduction in the number of larger operators as the sector consolidates
- Closer vertical and horizontal links between manufacturers, wholesalers and retailers
- A slower increase in the number of hypermarkets
- A rise in franchising
- Increased distance selling
- Networks of multifunction distribution centers
- Increased use of automation and information technology, especially e-marketplaces that bring buyers and sellers together electronically.
- New concept stores being introduced
- Moves towards internationalization and cross-border networks
- Growth in the Asianized dimension.

These trends, increasingly fueled by new media and communication technology (such as the Internet and e-marketplaces), create turbulence in employment within the distribution sector. The growing ease of ordering and selling via international communication networks and, increasingly, the Internet and communication sectors, indicates that some jobs will shift toward transportation and logistic flows. A substantial portion of this shift, in fact, will be the result of increased efficiencies associated with B2B (business-to-business) commerce, making many administrative and sales positions redundant. Today's e-marketplaces bring together logistics into seamless, electronic transactions and will affect other support sectors — banks and other service providers. See Exhibit 10.4.

Exhibit 10.4: THE REALITY OF B2B IN THE PHILIPPINES

In testimony before the U.S. House of Representatives Budget Committee, Federal Reserve chairman Alan Greenspan, in response to questions about the U.S. economy, suggested that the irrational exuberance that drove stocks — especially technology stocks — to such lofty values in the second half of the 1990s had given way to irrational pessimism. That pessimism raced around the world at Internet speed in the second quarter of 2000, when the Nasdaq began to falter.

Since then, "dot-com" — which had been taken as a sure sign of entrepreneurial millions for investors, geeks and dot-preneurs alike — has become something of a dirty word. In fact, dot-com enthusiasm helped pull many Asian economies out of the financial crisis that began in 1997, as lusty investors looked to replicate their Nasdaq successes in Asia's new-technology bourses, especially in Japan, South Korea and Hong Kong.

The Philippines, like other countries that once pinned many of their hopes on the fabled New Economy, is feeling that same irrational pessimism Mr Greenspan referred to in his testimony. While there is some optimism regarding the country's ability to become a multinational back-office for everything from call centers to software and Web-site development, there is little enthusiasm among investors for local technology initiatives in either the B2C (business-to-consumer) or B2B (business-to-business) sectors. The few technology stocks listed on the Philippine Stock Exchange (PSE) have suffered alongside their traditional sector contemporaries. Those listed in Singapore — a reasonable strategy considering the size of the PSE and its problems during the previous administration — haven't fared much better.

But as Mr Greenspan suggests, irrational pessimism probably blurs reality as much as irrational exuberance. It may even be as dangerous, since it may inhibit risk-taking and investment unnecessarily. That aversion to risk-taking and investment affects not only technology entrepreneurs, who begin to look for a more traditional environment, but it can also convince companies to put off much-needed initiatives, such as implementing an Internet strategy. From a business perspective, a meaningful Internet strategy is more likely to involve integration into an e-marketplace (which can often provide more opportunity for most businesses) than a company's own e-business Web site, although both are necessary.

In this regard, it's perhaps worth taking a look at BayanTrade.com, for example, whose success (despite the dreaded "dot-com" suffix) provides evidence that there's a lot more happening in Philippine business in the B2B sector than the prevailing irrational pessimism might have us believe. A number of companies were interviewed that have either integrated as buyers into the BayanTrade e-marketplace or been adopted as suppliers. While buyers were expected to be enthusiastic about the company's e-procurement service and the impact of lower procurement costs on the bottom line, they were more satisfied than anticipated. Although improved efficiency and productivity are the principal advantages cited by the buyers, other important benefits have become apparent.

The first of these is transparency, which enhances the integrity of the procurement process. Put bluntly, it's nearly impossible to cheat by way of channeling business to favored suppliers or accepting kickbacks. A second advantage is increasing the number of accredited suppliers, in significant part because BayanTrade helps buyers source new suppliers, a service called strategic sourcing. Third, there are fewer misunderstandings, because BayanTrade works with buyers and sellers to make sure that specifications are clear and comprehensive, including delivery and payment terms. As a result, some transactions — which range from hundreds of thousands to millions of pesos — involve medium-term agreements stretching as much as two years, making it easier for buyers and sellers to plan. One online auction involved the construction of an entire electrical substation, including equipment.

But real interest was in the sellers, and how they might feel about selling in an e-marketplace. It was feared they would be concerned about pressure on margins. While this is important to participating suppliers, the benefits appear to significantly outweigh that concern. One supplier confessed that moving into the e-marketplace was both exciting and scary: "[It] has taught us to be on our toes, which is really a fundamental element of business — you cannot be complacent."[1] He also claimed that benefits of being an adopted supplier are clear. For example, he was impressed with the visibility of his products to his client base. Even more telling was the number of calls he received from large conglomerates he hadn't previously done business with that were now interested in conducting business over the Internet.

What's been his success rate? In a short period of time, his company had transacted a deal of more than P20 million (US$389.8 million) and had immediately received inquiries from two other companies.[2] Other suppliers had similar experiences. The results were clear. Internet business was efficient and markets were expanding. In one instance, 80% of the supplier's transactions were with new customers.

So, while irrational pessimism can strike any country or industry, overreaction to Internet phobia can be fatal. Asian companies should not ignore this vital tool of transaction and communication. The progressive companies of the 21st century will be on the Web and will take Greenspan's comment as a warning to continue to grow their businesses via information technology.

Sources:

1 Adapted from Michael Alan Hamlin, "What's the Reality in Philippine B2B?," ITnetcentral (http://www.itnetcentral.com/article.asp?id=2236), viewed March 23, 2001. BayanTrade.com is a client of TeamAsia.
2 *Ibid.*

Despite the shifts in wholesale and retail distribution, places still benefit from high-profile retail institutions and probably always will. Famous stores in Asia can act as magnets to attract new businesses. Consider such department stores as David Jones in Australia, Central in Thailand, Lotte in South Korea, Takashimaya and Mitsukoshi in Japan, and SM Shoe Mart in the Philippines or the famous fashion stores, Kenzo, Issey Miyake and Giordano. Japan offers Yamaha and Sony for music enthusiasts. Singapore has Kinokuniya — a mecca for book lovers — the Japanese chain's largest bookshop in Southeast Asia. The biggest department stores in Asia are Yaohan Nextage in Pudong, Shanghai and

Seacon Square in Bangkok. The largest and most successful department store chain in the Philippines, Shoe Mart, more popularly known as SM, is currently building what will be the largest indoor shopping mall in the world. The "Mall of Asia" is being built on a 500,000 square-meter reclamation site and is scheduled to open in 2003.[10] These stores are considered the great treasures of Asian retailing and brand the entire shopping area.

Many places would like to attract stores that can contribute to an important retail cluster. To do so, they have to ask some fundamental questions: How can we attract retailers such as Kanebo, Shiseido, Red Earth, Aji Ichiban, U2, G2000, Wacoal, Giordano, The Swank Shop, Bossini and Billabong? More specifically, how can we combine them in a shopping mall? Or, on a much smaller scale, how can we attract McDonald's, Burger King or even 7-Eleven? The answers may lie in a combination of incentives, tax breaks, road construction or myriad other factors. The key issue for the place seller is to seriously improve the negatives, deal with the inevitable threats, and market the new position aggressively.

There are two major threats to the Asian retailing picture: discounters and virtual sales. The first is the trend towards large specialty operators moving into the fashionable, and often higher-priced, downtown shopping areas. The other is the increasing number of consumers willing to buy from mail order and the Internet. The discount threat demands that places decide on their markets and themes and work forcefully to maintain them. In New York City, the large discounters are buying factories and converting them to stores. Countries such as Australia, a major call center in the Asia-Pacific[11] which has many of the virtual stores,[12] are selling massive amounts of clothing and computers. In response to these threats, places will have to design their retail stores in such an attractive manner that customers will want to visit the stores and pay for the experience, selection and service. This demand on retail service requires more attention to the training of personnel, more depth and quality of stock, and a greater commitment to the place's image and long-term viability.

A Critique of Incentives

Asia's financial crisis, the slowdown in growth and higher unemployment have again raised the question of the willingness of Asian places to use financial incentives to attract businesses. Virtually every nation, region and community in Asia is using some sort of financial incentive. These include both large and small incentives: tax exemption, no-rent periods, completely free or subsidized work-force training, special electricity discounts, marketing projects paid for by the place, free parking space, accelerated depreciation, special tax-free reserves, interest subsidies, and so on.

There are no limits for national, regional and local innovation in this area. There are regions where structural challenges and economic crises, combined with a lack of local leadership, have left places bereft of any strong attractions. The only remaining attraction is financial incentives. In fact, some Asian countries can justifiably be called "Incentive Paradises." But if these places could generate true attractions they would have less need for financial incentives.

Asia is not alone in using financial incentives. In the U.S., cities and states have been in competition to provide tailor-made packages for various inward investors. BMW and Mercedes were the benefactors of biddings for their plants and found favorable deals in South Carolina and Alabama. European companies also used the bidding wars to their advantage.

Financial incentives offer a temporary advantage, a competitive edge, a kind of "early-bird-gets-the-worm" reasoning. As more nations, regions and communities join the incentives contest, competitive advantages diminish, as all benchmarking initiatives eventually do. The question in Asia is: What will happen to financial incentives in the years to come? Several factors are pointing toward a change:

1) Disappointed expectations because bidding wars indicate that incentives are not enough.
2) Negative media treatment of the players in the bidding wars. When General Motors selected Thailand over the Philippines as the locale for a regional manufacturing plant in 1996, the Philippines received bad publicity throughout Asia and the world. The tug-of-war between the two countries was highly publicized and resulted in negative media treatment of the Philippines, which lost the bid despite hard lobbying. Thailand then became known as the "Detroit of the East" and was chosen for its relatively strong domestic market and efficient infrastructure.
3) A slow shift in government support towards investment in less-developed regions. For example, China's corporate tax for companies locating in its poorer areas is 15%, as compared to 33% for the rest of the country.[13]
4) A growing recognition of other hard and soft factors, such as people and education.

5) The emergence of more professional place-marketing strategies in Asia.

Exhibit 10.5 outlines the pitfalls of incentive offers.

Exhibit 10.5: RUSSIAN ROULETTE: A GUIDE TO INCENTIVES

The changing competitive environment adds up to a different future environment for inducements. However, in the short term, places that do not have a straight-up competitive advantage will continue to offer companies incentives to move. There are four major issues for the place inducers to consider:

- Always study the company for the ability to sustain and market its products. When the state of Pennsylvania gave over its entire training budget to attract Volkswagen, it was betting on the company selling the new Rabbit. Sales in the U.S. bombed and so did the state's massive commitment when Volkswagen pulled out of the plant.
- The best inducements are aimed at companies that will find similar companies in the area. A large concentration of companies will encourage others to be attracted to the labor pool and the supportive community. The implementation of bio-regions in Australia is a good approach because it encourages a core of companies to establish a beachhead. It also enables banks and other financial houses to specialize in lending money to these enterprises.
- A bad environmental product will bring short-term jobs and long-term misery. Places that have attracted chicken plants, for example, frequently find that environmental effects are so devastating that desirable companies are not interested in moving in, and mobile, capable labor will leave.
- Offering incentives may be a zero-sum game for some places. If an inducement is offered, it needs to be strategic and not merely for the sake of increasing the pot. To high-tech start-up companies, available loans for non-collateral assets are essential. In most cases, without that one piece of

financial support, offers of cheap electricity or water are of little value.

■ Some companies move frequently to gain cost advantages. The moves become a profit center just like any other portion of their product mix. Places weighing offers to strategic movers should evaluate costs — infrastructure, new schools and environmental use — and then make a calculated decision. At the least, the contract should contain expensive move-out penalties.

In the real world of place attraction, how much you have to give up is generally related to how little you have. A place that wants to compete for targeted industries and services needs to build up its core infrastructure, to invest in workers' skills, to ensure citizen and financial support, and to select targets that have a reasonable chance of survival after the year 2000.

RETAINING AND EXPANDING EXISTING BUSINESSES

Most communities and regional bodies recognize the importance of retaining and expanding their existing businesses. They see this as their first line of defense. They know from today's challenging business environment that local business expansion does not occur automatically. They also know that external businesses might interpret bad performance among existing local businesses as an indication of a poor local business climate and anticipate that taxes will rise to compensate for revenues lost by move-outs or poor performers.

The active retention and expansion of local businesses is obviously a place-marketing act. Retention strategies are usually less manifest and dramatic than attracting external businesses. The strategies are normally more of a "drip-drip" character, without attracting much local media attention. However, sometimes the retention process can explode and become media-driven because of events such as:

■ A reduction in the number of production shifts
■ The announcement by an existing company of its decision not to invest in a previously planned project
■ A failure to recruit new employees
■ A business deciding to downsize or restructure
■ The business closing its plant and relocating.

Such situations do not occur out of the blue. Local representatives, if they are alert, can read the signs of impending problems and, where possible, assist these businesses. Each day a place should be continually monitoring existing businesses. The local business climate — comprising hard and soft factors — must be protected and improved by the place sellers. Building relationships with the local business community is an important element in the process, the main aim being to achieve maximum integration of the businesses. The more integrated they are, the less mobile the businesses become. Integration programs are a tool to encourage existing investors to grow, re-invest and create more jobs.

This integration strategy is probably one of the strongest trends in Asia in the aftermath of the financial crisis. Foreign investors who have already invested in countries such as Malaysia, the Philippines and Thailand are attracted to the lower costs of the China and Indochina markets. This cost disparity is a huge threat to countries that thought they were low-cost providers. Integration strategy is put into effect in millions of small day-to-day decisions within the local place market. Typical actions within these integration programs include:

- An informal dialogue between a manager of an enterprise and a community representative where the former may complain about local students' language skills. Such dialogue should lead to introducing new or stronger language programs in the local schools.
- Existing businesses are invited to participate in developing the place-marketing strategies. Participation provides an opportunity to integrate and develop a role and feeling of responsibility; and, of course, new ideas may emerge.
- The "keep in touch" dialogue can reveal a need to, say, find appropriate housing for certain categories of existing staff. The community can quickly set up a taskforce to find new attractive land to build on. The company and its staff would interpret the quick response positively. If good housing results, this is, of course, another positive factor.
- An important company informs the community about some dangerous threats on the horizon and, consequently, the community joins forces with the company to handle the threat. For example, software manufacturers in India, together with their community and regional leaders, are lobbying in Andhra Pradesh and other places to improve the standard of education in information technology and make it available to everyone.[14] The government of Penang also works closely with its foreign investors to enhance skills training in local schools.

In spite of close dialogue between existing businesses and a place, a company might decide to close a plant or relocate. Even here the place may manage to intervene, as we have already seen in the case of Penang. But when conditions have shifted so dramatically that a company has already decided to move, reversing that decision is almost always impossible. Although Johnson & Johnson's production facilities in the Philippines had earned worldwide recognition for its equipment design and packaging, the company still decided to move. Even retailing giant Hong Kong discovered that political and economic forces in the late 1990s caused large Japanese retailers to leave. The lesson to be drawn from these examples is that governments must never fall into the trap of closing the chapter on investment once a company has located within its borders. That will be especially true as China steps up in competition with Southeast Asia for foreign investment and the entire region liberalizes, increasing the attractiveness of central manufacturing.

While business retention and expansion strategies offer more potential than conventional business-attraction strategies, they also invite abuses. Retention policies and programs should be compatible with market forces and trends rather than be anti-market or cater to special interests.

PROMOTING SMALL BUSINESS AND FOSTERING NEW BUSINESS START-UPS

Many Asian communities run initiatives, plans and programs to promote small businesses and start-ups. Small- and medium-sized enterprises (SMEs) have long been a priority because they are, collectively, the most important contributors to generating employment and building economic growth. On an overall Asian level, this focus was visible during the 1993 Blake Island Leaders' meeting in Seattle, where SME development was discussed. "SMEs form the backbone of the economies of the Asia-Pacific Economic Cooperation (APEC) forum. They employ as much as 80% of the workforce, contribute 30–60% of the GNP and account for around 35% of total exports in the region. They also make up over 95% of all enterprises."[15]

In 1994 APEC identified five priority areas for SME development. These included human-resource development, finance, technology and technology sharing, access to markets and access to information. The SME Policy Level Group was also established with the aim of "helping SMEs improve their competitiveness and to facilitate their transition to a more open trade and investment environment."[16]

At the same time, APEC officials expressed deep concern over the weak performance of the Asian economy. As a result of the Asian financial crisis,[17] GDP for APEC economies fell from 3.7% in 1996 to 3.4% in 1997. At the seventh meeting of APEC Ministers responsible for SMEs, held in Brunei in 2000, the ministers agreed on a number of steps to facilitate SME growth. These included promoting the culture of entrepreneurship to students; conducting training programs in the areas of technology, management, and international trade; and encouraging cooperation programs for SME development. Ministers also agreed to develop and institute programs to enable SMEs to capitalize on e-commerce and to establish an APEC database to make the financial and capital markets more accessible to SMEs.[18]

These initiatives can be adopted in various ways at local and regional levels. Every place has its own unique SME and start-up culture. This can be illustrated by the fact that there are now more options available regarding how to approach SMEs and starts-ups. There are ambitious APEC programs, national policies, regional strategies and local plans. Their combination in a local setting is unique. How local strategies are worked out depends greatly on the type of local leadership present in a place. In Taipei, SME traditions are extremely strong and can therefore act as the best practice in a wider Asian context. This is likewise true in Japan. However, since each country or region has its own best practices, other place strategists need to visit those regions to learn possible improvement strategies.

Answering the questions set out in Exhibit 10.6 can lead to a better assessment of whether or not a place is actively supportive of new business development. Anything less than a passing score indicates that a place should reassess its commitment in this area.

Exhibit 10.6: BUSINESS CLIMATE TEST: MEASURING YOUR PLACE'S ENTREPRENEURIAL CLIMATE

During the 1990s, most places embraced a strategy to promote SMEs and starts-ups. The following ten questions inspired by *Inc.* magazine provide a rough approximation of where a community stands. With 10 points for each favorable answer, a passing grade is 60 points. Places can use the test to measure goals and achievements in new business developments.

1. When local civic leaders meet with business leaders, are there as many chief executive officers (CEOs) of SMEs as bankers and corporate executives?
2. Are SME CFOs invited to join important events within the community?
3. Do local newspapers follow the fortunes of start-ups and the growth of SMEs with the same intensity as they do with large corporations?
4. Are innovative SMEs able to recruit nearly all their professional workforce from the local area?
5. Do SME representatives often refer to easy access to venture capital?
6. Does the local college encourage its teachers and students to participate in entrepreneurial spin-offs?
7. Do CEOs from local SMEs hold even a quarter of the seats on the boards of the three largest banks?
8. Does the city's economic-development department spend more time helping local companies grow than it does chasing after branch facilities for out-of-the-region corporations?
9. Is there decent, affordable office and factory space available for businesses in the central business district?
10. Can you think of 10 recent spin-offs — SMEs started by entrepreneurs — which have left larger companies?

Source:

Inspired by the "Business Climate Test, Inc," March 1988, p. 81. Reprinted with permission, *Inc.* magazine, March 1988. Copyright 1988 by Goldhirsh Groups, Inc., 38 Commercial Wharf, Boston, MA 02110.

CONCLUSION

The worldwide competition for attracting and retaining business has passed through four phases in Asian place-development practices.

In the *first phase*, after the Second World War, Asia entered a period of reconstruction which continued until the 1960s. Key concepts were modernized, and expansion within manufacturing industries was a hallmark of the period.

In a *second phase*, starting in the 1970s, it became clear to developing Asia when economic and employment growth stalled that export substitution had failed as a development strategy. To create new jobs and restore growth, developing Asia adopted sweeping foreign-investment recruitment programs. Unlike the previous decade, these featured attractive incentives for investors, including tax holidays. Until that time, local attraction strategies were unknown and unwanted. For many places, it was a time of painful economic transition but, for most, the 1970s were the opening chapters of Asia's economic miracle. Development continued during the 1980s and much of the 1990s. During that time, Asia made the transition to a *third phase*, in which Japanese investment played an important role in developing manufacturing capacity in Asia on a scale never before seen, and intra-Asian trade became an important source of export revenue. But it was also a time when Asia, perhaps too slowly, began to think about where its economies were headed after years of building up relatively low value-added manufacturing and assembly capacity.

Putting off those decisions — and the failure to build stronger, independent institutions to regulate growth and investment — hit Asia hard in a *fourth phase*. In the late 1990s and in the early years of the 21st century, Asia has struggled to compete under new rules dictated by globalization and increasing liberalization. In much of Asia, place-marketing strategies are principally concentrated on how to attract higher value-added investment in services as well as manufacturing. The key concepts underlying these strategies are mergers and acquisitions with and by multinational corporations, and the expansion and development of the local business climate. At the same time, less-developed areas of Asia such as the south, Indochina and much of interior Mainland China are attracting low value-added manufacturing and assembly operations from North and Southeast China. Thus, retaining, expanding and reinvesting in higher value-added manufacturing by existing businesses has a top priority.

These developments are leading to vast experimentation with new programs. Intensive relationship-building measures between the community and existing companies are more common. Integration programs are appearing in which existing businesses participate in place actions. Public and private sectors are learning from each other. These learning processes include new partnerships, new institutions and new approaches to carrying out multiple, complex place-development activities.

This phase is also marked by the emergence of a more complex place-development strategy in which new technologies, employee education, intellectual infrastructure, high-tech centers, research parks and "Silicon strategies" are key concepts. In this multiple and complex place-development climate, financial incentives are one of several hard and soft factors. Bidding wars between places — offering mainly financial incentives — can be counterproductive for the image of the winning place. The real place winners are, rather, those that adopt long-term place-marketing strategies that can add new commercial value to existing businesses as well as to external place buyers.

As Asia makes the transition into the new century, signs of an eventual *fifth phase* are apparent — regionalization. The following steps have contributed to the shaping of new economic regions:

1. The improvement of production methods, transportation, communication and information technology.
2. The liberalization, deregulation and expansion of exports, which has resulted in the increase of inward FDI (especially into China) and thus in economic development.
3. Specialization in a particular field or set of fields.
4. The evolution of economic, political, educational and cultural regional institutions such as ASEAN and APEC (although many critics continue to complain that these organizations are developing too slowly in the context of globalization and liberalization trends).

The rapid economic growth of East Asia — Japan in the 1960s; Hong Kong, Taiwan, South Korea and Singapore in the 1970s and 80s; China, Thailand and Indonesia in the 1980s and 90s; and the "new" economies of the Philippines, Vietnam and Myanmar in the 1990s and beyond — provides a clear illustration of this fifth phase. This has resulted in the formation of the East Asia hub, a region's whose GDP share is now comparable to those of the European Union and North America. Many of these places have become, or are in the process of becoming, centers of electronics, information technology and finance. These positions have been further strengthened as individual countries become involved in regional institutions.

Other economic hubs in the Asia-Pacific include South Asia (India, Pakistan, Bangladesh, Sri Lanka, Nepal and Tibet), Southeast Asia (the Philippines, Cambodia, Myanmar, Thailand, Indonesia, Laos, Vietnam, Brunei, Malaysia and Singapore) and Northeast Asia (China, Mongolia, the Korean Peninsula, the Russian Far East and Japan). There is considerable pressure within ASEAN to establish a true free-trade region with a population — and therefore the market potential — to compete with China.

As a result of these fifth-phase changes, places are professionalizing their place marketing. Reaching a leading Asian place position today is as natural as it was to reach a leading national position only 10 to 20 years ago. In this competitive marketplace, effective targeting of specific groups can make the difference between winning and losing. Places need to examine their stories, adventures and attractions to package the most compelling message for their market. In this climate, there is an opportunity that can quickly emerge in an Asian region or hub. The appeal of the smallest and most peripheral place can now be distributed via the Internet and other cross-border media to an increasingly selective Asian market.

1 Laxmi Nakarmi, "Exodus of Disillusion: Despair over poor schools is pushing South Koreans to emigrate," *Asiaweek*, April 20, 2001, p. 42.

2 The World Bank, *World Development Report 2000/2001*, p. 297.

3 Gunter Pauli, *Double Digit Growth, How to Achieve it with Services*, (Berlaar: Pauli Publishing, 1991).

4 "The 2001 Index of Economic Freedom," The U.S. Heritage Foundation Web site, http://database.townhall.com/heritage/index/country.cfm?ID=63, viewed on February 19, 2001.

5 http://www.chinatopnews.com/xh/-01-2GAAiAaqXI.html, viewed on March 13, 2001.

6 http://www.abs.gov.au/Ausstats/ABS%40.nsf/e8ae5488b598839cca-25682000131612/e1ccd8eac9eaf770ca2568b7001b4598!OpenDocument, viewed on March 16, 2001.

7 http://www.tdctrade.com/main/economic.htm, viewed on March 16, 2001.

8 http://www.sgv.com.ph/~sgvweb/topnews/5_24/Credit.htm, viewed on April 2, 2001.

9 Ted P. Torres, "Diners Club eyes 20% hike in RP billings," *The Philippine Star*, April 6, 2001, p. B-3.

10 http://www.smprime.com.ph/announce.html, viewed on March 13, 2001.

11 http://malaysia.cnet.com/news/2000/05/09/20000509v.html, viewed on February 6, 2001.

12 http://malaysia.cnet.com/news/2000/05/09/20000509v.html, viewed on February 6, 2001.

13 http://www.globalbusinessmag.com/issues/200002/article3.html, viewed on March 8, 2001.

14 http://chronicle.com/free/v46/i45/45a04801.htm, viewed on March 8, 2001.

15 http://www.apecsec.org.sg/ecotech/span.html,viewed on February 23, 2001.

16 *Ibid.*

17 *Ibid.*

18 http://www.apecsec.org.sg/virtualib/minismtg/mtgsme2000.html, viewed on March 8, 2001.

11

Expanding Exports and Stimulating Foreign Investment

I n the global marketplace, more and more products are introduced with a clear place-brand origin. Most consumers know that quality tea originates in Sri Lanka (Ceylon), electronics are the hallmark of Japan, and fine Batik goods are crafted in Indonesia. Brands are often specific to the place where they are produced. Anchor products, for example, are synonymous with New Zealand. On the Anchor milk can the place of origin is made crystal clear: "Anchor Milk is made only from New Zealand milk. New Zealand milk is so good because cows in New Zealand eat fresh grass, drink cool clean water and breathe pure clean air." In the same way, Foster's beer is associated with Australia; Mikimoto Pearls are linked to Japan, and Lee Kum Kee consistently markets itself as the manufacturer of premier, authentic Chinese sauces.

Clearly, place-names can add extra value to products and services. A well-chosen place-brand makes the product or service more identifiable for the consumer and ties the country of origin to the product (see Figure 11.1).

Figure 11.1: Place-brand on the global market — three examples.

Figure 11.1a: Foster's of Australia

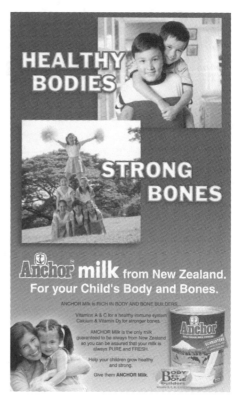

Figure 11.1c: Anchor Dairy Products of New Zealand

Figure 11.1b: Lee Kum Kee Chinese Sauces

Places can improve their economy by attracting tourists and business, but they can also grow by encouraging their businesses to export — perhaps showing their place of origin in a value-added manner. This type of value-added strategy is a form of co-branding. Export promotion has emerged as a major place-development strategy and it is likely to command an even more important position in the years ahead. This chapter is about how state and local governments and their officials can promote trade and foreign investment. We examine the following questions:

- How important are exports to a place's economy?
- What firms currently export and what goods and services produced in a place's economy have the greatest export potential?
- What programs, services and activities can be offered that most effectively assist existing exporters to expand and non-exporters to export?
- What strategies can a place use to enhance the image of its exportable products and to transfer a positive place identification to these products?

HOW IMPORTANT ARE EXPORTS TO A PLACE'S ECONOMY?

A place without exports is almost unimaginable. Imagine a place that grows only apples and consumes all of the apples locally. The same place needs to import other goods that it does not produce: food stocks, computers, automobiles, and so on. But then, how does this apple-growing place pay for the goods it imports? Ultimately, the place would have to develop some exports to pay for its imports.

Exports are the lifeblood of most cities, regions and nations in Asia. East Asia and the Pacific showed the highest growth of exports of goods and services in recent years. From 1990 to 1999, their exports increased 12.6%, while South Asia's exports grew 9.6%.[1] In 1999, exports of goods and services accounted for 39% of GDP in East Asia and the Pacific.[2] Merchandise exports accounted for 81% of total manufacturing in East Asia and the Pacific and 77% for South Asia in 1998.[3] In recent decades, as Asia has developed economically, intra-Asian trade has become an important component of regional export-oriented commerce. Historically, the living standards in Asian nations are closely linked to their export performances. There are places where export achievements have been extraordinary and where living standards are extremely high. The challenge in such places is to promote a climate where the existing export-driven companies can flourish.

The benefit that a place gets from foreign trade depends largely on whether its industries are export-oriented or import-competing. Places strong in export-oriented industries — aircraft, business services, lorries, chemicals, software and computers — benefit through the ripple effects of these exports on local employment and purchasing power. Places strong in import-competing industries — auto, textiles, consumer electronics, metal products and tires — are likely to be hurt by growing imports. Some places seek to export more (export promotion). Others seek to reduce current imports by producing the same goods and services at home (import substitution), although it's widely agreed that import substitution in a global economy is an unattractive development strategy.

From an individual place point of view, export and import flows can be dramatically influenced by the relationship between public and private sectors. This was especially true during Asia's "Miracle" decades, when public contracts were often awarded on the basis of political or economic favoritism. Now, new rules are being established, in part as a result of pressure to conform to World Trade Organization (WTO) rules on public procurement. WTO rules provide more genuine competition and, thus, lower costs. Technology is also having an important impact, as governments shift to government-to-business (G2B) electronic procurement, increasing transparency and rewarding bona fide best offers. Technology — especially the Internet — has also made services that provide information on government tenders and bidding procedures more visible, which has increased competition.

At least theoretically, and irrespective of geography and borders, every place or business in the internal market should have the same chance to export or import. The further opening of the public sector in Asia as a result of WTO membership, the Asia Pacific Free Trade Area agreement and globalization are discussed later in this chapter.

Some Asian nations are more export-driven than others. The Philippines, Malaysia and Thailand are among the most obvious examples of export-driven economies from developing Asia. Japan, South Korea, Singapore and Taiwan are corresponding examples from the more developed regions of Asia. These countries built modern economies on the strength of exports, and developing Asia intends to mimic their success. By contrast, Vietnam, Myanmar and Cambodia have been slow to develop export-oriented economies, but Vietnam is making progress and Cambodia is trying. Differences are even greater if we study regions and cities. Examples of such places with excellent export performance are Shenzhen, Ho Chi Minh City, Shanghai, Chennai, Rayong, Chittagong, Taichung and Port Moresby. On a micro level we can find very small communities or even individual villages where export is everything. Marikina in the Philippines, for example, is home to 542 footwear and bag manufacturers.[4] In 1994, export revenues from footwear — largely comprising sports and leather footwear — reached US$210.3 million.[5] More than half of the industrial output of Tokoname in Japan's Aichi prefecture, with a population of 52,000, is ceramics. Nishinomiya, a city in Hyogo prefecture, is the most famous sake-producing region in the country, and has been producing high-quality sake for centuries. In recent years, the city has become a residential suburb to larger surrounding enterprise centers, and its population has increased to around 450,000. But it is still home to 16 major sake manufacturers[6] who produce one-third of the country's total sake production.[7] As sake consumption has decreased in Japan, breweries have dedicated excess capacity to export markets.

"Export hot spots," where exports totally dominate a place's economy, can be found throughout Asia: the Japanese city of Toyota is the birthplace of the Japanese automobile industry and is a dominant supplier of cars. From a place-marketing perspective, it is important to note that the automobile brand is named after the city. Malaysia's "Pearl of the Orient," Penang island, is known — apart from its fine beaches — for electronic products and is home to over 148 manufacturers.[8] Bangalore has acquired the image of South Asia's version of Silicon Valley. It is Asia's foremost technology hub and leads the region in software exports. Johnson Electric, which has its regional headquarters in Hong Kong, is the world's foremost supplier and exporter of quality micromotors. The former Clark airbase in the Philippines hosts AOL's global call center and, along with other IT investment parks, is making the country Asia's predominant call center location. These call centers "export" information globally, 24 hours a day.

Developing into a "export hot spot" is a desired goal for most places. Higher living standards, low unemployment and a stable tax base are the inevitable rewards.

ASSESSING A PLACE'S EXPORT POTENTIAL

Export promotion begins with identifying who exports currently and who has the potential to export. One tool, *economic base analysis*, measures the presence of a particular industry in a specific place relative to its presence elsewhere in the country or some other relevant part of Asia. If the *export base ratio* in a place is greater than one, it suggests that the industry exports its goods or services; a ratio of less than one suggests that the industry's goods or services are partly imported. To illustrate, if 90% of Tokoname's workers are in the ceramics industry, and only 0.5%

of Japan's workers are in the ceramics industry, we can assume that Tokoname's ceramic industry is a major exporter of ceramics. This rough measuring device provides some indication of the export side of a place's economy as well as where it might have a competitive advantage.

The other task is to identify non-exporting companies and industries that have export potential. These companies can offer products or services that would possess some competitive advantage in another market, such as unique features or styling, high quality, high value for the money, or brand-image strength. Some of these companies start exporting on their own for a variety of reasons: excess capacity, unsolicited orders from abroad, a competitive attack from abroad, or the pursuit of economies of scale in production. At the same time, some companies hesitate because of perceived high costs, risks, or lack of export-management know-how. Here place sellers can play a positive role. They can help identify foreign opportunities for companies, assist them in finding distributors or importers, provide export training and offer export insurance and credit. Such efforts can work as a springboard for both large and small companies to improve their export performance.

WAYS TO ASSIST COMPANIES IN PROMOTING EXPORTS

Local, regional and national export-promotion networks and agencies face a difficult task both in converting non-exporters to exporters and in getting current exporters to expand their activities.

Export promotion agencies can play at least 10 roles in assisting and stimulating exports. They act as informer, broker, expediter, trainer and counselor, financier, host, targeter, promoter, facility developer, and new-technology developer.

Informer

Place developers can systematically provide existing businesses with information about export marketplaces. A network of export-experienced people can be gathered within the place. Such networks are rarely developed without assistance. There has to be a place-bound catalyst in the middle to bring them together. In Asia, it may be the chamber of commerce or the economic development unit of the community that acts as the catalyst — at least on the local and regional levels. Where there are stable clusters — for example, the shipping clusters of South Korea or the textile SME clusters in India — much of the export-related information is distributed within local and complex networks.

Broker

The WTO, the Asia Pacific Free Trade Agreement and globalization have dramatically increased pressure on Asian governments to level the enterprise playing field and provide equal opportunity to international competitors. Politically, governments must face up to liberalization pressures or risk their own access to important export markets, especially in North America. Market economics in an era of globalization dictate that strong, globally competitive companies are only created in competitive marketplaces.

Many places have responded to these pressures by performing a brokerage function in relation to export promotion. This could involve the provision of more specialized services for small exporters as well as larger companies. Brokering may entail finding names of specific contacts, agents and distributors. A special service such as India-Invest — a free business resource that promotes opportunities and tenders — is often appreciated in times when many companies lack competence to understand what is going on in various electronic marketplaces. AusAID provides tenders for community development. New Zealand's government tenders are provided by the Government Electronic Tenders Service. Japan External Trade Organization (JETRO), the Asian Development Bank (ADB) and the Asia-Pacific Economic Cooperation (APEC) forum also provide information on tenders and bidding procedures. The Internet and e-commerce technologies make such services increasingly important resources.

The Information Network Fully Online (INFO), an Australian organization, is a leader in electronic tendering and procurement systems. INFO carries tender notices from all levels of government, multi-national corporations and sole traders. The tender opportunities originate from public and private bodies throughout Australia and offer comprehensive and cost-effective solutions to subscribers who wish to purchase and/or supply goods and services. Notices are also included for other regions such as Asia, South Africa and Europe.[9]

Expediter

Export promotion also involves matching local businesses with foreign trade missions and trade shows. A place can invite specific companies to participate, offering, for example, to defray part or all of the costs of travel, displays, interpreters and other required services. During trade shows and trade missions, places have the opportunity to integrate other place-marketing messages and business offerings. Such integration could bring value-added effects for all participants. Classic examples of this can be seen in Asian trade shows in the tourism business where places organize a total concept within which various tourist and travel operators make up the content.

Trainer and Counselor

Places can conduct their own seminars, workshops, conferences and training sessions by working with existing export-driven enterprises, chambers of commerce and independent business experts. Education, training and counseling have all become an integral part of trade-promotion services offered by places seeking to promote export growth. The proposal by Asian economic ministers to form an East Asian Monetary Union has increased local and regional efforts to learn more about export markets.[10]

Singapore is clearly an Asian export success story, and it has tried to turn its strengths in infrastructure planning and development, facilities administration and quality management into a marketable export. The government exports its know-how in developing industrial parks and attracting businessmen and investors by investing in flagship projects in China, India, Vietnam and Indonesia.[11] However, China's Suzhou Industrial Park proved to be unsuccessful despite its high profile and sleek publicity. The Chinese attribute the failure of the Singaporean model, championed by Singapore's Senior Minister Lee Kuan Yew, to 'cultural differences.' The Singaporeans, however, point to a lack of support from the Chinese government, claiming that local and national officials favored locally developed industrial parks to the Singaporean investment. As a result, Singapore intends to transfer majority ownership of the park to state-owned Mainland developers.[12]

Financier

Asian countries in general — as well as the U.S. and Europe — have established systems for export loans and guarantees. Export credit has been an important factor in international trade for many years. Export credit agencies, some of which have been in existence for over 50 years, can play a decisive role in export trade. Official support may take the form of "pure cover," which means giving exporters or lending institutions insurance or guarantees without providing outright financial support. It may also be given in the form of "financing support" which is defined by the Organization for Economic Co-Operation and Development (OECD) as including direct credits to the overseas buyer, re-financing and all forms of interest-rate support. The Import-Export Bank of Japan, Nihon Yushutsunyu Ginko, is a financial institution that was created to encourage trade and overseas investment. It provides low-interest financing to Japanese exporters and importers as well as to less-developed countries to import Japanese products. The Export-Import Bank of India, the Export-Import Bank of Malaysia Berhad and the Export-Import Bank of Korea all fulfill similar functions.

A place needs to have a workable knowledge of the range of available finance schemes such as loans, guarantees and insurance. Financial know-how is a valuable competency in the highly competitive place market. In some places, a local bank can play a key role in providing financial know-how on a specific export market. The Trade & Development Bank of Mongolia, for example, assists in foreign trade operations and finance projects.

Host

Being a good host includes attracting foreign business visitors, sponsoring delegations and cultivating partner-city relations. The benefits of the tourism and hospitality business are multiple spillovers into trade and foreign investment as some places seek to convert tourists and guests into traders and investors. Places can actively encourage foreign businesses to visit local trade shows and exhibitions, and can arrange meetings and contacts with their local business counterparts.

Dating from the postwar period, partner-city relationships have expanded from a ceremonial and cultural exchange into place-to-place relationships where formal agreements focus on mutual trade opportunities, tourism, technology transfer, ASEAN-projects, education and culture. Sister-city arrangements are also supported by the Asia-Pacific Cities Summit[13] as a method for promoting deeper Asian integration.

An example of this can be seen in the SEAsia Regional Program of the Canadian International Development Agency which, with the help of ASEAN and APEC, aims at improving regional integration to promote sustainable development in the region. Other examples include the South Asian Association for Regional Cooperation (SAARC) and the South Asian Preferential Trade Agreement (SAPTA), which were formed to encourage cooperation and trade in the region.

Targeter

Rather than being all things to all businesses, more and more places are developing lists of target industries and target companies to pursue. Depending on organizational structure and resources, targeting can be by geographic area, by local clusters of industries and products, and by matching export-market opportunities to specific companies and their products. Many Asian places are promoting local products — tea products (China, India, Sri Lanka), wine (Australia, Japan's sake and Korea's chungju), dairy products (New Zealand), electronics (Malaysia, Japan, Singapore, Taiwan), beef and meat (Australia, Japan, New Zealand) rice (Japan, Thailand, India) or textiles (India, Thailand, Indonesia).

A basic precondition for effective local targeting is establishing a local place-marketing strategy to select the relevant targets.

Promoter

While all these activities and programs involve trade stimulation, places also need an overarching program for expanding public awareness of export opportunities. Just as some places invest heavily in tourism promotion, that same investment is required to reach broader audiences on trade. Such services include general ads, hot-line services, billboards, videos, Internet services, newsletters and promotional pieces. The marketing aspect of trade promotion is, in many cases, the weak link in export-development strategies. Places tend to over-invest in providing services and under-invest in the actual marketing of them.

More developed Asian places have been particularly eager to promote export strategies and, at the same time, market their services to place buyers. For example, the message from Invest Australia reads: "Australia — Invest for a Global Future." Of course, it's important that the message can be understood. The Thailand Board of Investment's slogan — "Challenge to the Future"[14] — provides an example of the confusion that can arise when the message you want to get across is not made clear.

Facility Developer

Obviously some places are better positioned for trade than others. They may share a border with a cooperative nation or possess a basic international trade base with ports or airfields. Some places have exploited these advantages better than others: Hong Kong, Singapore, Dubai, Pusan, Johor, Yokohama and Shanghai are excellent success stories. In some cases, places have managed to simplify customs procedures and re-train customs staff.

The case of Hong Kong is instructive, however. In recent years there have been concerns that slow customs procedures at the border might lead to Hong Kong being bypassed as the gateway to China. In fact, Hong Kong's exporters to China were finding it faster and cheaper to import supplies, components and materials direct to South China's less-efficient mainland ports. James Sparks, results manager of the Thomas Group, for example, observed that his company's clients "find that they can quickly get their products into Hong Kong, but that then they get stuck here."[15] Ironically, as a result, Hong Kong's competitiveness as a transshipment point to China has demonstrably eroded in comparison to its chief rival, Singapore, although it remained a key Asian transshipment port for other destinations. Singapore has the advantage of shipping directly to Mainland ports, bypassing customs processing at the Hong Kong border. This is a concern that Hong Kong leaders and businesses have taken seriously, since the former colony still considers its role in facilitating trade and business in China to be one of its chief competitive attributes.

Nevertheless, in 1999 global cargo growth was the highest in the Asia-Pacific region, with an increase of 13%,[16] and Hong Kong was largely responsible, despite its border difficulties. The Hong Kong advantage demonstrates the strategic importance for a place to host an air-traffic hub. With its huge international airport at Chek Lap Kok, Hong Kong is a classic illustration of how an Asian hub can improve place competitiveness. It ranked as the world's second-busiest cargo airport for 1999. Others on the list included Shanghai, Tokyo Narita, Singapore and Seoul.[17] Many smaller places are responding by eagerly promoting their regional air hubs as gateways for trade and export.

But it is not sufficient for such trade meccas to offer only ports and airfields. In order to attract buyers, places need an attractive combination of banks, consultants, export expertise, trading companies, and support services such as language and intercultural and legal competence. In the case of Hong Kong, efficient customs-clearance procedures on the part of the Mainland government are essential, something Hong Kong's government needs to negotiate with Beijing if it is to fight off tough competitors such as Singapore.

New-technology Developer

A place can systematically provide its companies with test grounds for various innovations. Such tests can then develop into important showcases for the export market. Investors and customers are welcomed to the pilot place in order to get a full, on-site understanding of the product or service. Pilot projects of this kind have become quite common as a result of the growing complexity of products and services.

The Taiwan Government is encouraging more innovation by giving tax breaks and grants to increase spending on R&D. Its Industrial Technology Research Institute (ITRI) is responsible for nurturing some of the country's most successful companies. The government spends

US$420 million in subsidies for ITRI and its sister company for software research.[18] The Hsinchu Industry Park, also a government initiative, was created in 1980 to attract investment in high-technology industries. It offers investors various benefits including R&D matching funds. The success of the Park led the government to create the Tainan science park in the mid 1990s. The spread of technology and science parks has created an industry dedicated to making them competitive (see Exhibit 11.1).

Exhibit 11.1: IT TAKES A "COOL" PLACE

Technology and science parks are a key component of a place's strategy to attract foreign direct investment. According to the non-profit Asian Technology Information Program (ATIP), there are around 200 science and technology parks competing for investment in Asia. Worldwide estimates vary from 600 to 1,000. About half of the science parks in Asia are in Japan, and local governments in China run half of the rest. India, despite its growing reputation as a technology hub — it exported over US$8 billion in software last year — has just a dozen or so.

What makes a science and technology park? In today's competitive environment, it takes a community. According to a recent report in *Asia-Inc.*, the International Association of Science Parks says to qualify as a science or technology park, a development must exhibit three qualities. First, it must have operational links — not just proximity — with universities, research centers and other institutions of higher education.

Second, the park must be "designed to encourage the formation and growth of knowledge-based industries or high-value-added tertiary firms."[1] Finally, the park must have "a steady management team actively engaged in fostering the transfer of technology and business to tenant organizations."[2] The report notes that by this standard, the number of bona fide science and technology parks in Asia shrinks.

Yet others say still more is required for a science park targeting high value-added investment to be truly competitive. David Crowe, chief operating officer of *Editor.com*, notes that park developers "are constructing grand projects in which a new generation of the technical elite can live and work in relative luxury, in modern homes, with community shopping centers, advanced technology laboratories, golf courses, and the occasional jacuzzi."[3]

The attempt is to make the place "cool," as Paco Sandejas, vice president of H&Q Asia Pacific, put it at the recent Cebu IT Summit.[4] Crowe says "the business model is all about 'work-play' combinations. The Singapore Science Park offers tenants a gymnasium, an aerobics studio, a swimming pool, tennis courts, food courts, cafés, restaurants, bus shuttles within the park, and shuttles to Singapore's MRT train stations."[5] And that's not all. Childcare and medical clinics are also available, as are business seminars, health programs and lunchtime entertainment.

As newer parks benchmark each other, the competition is fierce to provide the best environment for the best brains. The Philippines' IT investment zones in Eastwood City, Fort Bonifacio and RCBC Plaza potentially rival many of Asia's best parks in most work-play combinations, but not in the area of educational links. That's a critical, and missing, element of their marketing strategy. The Hong Kong Science Park does better. It has formal ties to six universities in Hong Kong. Hsinchu Science-based Industrial Park in Taiwan has links to 12 research facilities and two nearby national universities, and the Singapore Science Park sits next to the National University of Singapore and boasts 7,000 engineers and scientists within the park.

If science parks in other parts of Asia expect to attract high-value-added investment, it's imperative that educational infrastructure improve. Just as important, academe and parks must learn to link meaningfully and effectively to generate the research and the people required to drive development. And with developed economies also competing to attract developing Asia's best and brightest, institutions all over Asia must dramatically increase the number of technology and science graduates they produce each year.

Sources:

1 David Crowe, "Technology Parks," *Asia-Inc.*, April 2001, p. 43
2 *Ibid.*
3 *Ibid.* p. 42.

4 From remarks delivered at the Cebu Information Technology Summit
2001, March 30, 2001, in Cebu City, Philippines.
5 *Asia-Inc.*, p. 43.

"What Asia's Science and Technology Parks Have to Offer," *Asia-Inc.*, April
2001, pp. 44 & 45.

Other examples in Asia include the Hong Kong Productivity Board,
which serves to promote productivity excellence by managing, utilizing
and maximizing available resources to increase efficiency and
effectiveness and improve the quality of life of the people.[19] The Hong
Kong Science Park, fully funded by the government, aims at attracting
businesses in the electronics, IT, biotechnology and precision
engineering sectors. Aside from encouraging innovation, research and
development, it was built to attract knowledge-based industries and allow
the Special Administrative Region (SAR) to compete in the global
market. Another government organization, the Hong Kong Trade
Development Council, also protects and strengthens Hong Kong's
position as an Asian information hub, business center and gateway to the
mainland by actively promoting its goods and services. The government
of Victoria in Australia gives priority to science technology innovation
(STI) by focusing efforts on building world-class infrastructure and
developing the skills of its citizens to foster a culture of innovation and
position the state as a national and world leader in science.[20]

Pilot projects are uniting places and enterprises. We have already
discussed the Malaysian Multimedia Super Corridor, which serves as a
test-bed for new IT products and services. The Sultanate of Brunei is also
positioning itself as an information and communication technology (ICT)
hub in East Asia. It is scheduled to open a cyberpark, which aims to
position science, technology and IT as the country's growth sectors.[21]
The complexity of IT applications opens opportunities for full-scale pilot
projects of this sort in many Asian cities. This is probably one of the
reasons behind the positive response to initiatives such as cyberparks,
despite the recent downturn in technology stocks. In many countries,
such as the Philippines, investment into IT parks continues to grow
strongly.[22]

To stimulate IT-sector development, ASEAN offers research programs
as well as integrated regional-development programs. One example of an
initiative aiming at a wide use of IT applications is the establishment of
the eASEAN Task Force. Its objective is to develop the competencies in
ASEAN countries that will enable them to compete in the global

information economy. The Task Force is working on several pilot projects including the ASEAN Regional Internet Exchange, or ARIX, to serve as ASEAN's Information Infrastructure; the development of various e-commerce sites; the expansion of Internet services; and a program to educate officials on cyberlaws. As Exhibit 11.2 demonstrates, there are a number of locally based network programs operating.

Exhibit 11.2: A COMPETITIVE PLACE SERVICE: INTERNATIONAL TRADE NETWORKING

Networking on the international market can add a highly competitive edge to a place. In this exhibit we show four different approaches featuring four different actors. In each case, the service is tailored to the problems and the needs of the companies involved.

■ The World Trade Center in Singapore provides sophisticated telecommunication systems, worldwide Internet and direct Internet access. The networking service is linked to more than 300 World Trade Centers in over 90 countries. Their global network contains more than 500,000 companies. Trade education and integrated delegation services are also part of the service package. These services enable users to learn about and review trade opportunities.

■ Suntec City in Singapore has managed to attract a number of important high-tech companies such as Microsoft, Sun Microsystems, EMC, Oracle, NCR and Adobe Systems. Suntec prides itself on being a comprehensive facilities service provider (FSP), not a mere landlord, to the various companies in residence. A key element of the center's offerings is business networking. For example, Suntec has established strategic management alliances with Internet incubators located in established technology hubs, including Vancouver and Silicon Valley. These alliances serve to direct start-ups that are looking for strategic partners in Asia to Suntec, which helps companies that are setting up development centers to locate potential partners and to establish long-term relationships.

■ Many banks are offering international networks that can be of great value for trade. Bank of America offers trade and investment services. ABN Amro, recognized as a leader in packaging major FDI projects, focuses on emerging markets. ABN Amro managed a US$214-million financial package for the modernization of Turkmenistan's domestic natural-gas pipeline network. This project was covered by export credits from Czechoslovakia, Israel and the U.S. For Turkmenistan, international financial networking was vital for the implementation of the project.

■ In Asia, there are several local private and public companies that provide networking and advisory services to local exporters. The Reid Bracken Company in Thailand, Patwa Enterprises in India, and the Malaysia External Trade Development Corporation (MATRADE) are three companies that provide such services. MATRADE, for example, provides market intelligence and relevant advice, similar to Japan's JETRO. The following appear on its list of services :

- "Assist Malaysian exporters in searching for and developing new regional markets and niche markets overseas
- Match Malaysian exporters and foreign importers by organizing meetings between buyers and sellers
- Maintain an Import Register of overseas contacts for local exporters and an Export Register of Malaysian businesses
- Publish and disseminate trade information materials
- Organize outbound trade missions for local manufacturers and inbound trade missions for foreign importers
- Participate in international trade fairs to promote Malaysian products and to strengthen trade ties
- Plan and organize trade-related seminars and workshops for Malaysian exporters."[1]

A place that can incorporate a networking service into its place structure will have an advantage, especially in the future when access to trade and export intelligence will be even more decisive for a place and its enterprises.

Sources:

1   The Malaysia External Trade Development Corporation Web site, http://www.matrade.gov.my/Laman2000/Main/Public/Corporate/CorporateMain.html, viewed on March 20, 2001.

The World Trade Center — Singapore Web site, www.psa.com.sg/wtc, viewed on February 23, 2001; Suntec City Web site, www.suntec.com.sg, viewed on February 23, 2001; "Internet Incubation Centre Coming Up in Suntec City," *The Business Times*, April 28, 2000, http://www.internet-callcentre.com/Newsroom/coverage10.htm, viewed March 28, 2001; "Financial Report," Bank of America Web site, http://www.bankofamerica.com.hk/english/aboutus/result99.html, March 9, 2000; http://discport2b.law.utah.edu/cdroms/Energy/cd_rom/apps/cabs/turkmen.htm, viewed on February 27, 2001.

EXPLOITING THE PLACE-OF-ORIGIN IMAGE

If all the brands within a particular product category were perceived by consumers to be equal in quality and price, buyers would probably favor buying the brand that was locally or domestically produced. In this way, consumers would receive faster redress from the producer if they were dissatisfied and, at the same time, support local income and jobs. However, different brands in a product category are rarely perceived as delivering equal value. In fact, buyers make distinct brand evaluations based on their image of the place of origin (see Exhibit 11.3).

Exhibit 11.3: SONY QUALITY: A LAUNCHING PAD FOR OTHER PRODUCTS

In 1957, Japanese electronics company Sony developed the world's smallest transistor radio. Although Sony's pocket-sized transistor radio, the TR-63, wasn't the first, it was the most successful. The TR-63 is one of a wide range of unique, high-quality and innovative electronic products made by Sony and sold throughout the world. Sony products include flat-screen FD Trinitron® color televisions and computer displays, Memory Stick® IC Digital Media, Mavica® Digital Cameras, Digital-8™ Handycam® Camcorders, the Walkman® personal stereo, 3.5-inch floppy disks and MiniDisc systems for consumers and professionals, and Digital Betacam®, HD-CAM® and DV-CAM® products for professionals.

For the fiscal year ending on March 31, 2000, the Sony Corporation's consolidated earned income was US$63 billion, with US$19 billion (30%) accounted for by the United States alone. Sony products reached cult status and built credibility with the help of massive product advertising and marketing, which often focused on customer testimonials praising the longevity of Sony products and their quality.

So strong was the Sony brand that, once consumers understood that it was a Japanese company, the goodwill it generated migrated to other Japanese products, substantially enhancing the global image of Japan and its products. In that respect, Sony has helped sell many brands, even those of its competitors.

Many companies have tried to capitalize on the strong quality image associated with Japanese products that Sony and a handful of other Japanese companies symbolize. As a result, Japanese brands are often preferred to the exports of other countries. So it's not surprising that some companies have tried to create product names that mimic Japanese names, in an effort to associate themselves and their products with the country. They are, in effect, paying homage to Japan's brand effectiveness.

For example, a Philippines appliance maker, Hanabishi, has chosen a name composed of Japanese-sounding syllables which, to the unsuspecting consumer, might suggest that this manufacturer's products are of Japanese quality. This practice is not recommended, however, since companies that try to confuse consumers often suffer a severe backlash. Places serious about developing markets for their exports should put sufficient resources into developing their reputation for industry-leading companies and products.

Sources:

Steven E. Schoenherr, "Who's On First? A Note On The Transistor Radio," http://homestudio.thing.net/revue/content/transistor.html, viewed on February 28, 2001; Sony Corporation Web site, www.sony.com, viewed on February 28, 2001; Canada Computes Web site, http://www.canadacomputes.com/v3/print/1,1019,3246,00.html, viewed on March 21, 2001.

A product's place of origin can have a positive, a neutral, or a negative effect on non-resident and resident buyers alike. Most buyers — at least those interested in electronics — are favorably disposed to apparel bearing the label "Made in Japan." The "Made in Korea" origin for cars had a negative image in the U.S. until the recent improvement in the quality of Hyundai's automobiles.[23] Place-images can sometimes change or develop quickly. Only a few years ago, products stamped "Made in Taiwan," or bearing the names of some South Asian countries, generated negative quality signals because these countries were associated with sub-standard products. Today — although often a tortuous journey — new images have been created, as illustrated by the successful international computer brand, Acer, which originated in Taiwan.[24] As discussed earlier, Taiwan has also worked hard to associate its companies with international quality standards and has underwritten sleek and expensive international advertising campaigns.

Consumers form preferences for products from certain places based partly on personal experience but also through inferences about quality, reliability and service. Johnny Johansson contends that consumers use the "made-in" label as a cue to draw inferences about the product's worth.[25] Thus, buyers assume that a VCD (Video Compact Disc) player or a cellular phone made in Japan is of a higher quality than one made in China. Several place-of-origin studies have found the following:[26]

- The impact of place-of-origin varies with the type of product (for example, a car as opposed to oil).
- In highly industrial countries, consumers tend to rate their domestic goods high, whereas consumers in the developing countries tend to have a bias against products produced in their own or other developing countries.
- Certain countries and places have established a generally good reputation regarding certain goods: Tokyo for fashion, Dubai for gold, India for textiles, and Japan for electronics/cars. This reputation stems not only from a product's characteristics but also from accessibility, history and service reliability.
- The more favorable a place's image, the more prominently its name should be displayed in promoting the brand.
- Attitudes towards place of origin can change over time.

What can a place do when its products are competitively equal or superior but its place of origin turns consumers off? The place may resort to co-production or even a joint venture where the product is to be finished at another place that carries a more positive image. Products with a "Made in Europe" or "Made in the U.S.A." label often signify a higher grade or standard compared to a "Made in Asia" label. This is true even in the Asian continent. However, Asian products have, over the years, become more accepted in all parts of the world. Japan's image was boosted when successful brands such as Sony and Toyota entered the international market. The image of Taiwanese products as sub-standard also slowly faded with the introduction of brands such as Acer and Umax. Korean products are on their way to being accepted as high-quality, value-for-money products with booming brands such as Samsung and Hyundai. This achievement is despite the negative publicity associated with the overall financial viability and management of these firms following the Asian financial crisis.

Another strategy a place may pursue is to hire a well-known celebrity to endorse the product to overcome consumers' apprehensions. In seeking to introduce athletic footwear to Asia, Fila and Adidas used two of America's best-known professional basketball stars, Grant Hill and Kobe Bryant, respectively, to attract huge crowds to exhibits. A variation of this approach is the iconic visit. Respected Singapore senior minister Lee Kwan Yew's visits to Asian countries and elsewhere are carefully planned initiatives to build goodwill. Following in his wake are top Singapore bureaucrats and businesspeople whose job it is to establish new business contacts to recruit and facilitate investment into Singapore. Places and their companies often use similar strategies to upgrade their country-of-origin image through sponsoring art exhibitions, artistic tours, sport events and cultural shows.

Michael Porter argues that nations succeed in particular industries because their home environment is the most forward-looking, dynamic and challenging. Based on a four-year study of competitive successes in leading trading nations, Porter found that companies facing tough, effective competition at home are more likely to be successful abroad. Competitive advantages are generated whenever rivals are geographically concentrated and are vying for supremacy in innovation, efficiency and quality.[27] This competition allows places to align a name or region to its products (for example, Indian tea companies around the hill station of Darjeeling or palm oil companies around Sabah and Sarawak in Malaysia). Porter's argument accounts for how place names become associated with consumable products such as Ceylon tea, Korean kimchi, Japanese sushi, Australian wine and beef, Indian and Thai curry, Chinese herbs and Javanese coffee.

Various consumer groups have their own identification images and preferences. Many places are identified with images, which are mainly influenced by media. This is illustrated in Exhibit 11.4.

Exhibit 11.4: PLACE-OF-ORIGIN IMAGES IN ASIA

When a certain country is mentioned in conversation, it is only natural to conjure up images associated with that country. More often than not, these same image associations are those that these countries use to sell their country and its attractions. For example, Australia promotes itself as a premier location for beaches, surfing and sun, and it has used kangaroos, the movie character Crocodile Dundee and the koala bear as national symbols. According to the *Lonely Planet* Web site, Australia has "arguably the best beaches in the world."[1] The travel guide at the Excite.com Web site characterizes Australia as having a "beach culture."[2]

Hong Kong prides itself on being one of the best bargain-shopping places in the world, a center for entrepreneurship, the gateway to south coastal China and a business-friendly global city. Whenever bargain shopping is brought up in conversation, it's hard not to say "Hong Kong" in the same breath. For years, the city has played host to the greatest and grandest shopping festivals in Asia. The official Hong Kong tourism Web site says it all: "When it comes to a serious shopping experience, Hong Kong has everything in abundance."[3] Be it designer boutiques and malls or open-air markets, the city promotes itself as the best in shopping.

People visit India to soak up its exotic, spiritual ambience, but it has also gained a reputation as an educational and IT center. India has long been a sanctuary for those who are soul-searching and looking for spiritual guidance. Many know India as a land of spiritual development because the country is the birthplace of non-secular values and practices such as renunciation, meditation and Yoga.

Malaysia and Thailand are both known for their exceptional beaches, exotic cultures and historic sites. Bali is a romantic getaway not often associated with Indonesia, since its own international image for luxury leisure is so well recognized. Singapore is not just clean, efficient and honest; to many it is the most open economy in the world. Japan is a culinary and cultural treasure; the second-largest economy in the world is best known for sushi, the tea ceremony, soothing gardens, automobiles and electronic appliances. China is, in many respects, the center of Asian culture and its influence is seen throughout the world in food, architecture, art and furniture. However, not all associations are always positive.

Thailand may be well known for its many temples and religious artifacts but rampant prostitution and an extraordinarily high incidence of AIDS strike a serious blow to its positive image-building efforts. Like Thailand, Myanmar also has many religious places and charming tourist resorts, but its reputation as a major source of illicit drugs as well as a brutal military dictatorship discourages many potential tourists. While Angkor Wat is an astounding historic monument, the perception of Cambodia as a place of political instability and criminality keeps many tourists away.

While place-origin images can be formed by accident, in most cases places can control their development and impact. The key is anticipating the unexpected assaults and a willingness to launch and support aggressive campaigns on behalf of strengths.

___

Sources:

1 "Australia: An Introduction," *Lonely Planet* Web site, http://www.lonelyplanet.com/destinations/australasia/australia/, viewed on March 5, 2001.
2 Excite Travel Web site, http://travel.excite.com/show/?loc=2818, viewed on March 5, 2001.
3 Discover HongKong Web site, http://www.discoverhongkong.com/eng/shop/index.jhtml, viewed on March 5, 2001.

http://india.coolatlanta.com/GreatPages/sudheer/book.html, viewed on March 5, 2001; "Sexploitation?: Sex Tourism In Cuba," http://www.georgetown.edu/sfs/programs/isd/files/cases/Nhma.htm, viewed on March 5, 2001.

It is easy to distinguish the many place-bound links behind the image associations in Exhibit 11.3, which also reveals important place potentials. Place marketers can often use such associations to exploit their brand assets. Once a place's name becomes identified with a product or service category, it can seek to protect the integrity and exclusiveness of the product's benefits through regulatory and legal protections.

An important variation of aligning a place's name with its products involves cross-national marketing. Because of their historical, cultural and current ties with their American and European counterparts, certain Asian places target their export promotion and foreign-investment strategies to these places. Such marketing currently operates in both directions. Ethnic identification with products and place-of-origin can be a positive force in cross-national sales and marketing as well as within the growing and multicultural Asian home market.

CONCLUSION

Promoting foreign trade and investment has emerged as an important place-development strategy that has gained equal footing with business attraction, retention, start-ups and tourism-hospitality activities. Export place-development strategies will increasingly require more global thinking and strategic marketing to set apart a place, its people and businesses from other places or regions. Local responses to worldwide economic change will be the hallmark of national competition.

Table 11.1: Measuring your export climate

1. Can you name your place's leading manufacturing and service-industry exporters?

2. Does your local chamber of commerce or similar promoting body offer its members a program on export trade at least annually?

3. Does your local college or university provide any help to would-be exporters on identifying overseas markets and opportunities?

4. Is your major financial institution familiar with export financing, letters of credit and foreign-exchange protections?

5. Does your local economic-development agency sponsor trade seminars, trade shows and catalogs or provide marketing assistance?

6. Does your local export-development agency/organization identify, target and contact potential export companies to support trade facilitation?

7. If your place has a partner-city relationship, has it produced any new contacts or business ties between them?

8. Do your mayor and other local officials organize trade missions or travel overseas to promote contacts and trade?

9. Does your community/place have a well-defined understanding of its local economy with respect to trade composition or potential?

10. Can you identify any trade-facilitation strategies of your business community and/or economic-development agency? Does it have a plan?

As in other aspects of place development, businesses have responded to globalization and economic interdependence faster than most public organizations. However, Asian civic leaders have started to act on the Asian place market as well as overseas. They have become advocates and brokers for making places more competitive.

Places can gain an advantage by becoming known as the source of certain high-quality products and services. As we have seen, many such examples can be identified on the global market and include the transport, energy, banking, insurance and manufacturing sectors. Place-bound links are especially common in the food and drink business. Textiles, music and entertainment are other types of business where fashion may be integrated with a specific place.

Places can develop into "export hot spots", where place buyers and place sellers have managed, step by step, to establish trade excellence. A small town might be rescued when a company moves successfully into exporting. An entire region may become known for that product. The rewards for places are considerable, but require strong public/private partnerships, the removal of bureaucratic obstacles and a commitment to supporting local companies.

We conclude this chapter with a test that places might use to audit how they measure up to the challenge of export promotion (see Table 11.1). With 10 points for each favorable answer, a passing grade is 60 points.

---

1 *World Development Report 2000/2001*, The World Bank, p. 295.

2 *Ibid*, The World Bank, p. 299.

3 *Ibid*, The World Bank, p. 313.

4 http://www.marikina.com.ph/, viewed on March 21, 2001.

5 "Shoe Capital Targets Upmarket Niche for Women's Casual Shoes," December 8, 2000, Global Sources Web site, http://www.globalsources.com/MAGAZINE/BF/0102/WCSHOE.HTM, viewed on March 21, 2001.

6 http://www.kippo.or.jp/culture/water/food/sake/sake_h_e.htm, viewed on March 27, 2001.

7 http://www.bento.com/drinks/sake07.html, viewed on March 23, 2001.

8 http://www.cs.arizona.edu/japan/atip/public/atip.reports.96/atip96.107r.html, viewed on March 21, 2001.

9 http://www.tenders.net/, viewed on July 3, 2001.

10 http://www.jei.org/Archive/JEIR00/0012f.html#conclusion, viewed on March 22, 2001.

11 http://www.sedb.com.sg/why/wh_bi_gr_sf.html, viewed on March 22, 2001.

12 Ben Dolven, "Wounded Pride," *Far Eastern Economic Review*, July 8, 1999. http://www.feer.com/9907_08/p73investment.html, viewed on March 22, 2001.

13 http:// www.apsummit.org/overview.html, viewed on July 3, 2001.

14 http://www.boi.go.th/english/index.html, viewed on March 22, 2001.

15 Conversation with James Sparks, results manager, Thomas Group, March 7, 2001.

16 http://www.airports.org/media/mr_20000327.html, viewed on March 2, 2001.

17 *Ibid.*

18 Jonathan Moore, "Taiwan's New Grail: Innovation," *Businessweek,* August 25, 1997. Internet: http://www.businessweek.com/1997/34/b354189.htm, viewed on March 2, 2001.

19 http://www.hkpc.org/hkpc/html/nhome.asp, viewed on March 22, 2001.

20 http://www.innovation.vic.gov.au/programs/, viewed on March 23, 2001.

21 Veronica C. Silva, "Brunei Projects Itself as East Asia ICT Hub," *BusinessWorld Online*, November 12, 2000. Internet: http://apec.bworldonline.com/Articles/Nov2000/11122000a.html, viewed on March 23, 2001.

22 Ditas Lopez, "Philippine Export Zones Invest Php15.1B Jan-Apr 5," *Dow Jones Newswires* on WSJ.com, viewed April 19, 2001.

23 http://www.findarticles.com/m4PRN/1998_Jan_7/20119013/p1/article.jhtml, viewed on March 1, 2001.

24 http://www.brandingasia.com/cases/case1.htm, viewed on March 1, 2001.

25 Johnny K. Johansson, "Determinants and Effects of the Use of 'Made In' Labels," *International Marketing Review (UK)* 6, no. 1, pp. 47–58.

26 See Warren J. Bilkey and Erik Nes, 'Country-of-Origin Effects on Product Evaluations,' *Journal of Business Studies* 13, Spring–Summer 1982, pp. 89–99; P.J. Catin et al., 'A Cross-Cultural Study of "Made-In" Concepts,' *Journal of International Business Studies*, Winter 1982, pp. 131–41; and Gary M. Erickson, Johnny K. Johansson and Paul Chao, 'Image Variables in Multi-Attribute Product Evaluations: Country-of-Origin Effects,' *Journal of Consumer Research*, September 1984, pp. 694–99.

27 Michael Porter, *The Competitive Advantage of Nations*, (New York: The Free Press, 1990), pp. 3–4.

C H A P T E R

12

Attracting Residents

Places not only try to attract tourists, businesses and investors, they also undertake to attract and keep residents as part of building a viable community. In doing so, they seek to appeal to certain groups and to discourage others. The targeted groups typically include professionals, investors, the wealthy, young families, students, retirees and workers with special or relevant skills. At the same time, places may try to discourage low-income families, the unemployed, the homeless and certain immigrants. Understandably, policies that aim to attract certain people and exclude others remain controversial and are not always discussed publicly.

There are some compelling arguments for competing for residents:

- "The number of expatriates per company being sent to Asia has risen by 58% on average."[1]
- "The most popular regional destinations for expatriates are Asia (33%); Western Europe (26%); and the U.S. (16%)."[2]
- An Asian Intelligence Survey conducted in 1999 ranked Australia as the Most Desirable Location for expatriates, offering the highest quality of life in the Asia-Pacific region.[3] Singapore topped the 2000 survey conducted by the Political and Economic Risk Consultancy (PERC), which excluded Australia.
- PERC's 2001 report noted that many countries — China and South Korea, in particular — are losing their ranking as hardship posts, and that Asian countries in general are doing a better job promoting expatriate lifestyles because of the direct link with foreign investment.[4]

385

- There are still problems in promoting residential attractiveness. Although the PERC Quality of Life Survey reported that Bangkok had a much improved quality of life, the 1999 assassination of an expatriate accountant who was liquidating a local company drove home to many expatriates the risks associated with cleaning up Asia's less-desirable companies.
- Some countries send mixed messages. Despite the enormous difficulty in attracting expatriates to Indonesia in the violent aftermath of Asia's financial crisis and political change, the government intended to tax the foreign-earned income of expatriates, even though this was likely to have a negative impact on foreign investment.[5] Meanwhile, a confidential McKinsey & Co. report noted that management of Malaysia's Multimedia Super Corridor needed to provide "an attractive working and living environment," among other recommendations, to attract world-class companies and executives.[6]

A basic goal for APEC[7] and other Asian organizations has been to increase cross-border mobility. This goal creates new opportunities for place sellers to attract first-rate talent. Providing potential residents with professional services is a growing priority, and place sellers are initiating a number of *residential-place strategies.*

As enterprises move across Asia, residential preferences and conditions are becoming vital issues for more and more people. Their residential map consists of hard and soft factors. Place sellers, place-buying companies and special relocation-service companies are all trying to help the residential market answer questions related to hard and soft factors. The ability to provide quick and relevant answers to such questions is in itself an important attraction factor.

Settling down and building a new life in new surroundings is no easy matter. Each place raises its own set of relocation challenges for the potential resident. Therefore, a well-planned residential-place strategy is often welcomed by place buyers. This, in turn, can give rise to appreciative comments and good word-of-mouth recommendations from buyers. Messages such as: "In Singapore they have a tremendous residential service. My family and I were impressed," can play a decisive role for other people considering a residential move.

In discussing resident attraction, this chapter addresses the following questions:

- Why has resident attraction become important for place marketing?
- Whom do places want to attract and why? Within applicable laws, whom do places wish to encourage to relocate elsewhere?

■ What policies/programs can places use to attract/discourage certain population segments, and how do they market them?

WHY RESIDENT ATTRACTION IS IMPORTANT IN PLACE MARKETING

Places have always competed for certain people. During much of Asia's "miracle period" of development, North Asia actively recruited labor from Southeast and South Asia for construction, industrial and domestic work. Among the targets of labor recruiters were Indonesians, Filipinos, Thais and Sri Lankans. Workers from these countries were enticed primarily by the availability of jobs that paid more than they could expect at home. These efforts continue today, with advanced Asian economies like South Korea and Japan — previously highly resistant to importing outside workers — increasingly requiring workers to perform basic tasks that many of their own citizens are no longer willing to perform. The system to recruit such workers is based on relatively standardized and primitive mass-service.

Today, developed Asian economies such as Australia, Singapore, South Korea, Taiwan and Japan are also feverishly recruiting all kinds of professionals, especially engineers and technology specialists. So is China. For example, from Taiwan alone approximately "300,000 people, mostly managers, have moved to China, and Shanghai is the hottest destination. 'The more people leave, the faster China closes the technology gap,' worries Lee Tai-an,"[8] an official of the Taiwan Ministry of Economic Affairs' Industrial Development Bureau. And they are not all working at Taiwan ventures on the Mainland. Chinese companies are under pressure to build competitive businesses, and are competing for top management talent wherever they can find it.[9]

As a result of this competition for brains, the old job-recruitment mass-service has developed into highly selective headhunting and management-career planning. In fact, headhunting and place hunting go hand in hand. Many Asian hot spots are offering professional relocation services to target residents and their families. This is particularly true in the case of Singapore.

The free movement for goods and people on the internal market, the opening of new markets in Central and Eastern Asia, and the thirst of developed and developing economies alike for knowledge workers has led to more intense competition for talented people. Local access to intellectual capital represents one of the most important factors in place development. With fierce competition in the development of high-value-added products and services, the race actually boils down to the quality of the labor force. To attract people is therefore a strategic place investment.

A World Problem: Competing for Talent and Identity

A place should be concerned with the size and composition of its population. Losing population can be a serious economic threat in that it erodes the tax base and can quickly create a negative image if it continues. Therefore, maintaining or increasing the current number of citizens should be given a high priority. Nations and places are strategically positioning themselves on their ability to attract talented people.

On the world place market, of course, Asia is competing with thousands of places, regions and nations on other continents. Singapore aims to be the "Brain Capital of Southeast Asia" and advertises around the world to attract professionals with the objective of cementing its future as a high-tech center and exporter of expensive services to Asia and the rest of the world. The recruitment effort starts early in Singapore. The Ministry of Education offers secondary school and pre-university scholarships to students residing in ASEAN countries in the hope that they will remain in Singapore.

As we've already seen, the population picture in Asia is by no means homogeneous. While some places are struggling with congestion due to a serious shortage of land, others are confronted with growth restrictions that come with a low population density. In the latter case, existing infrastructure investments are not used enough, and the local market may be too small to attract place buyers. The extent of Asia's population differences can be seen in Table 12.1.

Asia's population is distributed unevenly, with the majority crowded into regions with 150 or more inhabitants per square kilometer. Central Asia and some Pacific countries, on the other hand, are characterized by generally low population densities. Several Southeast Asian countries, now opening for cross-border mobility, have a medium density with huge areas and too few residents. However, irrespective of current density figures, many Asian countries are marketing their attraction for skilled professionals.

Low- or medium-density places can easily be hurt in periods of recession or structural change. During the Asian financial crisis, many small and rural areas were severely hurt. In Fiji, several communities in the east and north have lost population. Citizens — especially the younger generations — have moved out. The result is that community viability is threatened. In spite of higher living costs in the larger cities, people leave small communities because jobs are scarce, salaries are low and other

Table 12.1: Asia's heterogeneous population (people per sq km)

Low Density (0–49)		Medium Density (50–99)		High Density (100–149)		Very High Density (150 and above)	
Australia	2	Uzbekistan	59	Indonesia	114	Nepal	164
Mongolia	2	Brunei	61	Thailand	121	Micronesia	165
Kazakhstan	6	Fr Polynesia	63	China	134	Pakistan	175
Papua New Guinea	10	Cambodia	67	Tonga	138	Korea, Dem. Rep.	194
Turkmenistan	10	Myanmar	68			Vietnam	238
New Zealand	14	Malaysia	69			Philippines	258
Solomon Islands	15					Guam	275
Vanuatu	16					Sri Lanka	294
Bhutan	17					India	336
Lao PDR	22					Japan	336
Kyrgyz Republic	25					Korea, Rep	475
Palau	40					Maldives	925
Fiji	44					Bangladesh	981
Tajikistan	44					Singapore	5,283
						Hong Kong	6,946
						Macau	23,450

Source: World Bank, *World Development Report 2000/2001*, p. 274.

opportunities may be virtually non-existent. As a result, prospects in such places are bleak. But this problem is not limited to low- and medium-density places. Even in Japan, one of Asia's most densely populated nations, rural areas are having difficulty maintaining their populations. Many Japanese farmers have taken to importing brides from Southeast Asia because so few local women choose to live in the rural areas.

The surprising thing is that so few places really try to work out proactive residential-place strategies to combat depopulation trends.

Approaches to Attracting Residents

Every place wants to boast of a high inflow of professionals, managers, technicians, senior officials, administrators and their families. Parallels can be drawn between marketing to attract foreign direct investment and marketing to attract new residents. Integrated approaches, which combine attractions for business and people in the same message, are common. The government of South Australia, for example, promotes the state this way: "South Australia is more than just an investment opportunity. It offers a quality of life that is hard to match in any other city, anywhere in the world. It provides an attractive lifestyle without the overcrowding, pollution and threats to personal security found in many larger cities."[10] Thus, residential offerings — security, cleanliness, convenience — are integrated into the overall place-selling package.

In the battle for talented people, places try a number of appeals. First, they can market their own unique access to talented people, as illustrated by the Philippines' claim: "English is taught in all local schools from the onset, making the Philippines the third-largest English-speaking country in the world. Every year, some 350,000 university graduates, a good number of them engineers, accountants, marketing professionals and IT specialists, join the workforce. Close to 100,000 enroll in IT courses yearly in 643 schools offering IT courses."[11] This theme became very popular throughout Asia in the late 1990s and companies are increasingly selecting well-trained workers over other factors.

Second, places can offer target packages directed towards specific people and their families. Such packages can include various mixes of hard and soft factors (see Figure 12.2). At one extreme, a place may offer very hard factors (no taxes) or it may emphasize soft factors (a lifestyle).

Lifestyle has become a determining factor for many decision-makers. Mark Langhammer, senior vice president of *The Economist*, says, "As an executive with Asia Pacific-wide responsibilities, Singapore is an ideal location to base myself. The positive aspects are well known — central location, excellent communication and business infrastructure, an excellent, well-educated workforce, a safe and clean environment. However, Singapore has also made significant strides to improve other quality-of-life issues such as culture, music and the arts. Given a few more years to develop, Singapore will be a center of excellence in these areas too. For me, lifestyle and balance of work and play is excellent."[12]

Third, a place can offer different levels of relocation services. Sometimes the service is organized and offered exclusively by a public place-selling agency. On the other hand, it may be organized by an independent private company (see Figure 12.1) or by one with a certain alliance to a public agency.

Relocation services will increase in importance in Asia and will be an integral part of other place-attraction programs, but there is no single model for organizing the service.

Figure 12.1: A private relocation service

Source: *Community Magazine*, January–February 2001, p. 4.

Figure 12.2: Two very specific target packages

Example one: Find a Home!

Example two: A World of Possibilities!

Sources:
1 http://www.asiaxpat.com.sg/, viewed on July 5, 2001.
2 http://www.contactsingapore.org.sg/, viewed on July 5, 2001.

DEFINING WHICH POPULATION GROUPS TO ATTRACT

Places vary in the target groups they can and choose to attract. In some cases, they may reach out for the growing (and monied) retirees market. More commonly, they seek skilled professionals and high-income earners. Lately, students have become another target group. Here we examine efforts to attract skilled professionals and certain lifestyle groups.

Targeting Skilled Professionals

A precondition for value-added production and services is the availability of skilled professionals. A place seeking excellence must therefore provide a maximum of attractions for this target group.

The following attractions will make a place desirable to this group: reasonable local taxes, attractive housing options, high educational quality, access to daycare centers, competitive social-security costs and conditions, a positive attitude to newcomers, and relocation services that include efforts to find job opportunities for spouses/partners. This last benefit is often undervalued by the seller. Since, in most families today, both parents are working, an unhappy spouse could discourage the move. Many places also worry that "brain drain" will counter their efforts to attract talent (see Exhibit 12.1).

Exhibit 12.1: REVERSING BRAIN DRAIN

An important issue for all Asian economies is the battle for highly skilled workers. Currently, there are severe and widespread shortages of trained people in the areas of information technology, the professions and the hard sciences. The drain doesn't stop with high-tech, as there are shortages of chefs. The term "brain drain" suggests a place is being sucked dry of its most talented and able people. The implications are ominous. "Countries, like companies, are finding out that having only physical assets won't make them great. It's the intellectual capital that provides the edge," says Boon Chong Na, a consultant with the international firm Hewitt Associates.[1] Consider these facts:

■ India and the Philippines claim that they are experiencing an erosion of talent, not only to the United States and the

European Union, but to other Asian countries as well. Jobs in these competing countries offer the prospect of upward mobility because of escalating salaries and promising business opportunities. According to the Information Technology Association of America, the U.S. IT industry needs an additional 800,000 skilled workers to fill half of the 1.6 million new jobs every year to sustain growth and development. Even India, previously considered a plentiful source of IT talent, will have 2,000,000 unfilled IT jobs by 2006 according to some estimates[2] as a result of the brain drain.

■ India, the Philippines and Malaysia particularly — the principal sources of English-speaking Asian IT talent — increasingly find themselves effectively subsidizing more advanced economies by training valuable IT engineers and programmers only to lose them to the United States, Singapore, Taiwan and South Korea.

■ The U.S., a large-scale importer of IT talent, has now acknowledged the importance of importing the world's brightest minds to maintain its leadership in the IT sector. As a result of intense lobbying by industry leaders such as Microsoft, Intel, Sun, Oracle and others, the U.S. Congress in 2000 almost doubled the number of technology visas issued annually. And although demand for fringe technology work declined after the dot-com bust (just as it did for content management and web design), demand for programmers, database administrators, project managers and system analysts remained strong.[3]

A worldwide battle for talent is on and the most gifted and mobile are looking for challenging opportunities. Filipino MBA graduate Joseph Lacson explained his reason for going to work at Microsoft's Seattle headquarters: "I wanted to work with people who are making a mark in history."[4] Other highly prized talent are attracted by high salaries, cultural environment and additional educational opportunities.

In such a competitive environment, what can a place do to plug the drain? There are places that are successfully addressing market needs and finding solutions. Singapore is attracting large numbers of Asian and East European IT workers because of its skilled, competitively priced workforce, international environment, cleanliness and organization, and proximity to many leisure destinations within Asia. The Singapore Science Park and others like it offer companies ready-made technical communities and make the new recruits comfortable moving into a new environment through a combination of first-rate relocation services, swift approval of visa applications, and an impressive array of leisure alternatives.

China is seeking to reverse its brain drain through serious economic reform, and by actively campaigning to convince talented young emigrants to return home. The government organizes regular visits to campuses and urban centers with large numbers of Chinese nationals as part of a recruitment campaign to lure them back home with the promise of a chance to play key roles in the nation's development.

The irony of the brain drain is that the International Labor Organization reports that many Asian countries have a high unemployment rate. For example, in 1999 India had 40,371,000 unemployed; China 5,750,000; Japan 3,170,000; and the Philippines 2,997,000. Many more were under-employed, filling jobs for which they were overqualified. Multilateral funding agencies such as the Asian Development Bank are moving to enhance job creation by including basic IT training in many of the educational-infrastructure support programs they provide throughout Asia.

The private sector is also investing significantly in IT education, often with multinational IT partners. One example of this is the initiative by IBM and the SM Group in the Philippines to build the Asia Pacific College, an IT training institution. The Reliance Group of companies in India opened the Institute for Information and Communication in Gujarat. The school will offer a high-quality IT education. On an even larger scale, Intel's 'Teach to the Future Program' trains teachers in China, Malaysia, India and other countries to build the capacity to integrate computer technology into classroom curriculum. The purpose of these initiatives is to match available jobs with the labor pool. These efforts demonstrate a commitment to convincing workers to pursue careers in areas in which there is a shortage of talented labor.

There is no sure cure for brain drain. In a fast-moving global economy, places need to find ways that ensure incentives for attracting and maintaining a talented workforce.

Sources:

1 Cesar Bacani, "I.T. Crunch Time: Brace yourselves. Asia's I.T. Crisis will not be solved by the death of the dotcoms and the U.S. slowdown," *Asiaweek*, May 18, 2000, p. 25.

2 *Ibid.*

3 *Ibid.*

4 Interview of Joseph Lacson, April 20, 1999, conducted by Michael Alan Hamlin.

Singapore Science Park. http://www.sciencepark.com.sg/, viewed on March 12, 2001; http://laborsta.ilo.org/cgi-bin/broker.exe, viewed on March 14, 2001.

The increasing number of expatriates in Asia makes them a special target group. Since places want to attract expatriates, a number of place-bound personal-tax concessions are offered by such countries as Malaysia, Taiwan and Singapore. These concessions are applicable only under certain conditions, such as a specified length of stay in the country. This development has taken place in spite of informal efforts to harmonize the general tax levels in Asia. These tax levels vary considerably — from 16% in Hong Kong[13] to as high as 40% elsewhere. Local and regional taxes also differ considerably and can become a major bargaining chip for retention of companies that need to rely on significant numbers of expatriate workers.

The private sector is also contributing significantly to the increasing level of options being made available to expatriates. In the mid 1990s, for example, Asia saw the rise of the serviced-apartment industry, which caters specifically to the needs of long-staying guests. Orientation seminars for expatriates, support groups for their spouses, and social activities are now more available, making adjusting to a new home easier. Surveys and published reports such as the annual *Asiaweek* Salary Survey, William M. Mercer's Quality of Living Survey and the PERC quality-of-life surveys serve as helpful guides for expatriates.

While taxes, housing and transportation are often primary factors in determining relocations, first impressions — such as conditions at the airport — can influence newcomers. Here are the observations of *Time* magazine's Daffyd Roderick on the potential impact of Asian airports on visitors:

> *"Hanging out at an airport is never what you want to be doing. Airports are simply places where you wait to get taken from where you are to where you want to be; they are not destinations, no matter how gussied*

up to look like shopping malls they may be. But delays are inevitable, and the differences between an awful transit airport and a good one are painfully obvious after you've spent a few minutes wandering around. So who has the best transit facilities and who has the worst? We've suffered through all of them, and here's what we think.

Hong Kong. *Open slightly more than two years, Chek Lap Kok is architecturally appealing and extremely efficient at processing travelers. But while it's a great airport if everything goes smoothly, it is deadly boring if you are delayed. Unless you have access to an airline lounge, the eating and drinking options are ridiculously limited. A decent cup of coffee? Not possible. A nice pub for a beer? Forget about it. An oyster at the Oyster Bar? Sorry, it doesn't sell oysters. Plaza Premium Lounge (www.pbc-asia.com) offers full lounge services for $33, including a passable buffet, drinks, Internet access, and resting chairs. Shopping, of course, is plentiful.*

Bangkok. *Don Muang's transit area is not a place you want to be stuck. The seats are uncomfortable — better designed for cleaning than for sitting, although they don't seem to be cleaned very often. And there is little to choose from in terms of food, unless you're a big Burger King fan. If you need to pick up a bottle of Johnny Walker or a carton of Marlboros, this is one of the cheapest sources in Asia. But finding a quiet place to make a phone call is a different story. Spending more than an hour here is as depressing as the poorly lit surroundings.*

Kuala Lumpur. *This colossal white elephant is not a bad place to do a little time. The seats are reasonably comfy, there is plenty of natural light and — since the facility is operating at about half its capacity — there is little in the way of crowds. As in Hong Kong, Plaza runs an airside lounge that includes Internet access, massage chairs, free-pour beer, and inviting chairs and sofas — all for $18. There are plenty of options for duty-free shopping, and it's possible to rent a hotel room by the hour.*

Tokyo Narita. *For years, transiting through Narita felt like punishment. But recent renovations have given the grim senior a face-lift. While the seats around the gates are still clogged with bodies, you can now escape the crowds, or at least avoid someone mistaking your lap for a headrest. On the third floor of Terminal 2, you'll find showers and day rooms as well as a video room. If you're traveling with kids, you can park them in the playroom in the satellite building, or accompany them to take advantage of the 10 Sony PlayStations.*

Seoul. *With the new Inchon airport scheduled to go into service this spring, Kimpo has done little to improve itself in the past few years and it shows. Seats are hard enough to numb your bum and decent distractions are painfully lacking. There are no free lounges and nothing seems to be* *open when you would expect it to be. Not as bad as Don Muang, but a close second with its grim-faced staff and tight security.*

Shanghai Pudong *is China's first attempt at building a modern airport. But while it looks good from the outside, on the inside it's still a work in progress, like a lot of Pudong. The airport is operating at less than 50% capacity, so there is a lot of space but little else. The old airport, Hongqiao, is busier and more convenient but equally dull.*

Singapore. *Changi airport is a testament to the fact that humans in transit don't have to wear a grimace. Simple touches like the separate TV lounges — sports, news and movies — as well as the infrared ports for accessing the Internet make this airport the best in Asia. The quiet areas are shockingly quiet, and the service people are professional and pleasant. It's not as glossy as the airports in Hong Kong or Kuala Lumpur, but Changi is living proof that killing time doesn't have to kill you."*[14]

A place's appeal is often judged on small, seemingly unrelated factors such as the airport. A critical impression can be formed by the scenery from the airport to the city, an unpleasant taxi ride or a rude shopkeeper. The successful place needs to inventory and upgrade the highly visible impressions but account for and fix incidental and accidental negative visitor experiences.

Place buyers' children are often a very important consideration within the family. Therefore, place buyers rank the local availability of top-quality schools very high. This has created competition among local and regional schools to enhance their images. The number of international schools in Asia is increasing, and a place with an international school has a distinct advantage. Table 12.2 indicates the number of international schools in different Asian countries. Many new schools are now in the planning stage.

Several places have adopted the so-called International Baccalaureate (IB) in order to provide a competitive curriculum at the upper secondary level. The founders of the IB were convinced that students needed much more international experience to meet international challenges. In an international community, it is also necessary to have standardized examinations that have worldwide acceptability. Today, 660 schools in over 80 countries have received accreditation to participate in the program, which has its headquarters in Geneva.

A recent trend among Asian countries is the inflow of foreign schools and universities. As Asian places realize the importance of education in boosting their workforce and image, and in creating an intellectual hub, they welcome renowned names in education. Singapore, for example, plays hosts to the University of Chicago Graduate School of Business,

Table 12.2: Number of international schools

Country	No. of Schools	Country	No. of Schools
Australia	23	Mongolia	1
Bangladesh	5	Myanmar	2
Brunei	3	Nepal	6
Cambodia	2	New Zealand	2
China	21	Pakistan	15
Fiji	2	Papua New Guinea	19
Guam	2	Philippines	12
Hong Kong	35	Singapore	16
India	21	South Korea	13
Indonesia	35	Solomon Islands	1
Japan	28	Sri Lanka	7
Kazakhstan	1	Taiwan	14
Kyrgystan	1	Thailand	20
Laos	2	Turkmenistan	1
Macau	1	Uzbekistan	2
Malaysia	19	Vanuatu	2
Marshall Islands	2	Vietnam	5

Source: International Schools The Database. http://www.earl.org.uk/isbi/
international/country/asia.html, viewed on March 5, 2001.

Massachusetts Institute of Technology (MIT), Johns Hopkins University, Georgia Tech and the European Institute of Business Management (INSEAD). Hyderabad in India has affiliations with the Wharton School of Business and J.L. Kellogg Graduate School of Management; while Hong Kong has the Harvard Business School and Kellogg.

A place must also have a good reputation for educational networks, competencies and educational mobility. University Mobility in Asia and the Pacific (UMAP) is an organization that aims for international understanding through increased university student and staff mobility. Through the UMAP Credit Transfer Scheme (UCTS), students are able to study in foreign institutions and gain appropriate credits.[15] The University Mobility in the Indian Ocean Region (UMIOR) program serves a similar function. There are also organizations working towards forming educational networks and improving educational standards. These include the Association of Universities of Asia and the Pacific (AUAP) and the Southeast Asian Ministers of Education Organization (SEAMEO). Most Asian countries also offer student-exchange programs such as the Global Youth Exchange (GYE),[16] Japan's Program of International Educational Exchange (PIEE), the Young Exchange Service (YES) of Thailand[17] and the Southern Cross Cultural Exchange of Australia.[18]

Exploiting such possibilities can lead to increasing a place's profile with education-seeking target markets.

Targeting Lifestyle Groups

In the information age, people have greater choice in where they want to live. As Peter Drucker observed, "It is now infinitely easier, cheaper and faster to do what the 19th century could not do: move information and, with it, office work, to where the people are."[19]

Peter Marsh concludes that, in today's large-scale societies, to a great extent *"you are where you live."*[20] Our place, housing, furnishings and so on, communicate our identity and reflect our values and ideals. According to Marsh, this is particularly important in large-scale, fluid societies where it is more difficult to categorize individuals reliably in terms of accent and clothes; their neighborhood then becomes an important clue to what they are like.

Based on an understanding of lifestyles, a place must learn how to market itself to various individual lifestyle segments. Demographics and a proliferation in types of lifestyle have led to an entire language characterizing attitudes and behaviors. What was a "Hippie" culture (often a rural and idealistic set of preferences) in the 1970s, turned into a "Yuppie" culture (Young Urban Professionals) in the 1980s. Yuppies had a strong preference for city life. Small cities and towns were certainly not on their shopping list. "Dinks" (Dual Income, No Kids) are the family version of yuppies. When they have children, they become "Dewks" (Double Earners With Kids).[21] More lately, the "Puppies" — Poor Urban Professionals — entered the picture during the Asian financial crisis. The Popcorn Report[22] defines yet another powerful lifestyle group: the "Woofs" (Well-Off Older Folks). These middle-aged and wealthy people, born in the boom of the 1940s and rapidly increasing in number, can be a highly attractive target group for many places in Asia.

Another consideration for places involves the impact of information technologies on lifestyles. Futurists ponder on a world consisting of an office-less city where more people are employed at home as independent contractors or tele-workers. The exodus from cities to suburbs as a place of residence and work can already be seen in some Asian cities and regions (although developing Asia suffers from the reverse: too many unskilled rural poor moving to cities). The marketing challenge for large cities is how to slow the exodus and retain certain segments of the urban population. In addition, large cities seek to capture a share of the city-to-city migration of professionals and to bring certain suburbanites back into the city.

Places must adapt to an Asia of movers. While in the past migration tended to result in rural depopulation, more recent evidence indicates a more complicated pattern.[23] Young people entering the labor market tend to migrate from rural areas to regions with more dynamic labor markets and cultural life. At around 30 years of age, there is some reverse migration to native regions. This could give a place — even a remote one — opportunities if there is a strategy in place to provide specific target packages.

Place marketers must constantly segment markets according to consumer attitudes, behavior and lifestyles. Changes in attitudes must also be monitored.

Here are some examples of the kinds of lifestyle interests that can be targeted:

- A drift back to South Korea and other Asian countries was reported in 2000 where a property market weakened by the financial crisis has attracted many foreign place buyers.[24] *(Interest in business)*
- The Asian attraction to gardening (particularly in New Zealand) has increased buying and moving to places where there is a garden tradition. *(Interest in gardening)*
- The massive interest in golf in Asian countries is pushing places and huge regions to exploit special offerings where golf and residential attractions are combined. Thailand, the 'Golf Capital of Asia', actively promotes its golf regions — Bangkok, Pattaya, River Kwai, Hua Hin, Phuket, Chiang Mai and Chiang Rai. *(Interest in golf)*
- Hill Stations/Resorts in Malaysia — the Genting Highlands, Fraser's Hill, the Cameron Highlands and Bukit Larut — and other Asian countries are built for those who wish to escape the overcrowded cities to unwind in a resort. The beach is also a common holiday destination for many in Asia, where beautiful coastlines abound. Beach resorts, homes and villas are actively promoted to city dwellers as weekend getaways. These places are marketed by the countries' national tourism boards. *(Interest in quality of life)*
- The trend towards so-called "Village life in the heart of the big city" is meeting the needs of many young urban professionals. But there are also many older, empty-nesters/Woofs who want to combine city living with some of the best aspects of village life. For example, the outlying islands of Hong Kong (Cheung Chau, Lantau, Lamma and Peng Chau), although sparsely populated in comparison with the main islands, are developing into popular residential areas, attracting those who fancy a slower-paced lifestyle. *(Interest in fashionable village life)*

- Many professionals are looking for residential solutions which can combine a central Asian position and, at the same time, provide all the necessary family conveniences. For example, Whyalla, South Australia's second-largest city, calls itself 'Education City' and boasts a comprehensive selection of educational institutes — from kindergarten through to university — two major shopping centers and numerous shopping districts, and a clean, pollution-free environment. *(Interest in convenient family life)*

CONCLUSION

On the world place market, there is a silent war to attract professionals of all sorts. Asia is part of this global competition, where thousands of overseas places, regions, nations, and continents are trying to promise residential paradise.

Attracting people is likely to become an even more important component in place competition in the years ahead. To be a winner in this competition, place sellers need to understand the underlying dynamics and lifestyles that determine residential market decisions. The place that is successful in attracting highly recruited sectors will benchmark its schools, transportation and people skills against the best of the global competitors.

---

1 http://www.relojournal.com/oct99/expatcenter.htm, viewed on March 7, 2001.

2 *Ibid.*

3 http://www.dsd.tas.gov.au/technology/lifestyle.html, viewed on March 14, 2001.

4 "North-South Divide Gaping in Asian Expatriate Life Too," *The Asian Wall Street Journal*, Internet edition, viewed March 26, 2001.

5 "Government sticks to plan to tax foreigners' overseas income," *Jakarta Post*, Dow Jones Publications Library (Internet), viewed on March 26, 2001.

6 Chen May Yee, "Glitches Zap Malaysian Tech Corridor: Study Says Project Needs to Attract More Key Companies to Achieve Goals," *The Asian Wall Street Journal*, March 26, 2001, p.1.

7 http://apecsec.org.sg/chap2.html, viewed on March 7, 2001.

8 Matthew Forney, "Taipei's Tech-Talent Exodus — It's one China when it comes to getting rich: Taiwan's top brains are crossing the strait," *Time*, May 21, 2001, p. 30.

9 Kathy Wilhelm, "Breaking All Barriers: Mainland Chinese companies are under pressure to build competitive, world-class businesses. For some, it means defying tradition by seeking top managerial talent from abroad," *Far Eastern Economic Review*, April 26, 2001, p. 32.

10 http://www.business.sa.gov.au/quality_living/quality.htm?, viewed on March 6, 2001.

11 http://www.i-philippines.ph/E-Services_Hub_of_Asia/body_e-services_-hub_of_asia.html#Phil, viewed on March 6, 2001.

12 Interview with Mark Langhammer by Michael Alan Hamlin on May 22, 2001.

13 http://www.cfoasia.com/_others/tax.pdf, viewed on March 6, 2001.

14 Daffyd Roderick, "Killing Time: A Guide to Asia's Airports," *Time*, January 8, 2001, p. 6.

15 http://www.umap.org/, viewed on March 9, 2001.

16 http://www.mofa.go.jp/policy/culture/gye/, viewed on March 12, 2001.

17 http://www.y-yes.com/, viewed on March 12, 2001.

18 http://www.scce.com.au/, viewed on March 12, 2001.

19 Peter F. Drucker, "Information and the Future of the City," *Wall Street Journal*, April 4, 1989, p. 14.

20 Peter Marsh, *Life Style — Your Surroundings and How They Affect You*, (London: Sidgwick & Jackson, 1990), p. 144.

21 Diane Crispell, "Guppies, Minks, and Tinks," *American Demographics*, June 1990, p. 51.

22 Faith Popcorn, *The Popcorn Report*, (New York: Harper Business), 1992, p. 46.

23 *Europe 2000, Outlook for the Development of the Community's Territory*, Commission of the European Communities, Brussels, 1991, p. 156.

24 Mark Mitchell, "Property Starts to Stir Again," *Far Eastern Economic Review*, November 9, 2000.

25 http://www.hotelthailand.com/thailand/golfing.html, viewed on March 9, 2001.

26 http://www.whyalla.sa.gov.au/default.htm viewed on March 9, 2001.

C H A P T E R 13

Organizing for Change

I n this book, we have argued that many Asian places — cities, states, regions and entire nations — are facing growing crises and opportunities. As people and businesses become more mobile, they will move toward attractive places and leave unattractive places. The shrinking of time and distance in the global marketplace means that developments in other parts of the world can affect the fortunes of places once thought to be safe. This raises fundamental questions about what places can do to survive and prosper.

Places must routinely re-assess whether they are meeting the needs of their citizens and businesses. Each place must be continually involved in a value-added process. What benefits and attractions need to be added? How is the place helping local citizens and businesses find and create new value? Is the place providing distinctive benefits compared to other places?

Places also have to visualize clearly the roles they play in the local, national and global economy. They have to ask themselves "Who will want to live and work here, under what conditions, and with what expectations?" A place that fails to critically examine its prospects and potential is likely to lose to more attractive competitors.

In this last chapter, we summarize the key challenges facing places and suggest ways in which they might meet these challenges. We specifically address three issues:

- What key challenges are places facing?
- How can places respond positively to these challenges?
- Why is market-oriented planning necessary?

WHAT KEY CHALLENGES ARE PLACES FACING?

Asian places face four major challenges:

Challenge One: **Places are increasingly at risk as a result of the accelerating pace of change in the global economic, political and technological environment.**

There was a time when place residents expected their city, community or region to maintain a permanent business and industrial character. Tomorrow would be much like today. Hong Kong would remain an Asian financial center and manufacturer of low-cost toys, garments and electronics. Singapore would be a contract manufacturer, a components exporter and an Asian meeting place. Japan would continue to be a center for Asian and global electronics and cars. Today, however, place residents have learned that change, not stability, is the only constant. As a result, Hong Kong, Singapore and Japan are in a constant battle to leverage their past successes to enhance their future competitiveness.

The fact is that the locations of global industries keep shifting. Increasingly mobile companies are drawn to places with lower costs, better skills and/or a higher quality of life. China is becoming a huge magnet, "vacuuming foreign investment"[1] (as Philippines secretary for Trade and Development Manuel A. Roxas described it), as well as people and industries. As a result, other Asian countries are now feeling pressure as investments in China grow to around US$45 billion annually, complicating their struggle to re-attain pre-crisis levels of investment. Under these difficult competitive circumstances, other countries (the Philippines, India and Vietnam, among others) must demonstrate their attractiveness to investors as never before.

Privatization and liberalization have taken hold relatively quickly in much of post-crisis Asia and, either by choice or *fait accompli*, it has increasingly welcomed foreign strategic investors in formerly protected sectors. There have been exceptions, notably Malaysia, but how long those exceptions will remain so is a question of increasingly open debate, with other countries, principally Singapore, anxious to pursue free-trade liberalization initiatives.

That pressure to "operationalize" an ASEAN free-trade area and the economies of scale that would result have benefited traditional sectors — though not always the traditional players — which are experiencing new life from an inflow of Greenfield investments. In Rayong province in Thailand, for instance, General Motors, Ford, Toyota and BMW have established major auto-manufacturing plants. More will certainly come and, in the process, will change the Asian map of tomorrow. Meanwhile, once-safe local appliance-makers, garment manufacturers and food processors are under serious threat as a result of the trend toward free trade. Progress demands tradeoffs and, increasingly in Asia, new investments take priority over inefficient domestic producers who don't make the investments required to develop world-class competitiveness — and create jobs.

These local companies frequently try to move elsewhere in their search for lower costs rather than higher productivity at home and also when they are outperformed in their own local area. Companies that once had assured markets now face tough competition from invading multinational organizations, which possess greater resources and offer better products at lower prices.

The heightened mobility of industry is largely due to dynamic advances in information systems, which has facilitated the movement of goods, services, technology and capital across Asian borders. The result has been a dramatic weakening of the traditional barriers of time and distance. Places can no longer expect to retain all their major industries and businesses. They must be ready to abandon shrinking or non-competitive ones and replace them with new and more value-added businesses. When places suddenly discover that there is no way to rejuvenate old steelworks or shipyards — or sustain uncompetitive monopolies — the impact can be traumatic. They must take action before it is too late *and* develop new strengths in advance of reversals.

In the old economy, goods were produced in certain places that enjoyed least-cost advantages. They had distinctive national and often specific place identities. In the new complex economy, goods can be produced in several locations and then assembled in even more places. Robert Reich has observed that "Precision ice-hockey equipment is designed in Sweden, financed in Canada, manufactured out of alloys whose molecular structure was researched and patented in Delaware, fabricated in Japan, and assembled in Cleveland and Denmark for distribution in North America and Europe."[2]

In these complex production situations, the main owner of the ice-hockey brand has the potential to co-brand in more than one place. As Foster's of Australia has accomplished successfully with beers, Sony of Japan with electronics, GM and Ford of the U.S. with automobiles and trucks, the ice-hockey brand can link to any place with a natural winter-sports image.

While processing, interpreting and analyzing the information in other places, service producers can also draw information from multiple places and disseminate the information to still other places. Twenty-four hours a day, the Hong Kong office of discount brokerage Charles Schwab transfers information to its San Francisco offices so that Asia-based clients can execute and pay for securities trades. AOL's call center at the former Clark airbase in the Philippines answers calls all night long from around the world. TrendMicro's anti-virus experts attack the latest viruses in Manila almost as fast as rogue software programmers build and release them.

The initial trend was for corporations to move their back-office operations from cities to suburbs. Under increasing cost pressures, they moved these offices to low-cost regions. Many of these regions have managed to provide high productivity and even world-class excellence in their new niche. Clusters of back-office companies have settled in certain parts of Asia and given these places a new industry and a new image. An increasing number of large companies are outsourcing their information systems to capture value from specialized firms and technologies. This move opens additional opportunities for places with excellent service clusters.

Places are further influenced by significant political developments. The end of the Cold War meant the political decentralization of the socialist government of the Soviet Union. In the months before the formal decentralization and dissolution of the U.S.S.R. in December 1991, the states in Central Asia declared their independence one by one. The newly formed independent countries had initial success in handling their newfound freedom from the centralized Soviet government, but deep-rooted problems, especially in the political and economic arena, continue to delay any positive developments in the area. Especially in this area, strategic place marketing is essential and new niches must be developed.

For most of the rest of Asia, the collapse of the Soviet Union resulted in the rapid evolution of a major competitor — China — as the limitations of a closed, centrally planned economy gave way to a rapidly opening market economy. The government of China had no intention of making the same mistake as the old U.S.S.R. Suddenly, the risk of balancing economic freedom against political freedom was no longer worth taking: there seemed to be no other choice.

The fundamental point is that external forces change rapidly and often unexpectedly, transforming the fate and fortunes of places. Industry and market cycles, trade policies and fluctuating national currencies add to these uncertainties.

Challenge Two: **Places are increasingly at risk as a result of the inevitable process of urban evolution and decay.**
Most places started off as rural-agricultural communities, became towns

and then grew into cities and metropolitan areas. In the modern period, cities transformed from trade centers to industrial centers and then to service producers. As problems within the city expand — pollution, crime, congestion, traffic gridlock, poor schools and services, higher taxes and unemployment — an increasing movement to the suburbs occurs. However, as a result of ambitious public and private urban-redesign projects, more recent trends suggest a return to the inner cities of developed Asia.

Meanwhile, metropolitan growth continues from inner-ring suburbs to outer-ring exurbs. As factories and offices move farther out, clean well-functioning "edge cities" emerge around the core city. In many cases, such "edge cities" have begun forming their own urban identity. A century ago, major technological changes occurred that transformed and benefited urban growth: electricity, the internal-combustion engine, subways, indoor plumbing and sanitation systems, elevators, and steel-structured buildings. Today, new technologies have emerged that allow economic activity to occur almost anywhere: satellite communications, fiber optics, mobile phones, the Internet and microcomputers. Most Asian places have worked to adopt these technological breakthroughs early on and, as a result, are managing to turn the challenge into a competitive edge.

Challenge Three: **Places are facing a growing number of competitors in their efforts to attract scarce resources.**
In the face of mounting problems, places have responded by establishing specialized economic-development agencies — planning, financing, marketing, tourism, exports — all related to place improvement. At least 1,000 regional and national agencies operate in Asia today. Nobody has managed to calculate exactly how many there are at the local community level. As a rule, however, at least some rudimentary organization exists within most communities. These agencies and units spend public funds for advertising and send salespeople on missions at home and abroad to attract resources to their area. But they soon discover that other places are matching or exceeding their own efforts and level of sophistication. The stark reality is that there is a superabundance of place sellers hunting for a limited number of place buyers.

Place buyers have access to a growing number of information sources about places — including place ratings, real-estate interests, consultants, and new software technologies that provide highly sophisticated and usable data. They make careful comparisons of what each place seller offers, including costs of doing business, inducements and quality-of-life benefits. Place buyers may end up demanding such high concessions from a place that what appears to be a final winner may in fact turn out to be a loser. Place-inducement battles occur on all continents. In Asia, such battles have exploded as a consequence of Asia's financial crisis, globalization and political pressures to liberalize protected markets and sectors. For instance, Malaysia has frequently sought to slow the transition to free trade, particularly in the automotive sector. Its intent is to protect its money-losing national car program. In doing so, it is irritating Thailand and, potentially, exposing itself to World Trade Organization sanctions requiring that it compensate its neighbor. When Singapore became frustrated with the slow pace of reform, it began negotiating bilateral free-trade agreements with New Zealand — signed in 2000 — and Australia, as well as with the U.S. It already had free-trade agreements with Canada, Mexico and Israel. Despite efforts to slow reform, Asian places are responding to the competitive marketplace with an ever-widening array of agreements. As a result, the slower players may be left without favorable trade agreements and, ironically, free trade may be constrained.

Places have to rethink the premises upon which they base their future. More importantly, they have to learn more about targeting customers if they are to be successful in attracting and retaining businesses and people, exporting their products, and promoting tourism and investments. Every place must recognize the nature of a free market rivalry and hone its skills as a competitor.

To win, places must respond to change rather than resist it; adapt to market forces rather than ignore them. This is not an easy task for Asian community organizations, which traditionally have very little experience with market orientation, the investment climate and business life in general. In many cases, the local public sector tends to live a separate life from the private sector. This is often considered to be the classical Asian situation. It has to change, fast.

Challenge Four: **Places have to rely increasingly on their own local resources to face growing competition.**
Current trends and forces pull businesses, much like nations, in two directions simultaneously. "Think globally — act locally" represents the new paradigm in which businesses must practice and apply globalism in outlook and operation, and localism in business practices and market differences. Asian nations are pulled together by the imperatives of trading blocs and the need for common rules, but are pulled apart by parochial interests and provincial needs. Places also encounter the full force of these centripetal and centrifugal pressures from business and higher government levels that end up producing a reversal of the

preceding maxim: "Think locally — act globally." The place paradigm requires, first, an understanding of what a place has or can have that someone else needs or wants and, second, a translation of these advantages to broader selected audiences.

Because many Asian governments are preoccupied with a huge debt burden, they are less able than in previous decades to provide substantial direct aid to local communities. Even if such resources existed, the ability of national government and other central bodies to target and tailor specific resources to meet individual place needs is fraught with distribution and equity considerations. Furthermore, since all business originates in a specific place, it is impossible to grasp such combinations from a central position outside the particular place. Business intelligence can be generated on a global level, but its commercial exploitation is always made locally. How a place meets these global opportunities can be called the "business intelligence" of a place.

HOW MUST PLACES RESPOND TO THESE CHALLENGES?

We have seen earlier how places can be transformed: Bangalore from Garden City to South Asia IT hub; Taiwan from low- to high-quality, globally competitive electronic and high-tech products; Sepang from a palm-oil plantation to the site of the F1 Circuit and the new Kuala Lumpur International Airport; Thailand from a one-sided dependence on tourism to a broadened industrial base with a dominant automobile sector. Such Asian lessons are quickly disseminated and serve to substantiate the fact that places can deliberately affect their mix of business.

A place's condition is never hopeless; all places have some actual or potential resources to exploit. To turn fortunes around, places must think in the longer term and choose their short-term actions to deliver their long-range perspective.

To assist Asian place development in the years ahead, we propose the following ten responses that constitute a framework for navigating place development in the 21st century.

Response One: **Places need to establish a strategic vision to face these challenges.**
Very few places today can articulate a strategic vision of what they are aiming to be in the next 10 or 20 years. Asia has hundreds of major and minor ethnic groups who want prosperous industries, increased real incomes and a better quality of life. But this is a wish or hope, not a vision. A vision must define a realistic picture of what they can become in the next decade and beyond as a place to live, work and play. A vision

goes beyond simply targeting specific businesses that the public would like to see locate in a place. On the other hand, a strategic vision should not be so general that it fails to create a precise goal around which people can organize. The articulation of the vision should be localized to the specific place. If most other Asian places can identify with the same vision, it is in some ways meaningless for the specific place — even if it "sounds good." Exhibit 13.1 is an example of a carefully crafted vision.

Exhibit 13.1: VISION AND THE COMMITTEE ON SINGAPORE'S COMPETITIVENESS

Singapore is a "wired" island. The rapid development of telecom and Internet infrastructure in Singapore is the product of several factors. First, it's a small nation, both in physical and population terms. A national infrastructure-development program for Singapore naturally can take place much faster than it would, say, in Indonesia, a vast land with a diverse population. Second, Singapore has had very clear ideas of what it wants to be. For example, the Committee on Singapore's Competitiveness (CSC) — a joint public- and private-sector initiative — was charged with developing a vision for making the island's economy world class. Its national vision has just three components:

1. It is globally competitive.
2. It is knowledge-based.
3. It has manufacturing and services as the twin engines of growth.

In a statement announcing its vision, the committee explained: "the CSC's vision is for Singapore to develop into an advanced and globally competitive knowledge-economy within the next decade, with manufacturing and services as the twin engines of growth. To realize this vision, we require a quantum jump in capabilities while managing our cost competitiveness."[1]

If it's able to achieve this, CSC's vision continues, Singapore, as a knowledge-based economy, "will have a strong entrepreneurial base; an open cosmopolitan society attractive to global talent and well-connected to other global knowledge nodes. Companies operating in Singapore will be able to leverage a cost-competitive, motivated workforce with world-class capabilities in business management, technology, innovation, production and services, and international market development."[2]

This vision is straightforward, readily understandable and, most importantly, balanced nicely between an approach that is too detailed and one that runs the risk of being too general. Aside from these broad goals, the vision is broken down into eight strategic initiatives:

1. Promote manufacturing and services as the twin engines of growth, reducing vulnerability and providing a broader economic base.
2. Globalize Singapore's economy through expansion and acquisition of resources outside the country.
3. Require local companies to be world-class.
4. Develop mid-market enterprises.
5. Develop the value-added attributes (skills, conceptual thinking innovation, R&D) of the workforce.
6. Leverage science, technology and innovation as competitive tools.
7. Optimize allocation of scarce resources.
8. Encourage government to play a supportive, but active, role in development.

These elements together combine to ensure that the vision is a serious effort.

Sources:

1 Committee on Singapore's Competitiveness, http://www.gov.sg/mti/competitiveness/content-1.html, viewed April 24, 2001.
2 *Ibid.*

Strategic initiatives paraphrased from: Committee on Singapore's Competitiveness, http://www4.gov.sg/mti/cscrel.html, viewed April 24, 2001.

Response Two: **Places need to establish a market-oriented strategic planning process to face these challenges.**

All places engage in some form of planning whether driven by fiscal, physical or social needs. Some places suffer from too many plans and planning groups. Over-planning can occur when planning replaces leadership. So long as "plans are being made," some organizations can avoid dealing with real problems and conflicts of implementation and, consequently, never become fully and effectively market-oriented.

Fundamental differences exist between the public and the private sectors in their relation to resource allocation. Most public organizations get their resources via complex budget processes with little or no direct dialogue with customers. Businesses, on the other hand, are influenced by their customers every day. Elected public officials receive their customers' opinions every third or fourth year and, in many cases, these opinions emanate from organized groups with specific interests. These characteristics of public organizations can work against long-term planning and a broader place perspective.

Consequently, in a place's desperation to find planning answers, various quick fixes emerge to span a short-term planning horizon and placate various interest groups. The most common ones are business attractions such as a new plant; major capital projects ranging from sports stadiums to convention centers; a new tourist attraction such as a festival market; reorientation of retail operations into a mall; or casino gambling; or theme parks. Often certain interest groups, a developer, an entrepreneur or a potential place buyer initiates such projects. When the prospect of lost opportunities is felt, it is tempting to take immediate action.

These initiatives have the virtue of appearing to address one or more problems. They often deliver symbolic comfort to the citizens that specific action is being taken to secure a better future. After all, the message of immediate jobs is far more persuasive than the message of receiving durable or higher-paying jobs in the future. Yet, many such actions turn out to be boondoggles or white elephants. More often than not, they fail to meet most tests of a viable plan for improving the community. Often such stopgap measures offer a vague hope of triggering a host of other improvements that may or may not follow. Yet the "build and they will come" appeal makes no more sense for real-estate development than it did for overall place development in the 1980s. Rarely do these proposals deliver a full solution to the community's problems. They do not deal with, but seek to avoid, more basic issues such as suburban flight, rural depopulation, increasing unemployment, deteriorating educational and transportation systems, and inadequate housing.

Clearly, places need to assign higher importance to the strategic-planning process that moves beyond meeting the electoral needs of the moment to incorporating the broader perspectives of the marketplace into place planning. Strategic market planning can serve as the guiding force in developing a place's future — as a screen for both filtering and ranking specific actions or proposals that inevitably arise. Places need to keep themselves from habitually reacting to proposals for change and strive to be proactive in what they can do. This is not to ignore the reality of politics but, rather, to balance political needs with market forces. The place needs to identify its resources, opportunities and natural customers. It must construct scenarios of its potential futures and determine a path that will confer competitive advantages.

***Response Three*: Places must adopt a genuine market perspective toward their products and customers.**
Asia is moving toward a more market-oriented, consumer-driven economy. Each place must understand its potential customers' needs, perceptions, preferences and buying decisions. Even publicly owned airlines, telecommunications companies and energy utilities are becoming increasingly market-driven, while many are becoming privatized in order to speed or facilitate this transformational process. The speed of change is often dramatic in both developing and developed Asian economies.

In an era when the public sector is asked to do more with less, governments and communities are compelled to think and plan more like businesses. They need to calculate the actual costs of their services and apportion them through prices to determine demand levels. They must generate more of their own resources through the sale of services and seek to reduce costs through user fees and contracted services — though not at the expense of quality. They also may need to get out of certain public businesses and eliminate programs that no longer meet the public's needs. They are learning the business of converting *spending* thinking into *investment* thinking, whether through preventive actions to avoid more costly remedies later or through allocating resources to where they have highest returns. With a market orientation, a place sees itself as serving and meeting the needs of customers and directing resources towards the welfare of its citizens.[3]

Places ultimately thrive or languish based on what they do to create skilled, motivated and satisfied citizens. Human capital is emerging as the most vital resource places possess or can develop in place competition. Places that turn unskilled workers into skilled labor, promote innovation and entrepreneurship, and provide lifelong education and training gain a competitive advantage in the new economic order. The important industries of the future that specialize in the commercial application of new technologies will locate places that have a supply of skilled workers. Places that do little else but nurture an educated and trained labor force may do far more to enhance their competitive advantages over the longer run than those making a series of one-time investments in a single employer or a single capital investment.

Genuine market perspectives must be integrated in the place-marketing strategies. This can be difficult when true market orientation has such a short tradition and where a market approach might be greeted with the political distrust that can still be found within many Asian places.

Response Four: **Places have to build quality into their programs and services to compete with other places.**

On a day-to-day basis, people judge a place by the quality of its everyday services, not so much by its grand vision. Their impressions come from how easily the traffic moves, how clean the city air and streets are, how good the education system is, and how accessible cultural and recreational amenities are. Quality services are noted by the residents and business firms but also by those considering moving to, visiting or investing in a place. The same principle holds true for the tourism-hospitality business where competition intensifies as more places make the physical investments necessary to enhance their relative attractiveness. Beyond infrastructure, success turns increasingly on the quality of the services provided by industry and public sectors alike.

When standards of living rise, citizens generally develop higher expectations of performance. In weighing relocation decisions, businesses place increasingly more value on quality-of-life considerations than on cost factors alone. Service quality, therefore, requires continuous investments in infrastructure as well as in various amenities — museums, theaters, sports, entertainment, libraries, recreation facilities — to maintain a competitive posture. The fact that tax revenues and borrowing often do not accommodate such needs makes it even more necessary to adopt a market-planning perspective. Those places that figure out how to create and deliver high quality in their various services are much more formidable competitors in place competition. It is striking how small a role quality service has taken in Asian place-marketing strategies. This inattention is apparent in personal service, and the handling of cases, applications and requests for assistance and information in local governmental organizations. Quality in these instances is important in setting the image of a place.

For many places, the transition to a strategic market-planning perspective is an evolutionary one. It often begins with opening up public services to competition, moving to some privatization and adopting total quality management (TQM) principles for service delivery, and even learning how to manage and strengthen relationships with customers: the public. Once the skills of greater competitiveness and customer orientation are internalized, places are far more likely to adopt a customer orientation in marketing themselves externally. The mindset of markets and the meeting of identifiable needs can carry over from one to the other (see Exhibit 13.2).

Exhibit 13.2: IMPROVING PUBLIC-SECTOR SERVICE QUALITY

Public organizations, being largely monopolistic in character, often have problems with being responsive to the needs and service requirements of their citizens. A number of mechanisms can help the public sector become more responsive:

1) *Outsourcing* various public service functions in order to buy the best available solution on the market. For example, consider the community switchboard. A dramatic improvement in service quality can be secured via the city call center, which can be turned into a professional call center. To the delight of citizens, public services can be delivered even after 5 pm. The call center can provide a multitude of services in a coordinated way: answering questions regarding building codes, providing information about the minutes and protocols of a community meeting, elderly care, day care, utility bills, and so on. Tourism information and reservations — in different languages — are other quality improvements within reach via a place-related call center.

2) *A voucher system*, where citizens receive a basic credit that they can choose to spend on the public service or a competing private service. With Internet access, citizens are able to scan the regional or local market in a much easier and more convenient way.

3) *Warranties*, where a public agency is required to compensate aggrieved citizens for personal losses or inconveniences caused by the agency. Here are some warranties that already exist in Asia:

- If the Japanese *Shinkansen,* or Bullet Train, cancels trains or runs them excessively late, passengers may be compensated for their ticket cost by receiving a voucher for off-peak travel.
- Maintenance and repairs or replacement of garbage bins are taken care of by the Monash City Council (Australia) at no cost where bins have been subject to normal deterioration.

4) *Decentralization,* the classic approach to improving service quality. Quicker and more flexible responses are major advantages flowing from decentralization.
5) *Total quality management,* sometimes introduced in a systematic way within communities.
6) *Quick service,* an appreciated way of giving a public authority a positive image. One such example is the immediate processing and issuance of 30-day tourist visas for most visitors arriving at the Maldives' Airport.

A place searching for an identity can maximize its relationships with its citizens by introducing often low-cost, commonsense remedies that will pay big dividends.

Sources:

Shinkansen *Frequently Asked Questions* Web page, http://www2.neweb.-ne.jp/wc/dolittle/byunbyun/faq.htm, viewed on March 29, 2001; *Monash City Council* Web site, http://www.monash.vic.gov.au/services/garbage1.html; Maldives — Consular Information Sheet, February 22, 2001, www.travel.state.gov/maldives.html, viewed on March 29, 2001.

Response Five: **Places need skill to communicate and promote their competitive advantages effectively.**

Having quality and being attractive is one thing; communicating the special quality of a place to others is quite another. Places must skillfully position themselves for those various buyers who may wish to locate, invest, live or do business there. They must adapt their messages to highly differentiated place buyers and, at the same time, develop a core image of what the place basically offers. Take, for example, two concepts mentioned earlier: Siargao, "Surfing Capital of Asia," and West Bengal,

"Gateway to the East." For specific target groups, such concepts have a distinct meaning. The Philippines is marketing itself as the "Call Center Hub of Asia." This is not only a highly visual image, it is also an emerging, virtual trademark. Hong Kong markets itself using an actual image: a dragon symbol accompanied by the tagline "Asia's World City".

Many Asian places have summarized their attractions in a concept that is consistently communicated. The concept must be built on a combination of unique place attractions and must be drawn from actual attributes of the place.

A place concept must be carefully handled. As we have illustrated through product brands such as Foster's of Australia, Anchor Dairy of New Zealand, Tiger Beer of Thailand, Lee Kum Kee of China (Hong Kong), and Mikimoto Pearls of Japan, a strong place concept has enormous value. A code of usage should surround the chosen place concept. Communication programs should be carefully planned and coordinated by a local or regional body that has a high degree of acceptance among influential public and private organizations.

Response six: **Places need to diversify their economic base and develop mechanisms for adapting flexibly to changing conditions.**
Places cannot rely on one or a few miscellaneous industries or businesses on which to base their future. Industries quickly rise and fall with technological changes, and they can respond quickly to productive advantages found elsewhere in Asia or on the global place market. The challenge that places must take up is that of building a well-balanced portfolio of businesses.

Porter identifies the challenge: "Nations succeed not in isolated industries, but in clusters of industries connected through vertical and horizontal relationships."[4] *Clustering* has become a key concept for positioning a place's business mix. Developing clusters is usually the responsibility of local and regional places rather than nations, which are usually too distant from commercial realities. By "clustering" we do not mean the old notion of similar industries gathered in one place. Modern clustering involves the sharing of new technologies, services and infrastructures across industries. Such sharing can be organized in a unique way and thereby create a set of competitive advantages for a place.

Places must identify trends and emerging needs that can influence new cluster developments. Effective local leadership must be concerned, at least partly, with the question of how competitive place intelligence can be stimulated and exploited.

Response Seven: **Places must develop and nurture entrepreneurial characteristics.**

Place development is spurred by entrepreneurial people and organizations. Most observers, irrespective of their political alignment, agree that in the shadow of high Asian unemployment and the lack of a dynamic labor market, places need to attract small business and entrepreneurship. Neil Peirce and Robert Guskind identified the ten best-managed cities in the U.S. The major feature that these cities had in common was the nurturing of an entrepreneurial spirit, where city mayors and managers matched their private-sector counterparts in market-driven thinking. "Most important," noted the authors, "all of the nation's best-run cities are characterized by managerial leadership that has set the stage for economic advances that make these cities masters of their own destiny."[5]

The talent of local leadership is consistently found to be the key explanation behind winning places in Asia. Some characteristics of entrepreneurial places and their public-sector orientation are shown in Tables 13.1 and 13.2.

Response Eight: **Places must rely more on the private sector to accomplish their tasks.**

Increasingly, local and regional businesses are participating in strategic place-marketing processes. Even now in Asia, the most common scenario is — at least in practice — that the public sector works within its own references, although there is some evidence that this is changing, especially in such places as Hong Kong, Singapore and the Philippines. Even Japan is coming around. Still, while the business sector and its representatives have contacts with the public sector, close and joint place

Table 13.1: Characteristics of entrepreneurial places

Economy	Open, fluid, low barriers to start-ups.
Social structure	Dynamic, mobile, outsiders welcome.
Business	No dominant employer, competitive.
Financial	Competitive banks, access to venture capital.
Labor	Skilled labor, professional workforce, support.
Government	Support small business, start-ups.
Innovation	Large university, corporate research center.
Media	Attention to entrepreneurs, new business.
Jobs	Grow new businesses, small business growth.
Amenities	Good quality of life, culture/recreation.

Sources: David L. Birch, "Thriving on Adversity," *Inc.*, March 1988, pp. 80–84, and Joel Kotkin, "City of the Future", *Inc.*, April 1987, pp. 56–60.

Table 13.2: Characteristics of an entrepreneurial public sector

Finances	Modest taxes, high bond ratings.
Managers	Thinkers, visionaries, politicians, salespersons.
Services	High quality, innovative, competitive.
Culture	High citizen participation, open.
Styles	Professional, results oriented.
Bureaucracy	Entrepreneurial, new ways to do things.
Spending	Investments, performance, outcomes.
Citizens	Consumers, stockholders.
Planning	Anticipation multiyear, strategic.
Responsiveness	Good listeners, negotiators, accountability.

Source: Adapted from Neil Peirce and Robert Guskind, "Hot Managers, Sizzling Cities," *Business Month*, June 1989, pp. 36–53.

development is not particularly common. Where this does exist, it is often as a mechanism intended to demonstrate private-sector support for government policy. (For years, Japan's Ministry of International Trade & Industry claimed to dictate to the private sector strategies for development, but that was hardly a truly joint effort. Nor was it particularly successful, as Porter and Hirotaka Takeuchi demonstrate).[6] Too frequently, close relationships between the public and private sectors represented the channeling of opportunity to favored corporations and their executives by government.

Public-private partnerships emerged in the 1960s and 1970s in the U.S. In Asia, a genuine cross-sector approach at the local and regional levels began to appear in the early 1990s, and accelerated somewhat after the 1997 Asian Financial Crisis. Today, we can see joint approaches where public place representatives are forming partnerships with banks, utilities, leading local enterprises, chambers of commerce, and other regional or local business organizations. In 1997 — after many years of only slow growth in any truly meaningful public-private sector cooperation in Asia — the Pacific Economic Cooperation Council hosted the first Asia Pacific Information Technology Summit. One of the aims of the summit was to provide a venue for corporate business leaders and government officials to discuss the development and promotion of IT in the region, as well as to suggest measures to enhance Asia's competitiveness as a base for IT. Such initiatives from the industrial sector marked the growing broader interest of businesses to participate, on a practical level, in areas that traditionally had been reserved for the public sector. A new climate has slowly developed where joint efforts — local, regional and national — have become more natural.

Such joint efforts are more common in Asian places today. Yet there are still many places where public-sector actors often cling to old roles as custodians of public works driven by outdated values inconsistent with today's economic and commercial realities. Risk-taking, competitiveness, entrepreneurship and leadership are neglected and even avoided. These things, too, are often assumed to be things "taken care of by the business community." In some nations and regions in Asia, far-reaching privatization programs have changed the traditional roles completely. This is especially true in China where, before 1989, state-owned industries "accounted for about two-thirds of economic output,"[7] but by 2000 accounted for just 28%. "The once-minuscule private sector now accounts for one-third of output and is the main driver of job growth."[8]

Response Nine: **Each place needs to develop its unique change processes that arise from differences in its culture, politics and leadership processes.**
Different places cannot simply apply formulaic approaches to planning their future. Each place has its own history, culture, values, public bodies, institutions, leadership, and systems of public and private decision-making. Strategic market planning inevitably takes a different form in Xiamen than in Karachi. Each place has to sort out how best to promote innovation, how to take the necessary actions to produce change and how to form alliances that will get various publics to accept and support change. The need for vital services can sometimes have surprising results (see Exhibit 13.3).

Exhibit 13.3: IT TAKES A VILLAGE

That title is not original. It first appeared, in this form at least, as the headline of an article in the January 12, 2001 issue of *Asiaweek*. The article chronicled the surprisingly high-tech story of Yamada Village in Japan, a small town with an aging population where residents are snowed into their homes through most of every winter. The citizens have embraced the Internet because it allows them to communicate with each other, and the outside, during those lonely months. The technology also assures elderly villagers of regular medical attention in the comfort of their homes, dramatically reducing time-consuming, costly, and frequently very difficult trips to a clinic or hospital.

The story is an example of how circumstances often conspire to bring about unexpected results. Although Internet penetration is high in Japan and continues to grow dramatically — in large part because of the popularity of NTT DoCoMo's all-the-time wireless i-mode Internet service — New Economy stereotypes don't associate leading-edge technology with quaint mountain villages populated mostly by senior citizens. Instead, we think of ambitious projects such as Singapore One, the island-nation's broadband network; Malaysia's Multimedia Super Corridor (MSC); and Pacific Century Cyberworks' (PCCW) CyberPort.

The problem with these modern stereotypes, of course, is that they aren't very accurate. Singapore One signed up just 12,000 subscribers in its first year. It had expected 400,000 households to be connected. Despite the popularity of dial-up access — penetration is the highest in Asia at 49.1% — the practical benefits of the more expensive broadband technology just aren't apparent to most Singaporeans. The MSC is largely uncompleted, and investment is a fraction of what was originally projected. The CyberPort won't begin operations for another two years, and there are concerns over whether its parent will be much more than a telecom player and real-estate developer before it is completed, rather than the pan-Asia Internet, technology, and entertainment powerhouse investors originally expected.

Most of Asia's governments, as elsewhere, agree that Internet penetration is an indicator of prosperity, educational attainment and what might be called New Economy aptitude, or the capacity to continuously embrace technology-driven change and its impact on work and lifestyle. But what does it take to catalyze consumer acceptance of the technology?

In Yamada Village, it was the promise of interaction and access to medical and other services during the long, lonely winter months. But once the technology became a way of life, it became a fixture of life all year long. The popularity of DoCoMo's i-mode provides another glimpse into what stimulates people to embrace technology: meaningful, relevant interaction any time and all the time users want. Aside from always being on, services are practical, simple and plentiful. But for others, especially in developing Asia, Internet-based services can be the difference between life and death. Take for example the case of Thoung Pou, a resident of the hamlet of Robib in northern Cambodia. Two years ago, Robib, six hours from Phnom Penh, was inaccessible to outsiders. Recently, however, Thoung Pou and about 30 other residents sent their medical information and digital photos to a medical facility in Boston over the Internet. As a result, Thoung Pou's 10-month-old daughter was immediately diagnosed with life-threatening tuberculosis, and arrangements were made to transfer the infant to a provincial hospital.

"I don't know what the Internet is," says Thoung Pou; "I just know my situation would have been hopeless [without the project]."[1] The project is an effort by journalist-turned-philanthropist Bernard Krisher to bridge the digital divide with the help of American Assistance for Cambodia and Japan Relief for Cambodia. Together, they've brought computers — powered by solar panels and generators — and the Internet — via a satellite dish donated by a Thai communications company — to tiny Robib.

Aside from the medical benefits, Robib's schoolchildren connect to the outside world using e-mail and the Web, and villagers participate in e-commerce through their own Web site, www.villageleap.com. The first US$6,000 raised through selling handcrafted silk products to overseas buyers was used to set up a pig farm. "The Internet is helping develop a whole village in a remote area of Cambodia,"[2] says Krisher.

Such efforts are increasingly common in Asia, which already accounts for 33% of the world's Web surfers, more than Europe or America. In India, M.S. Swaminathan brought the Internet to the Indian village of Veerampattinam, along with crop prices, e-mail and weather forecasts, which are broadcast by a volunteer over a public address system. Pannerselvan, a village fisherman, remarks, "When the computer says that there will be a storm, there has always been a storm. We all believe in it."[3] And all are much safer as a result.

Former bureaucrat turned activist Lin Mui Kiang installed computer kiosks in the small Malaysian village of Kampung Raja Musa, 120 kilometers south of Kuala Lumpur. "Guided by icons, villagers use the terminals to access a database that covers subjects like dressmaking and farm management. The ease with which the database can be navigated fulfills a vital criterion: that the terminals be accessible not only to the computer-literate, but to the illiterate, period."[4]

While efforts like these are certainly generous, they also make good business sense according to Grameen Bank founder Muhammad Yunus: "Imagine if the three billion people who live on less than US$2 a day could come into the market, not just as consumers but as producers too — imagine how big the market would be."[5] What appears to drive technological change is not the need for large corporations to maximize profits with huge installations; rather, it's a fundamental need for people to communicate and to solve important problems.

Sources:

1 "Bernard Krisher: Healing the Killing Fields," *Asiaweek*, June 29, 2001, p. 40.

2 *Ibid.*

3 Sanjay Kapoor, "M.S. Swaminathan: Brain Food for the Masses", *Asiaweek*, June 29, 2001, p. 35.

4 Arjuna Ranawana, "Lin Mui Kiang: Defender of the Poor," *Asiaweek*, June 29, 2001, p. 36.

5 Yasmin Ghahremani, "Heroes of the Digital Divide," *Asiaweek*, June 29, 2001, p. 34.

Mutsuko Murakam, "I.T. Takes a Village," *Asiaweek*, January 12, 2001, p. 46; edited by Gabelle Lam and Kelvin Fung, "Asia's Growing Digital Divide," *Asiaweek*, June 29, 2001, p. 48.

Most places experience common barriers to change: inertia, lack of vision and political consensus, a scarcity of resources, and inadequate organizational machinery and skills that will lead to change. Overcoming barriers depends on favorable events, trends and various catalysts for change — an election, new leaders, the media, and new organizations or the evolution of older ones.

In spite of their differences, all places have to pay attention to certain basic imperatives:

1) Scarcity of resources necessitates a certain *consolidation* of place-development activities, both within the community organization and

between the community and the private sector. Consolidation provides opportunities to broaden participation, refine and focus place-development strategies, pool resources and better leverage transactions.

2) Places need greater *continuity and consistency* in their approaches to place development, which means institutionalizing ways for leadership to emerge. Through consolidation, partnerships and the emergence of lead organizations, the professionalization of both public and private leaders can develop. Place development is frequently associated with recognized leaders who come from a variety of sectors.

3) Places need to *reach beyond their geopolitical boundaries* to leverage their resources, attack common problems and share collective benefits. Tourism, convention businesses, airports, bridges, and so on, often consolidate activities beyond the community areas. An individual region, or some regions in a joint effort, may support such a project. In some cases individual projects go far beyond national boundaries, as with the Malaysia-Singapore Second Crossing. Concept-building — for example, Australia and New Zealand Wine Tours (in several wine-producing regions of each country); Star Cruises (cruises around Asia-Pacific countries); Orient-Express Trains and Cruises (luxury train journeys in historical and exotic Southeast Asian destinations) — has increasingly extended beyond an individual community because of the necessity to share resources and develop a critical mass. More complex structures are also emerging. For example, "The Silk Road" is a joint concept made up of the World Tourism Organization and 19 participating countries covered on the historical route. In 1994, the Samarkand Declaration on Silk Road Tourism was adopted and a long-term tourism program was launched. Such programs, involving innovative regional networks that extend beyond traditional boundaries, will certainly grow in number and importance in the future.

Response Ten: **Places must develop organizational and procedural mechanisms to sustain place development and maintain momentum once it has begun.**

Strategic market planning requires patience and persistence. It will be many years before Malaysia and Hong Kong will see results from investments in building and marketing their image as information-technology hubs. Even though it will take decades for China to change its image and completely transform itself into a market economy, we are witnessing huge investments in Guangzhou, Shanghai and other areas.

Other places undergoing change are the resort regions of Thailand — Pattaya, Phuket, Chiang Mai and Hat Yai — which are expanding their hospitality industry to make room for conventions and exhibitions. Such a transformation will require time and skillful organizational effort.

There is a danger that an impatient public can become discouraged, change its elected leaders and revert to preferences for quick fixes. Because there is no magic formula for place development, we can only learn from the past successes and mistakes of others and ourselves. As historians have long noted, democracies tend to meet crises effectively, which therefore enables leaders to lead and allows power to be temporarily concentrated. This pattern is apparent when we study local political leaders in places where huge structural crises have occurred. On the other hand, democratic institutions tend to work poorly in places that are not in crisis. There, checks and balances can create stalemates, if not paralysis.

Sustaining momentum can be difficult in the face of success. As a community experiences some initial progress, it may become complacent and relax its efforts. Soon longer-term goals are forgotten and momentum is lost. The challenge here is to keep the goal foremost in the public's minds, to allow them to revisit the strategic plan and to provide a constant flow of information on the progress achieved to date. Regrettably, implementation may be the least exciting aspect of change, but it remains the most important.[9] To sustain interest and approval means the public must be convinced that various investments are producing results, that accountability is being maintained and that further progress will be achieved.

Asian communities always face the risk of not attaining *critical mass* in their place-development projects. Many ambitious plans and projects are started without sufficient consideration for building and maintaining resources, energy and organizational momentum. In order to reach critical mass, places often need to associate with larger networks regionally, nationally or even internationally. Exhibits 13.4 and 13.5 provide examples of how implementation requires careful attention to maintain a strong initiative.

A last organizational aspect — often forgotten — is the issue of *aftercare*. The main aim of a place's aftercare program is to help and encourage new and existing investors to adapt and grow, to re-invest and to create more jobs. According to Michael J.T. Rowse, director-general of InvestHK, 60% of all investment in some countries is actually reinvestment by existing investors. "We fell short in Hong Kong in terms of investor aftercare services, and part of my job is to fix that."[10] The program must be systematic. All new investors should move into the aftercare program immediately after they start operations. Continuity of contact is important and the personal dimension should not be neglected. Because settling down and building a life in new surroundings is not easy, a place must meet both the investor and his/her family members. Place buyers rank aftercare efforts high.

Exhibit 13.4: OSAKA WRESTLES WITH A FAILED OLYMPIC BID

When the International Olympic Committee (IOC) issued a negative report on Osaka's bid for the 2008 Olympics, the reaction was predictable. The excuses ranged from lack of government support, misunderstandings with the committee, poor communication with the media and inexperience in bidding for such a prize. The bottom line was that Osaka was ill-prepared strategically to take on such formidable contenders as Paris, Toronto and Beijing.

Let's look at the situation. Osaka is the second-largest city in Japan (with a population of 8.8 million) and, because of its geographical remoteness and a commercial background dating back to medieval times, it has a distinct culture. Although an energetic manufacturing city known for its excellent cuisine and a friendly, accessible lifestyle, it lives in the shadow of Tokyo. The Olympics for Osaka, not unlike our earlier example of Sydney, represented a quantum step toward leadership and respectability in Asia.

Osaka, in its determination to emerge from the shadows, has made some excellent progress. The city's crown jewel is the Universal Studios Japan (USJ), which opened in 2001. The location of USJ in Osaka has set off a number of building projects including roadways, hotel construction and train stations. In addition, there is impressive local activity such as the planned renovation of the once-thriving Chinatown. The Chinatown development group consists of an ambitious association of shop owners and other local residents. Moreover, Osaka already had two-thirds of the Olympic sites in place, which represented a substantial cost saving in the overall plan. The news in Osaka was bright and optimistic.

So what happened in the battle for the Olympic site? Osaka could be faulted on a number of issues that are clearly part of a strategic marketing plan. The IOC criticized the city for possible congestion problems resulting from an ambitious plan to transport athletes around the three island Olympic sites. Moreover, the large amount of city investment was taken as evidence of a lack of country support. Osaka should have anticipated these objections and countered with effective arguments. The state of the traffic infrastructure needed to be carefully outlined, and the Osaka message required a consistent and clear strategy. Kimihide Harada, director of international affairs for the Osaka bid, admitted, "We have been very active promoting Osaka at home, but I'd like to see more output from us towards the press abroad. That, too, has been part of the learning process for us."[1]

Stated succinctly, Osaka did not communicate its story because it never really got it out. The city also needed an effective theme to communicate. The competition was stiff, as Paris marketed its unparalleled ambiance and charm, Toronto its conveniently sited athletic facilities, and Beijing its economic and political positioning. Osaka was inevitably paired against Beijing, which mounted a massive effort to convince the marketplace of the legitimacy of its bid. Osaka's lukewarm effort that only belatedly included the government and failed to generate overwhelming enthusiasm from its skeptical citizens was not going to win.

Osaka is in a favorable position for the future and is optimistic that the 2008 setback can serve as a launching pad for a winning bid. The lesson here is that strategic marketing planning is not only building attractions, but is often lost or won on mounting strong internal and external support, anticipating objections and getting out the message.

Sources:

1   Alastair Himmer, "Japan: Olympics-Osaka putting positive spin on 2008 vote," *Reuters English News Service*, http://ptg.djnr.com/ccroot/asp/ pub...wMTA3MDkxNjQ0MjYAAAAN&referer=true, July 8, 2001, viewed on July 10, 2001.

"Osaka Chinatown Revival Planned," *The Yomiuri Shimbun / Daily Yomiuri*, http://ptg.djnr.com/ccroot/asp/pub...wMTA3MDkxNzQwMjQAA- AAM&referer=true, May 20, 2001, viewed on July 10, 2001; "IOC Evaluation on 2008 Games Bidding Cities," Xinhua News Agency, http:// ptg.djnr.com/ccroot/asp/pub...wMTA3MDkxNzQwMjQAAAAM&- referer=true, July 8, 2001, viewed on July 10, 2001.

Exhibit 13.5: BEIJING VAULTS OVER OLYMPIC OPPOSITION

Beijing is the winner of the high-stakes competition to host the 2008 Olympic Games. The city had a brilliant strategic marketing plan that not only featured its virtues and corrected its weaknesses, but effectively countered an aggressive attack on its human rights policies. The marketing plan, however, is just phase one; Beijing must now deliver on its promises. The energy and focus necessary to complete the Olympic commitment illustrates how important implementation is to a successful strategic marketing plan.

There were three key elements to Beijing's successful bid. The first was the massive efforts to match the criteria of the International Olympic Committee (IOC) on 17 themes, including environmental protection, transportation, and popular and governmental support. The Beijing response was comprehensive and conclusive. It will spend US$12.2 billion on environmental clean-up alone. Beijing is rebuilding the entire public lavatory structure and training taxi drivers and subway workers in English language competence. Over 90% of its citizens support the bid. The second component was a large-scale government and corporate effort to demonstrate the solidarity and resolve of China and Beijing to the Games. The third component was the political reality of the Games being hosted in a previously under-represented sphere of the world. Beijing lost the 2000 Games by two disputed votes to Sydney and there was a strong feeling that this injustice should be corrected. All three elements combined to make that portion of the plan work.

Beijing now faces implementation issues on a scale previously unprecedented in Olympic history. As in most strategic marketing plans, there is the Monday morning question: "It is nine a.m. and who is going to do what?" This question includes what experts will be hired, at what cost, when it will be done, and what will happen if deadlines are not met. For example, the air in Beijing is often so toxic many people simply cannot tolerate it. The image of Olympic marathon runners gasping for breath and dropping like flies is not one that ennobles the reputation of a city. A public relations campaign that promises a cooperative and friendly city can be quickly shattered by human rights violations such as executions of political prisoners. World opinion will also be harsh if demonstrators are treated roughly or dissenters are banished from the Olympic site. Beijing has the difficult task of showcasing its new face while proving real reform before the world's television cameras.

Besides the enormous value of an improved image, the entire Chinese economy will receive a tremendous boost. Gross domestic product, according to Goldman and Sachs analyst Fred Hu, could rise by "0.3% per year from 2002 to 2008."[1] There will be a tremendous demand for services and construction that accompanies such a large-scale endeavor. China and Beijing are facing a great challenge. They made all the right strategic marketing moves to capture the bid. Now, the world will watch as they work to deliver the rest of the plan.

Sources:

1 Jeremy Page, "Russia: Olympics-Big Business Drools Over Beijing Prospects," *Reuters English News Service*, http://ptg.djnr.com/ccroot/asp/publib/story.asp, July 10, 2001, viewed on July 12, 2001.

"IOC Evaluation Commission Rates Beijing Olympic Bid," *Asia Pulse*, http://ptg.djnr.com/ccroot/asp/publib/story.asp, May 17, 2001, viewed on July 12, 2001; "China: Olympic Dreams," *Newsweek International*, http://ptg.djnr.com/ccroot/asp/publib/story.asp, February 26, 2001, viewed on July 12, 2001; "Beijing Steps Up Solid Waste Controls to Increase Chances for Olympics Bid," Gale Group Inc, http://ptg.djnr.com/ccroot/asp/publib/story.asp, March 1, 2001, viewed on July 12, 2001.

THE NECESSITY OF MARKETING PLACES IN ASIA

For much of its modern history, Asia was a source of valuable resources, from gold to spices, which were often paid for with opium. As a result, Asia's largest society was crippled by global trade, rather than developed. With most of the region in colonial shackles, administrators were more concerned with exerting control than with increasing prosperity. But now, Asia is the world's fastest-developing market. And thanks to liberalization and globalization trends catalyzed by the decade-long U.S. boom, never before in global history has there been such strong market pressure to be competitive.

In order to compete effectively, Asian places must develop an effective marketing approach. Places must produce products and services that current and prospective citizens, businesses, investors and visitors want or need. Places must sell products and services internally and externally, nationally and internationally.

The task of marketing places undergoes constant change as new industries form; new technologies emerge; companies expand; and old businesses shrink, merge or consolidate. As conditions and customers change, products must be upgraded and refined and new products and services must be designed to meet new needs. In Asia, many places have responded to changing market demands by leveraging new market and technology trends: in South Korea, the Internet and "technopreneurship;" in Tokyo, the fashion industry and mobile wireless technology; in Hong Kong, the service sector and entertainment; in Bangalore, the technology sector; in Singapore, financial services and high-tech manufacturing. Still, the Asian challenge is to be competitive, not only throughout Asia but around the world.

Opportunities for selling abroad are expanding greatly as global markets grow. Places are becoming more aggressive in financing and facilitating exports through information assistance, trading companies and trade centers. Entering the 21st century, Asian communities more than ever before need to help their local business firms develop market opportunities in specific national and international markets; to conduct on-line searches for buyers and agents; and to engage in cultural, scientific and educational exchanges. These communities need the support of "their" commercial bank, chamber of commerce, trade clubs and other export intermediaries.

However, the single greatest challenge that places face involves marketing their various activities to their own residents and voters. Marketing to internal consumers is not so much a technical marketing problem of methods, messages and targets as it is a political problem of embedding place-development values in the public's mind.

Now we are back to the point at which we began. *All places are in trouble, if not now, certainly in the future.* The globalization of the world's economy and the accelerating pace of technological change are two forces that require all places to learn how to compete. Asian places must learn — in spite of very limited experience in this area — how to think more like businesses and to develop the local business climate, products, markets and customers, all in a global context. The winners in Asia will also emphasize joint efforts between public and private sectors to build meaningful relationships.

The central tenet of *Marketing Asian Places* is that, in spite of the powerful external and internal forces that protect them, places have within their collective resources and people the capacity to improve their relative competitive positions. Their responses to the new bottom-up economic order are as important as national responses to the competitive challenge. A strategic market-planning perspective provides places with the marketing tools and opportunities to rise to that challenge.

---

1 Remarks by Manuel A. Roxas to the Management Association of the Philippines, Manila June 4, 2001.

2 Robert Reich, "The Myth of Made in America," *Wall Street Journal*, July 5, 1991, p. 14; see also Reich, *The Work of Nations: Preparing Ourselves for 21st Century Capitalism*, (New York: Knopf, 1991).

3 David Osbourne and Ted Gaebler, *Reinventing Government*, (Reading, Massachusetts: Addison-Wesley), 1992, Chapter 10.

4 Michael E. Porter, *The Competitive Advantage of Nations*, (New York: The Free Press), 1990, p. 73.

5 Neil Peirce and Robert Guskind, "Hot Manager, Sizzling Cities," *Business Month*, June 1989, p. 38.

6 Michael E. Porter, Hirotaka Takeuchi and Mariko Sakakibara, *Can Japan Compete?*, (Macmillan Press Ltd), 2000.

7 Mark Clifford and Dexter Roberts, "China: Coping with Its New Power," *BusinessWeek*, April 16, 2001, p. 40.

8 *Ibid.*

9 John Gunther-Mohr and Bert Winterbottom, "Implementation Strategies, Turning Plans into Successful Development," *Economic Development Commentary*, Summer, 1989, pp. 23–31.

10 Interview with Michael J.T. Rowse, September 16, 2000.

Index

433